LSAT® Advanced
Second Edition

Other Kaplan Books Related to Law School Admissions

Kaplan LSAT: Strategies, Practice, and Review

Kaplan LSAT: Premier Live Online

Kaplan LSAT Logic Games Workbook

Kaplan LSAT Logic Games in a Box

LSAT Direct

Kaplan LSAT Writing Workbook

Get Into Law School: A Strategic Approach

First Year Law Student: Wisdom, Warnings,
and What I Wish I'd known My Year as a 1L

LSAT® ADVANCED
Second Edition

The Staff of Kaplan Test Prep and Admissions

PUBLISHING

New York

Published by Kaplan Publishing, a division of Kaplan, Inc.
1 Liberty Plaza, 24th Floor
New York, NY 10006

Printed in the United States of America

10 9 8 7 6 5 4 3 2 1

ISBN-13: 978-1-60714-691-9

Kaplan Publishing books are available at special quantity discounts to use for sales promotions, employee premiums, or educational purposes. Please email our Special Sales Department to order or for more information at kaplanpublishing@kaplan.com, or write to Kaplan Publishing, 1 Liberty Plaza, 24th Floor, New York, NY 10006.

Table of Contents

kaptest.com/publishing

The material in this book is up-to-date at the time of publication. However, the Law School Admissions Council may have instituted changes in the test or test registration process after this book was published. Be sure to carefully read the materials you receive when you register for the test.

If there are any important late breaking developments—or changes or corrections to the Kaplan test preparation materials in this book—we will post that information online at kaptest.com/publishing. Check to see if there is any information posted there regarding this book.

kaplansurveys.com/books

If you have comments and suggestions, we invite you to fill out our online form at **kaplansurveys.com/books**. Your feedback is extremely helpful as we continue to develop high-quality resources to meet your needs.

About the Authors

Gar Hong is the Lead Instructor at the State College Kaplan Center. He teaches classes and tutors students in Kaplan's LSAT, GRE, GMAT, SAT, DAT, TSS, and GESS courses. He has also written test prep material for the LSAT, GRE, SAT, PSAT, ACT, ISEE, SSAT, BMAT, and the UKCAT. Gar was named Kaplan Teacher of the Year in 2005 and 2006, and was one of a handful of instructors selected to help create Kaplan's LSAT Advanced course in 2008.

Julie Lamberth received her Juris Doctorate from UNC-Chapel Hill. She began teaching for Kaplan in Chapel Hill Center shortly before embarking upon law school, and has taught classes in Kaplan's LSAT, GMAT, GRE, and SAT courses, including the LSAT Extreme course. She has also been LSAT Product Manager for the national curriculum team, and is now an Editor for PMBR, Kaplan's full-service bar exam review division. When not working for Kaplan, Julie spends her time rooting for the Yankees and the Tar Heels, and scouring the city for a restaurant that can replace her favorite Franklin Street hangout.

The Perfect Score

Ah, *perfection* . . .

We humans are a demanding bunch. We don't bound out of bed in the morning aspiring to mediocrity, but rather striving for *perfection*. The *perfect* job. The *perfect* shoes to go with the *perfect* outfit. We head to the beach on a *perfect* summer day to find the *perfect* spot to get the *perfect* tan.

Webster's defines perfection as "the quality or state of being complete and correct in every way, conforming to a standard or ideal with no omissions, errors, flaws or extraneous elements."

The LSAT test makers define perfection as a score of 180. If that's what you're after, then you've come to the right place. We at Kaplan have been training test takers to ace the LSAT for over 30 years. We understand your desire for the highest possible score. For those of you shooting for the moon, we salute your quest for perfection. The *perfect* LSAT score. The *perfect* law school. The *perfect* career.

WHAT IS THE LSAT AND HOW IS IT STRUCTURED

The LSAT is a half-day (220-minute) test designed to measure skills considered essential for success in law school: reading, organization and management of information, and reasoning. It consists of four scored 35-minute sections of multiple-choice questions and one unscored "variable" section used to pretest new test items. A 35-minute, unscored writing sample is administered at the end of the test.

The four scored sections include:
- One Reading Comprehension section (26–28 questions based on 4 passages: three single passages, each about 450–550 words, and a pair of passages that together total about 500 words)
- One Analytical Reasoning or "Logic Games" section (22–24 questions based on 4 games)
- Two Logical Reasoning sections (24–26 questions each, consisting of short arguments followed by 1 or 2 questions)

The "variable" section will look like one of those other sections and have 22–28 questions. The number of scored questions you answered correctly is your "raw score." The score scale is 120 to 180.

You must register for the test in advance, so try to get your hands on the *LSAT/LSDAS Registration and Information Book* as soon as possible. It's available at most colleges and law schools. You can also download a copy at *www.LSAC.org* or order it by calling (215) 968-1001. The earlier you register, the better your chances are of being assigned to your first or second choice test center.

Since you are aiming for a perfect score, we assume that you are familiar with the LSAT question types and believe you can already do well on the test—that you are looking for the tools to help you edge your score up from good to perfect.

WHO SHOULD USE THIS BOOK

We should warn you up front: This book is not for the faint of heart. It assumes you've already learned the basics, so it consists exclusively of examples of the toughest material you're likely to see on the LSAT (though we do define some basic terms.) No easy stuff, no run-of-the-mill strategies—just killer games, passages, and questions, complete with Kaplan's proven techniques to help you transcend "above average" and enter the rarefied arena of LSAT elite. If you're entertaining the notion of pulling off the perfect 180, then you're going to have to face down the most brutal material the LSAT test makers have to offer. Even if a perfect score is not your immediate goal, diligent practice with the difficult material in this book can help develop your skills and raise your score.

If you're looking for a more fundamental introduction to the LSAT, or practice with questions ranging from easy to difficult, then we recommend working through the Kaplan LSAT Premier Program or Comprehensive Program as a prerequisite for the highly challenging material contained in this volume. You can find the latest edition of these books in stores nationwide, as well as by visiting us at KaplanPublishing.com or through other online retailers.

HOW TO USE THIS BOOK

This book is divided into three sections corresponding to the three question types: Logic Games, Logical Reasoning, and Reading Comprehension. (The Writing Sample is not included in this book because it doesn't contribute to your 120–180 score, and no Writing Sample prompt is written to be any more difficult than any other.)

Each section provides detailed guidelines on how to make the most of the material. Jump right to the section that gives you the most trouble, or work through the sections in the order presented— it's up to you. You'll notice that the habits and thought processes of top test takers are highlighted throughout the book. Study these thoroughly, and make these effective techniques your own.

No matter what you do, try not to overload; remember, this is dense, complicated material, and not representative of the range of difficulty you'll see on Test Day. One thing's for sure: If you can ace this stuff, the real thing will be a breeze.

Good luck!

section one

LOGIC GAMES

CHAPTER ONE

The Logic Games Challenge

A college dean will present seven awards for outstanding language research. The awards—one for French, one for German, one for Hebrew, one for Japanese, one for Korean, one for Latin, and one for Swahili—must be presented consecutively, one at a time, in conformity with the following constraints:

The German award is not presented first.
The Hebrew award is presented at some time before the Korean award is presented.
The Latin award is presented at some time before the Japanese award is presented.
The French award is presented either immediately before or immediately after the Hebrew award is presented.
The Korean award is presented either immediately before or immediately after the Latin award is presented.

1. The order in which the awards are presented is completely determined if which of the following is true?

Who knows? Who cares?

Well, for starters, the admission boards at most accredited law schools do—and if you're reading these words, chances are you're someone who's looking to impress that particular crowd. To most law school admission officers, the LSAT Logic Games section is not some arbitrary exercise in tortured logic (as it no doubt may seem to some test takers), but rather a realistic test of the kinds of reasoning skills necessary to think through complex legal issues and situations.

Above-average difficulty games appear often on the LSAT. Unfortunately, the advice to "just skip the tough ones and do the best you can on the others" simply won't cut it for those aspiring to enter 180 territory. If that's your quest, then you have no choice but to muster all your skill, speed, and stamina to face these killers head-on. For those of you simply interested in improving your gaming techniques, cutting your teeth on the hardest games will certainly help you to hone your skills and raise your score.

It is in this spirit, and with these objectives in mind, that we present the Logic Games in this book.

USING THE LOGIC GAMES IN THIS BOOK

The Logic Games in this book are broken up into four categories:

- Supercharged Standards
- Time Warps and Assemblies
- Volatile Mixtures
- Huh . . . ?

Together, these represent the full range of the types of difficult games you may encounter on your test. You'll find descriptions of these categories at the beginning of each chapter. You're probably best off working your way up to the games in the final chapter, which, as the name implies, are particularly nasty. You can do the games one at a time before reviewing the explanations, or plow through a bunch before coming up for air—really, it's up to you. You'll also find blank "Notes" pages in the back of the book that you can use for sketching. A few suggestions, however:

Observe timing guidelines. You'll surely get the right answers eventually if you take an hour to do each game. The point, however, is how well you can handle the tough stuff under true LSAT conditions. You don't have to go so far as to hire a proctor to stand over you with a timepiece (although that probably couldn't hurt), but make sure you spend no more than nine and one-half minutes per game. Four games in 35 minutes allows for roughly eight and one-half minutes per game, but considering the difficulty level of these, it's reasonable to allow a little extra time.

Devise a plan of attack. The LSAT tests many things—one of which is ingenuity. How is that tested? By presenting questions in a less-than-ideal sequence to ensnare test takers who rush into battle without a plan. How is it overcome? By doing these questions in the most efficient order—*not* in the order printed.

Read the explanations. Review the keys to each game, comparing your own approach to the insights provided. Notice whether you are consistently coming up with the same deductions as us, and recognizing the same factors that cut these killers down to size. Take special note of the thought processes and habits of Advanced test takers highlighted throughout the explanations.

Have fun. Remember, these are games. Games are meant to be fun!

An Advanced test taker approaches the Logic Games section with good humor, a positive attitude, and enthusiasm for the challenge of facing the toughest material the test makers have to offer.

Oh, by the way: Regarding the language awards, one way the presentation order would be fully known is if German was presented immediately before French and Latin was presented immediately before Japanese.

But you already figured that out, right?

CHAPTER TWO

Supercharged Standards

What makes a Logic Game hard? Certainly games that contain very unusual game actions are difficult to manage. Games that consist of a mixture of multiple game actions can also be cumbersome and trying. Have no fear: You'll see plenty of examples of these later on. But some Logic Games that seem fairly straightforward at first glance, by virtue of complicating elements, must be counted among the killer elite as well.

Each of the games in this first Logic Games chapter involves one of four single standard game actions: Sequencing, Matching, Distribution, or Selection (the last two are referred to collectively as Grouping Games). For this reason, they may not seem as nasty as what's to come later, but beware: While these games represent standard LSAT fare, they are nonetheless deceptively difficult.

Keep your guard up.

LOGIC GAME 1

Eight people—Fiona, George, Harriet, Ingrid, Karl, Manuel, Olivia, and Peter—are sitting, evenly spaced, around a circular picnic table. Any two of them are said to be sitting directly across from one another if and only if there are exactly three other people sitting between them, counting in either direction around the table. The following conditions apply:

Fiona sits directly across from George.

Harriet sits immediately next to neither Fiona nor Karl.

Ingrid sits immediately next to, and immediately clockwise from, Olivia.

1. Which one of the following could be the order in which four of the people are seated, with no one else seated between them, counting clockwise around the table?

   (A) George, Peter, Karl, Fiona
   (B) Harriet, Olivia, Ingrid, Karl
   (C) Ingrid, Fiona, Peter, Manuel
   (D) Olivia, Manuel, Karl, George
   (E) Peter, Harriet, Karl, Fiona

2. If Harriet and Olivia each sits immediately next to George, then which one of the following could be the two people each of whom sits immediately next to Peter?

   (A) Fiona and Karl
   (B) Fiona and Olivia
   (C) Harriet and Ingrid
   (D) Harriet and Karl
   (E) Karl and Manuel

3. If George does not sit immediately next to Harriet, then which one of the following could be the two people each of whom sits immediately next to Manuel?

   (A) Fiona and Harriet
   (B) Fiona and Peter
   (C) George and Karl
   (D) George and Peter
   (E) Harriet and Peter

4. If Manuel sits immediately next to Olivia, then which one of the following people must sit immediately next to Fiona?

   (A) Harriet
   (B) Ingrid
   (C) Karl
   (D) Manuel
   (E) Peter

5. What is the minimum possible number of people sitting between Ingrid and Manuel, counting clockwise from Ingrid around the table?

   (A) zero
   (B) one
   (C) two
   (D) three
   (E) four

6. If Karl sits directly across from Ingrid, then each of the following people could sit immediately next to Olivia EXCEPT:

   (A) Fiona
   (B) George
   (C) Harriet
   (D) Manuel
   (E) Peter

7. If Karl sits directly across from Harriet, then what is the minimum possible number of people sitting between George and Karl, counting clockwise from George to Karl?

   (A) zero
   (B) one
   (C) two
   (D) three
   (E) four

Logic Game 1: Picnic Table

What Makes It Difficult?

The setup tells us we must position (or *sequence*) eight entities at a picnic table. With eight people to eight spots and an innocent set of rules, this seems like a fairly straightforward game at first glance.

Sequencing game
Ordering entities with respect to defined positions or with respect to each other.

If the test maker left it at that, this game would've been a picnic (pardon the pun). However, if you scanned through the opening paragraph before starting to sketch anything out, you would've noticed the lone fact that earns the game a spot in this book—the table is *round*. How can a round sketch have a beginning or end? How can I place anyone in such a sketch?

Grab onto something. Your head is about to spin.

Keys to the Game

"Directly across" means exactly three in between. While this is mentioned verbatim in the opening paragraph, it merits notice as lesser test takers will miss this *precisely* because it's buried in the opening paragraph.

An Advanced test taker knows that the opening paragraph to a tough Logic Game is just as good a place for additional rules as the indented list that follows.

Circular Sequencing needs a circular sketch. Circular sequencing behaves much like any other Sequencing game, but with these additional wrinkles thrown in: You have to consider who's *across* from whom, not just who's next to whom, and you have to consider "clockwise" vs. "counterclockwise." In any circle game involving entities across from others, instead of drawing a simple circle, draw the *diameters* that define "acrossness":

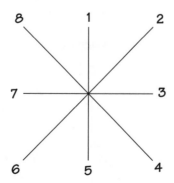

It is important to note that we are numbering the seats solely for your convenience in following these explanations. A circle has no beginning and no end, so any seat can, in theory, be called #1.

OI is a set sequence. Rule 3 says that Ingrid is immediately clockwise from Olivia. Since a circle has no beginning or end, we'll place them in seats 1 and 2, respectively.

H doesn't have too many friends. Rule 2 is one of those irksome "negative rules" and doesn't permit very much more deduction because it simply reminds us what we must *avoid*: We can never have either "HF" or "HK" anywhere in the circle.

M and P are Floaters. A Floater is an entity that isn't mentioned in the rules. While Floaters do not have a direct impact on the other entities in the game, they do tend to end up on a test taker's "forget" list, and that can make them dangerous in the hands of the test maker.

Neither M nor P is mentioned in the rules, but they have just as much of a right to be at this picnic as the others. Don't focus on them, but don't forget about them either.

F and G are Key Players that allow us to set up limited options. A Key Player is an entity or set of entities that first, is limited to two or three slots, and second, substantially affects the placement of other entities (in a domino-effect manner), depending on its placement. Any time you realize an entity is limited to one of two or three locations, check to see whether it strongly impacts other entities. If so, then automatically presume it's worthwhile to map out both or all three possible configurations for that entity (we say "presume," because most test takers are intimidated by what they incorrectly imagine to be a nearly infinite set of options).

With Olivia and Ingrid occupying two consecutive spots at the round table, the only remaining pairs of seats available to Fiona and George, who must sit across from one another according to Rule 1, are spots 3 and 7 or spots 4 and 8. So our limited options look like this:

Option I

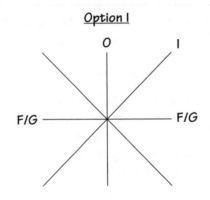

Option II

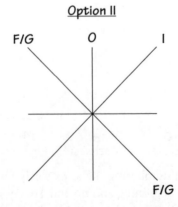

Never HK
Never HF

With our preliminary sketches complete, we can now march confidently on to the questions.

> An Advanced test taker knows that almost every Logic Game battle starts before the first question is read. Spending time up front making deductions and recognizing restrictions translates into quick points later on.

Question Tally

Seven questions: one Partial Acceptability, five Ifs (one of which contains a negative premise), and one Minimum Number.

Battle Plan

The key to a good battle plan is to attack the questions in the correct order. Questions of the Acceptability variety confirm our understanding of the rules and should always be tackled first. Strategies beyond that depend on the individual game itself but the general idea is to get quick sketch-producing If questions done earlier so that sketch-reliant questions can benefit from them.

A quick look at the five Ifs reveals that one of them—question 3—seems rather open. Such a hypothetical tends to be harder than most due to the sheer number of possibilities available to them, so it would be prudent to do it at the end of the If queue. Our plan of attack is as follows:

- #1 first.
- #2, #4, #6, and #7 second.
- #3 third.
- #5 last.

> An Advanced test taker *never* rushes blindly into battle without a plan.

Answers and Explanations

1. C   2. D   3. A   4. C   5. A   6. B   7. C

Question Order: 1, 2, 4, 6, 7, 3, 5

1. C

The Acceptability only focuses on half of the picnic goers. Most of the time, questions that focus on only one half of the sketch rely heavily on what each choices forces into place in the other unseen half. When you've gone to the trouble of listing limited options, you get a big payoff with questions like these. Rule 1 knocks out (A), as Fiona and George aren't placed far enough apart to sit opposite each other. (E) has Harriet and Karl sitting next to each other, which violates Rule 2. (D) puts Manuel clockwise from Olivia, which goes against Rule 3. Finally, (B) can be eliminated as our limited options make it clear that one of Fiona or George must either be immediately clockwise from Ingrid (Option I) or immediately counterclockwise from Olivia.

Acceptability questions

These ask which choice could be a possible sequence or arrangement (that is, which doesn't break any of the rules).

2. D

The only way Harriet and Olivia could both sit immediately next to George is if they flank him to either side. This is only possible in Option II, in the following way:

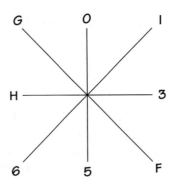

To flank Peter on both sides, we'll need two people with exactly one seat between them. That rules out (B) and (C). (A) could only work by placing Karl in seat #6, but that would violate Rule 2. The only person Karl and Manuel could flank together is Fiona, so (E) is out as well. That leaves (D), the correct answer.

4. C

Manuel can only sit next to Olivia in Option I. Once he takes his seat, we have:

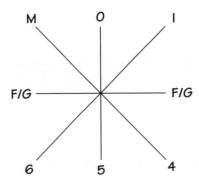

Sketching that out allows us to see the Harriet/Karl situation (Rule 2) rather starkly. To separate them, we'll have to place them in seats 4 and 6. And since we have to keep separating Harriet and Fiona (who invited them both anyway?), it'll have to be George next to Harriet and—choice (C)—Karl next to Fiona.

6. B

This premise works with either sketch so work them both out:

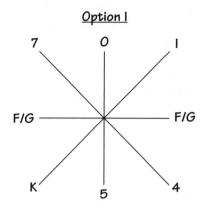

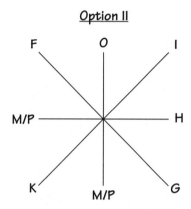

Option I is pretty wide open, but Harriet can only take seat 3 in Option II. This puts George in 4 (as Harriet cannot sit next to Fiona), Fiona in 7, and Manuel and Peter in the two remaining spots. With George forced out of seat 7 in Option II, he is the one who cannot sit next to Olivia in either sketch.

7. C

Karl can sit across from Harriet in either option, so work out both sketches:

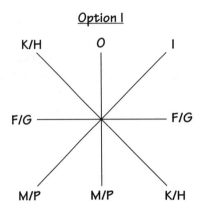

The shortest clockwise path from George to Karl that avoids putting Harriet next to her nemeses Fiona and Karl comes from Option II:

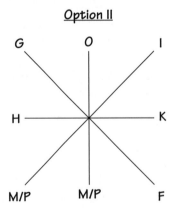

That makes (C) correct.

3. A

Since neither George nor Harriet, the principals in this "if" clause, is definitely placed, this new negative rule appears to make life exceptionally difficult—precisely why we're doing it *after* the easier Ifs. Unfortunately, Harriet has been clinging to George in the other questions, so our strategy doesn't pay off this time. The key here is to realize how perfectly it links up with Rule 2. Harriet is either wildly unpopular or terribly hard to please, because we now have to separate her from *three* other people: Karl, Fiona, and George. Given that either sketch seems just as likely to work, let's sketch one out and see if it answers the question:

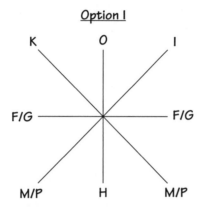

Harriet is forbidden from seats 4, 6, and 7, so she must occupy 5. To separate her from Karl, he must take 7, which leaves 4 and 6 for Manuel and Peter. This shows that (A) is correct, and there is no need to do any additional work.

> An Advanced test taker does not do more work than is needed to answer the question.

5. A

An astute test taker saves questions without a new "if" clause for last as previous work can greatly reduce the amount of work needed to answer the question. So far, the sketch from question 3 proves that (B), one, is possible. Can it be zero? If (A), zero, is correct, then we're in Option II with Manuel in seat 3. Can we place Harriet in accordance with Rule 2? Yes. Give her 5, with George in 4. Put Peter on her left in 6, with Karl in 7, and Fiona, across from George as always, in 8. Case closed. Ingrid and Manuel can sit next to each other, choice (A).

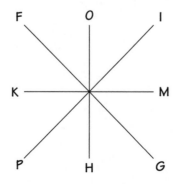

An Advanced test taker conquers the toughest questions in a Logic Game by doing them last.

What's Next?

Head still spinning around the picnic table? Or did that merely whet your appetite for more? If so, here comes another Sequencing game for you to try! Don't worry; this one won't have you running in circles. We promise.

LOGIC GAME 2

Gutierrez, Hoffman, Imamura, Kelly, Lapas, and Moore ride a bus together. Each sits facing forward in a different one of the six seats on the left side of the bus. The seats are in consecutive rows that are numbered 1, 2, and 3 from front to back. Each row has exactly two seats: a window seat and an aisle seat. The following conditions must apply:

Hoffman occupies the aisle seat immediately behind Gutierrez's aisle seat.

If Moore occupies an aisle seat, Hoffman sits in the same row as Lapas.

If Gutierrez sits in the same row as Kelly, Moore occupies the seat immediately and directly behind Imamura's seat.

If Kelly occupies a window seat, Moore sits in row 3.

If Kelly sits in row 3, Imamura sits in row 1.

1. Which one of the following could be true?

    (A) Imamura sits in row 2, whereas Kelly sits in row 3.
    (B) Gutierrez sits in the same row as Kelly, immediately and directly behind Moore.
    (C) Gutierrez occupies a window seat in the same row as Lapas.
    (D) Moore occupies an aisle seat in the same row as Lapas.
    (E) Kelly and Moore both sit in row 3.

2. If Lapas and Kelly each occupy a window seat, then which one of the following could be true?

    (A) Moore occupies the aisle seat in row 3.
    (B) Imamura occupies the window seat in row 3.
    (C) Gutierrez sits in the same row as Kelly.
    (D) Gutierrez sits in the same row as Moore.
    (E) Moore sits in the same row as Lapas.

3. If Moore sits in row 1, then which one of the following must be true?

    (A) Hoffman sits in row 2.
    (B) Imamura sits in row 2.
    (C) Imamura sits in row 3.
    (D) Kelly sits in row 1.
    (E) Lapas sits in row 3.

4. If Kelly occupies the aisle seat in row 3, then each of the following must be true EXCEPT:

    (A) Gutierrez sits in the same row as Imamura.
    (B) Hoffman sits in the same row as Lapas.
    (C) Lapas occupies a window seat.
    (D) Moore occupies a window seat.
    (E) Gutierrez sits in row 1.

5. If neither Gutierrez nor Imamura sits in row 1, then which one of the following could be true?

    (A) Hoffman sits in row 2.
    (B) Kelly sits in row 2.
    (C) Moore sits in row 2.
    (D) Imamura occupies an aisle seat.
    (E) Moore occupies an aisle seat.

Logic Game 2: Bus Riders

What Makes It Difficult?

The game itself—sequencing six people to six seats on a bus—seems pretty tame. It's the rules that are nasty: With the exception of the first, every rule in this game is a formal logic statement, and that alone makes this game challenging.

Rules 2, 4, and 5 are classic formulations of the "if-then" constraint that appears on the LSAT frequently. The test makers most likely use and reuse this formulation because so many people misinterpret these rules to mean that M is always in the row 3 aisle seat, H is always with L, K is always in the row 3 window seat (next to M), and I is always in row 1. Not so.

Rule 3 takes the formal logic concept even further with an extremely ugly rule.

Rule 1 offers up limited options. Test takers who miss this fact will find the game next to impossible, but those who notice it aren't exactly treated to a smooth ride either.

Hope you've got your ticket. It's time to get on the bus.

Keys to the Game

Rule 2 means neither "M is always on an aisle seat" nor "H is always with L." The contrapositive of this if-then rule is, "If Hoffman is not with Lapas, then Moore occupies a window seat." Together, these statements mean that anytime Moore gets an aisle seat, Hoffman will sit with Lapas; anytime Hoffman and Lapas are separate, Moore gets a window seat. But if Hoffman is sitting next to Lapas, that doesn't tell us anything about Moore. Similarly, if Moore is at a window seat, that tells us nothing about Hoffman or Lapas.

"Contrapositive"
To contrapose an if-then statement, do the following:

1) Flip both sides around.
2) Negate every entity.
3) Change all instances of "AND" to "OR" and vice versa.

So, "If A, then B" becomes "If No B, then No A" and "If D AND No E, then No F OR G" becomes "If F AND No G, then No D OR E."

Rule 4 means neither "K is always on a window seat" nor "M is always in row 3." We do know that if Kelly gets a window seat, Moore sits in row 3 and that if Moore is *not* in row 3, then Kelly gets an aisle seat. However, this rule doesn't tell us anything more than that.

Rule 5 means neither "K is always in row 3" nor "I is always in row 1." Similar to the previous point, if Kelly sits in row 3, Imamura will be in row 1 and if Imamura *isn't* in row 1, Kelly won't be in row 3, either. Beyond this, we know nothing else about either from this rule.

G and H are Key Players that allow us to set up limited options. Hoffman occupying the aisle seat behind Gutierrez's aisle seat can only happen in one of two ways.

An Advanced test taker is always on the lookout for Key Players that reduce the game to a couple of limited options.

Rule 3 leads to one completed sketch. The "then" portion of this rule can only happen in Option I.

Putting all of this together, our Master Sketch looks like this:

	Option I			Option II	
	w	a		w	a
1	___	G	1	___	___
2	___	H	2	___	G
3	___	___	3	___	H

If $\underline{KG}$, then ......

$M_{aisle} \rightarrow \underline{LH}$		w	a
No $\underline{LH} \rightarrow M_{window}$			
$K_{window} \rightarrow M_3$	1	K	G
$M_{1 \, or \, 2} \rightarrow K_{aisle}$	2	I	H
$K_3 \rightarrow I_1$	3	M	L
$I_{2 \, or \, 3} \rightarrow K_{1 \, or \, 2}$			

Question Tally

Five questions: four Ifs and one Could be True.

Battle Plan

With four Ifs, we are guaranteed to end up with plenty of sketches that will make question 1 easier. The first If seems very open ended as it doesn't allow us to definitively place anyone, so do that at the end of the If "queue."

- #3, #4, and #5 first.
- #2 next.
- #1 last.

Answers and Explanations

1. E   2. A   3. D   4. B   5. C

Question Order: 3, 4, 5, 2, 1

3. D

Moore sits in row 1 but which seat? Well, it can't be the aisle seat as that gives Moore, Gutierrez, and Hoffman aisle seats, which puts Kelly in a window seat and violates Rule 4 in the process. So Moore must take row 1's window seat and Rule 4's contrapositive kicks in. Since Moore is in row 1, Kelly must take an aisle seat, and that's only possible in Option II (in this way):

	w	a
1	M	K
2	I/L	G
3	I/L	H

That makes (D) correct.

4. B

This premise places us definitively in Option I like so:

	w	a
1	I	G
2	M/L	H
3	M/L	K

Hoffman *could* sit with Lapas but doesn't have to. That's (B).

"EXCEPT"

A common problem in Logic Games is doing all the right work only to answer the wrong question. When faced with a "must/could" be "true/false" EXCEPT question, swap the first and second pairs of words and remove the "EXCEPT." So a "must be true EXCEPT" becomes "could be false" and a "could be true EXCEPT" becomes a "must be false."

---

5. C

With Gutierrez out of row 1, we're definitely in Option II, and (A) and (D) are impossible. With Imamura out of row 1, Kelly cannot sit in row 3 (contrapositive of Rule 5). Can she sit in row 2 next to Gutierrez? No, because that would violate Rule 3 (with row 2 completely full, the vertical IM block would be impossible). This means Kelly must sit in row 1 and (B) is out. With two choices left, simply pick one and sketch it out. If Moore sat in row 2 (C), we *could* have . . .

	w	a
1	K	L
2	M	G
3	I	H

The sketch works, so (C) is correct.

2. A

That the question stem doesn't hint at **which** window seats, and that Lapas and Kelly can take window seats in both Options, means that there are lots of possibilities. Your first instinct should be to check your previous sketches but, unfortunately, that strategy doesn't pay off this time. Therefore, the fastest way to answer this question is to simply test the choices. If (A) were correct, it would be in Option I. Placing M triggers Rule 2, and Hoffman and Lapas must therefore share row 2. We can't assign Gutierrez and Kelly in row 1 here (Rule 3), so it'll be Imamura and Gutierrez in row 1, which results in the following sketch:

	w	a
1	K	G
2	L	H
3	I	M

That works, so there is no need to test any other choices.

An Advanced test taker doesn't waste time testing the remaining choices once the correct answer has been found.

---

1. E

Ahh . . . the dreaded "could be true" that comes without any additional information. While such a question can zap an obscene amount of time from the average test taker as he makes sketch after sketch to narrow down the choices, *you* will be spared such an ordeal if you followed the Battle Plan and attacked it last. A quick scan of our previous work reveals that the sketch for question 4 makes (E) possible.

What's Next?

Never thought Sequencing could be so exhilarating, huh? Don't put that pencil down yet, here come some Matching games for you to enjoy.

LOGIC GAME 3

Two mannequins—1 and 2—will be dressed for display in outfits chosen from ten articles of clothing. Each article is in exactly one of three colors: navy, red, or yellow. There are three hats—one in each color; three jackets—one in each color; three skirts—one in each color; and one red tie. Each mannequin wears exactly one of the hats, one of the jackets, and one of the skirts. Furthermore, their outfits must meet the following restrictions:

Neither mannequin wears all three colors.
Each mannequin wears a hat in a different color from the jacket it wears.
Mannequin 2 wears the navy skirt.
Mannequin 1 wears the tie.

1. Which one of the following could be complete outfits for the two mannequins?

   (A) mannequin 1: navy hat, red jacket, yellow skirt, red tie; mannequin 2: red hat, navy jacket, navy skirt
   (B) mannequin 1: red hat, red jacket, yellow skirt, red tie; mannequin 2: yellow hat, navy jacket, navy skirt
   (C) mannequin 1: red hat, yellow jacket, red skirt, red tie; mannequin 2: yellow hat, navy jacket, yellow skirt
   (D) mannequin 1: yellow hat, red jacket, yellow skirt, red tie; mannequin 2: red hat, navy jacket, navy skirt
   (E) mannequin 1: yellow hat, yellow jacket, red skirt; mannequin 2: red hat, navy jacket, navy skirt

2. Which one of the following could be true of the mannequins' outfits?

   (A) Mannequin 1 wears the navy jacket and the yellow skirt.
   (B) Mannequin 2 wears the red hat and the red jacket.
   (C) Mannequin 1 wears exactly one red article of clothing.
   (D) Mannequin 1 wears exactly three yellow articles of clothing.
   (E) Mannequin 2 wears no red articles of clothing.

3. If mannequin 1 wears the navy jacket, which one of the following could be true?

   (A) Mannequin 1 wears the yellow hat.
   (B) Mannequin 1 wears the yellow skirt.
   (C) Mannequin 2 wears the red hat.
   (D) Mannequin 2 wears the yellow hat.
   (E) Mannequin 2 wears the yellow jacket.

4. If all four of the red articles of clothing are included in the two mannequins' outfits, which one of the following must be true?

   (A) Mannequin 1 wears the red hat.
   (B) Mannequin 1 wears the yellow jacket.
   (C) Mannequin 2 wears the navy jacket.
   (D) Mannequin 1 wears no navy articles of clothing.
   (E) Mannequin 2 wears no yellow articles of clothing.

5. If mannequin 2 wears the red jacket, then mannequin 1 must wear the

   (A) navy hat
   (B) red hat
   (C) yellow hat
   (D) red skirt
   (E) yellow skirt

6. If all three of the yellow articles of clothing are included in the two mannequins' outfits, which one of the following could be true?

   (A) Mannequin 1 wears the navy jacket.
   (B) Mannequin 1 wears the yellow jacket.
   (C) Mannequin 1 wears the red skirt.
   (D) Mannequin 2 wears the red hat.
   (E) Mannequin 2 wears the red jacket.

7. If mannequin 1 wears the skirt that is the same color as the jacket that mannequin 2 wears, which one of the following must be true?

   (A) Mannequin 1 wears the yellow hat.
   (B) Mannequin 1 wears the yellow jacket.
   (C) Mannequin 2 wears the navy hat.
   (D) Mannequin 2 wears the red hat.
   (E) Mannequin 2 wears the red jacket.

Logic Game 3: Mannequin Outfits

What Makes It Difficult?

Like most other games in this Supercharged Standards chapter, the real-life situation depicted in this game is hardly difficult to comprehend—we're just dressing up mannequins, after all. Hats, jackets, and skirts, oh my!

Matching Game
Matching two kinds of entities to each other.

With ten different articles of clothing (three each of the hats, jackets, and skirts, plus one red tie), it can be quite a challenge juggling around all that apparel. The test maker was generous enough to nail two pieces down for you (mannequin 2's skirt and the fact that mannequin 1 wears the tie) but the generosity ends there. We desperately need a way to figure out the remaining colors worn but the rest of the rules are vague at best. To make matters worse, only seven of the ten articles of clothing will be used, which only seems to add to the number of possibilities in this game.

The questions seem like a helpful enough bunch, with a full five hypothetical Ifs, but if you thought that meant you didn't need deductions, you'd be in for quite a surprise. The game takes this deception further by not having *any* not-If "Must be True" questions, which seems to further assure the unsuspecting test taker that it's as open as it appears.

Hope you brought a change of clothes. You'll need it after this one.

Keys to the Game

Each mannequin wears exactly two colors. This is the result of combining Rules 1 and 2. Since no mannequin wears all three colors (how gauche!), but each wears a hat in a different color from the jacket it wears, each mannequin must wear exactly two colors.

An Advanced test taker turns vague numerical restrictions into concrete numbers.

Mannequin 1 must wear either the red hat or the red jacket, but not both. With the hat and jacket in different colors and each mannequin wearing exactly two colors, both must be represented in these two articles of clothing. Rule 4 places the red tie on mannequin 1, so one of these two articles must also be red.

Mannequin 2 must wear either the navy hat or the navy jacket, but not both—for the same reason as the above, since Rule 3 assigns the navy skirt to mannequin 2.

Mannequin 1's skirt is either red or yellow. With mannequin 2 wearing the navy skirt, this is all that remains for mannequin 1.

Our master sketch looks like so:

Colors: N R Y

	#1 R + ?	#2 N + ?
(dif ↓) hat		
(dif ↑) jacket		
skirt	R/Y	N
tie	R	None

#1 has red hat or red jacket
#2 has navy hat or navy jacket

Question Tally

Seven questions: one Acceptability, five Ifs, and one Could be True.

Battle Plan

The game contains a whopping seven questions, and because none of them seem particularly nasty with our setup, we'll be following the standard mode of attack on this one:

- #1 first.
- #3–7 next.
- #2 last.

Answers and Explanations

1. D   2. E   3. E   4. E   5. B   6. B   7. C

Question Order: 1, 3, 4, 5, 6, 7, 2

1. D

First up is a standard acceptability question. Rule 1 kills (A), which gives all three colors to mannequin 1. Rule 2 knocks out (B) and (E)—both contain a mannequin with the same color hat and jacket. Finally, Rule 3 eliminates (C), which gives mannequin 2 a yellow skirt.

3. E

If mannequin 1 gets the navy jacket, then its colors are red and navy. Mannequin 2 needs either a navy hat or a navy jacket but the latter is taken by mannequin 1, so mannequin 2 gets the navy hat and the sketch works out like this:

	#1 R + N	#2 N + ?
(dif ↓) hat	R	N
(dif ↑) jacket	N	R/Y
skirt	R	N
tie	R	None

Of the choices, only (E) could be true.

4. E

The premise requires the red hat, red jacket, red skirt, and red tie to all be worn. Putting the red jacket on mannequin 2 in question 3's sketch meets this requirement and eliminates (B), (C), and (D) in the process!

We *could* draw out a sketch to test the remaining two choices but a quick bit of critical thinking makes this unnecessary: Having all four red articles in play means that mannequin 2's colors must be navy and red (as mannequin 1 can't wear all the red by herself). This means (E) must be true.

> An Advanced test taker has the ability to "brute force" the answer when it's needed . . . and the awareness to recognize when it's not.

5. B

Inputting the premise into our trusty sketch from question 3 once again satisfies the requirements while eliminating three choices—(A), (C), and (E). With the red jacket on mannequin 2 and mannequin 1 needing a red article in either the hat or the jacket, (B) must be true.

> An Advanced test taker milks a previous sketch for all it's worth for maximum efficiency.

6. B

With three yellow articles of clothing in play, we must unfortunately retire the venerable question 3 sketch. With all three yellow articles, mannequin 1 must wear red and yellow and mannequin 2 must wear navy and yellow like so:

	#1 R + Y	#2 N + Y
(dif ↓) hat	R/Y	N/Y
(dif ↑) jacket	R/Y	N/Y
skirt	Y	N
tie	R	None

Of the choices, only (B) works.

7. C

If mannequin 1's skirt is the same color as mannequin 2's jacket, what color can that be? It can't be navy, since mannequin 2's skirt is navy, so it must be either red or yellow. Since mannequin 2 needs either a hat or a jacket in navy, she must wear the navy hat. That's (C).

2. E

Once again we arrive at the "could be true" and once again our sketches save us from doing any actual work: the sketch for question 6 proves that (E) is quite possible and therefore correct.

What's Next?

Did you like the outfits we came up with? Now that we're all dressed up, let's attend some conferences . . . in the next Matching game.

LOGIC GAME 4

Exactly three employees of Capital Enterprises—Maria, Suki, and Tate—attend a three-day conference together. Each day, there are exactly three sessions on the three topics of the conference—one on hiring, one on investing, and one on regulations. The following rules govern the conference:

Each conference participant attends exactly two sessions, which are on different topics and on different days.

Neither Maria nor Suki attends any session on investing.

Tate does not attend any session on the third day.

At most two Capital employees attend any given session together.

1. What is the maximum number of sessions attended by at least one Capital employee?

   (A) three
   (B) four
   (C) five
   (D) six
   (E) seven

2. Which one of the following must be false?

   (A) Maria attends sessions only on the first two days.
   (B) Suki attends sessions only on the last two days.
   (C) Exactly two Capital employees attend a session together on the second day.
   (D) Exactly one session is attended by one or more Capital employees on the second day.
   (E) Exactly three sessions are attended by one or more Capital employees on the third day.

3. If exactly two sessions on the third day are attended by one or more Capital employees, then which one of the following must be true?

   (A) Exactly two sessions on the first day are attended by one or more Capital employees.
   (B) Exactly two sessions on the second day are attended by one or more Capital employees.
   (C) Maria and Suki do not attend any session together.
   (D) Maria and Tate do not attend any session together.
   (E) Tate attends a session on investing.

4. Each of the following is possible EXCEPT:

   (A) Every session attended by at least one Capital employee is attended by exactly one Capital employee.
   (B) Every session attended by at least one Capital employee is attended by exactly two Capital employees.
   (C) Every session attended by Maria is also attended by Suki.
   (D) Every session attended by Suki is also attended by Tate.
   (E) Every session attended by Tate is also attended by Maria.

5. If all three sessions on the first day are attended by one or more Capital employees, then which one of the following must be false?

   (A) Maria and Suki attend a session together on the third day.
   (B) Suki and Tate attend a session together on the second day.
   (C) Maria attends a session on hiring on the second day.
   (D) Suki attends a session on regulations on the third day.
   (E) Tate attends a session on investing on the first day.

6. If Maria and Tate are the only Capital employees to attend a session on the first day, then each of the following could be true EXCEPT:

   (A) Maria and Suki attend exactly two sessions together.
   (B) Maria and Tate attend exactly two sessions together.
   (C) Suki and Tate attend exactly one session together.
   (D) Maria attends a session on regulations on the second day.
   (E) Tate attends a session on hiring on the second day.

Logic Game 4: Conference Attendees

What Makes It Difficult?

The game starts out quite harmlessly—three people attending a three-day conference together. A quick glance at Rule 1 reveals that each person goes to exactly two sessions, for a total of six attendances.

However, that's where its innocence ends as we're immediately told that each day of the conference consists of three possible sessions. "That's not so bad," you might say, as six attendances in nine spots just means that three will be blank. Unfortunately, Rule 4 removes all hope for a simple game: Each session can have at most two Capital employees. So the sessions can each have more than one attendee! While that's great for the person hosting the session (a conference of one is pretty sad), it's not so good for us.

Ready to go? The conference is in session.

Keys to the Game

Each session will have either one or two attendees. This is the heart of Rule 4.

Maria and Suki must attend *both* Hiring and Regulations. This is essentially the positive version of Rule 2. Since neither attends Investing, and each employee attends exactly two sessions, both must attend Hiring and Regulations. If anyone attends Investing, it'll have to be Tate.

An Advanced test taker always turns negatives into positives whenever possible.

Tate attends a session on each of days one and two—the positive implications of Rule 3.

Our Master Sketch looks like this:

Employees: m m s s t t

```
                    t             t
                    1             2             3
          H   ____ / ____    ____ / ____    ____ / ____

(No m, s) I   ____ / ____    ____ / ____    ____ / ____

          R   ____ / ____    ____ / ____    ____ / ____
```

Question Tally

Six questions: one Maximum number, one Must be False, one Could be True EXCEPT, and three Ifs.

Battle Plan

With half of the game's questions possibly benefitting from previous sketches, the most efficient approach is to do the Ifs first and hope that they can reduce your workload on the remaining three.

- #3, #5, and #6 first.
- #1, #2, and #4 last.

Answers and Explanations

1. D   2. E   3. C   4. B   5. A   6. A

Question Order: 3, 5, 6, 1, 2, 4

3. C

Since Tate never attends day 3 sessions (Rule 3), the question must be referring to Maria and Suki. Neither of them attend Investing, so one must attend Hiring and the other must attend Regulations on day 3. Since no one sees the same session twice (Rule 1), Maria and Suki must each attend the *other* session on either of days 1 or 2, which prevents them from going to anything together. That's (C).

5. A

If all three day 1 sessions are attended, the sketch would look like this:

As in question 3, splitting Maria and Suki up once means splitting them up both times, since neither can see Investing and neither can see the session they already saw again. (A) is therefore impossible.

6. A

Translate the EXCEPT and we end up with a "Must be False," so the correct answer is a choice that is impossible. There are only two possibilities here: Either Maria and Tate attend Hiring or Regulations together or Maria attends one of them while Tate attends Investing alone. Either way, Suki must attend a session on each of days 2 and 3, and Maria only has one session left, so (A) is impossible.

1. D

To maximize the number of sessions, we want to minimize the number of shared sessions—so that'll be zero; Rule 4 *permits* two employees to share but doesn't mandate it. So three employees times two sessions each = six, and that's (D). As long as Tate stays out of day 3, Maria and Suki stay out of Investing, and everyone attends solo, six of the nine sessions can be attended.

2. E

We may be lacking in sketches but oftentimes the previous *questions* themselves can be just as helpful: (A) is possible in question 5 if Maria has her second session on day 2; (B) must be true in question 6; and (C) and (D) are both possible in question 6 if Suki and Tate attend a session together on day 2 and Maria has her second session on day 3. That leaves (E) as impossible—indeed true as Tate isn't allowed to attend day 3.

An Advanced test taker knows that "previous work" doesn't *have* to mean "previous sketches."

---

4. B

Translate the EXCEPT and we end up with a "Must be False," so the correct answer is a choice that is impossible. (A) is proven possible in question 1. (C) is possible as long as Maria and Suki never split up. (D) and (E) are both possible if Tate stays out of Investing.

What's Next?

That's enough Matching for now. Next up are some Grouping games of the Distribution variety.

LOGIC GAME 5

A total of six books occupies three small shelves—one on the first shelf, two on the second shelf, and three on the third shelf. Two of the books are grammars—one of Farsi, the other of Hausa. Two others are linguistics monographs—one on phonology, the other on semantics. The remaining two books are novels—one by Vonnegut, the other by Woolf. The books' arrangement is consistent with the following:

There is at least one novel on the same shelf as the Farsi grammar.

The monographs are not both on the same shelf.

The Vonnegut novel is not on the same shelf as either monograph.

1. Which one of the following could be an accurate matching of the bookshelves to the books on each of them?

    (A) first shelf: Hausa grammar; second shelf: semantics monograph, Vonnegut novel; third shelf: Farsi grammar, phonology monograph, Woolf novel

    (B) first shelf: semantics monograph; second shelf: Farsi grammar, Vonnegut novel; third shelf: Hausa grammar, phonology monograph, Woolf novel

    (C) first shelf: Vonnegut novel; second shelf: phonology monograph, Farsi grammar; third shelf: Hausa grammar, semantics monograph, Woolf novel

    (D) first shelf: Woolf novel; second shelf: phonology and semantics monographs; third shelf: Farsi and Hausa grammars, Vonnegut novel

    (E) first shelf: Woolf novel; second shelf: Farsi grammar, Vonnegut novel; third shelf: Hausa grammar, phonology and semantics monographs

2. Which one of the following CANNOT be true?

    (A) A grammar is on the first shelf.

    (B) A linguistics monograph is on the same shelf as the Hausa grammar.

    (C) A novel is on the first shelf.

    (D) The novels are on the same shelf as each other.

    (E) Neither linguistics monograph is on the first shelf.

3. Which one of the following must be true?

    (A) A linguistics monograph and a grammar are on the second shelf.

    (B) A novel and a grammar are on the second shelf.

    (C) At least one linguistics monograph and at least one grammar are on the third shelf.

    (D) At least one novel and at least one grammar are on the third shelf.

    (E) At least one novel and at least one linguistics monograph are on the third shelf.

4. If both grammars are on the same shelf, which one of the following could be true?

    (A) The phonology monograph is on the third shelf.

    (B) A novel is on the first shelf.

    (C) Both novels are on the second shelf.

    (D) The Farsi grammar is on the second shelf.

    (E) The phonology monograph is on the first shelf.

5. Which one of the following must be true?

    (A) A linguistics monograph is on the first shelf.

    (B) No more than one novel is on each shelf.

    (C) The Farsi grammar is not on the same shelf as the Hausa grammar.

    (D) The semantics monograph is not on the same shelf as the Woolf novel.

    (E) The Woolf novel is not on the first shelf.

6. If the Farsi grammar is not on the third shelf, which one of the following could be true?

    (A) The phonology monograph is on the second shelf.

    (B) The Hausa grammar is on the second shelf.

    (C) The semantics monograph is on the third shelf.

    (D) The Vonnegut novel is on the third shelf.

    (E) The Woolf novel is on the second shelf.

7. If the Hausa grammar and the phonology monograph are on the same shelf, which one of the following must be true?

    (A) The phonology monograph is on the third shelf.

    (B) The Vonnegut novel is on the second shelf.

    (C) The semantics monograph is on the second shelf.

    (D) The semantics monograph is on the first shelf.

    (E) The Woolf novel is on the third shelf.

Logic Game 5: Shelving Books

What Makes It Difficult?

The action in this game—*distributing* six books among three shelves—is straightforward.

Grouping: Distribution Game
Dividing a large group of entities into several smaller groups.

With three types of books, this is indeed no simple distribution. To make things worse, the rules aren't particularly helpful. Rule 1 references (no pun intended) one of the Farsi grammar's shelf buddies. Rules 2 and 3 are no better—they merely tell us what *can't* be together. With a whopping seven questions, this game becomes a "must do" for *anyone* aiming for a high score, let alone the Advanced test taker.

It's time to hit the books.

Keys to the Game

F is a Key Player that allows us to set up limited options. Since the Farsi grammar must share a shelf with at least one novel, it's limited to either the second or third shelf. We can sketch both possibilities like so:

	Option I			Option II		
Grammars: F H	____			____		
Monographs: p s	F ____			____	____	
Novels: V W	____	____	____	F ____	____	____

An Advanced test taker finds limited options in Distribution games by driving the numbers to the definite.

The Vonnegut lies on shelf 2 in Option I. Rule 2 splits the monographs. Since the Vonnegut cannot share a shelf with either monograph, it must share with the Farsi in Option I. This leads to . . .

The Woolf and the Hausa lie on shelf 3 in Option I. With the monographs split and the Vonnegut occupying the remaining spot on shelf 2, only two spots remain for the Woolf and the Hausa—and they're both on shelf 3.

Our Master Sketch is as follows:

		Option I			Option II		
Grammars: F H	p/s				___		
Monographs: p s	F	V			___	___	
Novels: V W	p/s	W	H		F	V/W	___

Never ps
Never Vs
Never Vp

We weren't so lucky in Option II but, with one near complete sketch, we're still in excellent shape to tackle the questions.

Question Tally

Seven questions: one Acceptability, one Cannot be True, two Must be True, three Ifs.

Battle Plan

With limited options set up, we're in pretty good shape, but it still can't hurt to build good habits by approaching the questions in the most efficient order. Our plan of attack is:

- #1 first.
- #4, #6, and #7 second.
- #2, #3, and #5 last.

> An Advanced test taker knows that good, efficient habits are every bit as important as good, efficient strategies.

Answers and Explanations

1. B   2. A   3. D   4. E   5. E   6. C   7. E

Question Order: 1, 4, 6, 7, 2, 3, 5

1. B

Whenever your limited options produces at least one complete sketch, always take a moment to see if that sketch is in the choices of the Acceptability question before checking the rules one at a time. As it turns out, Option I matches (B) exactly and there's no need to do any further work.

> An Advanced test taker uses every advantage at his disposal to breeze through the Acceptability question.

4. E

Both grammars can only be on the same shelf in Option II and only on the third shelf at that. Since the Vonnegut cannot share a shelf with either monograph, it too must be on the third shelf, leaving the lone spot on shelf two for the Woolf:

p/s		
p/s	W	
F	V	H

With a completed sketch, a "could be true" question tends to refer to an entity that hasn't been definitively placed yet (either of the monographs, in this case). A quick scan of the choices reveals that only (A) and (E) mention monographs. Since they can be on the first shelf, (E) is correct.

6. C

The Farsi *not* on the third shelf should be music to your ears, as this means we're in Option I. Could be true refers to the monographs (as neither has been placed yet). (A) and (C) both mention monographs, but only (C) can be true.

An Advanced test taker gravitates towards the least restrictive entities for "could be" questions.

---

7. E

The Hausa and the phonology must share either shelf 2 or shelf 3. The latter can happen in Option I if the semantics monograph is on shelf 1. Unfortunately, that only eliminates (C). With four choices remaining, we have no choice but to sketch out the other option:

s		
p	H	
F	V	W

If the Hausa and the phonology share the second shelf, semantics needs to occupy the first shelf as it cannot share with the Vonnegut (Rule 3). Therefore, the remaining spot on the third shelf is for the Woolf—choice (E).

2. A

With plenty of sketches at our disposal, the fastest way to answer a "Cannot be True" is simply to check the choices against them: Any choice that shows up in even one working sketch can be eliminated. (B) works in our Option I sketch. (D) works in question 7's sketch. (C) works in question 7's sketch if you swap the Vonnegut and the semantics.

You *could* draw out one of the remaining two choices to find the answer but there's no need: if we *could* place a grammar on the first shelf (A), then (E) would also work at the same time, leaving us with no correct answer. However, it doesn't work the other way around—*not* placing a monograph on the first shelf doesn't necessarily mean that a *grammar* must go there. Therefore, (A) must be the one that's impossible.

3. D

The correct answer to a "Must be True" must work in *every* valid sketch. Our Option I sketch rules out (A). (B), (C), and (E) can all be eliminated by question 4's sketch. That leaves us (D), the correct answer.

5. E

Once again, the most efficient way through a "Must be True" is to check your previous work. Our Option I sketch rules out (D). Question 7's sketch removes (B). Swapping the Vonnegut with the semantics in question 7's sketch knocks out (A). Question 4's sketch eliminates (C). This leaves (E), the correct answer.

Must be True/Cannot be True

A non-If "must be true" by definition means that it must work in every sketch. On the other hand, a non-If "must be false" by definition is prohibited in every sketch. Therefore, a wrong choice for the former need only be *impossible* in one sketch and a wrong choice for the latter need only *work* in one sketch.

What's Next?

If you found the bookshelves tough, you most likely did not discover the keys to the game. The next game, however, is tough even if you *do* find them.

LOGIC GAME 6

A breeder has ten birds:

Kind	Male	Female
Goldfinches	H	J, K
Lovebirds	M	N
Parakeets	Q, R, S	T, W

The breeder exhibits pairs of birds consisting of one male and one female of the same kind. At most two pairs can be exhibited at a time; the remaining birds must be distributed between two cages. The breeder is constrained by the following conditions:

Neither cage can contain more than four birds.
Any two birds that are both of the same sex and of the same kind as each other cannot be caged together.
Whenever either J or W is exhibited, S cannot be exhibited.

1. Which one of the following is a possible assignment of the birds?

	First Cage	Second Cage	Exhibition
(A)	H, M, N	J, K, S	Q, R, T, W
(B)	K, M, Q	N, R, W	H, J, S, T
(C)	K, Q, S	R, T, W	H, J, M, N
(D)	H, J, M, R	K, N, S, W	Q, T
(E)	H, J, M, R, W	K, N, S	Q, T, W

2. Which one of the following lists two pairs of birds that the breeder can exhibit at the same time?

   (A   H and J; M and N
   (B) H and J; S and T
   (C) H and K; M and N
   (D) H and K; R and W
   (E) M and N; S and W

3. If Q and R are among the birds that are assigned to the cages, then it must be true that

   (A) H is exhibited
   (B) K is exhibited
   (C) N is exhibited
   (D) J is assigned to one of the cages
   (E) T is assigned to one of the cages

4. If Q and T are among the birds assigned to the cages, which one of the following is a pair of birds that must be exhibited?

   (A) H and J
   (B) H and K
   (C) M and N
   (D) R and W
   (E) S and W

5. Which one of the following CANNOT be true?

   (A) One pair of parakeets are the only birds exhibited together.
   (B) One pair of goldfinches and one pair of lovebirds are exhibited together.
   (C) One pair of goldfinches and one pair of parakeets are exhibited together.
   (D) One pair of lovebirds and one pair of parakeets are exhibited together.
   (E) Two pairs of parakeets are exhibited together.

6. If S is one of the birds exhibited, it must be true that

   (A) H is exhibited
   (B) M is exhibited
   (C) K is assigned to a cage
   (D) N is assigned to a cage
   (E) R is assigned to a cage

Logic Game 6: Birds on Display

What Makes It Difficult?

The action—distributing birds between the exhibition and the cages—is fairly straightforward. Unfortunately, it's also the *only* thing that's straightforward. There are ten birds to keep track of and, as if that wasn't bad enough, each bird is one of three types and one of two genders. It gets worse—there <u>is</u> an exhibition and *two* cages, with different restrictions for the former and latter.

The rules aren't much better. There aren't that many of them and none of them really give us anything concrete to work with. Rule 3 is the only one that tells us anything about specific birds, but its formal logic nature makes it not very useful.

Seems this one is really for the birds.

Keys to the Game

If S is exhibited, both J and W are in cages. This is the contrapositive of Rule 3.

One of the exhibited pairs of birds must be parakeets—the major deduction in this game. With three male parakeets and no two birds of the same sex and species able to share a cage (Rule 2), the only way to ensure that two of them don't end up in the same cage is to exhibit at least one.

An Advanced test taker *applies* the rules given to her, rather than simply reading and jotting them down.

At least one of T or W must be exhibited. Birds are exhibited in pairs. With one of the exhibited pairs being parakeets, at least one of these two ladies must be in the exhibition.

Not much to go on but it'll have to do. The final sketch looks like this:

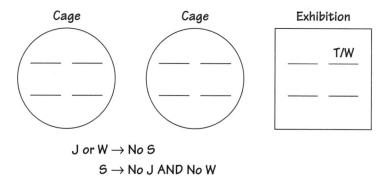

J or W → No S

S → No J AND No W

Same sex and kind cannot be in same cage.

Our sketch uses 12 slots but only ten of them will be filled, so remember to use two Xs as placeholders.

Question Tally

Six questions: one Acceptability, one Can be True, three Ifs, one Cannot be True.

Battle Plan

None of the hypothetical questions seem particularly difficult to implement, so our standard plan of attack applies:

- #1 first.
- #3, #4, and #6 second.
- #2 and #5 last.

Answers and Explanations

1. D **2. D** **3. D** **4. D** **5. B** **6. E**

Question Order: 1, 3, 4, 6, 2, 5

1. D

An acceptability question, so check each rule against the choices: The opening paragraph (*pairs* of birds are exhibited), as well as Rule 1 eliminates (E). Rule 2 axes (A) and (C). Rule 3 removes (B). That leaves (D), the correct answer.

3. D

With two of the three male parakeets assigned to cages, the remaining male parakeet, S, must be exhibited:

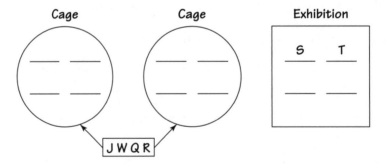

The contrapositive of Rule 3 tells us that J and W cannot be exhibited and must be caged. Of the choices, (D) must be true.

4. D

With T caged, our only remaining female parakeet, W, must be exhibited. Since Q is also caged and W cannot go with S, R must be the male parakeet in the exhibit:

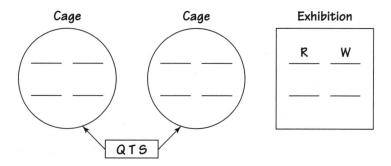

That's choice (D).

6. E

Since S *is* exhibited in question 3's sketch and the question is asking for a "must be true," we can simply refer to that sketch. Of the choices, only (E) *must* happen in that sketch, so it is correct.

Previous Work

Previous work can be a huge timesaver, but when is it safe to use a previous sketch for another hypothetical If and when is it not? Since "must be" questions ask for something in *every possible sketch that meets this criteria* and "could be" questions ask for something in *at least one possible sketch that meets this criteria*, it is safe for the former and not for the latter.

---

2. D

And so we arrive at the innocent-looking "could be true." Unfortunately, none of our previous sketches help us since they focused exclusively on placing parakeets. We'll simply have to do this the long way. (A) and (C) can be eliminated because neither contains a pair of parakeets. (B) has S with J and (E) has S with W, so these need to go as well. That leaves (D), the correct answer.

5. B

This "cannot be true" is asking for types of birds that are exhibited. The only concrete thing we know is that one of the types must be parakeets and that makes (B) impossible.

An Advanced test taker is proactive. She gives some thought to what the right answer might look like.

What's Next?

Whew, be glad that one's over! That's enough distribution for now. In the final game type for this chapter, you'll only have to select a group of items from a larger group. Sounds simple, right? Well, by now you know that if it was, it wouldn't be here.

LOGIC GAME 7

From among ten stones, a jeweler will select six, one for each of six rings. Of the stones, three—F, G, and H—are rubies; three—J, K, and M—are sapphires; and four—W, X, Y, and Z—are topazes. The selection of stones must meet the following restrictions:

At least two of the topazes are selected.

If exactly two of the sapphires are selected, exactly one of the rubies is selected.

If W is selected, neither H nor Z is selected.

If M is selected, W is also selected.

1. Which one of the following could be the selection of stones?

   (A) F, G, H, M, X, Y
   (B) F, G, J, K, M, W
   (C) F, G, J, K, W, X
   (D) G, H, J, X, Y, Z
   (E) G, H, K, W, X, Z

2. Which one of the following most be true?

   (A) G is selected.
   (B) J is selected.
   (C) X is selected.
   (D) Of at least one of the three types of stones, exactly one stone is selected.
   (E) Of at least one of the three types of stones, exactly three stones are selected.

3. If Z is selected, which one of the following could be true?

   (A) All three of the sapphires are selected.
   (B) Both J and M are selected.
   (C) Both K and M are selected.
   (D) None of the rubies is selected.
   (E) None of the sapphires is selected.

4. If exactly two rubies are selected, which one of the following must be true?

   (A) H is selected.
   (B) J is selected.
   (C) Z is selected.
   (D) Exactly one sapphire is selected.
   (E) Exactly two topazes are selected.

5. Which one of the following must be true?

   (A) The selection of stones includes at least one ruby.
   (B) The selection of stones includes at most two rubies.
   (C) The selection of stones includes either F or Z, or both.
   (D) The selection of stones includes either X or Y, or both.
   (E) The selection of stones includes either X or Z, or both.

6. If J and M are the only sapphires selected, which one of the following could be true?

   (A) F and G are both selected.
   (B) F and X are both selected.
   (C) G and H are both selected.
   (D) G and K are both selected.
   (E) Y and Z are both selected.

Logic Game 7: Jeweler Stones

What Makes It Difficult?

The action in this Grouping game is fairly simple—to *select* six stones out of 10.

Grouping: Selection Game
Choosing one small group out of a large one.

Difficulties abound. For one thing, there are ten stones to choose from—three rubies, three sapphires, and four topazes. That alone makes the choices fairly cumbersome. The ambiguity is heightened by what we're not told, namely: How many of each type of stone should we choose? It's always easier when we have an exact number to shoot for.

The rules only serve to further complicate matters. Rule 1 seems nice enough, but Rule 2 gives us a number restriction in formal logic. "Why can't you just *tell* me the bloody numbers outright?!" you might say. Rule 3 is presented in a "neither-nor" format, which requires a bit of translation. Rule 4 is pretty straightforward but even it doesn't help us nail anything down. With all the trouble we're going through selecting these stones, it better be a *really* nice ring.

Did you spot the keys? Leave no stone unturned.

Keys to the Game

If we have H or Z, we can't have W and we can't have M—the contrapositives to Rules 3 and 4.

Either two or three topazes will be selected—a combination of Rules 1 and 3. Rule 1 requires at least two, but Rule 3 prevents topazes W and Z from being selected together.

An Advanced test taker can draw the correct interpretations from formal logic statements and then combine those interpretations with other rules to form larger deductions.

In fact, knowing that there are either two or three topazes allows us to take the numbers further: If we have two topazes, we'll need three of one type (ruby or sapphire) and one of the other. If we have three topazes, we'll need either two of one type (ruby or sapphire) and one of the other, or three of one type (ruby or sapphire) and none of the other.

An Advanced test taker works out the number combinations whenever possible.

Our final sketch looks like this:

Ruby: F G H   _____   _____   _____   _____   _____   _____
Sapphire: J K M   t   t
Topaz: W X Y Z

Topazes = 2 or 3
Exactly 2 sapphires → exactly 1 ruby
Not exactly 1 ruby → Not exactly 2 sapphires
W → no H and no Z
H or Z → No W
M → W
No W → No M

Question Tally

Six questions: one Acceptability, two Must be True, three Ifs.

Battle Plan

A standard mix of questions: The Ifs don't seem hard to implement, so apply the standard order:

- #1 first.
- #3, #4, and #6 next.
- #2 and #5 last.

Answers and Explanations

1. D   2. E   3. E   4. D   5. D   6. B

Question Order: 1, 3, 4, 6, 2, 5

1. D

(B) is short one topaz (Rule 1). (C) has one too many rubies (Rule 2). (E) has W *and* the HZ pair (Rule 3). Finally, (A) has M without W (Rule 4). And just like that, (D) is correct.

3. E

If Z is selected, we cannot have W (contrapositive of Rule 3) and therefore no M (contrapositive of Rule 4):

Z	X/Y	_____	_____	_____	_____
t	t	r			

With a maximum of three topazes possible and one of the sapphires, M, already nixed, there must be at least one ruby in the lineup. That is enough to eliminate (A) through (D), leaving (E) as correct.

4. D

If *exactly* two rubies are selected, we cannot have exactly two sapphires (Rule 2), so the number of sapphires is either one or three. With at least two guaranteed topazes, three sapphires is too many, so we must have two rubies, three topazes, and—choice (D)—one sapphire.

An Advanced test taker is comfortable working out all kinds of deductions, be they numbers, specific entities, or otherwise.

---

6. B

If you missed the "only" here, it's fairly hopeless. Otherwise, it's not so tough: With J and M as the *only* sapphires selected, Rule 2 kicks in and we can only have one ruby and three topazes to round out the six:

X	Y	W	J	M	F/G
t	t	t	s	s	r

With three topazes, either W or Z must be rejected (Rule 3). Since M is selected, the lucky topaz must be W (Rule 4), which makes H ineligible for selection as well (Rule 3). So the ruby must be either F or G, the former of which, along with X, is choice (B).

An Advanced test taker takes careful notice of "keywords"—structural signals that authors employ in order to help convey their ideas.

---

2. E

(A), (B), and (C) while possible, do not need to be selected in question 3's sketch. For the remaining two choices, we would simply need to work out the numbers. (D) does not have to be true as three topazes can be paired with three rubies (if W isn't selected) or three sapphires (if W *is* selected). (E), however, *must* be true: with two topazes, the 2-2-2 combination isn't allowed as that would violate Rule 2, so there would need to be either three rubies or three sapphires. And with three topazes, the requirement in (E) has already been met.

5. D

In question 2, we determined that three topazes *can* be paired with either three sapphires or three rubies, which eliminates (A) and (B), respectively. Question 6's sketch proves that (C) does not need to be true. As for the remaining two, we'll simply need to test one: With a minimum of two topazes, (D) *does* need to be true as the remaining two topazes, W and Z, cannot be selected together, so we are forced to take either X or Y. (E), however, need not be true as W and Y is a perfectly valid selection for a two-topaz ring.

What's Next?

Selection's got a nice ring to it, doesn't it? Let's try that again with people on a panel in our final "Supercharged Standards" game.

LOGIC GAME 8

In each of two years exactly two of four lawmakers—Feld, Gibson, Hsu, and Ivins—and exactly two of three scientists—Vega, Young, and Zapora—will serve as members of a four-person panel. In each year, one of the members will be chairperson. The chairperson in the first year cannot serve on the panel in the second year. The chairperson in the second year must have served on the panel in the first year. Service on the panel must obey the following conditions:

Gibson and Vega do not serve on the panel in the same year as each other. Hsu and Young do not serve on the panel in the same year as each other. Each year, either Ivins or Vega, but not both, serves on the panel.

1. Which one of the following could be the list of the people who serve on the panel in the first year?

   (A) Feld, Gibson, Vega, Zapora
   (B) Feld, Hsu, Vega, Zapora
   (C) Feld, Ivins, Vega, Zapora
   (D) Gibson, Hsu, Ivins, Zapora
   (E) Hsu, Ivins, Young, Zapora

2. If Vega is the chairperson in the first year, which one of the following is a pair of people who must serve on the panel in the second year?

   (A) Gibson and Young
   (B) Gibson and Zapora
   (C) Hsu and Ivins
   (D) Ivins and Young
   (E) Vega and Young

3. If Hsu is the chairperson in the first year, which one of the following could be the chairperson in the second year?

   (A) Feld
   (B) Gibson
   (C) Hsu
   (D) Ivins
   (E) Young

4. IF Feld serves on the panel in a given year, any one of the following could serve on the panel that year EXCEPT:

   (A) Gibson
   (B) Hsu
   (C) Ivins
   (D) Vega
   (E) Young

5. If Ivins is the chairperson in the first year, which one of the following could be the chairperson in the second year?

   (A) Feld
   (B) Gibson
   (C) Hsu
   (D) Vega
   (E) Young

6. Which one of the following must be true?

   (A) Feld is on the panel in the second year.
   (B) Hsu is on the panel in the first year.
   (C) Ivins is on the panel in both years.
   (D) Young is on the panel in both years.
   (E) Zapora is on the panel in the second year.

Logic Game 8: Legal Science Panel

What Makes It Difficult?

The game starts generously: We're selecting *exactly* two of four lawmakers and *exactly* two of three scientists (don't you just love the sound of that word?) for a four-person panel. Unfortunately, that seems to be it in terms of freebies for this game. Almost in the same breath, the test maker decides to throw in a semi-red herring (a pink herring maybe?): There's a chairperson in each of the two years and the chair of the first year can't participate in the second. While the chair *is* mentioned in some of the questions, focusing on this rule early can actually make the setup *harder* to complete.

Rules 1 and 2 aren't much help as each only tells us who *can't* serve together. Rule 3 is one of those rules that just "feels" important and is therefore a great place to start.

Hope you like voting. It's time to elect some panel members.

Keys to the Game

I and V are Key Players that allow us to set up limited options. The "but not both" in Rule 3 is a clear sign of limited options. With only two years and "Ivins but not Vega" in one and "Vega but not Ivins" in the other, there are only two possible ways that can work out:

(2 *of* 4) Lawmakers: F G H I
(2 *of* 3) Scientists: v y z

	Option I				Option II			
I	___	___	___	Year 1 v	___	___	___	
v	___	___	___	Year 2 I	___	___	___	

> An Advanced test taker recognizes key phrases that lead to major deductions.

Focus on who *can* go together, rather than who *can't*. Rules 1 and 2 aren't much help in their current form but their implications are profound:

If I is selected, then v isn't (Rule 3), but then the other two scientists, y and z, must be selected. If y is selected, then H isn't (Rule 2). The last member could be either F or G.

If I *isn't* selected, then v is (Rule 3), and therefore G isn't (Rule 1). With I and G out, the two lawmakers on the panel must be F and H, since they're the only ones left. Since H is in, y is out (Rule 2), and therefore z must be selected, since z is the only scientist left. This leads us to our final key…

z will always be on the panel. As one of two people who can serve with anyone, Zapora will always be on the panel for both years.

Putting all of this together into our Master Sketches results in the following:

(2 of 4) Lawmakers: F G H I
(2 of 3) Scientists: v y z

	Option I						Option II		
I	y	z	F/G	Year 1	v	F	H	z	
v	F	H	z	Year 2	I	y	z	F/G	

An Advanced test taker invests the time for deductions upfront to reap the rewards once the questions begin.

Question Tally

Six questions: one Acceptability, four Ifs, one Must be True.

Battle Plan

With two completely worked out sketches as the *only* sketches for this game, there's no reason why we *can't* go in order. The test maker must have realized the futility in trying to slow you, the elite test taker, on this set as the questions happen to be printed in the most efficient order anyway!

You worked hard on setting this sketch up to be as complete as it is, so get in there and collect your reward!

Answers and Explanations

1. B   2. D   3. A   4. A   5. A   6. E

Question Order: 1–6

1. B

First up, the Acceptability. A look at our sketch reveals (B) to be correct!

For the record: (A) is out as Gibson and Vega cannot serve together (Rule 1); (E) is out as Hsu and Young cannot serve together (Rule 2); (C) has Ivins serving with Vega (Rule 3); and (D) has too many lawmakers and is one scientist short of a full panel.

2. D

If Vega is the chair in the first year, we're in Option II. Of the choices, only (D) must be true.

3. A

Hsu as chair in the first year puts us in Option II again. The chair for the second year needs to have served during the first. That's Zapora or Feld, the latter of which is choice (A).

4. A

Feld can serve in either year, so anyone who can serve with Feld at any time can be eliminated. Of the choices, only Gibson cannot, as he can only do so by replacing Feld.

5. A

Ivins as the chair in the first year puts us in Option I. The chair for the second year needs to have served during the first. That's Zapora or Feld, the latter of which is choice (A).

6. E

With our detailed Options, this one is a snap: (A) and (B) each depend on a particular Option, so both are out. (C) directly violates Rule 3. (D) happens in neither Option. This leaves (E), which must be true as Zapora serves in *both* years.

An Advanced test taker milks his hard-earned deductions to the fullest extent possible.

What's Next?

This concludes our Logic Games warm-up, as we move on to more challenging material. Perhaps you found these to be pretty tough already—tough maybe, but not quite brutal. Despite some complexities, all the games in this chapter revolve around a single game action, which is almost always easier than handling multiple tasks at once. Furthermore, all are amenable to a few key deductions and a little cleverness.

But perhaps you breezed through the games in this chapter, wondering to yourself, "I thought these were going to be difficult. What gives?" Have no fear. It gets worse, much worse.

CHAPTER THREE

Time Warps and Assemblies

Once upon a time the LSAT test makers introduced aspiring law students to the wonderful world of what we at Kaplan call Process games and Mapping games.

Process, or Time Warp, game
Fit behavior to a prearranged plan or pattern.

A key skill tested in this game type is your ability to think forward and backward in time, so we also call these "Time Warps."

Mapping, or Assembly, game
Build a map by connecting entities together.

The goal of this type of game is to construct a framework by connecting individual entities together, so we also call these "Assemblies."

While process games appeared regularly from LSAT PrepTest X through LSAT PrepTest XVI (1994–1995), mapping games were a bit rarer. Both have pretty much been absent since then, but there are a few good reasons to wrack your brain with these game types. First, there's no guarantee that they won't appear again; in fact a Process game *did* appear in an undisclosed test in 1998 and a Mapping game appeared on LSAT PrepTest XL (June 2003). And second, there's always a chance that you'll see a game on your test that doesn't fit into one of the standard categories. In fact, an Advanced test taker *needs* to be ready for the unexpected. Pitting your wits against games that are *unusual* can't hurt, and will almost certainly help prepare you for any type of oddball that you may encounter.

Before you begin, here are some useful questions to think through when faced with a Time Warp game:

- What is the situation at the start?
- How often do changes occur?
- What specifically happens during a change?
- How is the situation different after the change?
- Hypothesize: What could happen? Go through some "what ifs" about the game to get a feel for how the process works.

Also consider the following for an Assembly game:

- How are the entities arranged at the start?
- Which entities *can* or *cannot* connect with the other entities?
- Are there any restrictions on the *number* of connections allowed?
- Does the actual position of the entities matter?
- Hypothesize: How many ways can the key entities connect? Map out a few possible connections to get a feel for how the entities interact.

LOGIC GAME 9

A science student has exactly four flasks—1, 2, 3, and 4—originally containing a red, a blue, a green, and an orange chemical, respectively. An experiment consists of mixing exactly two of these chemicals together by completely emptying the contents of one of the flasks into another of the flasks. The following conditions apply:

The product of an experiment cannot be used in further experiments.

Mixing the contents of 1 and 2 produces a red chemical.

Mixing the contents of 2 and 3 produces an orange chemical.

Mixing the contents of 3 with the contents of either 1 or 4 produces a blue chemical.

Mixing the contents of 4 with the contents of either 1 or 2 produces a green chemical.

1. If the student performs exactly one experiment, which one of the following could be the colors of the chemicals in the resulting three nonempty flasks?

   (A) blue, blue, green
   (B) blue, orange, orange
   (C) blue, orange, red
   (D) green, green, red
   (E) green, orange, orange

2. If the student performs exactly two experiments, which one of the following could be the colors of the chemicals in the resulting two nonempty flasks?

   (A) blue, blue
   (B) blue, orange
   (C) blue, red
   (D) green, red
   (E) orange, orange

3. If the student performs exactly one experiment and none of the resulting three nonempty flasks contains a red chemical, which one of the following could be the colors of the chemicals in the three flasks?

   (A) blue, blue, green
   (B) blue, green, green
   (C) blue, green, orange
   (D) blue, orange, orange
   (E) green, green, orange

4. If the student performs exactly one experiment and exactly one of the resulting three nonempty flasks contains a blue chemical, which one of the following must be the colors of the chemicals in the other two flasks?

   (A) both green
   (B) both orange
   (C) both red
   (D) one green and one red
   (E) one orange and one red

5. If the student will perform exactly two experiments and after the first experiment exactly one of the resulting three nonempty flasks contains an orange chemical, then in the second experiment the student could mix together the contents of flasks

   (A) 1 and 2
   (B) 1 and 3
   (C) 1 and 4
   (D) 2 and 3
   (E) 3 and 4

6. If the student performs exactly one experiment and none of the resulting three nonempty flasks contains an orange chemical, then the student must have mixed the contents of

   (A) flask 1 with flask 2
   (B) flask 1 with flask 4
   (C) flask 2 with flask 4
   (D) flask 2 with one of the other flasks
   (E) flask 4 with one of the other flasks

7. If the student performs exactly two experiments and exactly one of the resulting two nonempty flasks contains an orange chemical, then it must be true that the contents of the other nonempty flask is

   (A) obtained by mixing flasks 1 and 2
   (B) obtained by mixing flasks 2 and 4
   (C) blue
   (D) green
   (E) red

Logic Game 9: Rainbow Flasks

What Makes It Difficult?

The opening paragraph seems to be standard fare until we hit the bit about an experiment. A quick glance at the rules confirms that this is indeed a Time Warp game. There are plenty of rules, which initially suggest an endless array of colorful concoctions.

The questions pose the usual difficulties found in these kinds of games. Some questions ask you to look forward in the process and follow the steps through to a result, while others—generally the tougher ones—tell you what the result was, and ask you to work backwards to reconstruct the situation that made this result possible. Another difficulty is that there are no big deductions to make up front. We simply have to bang out the questions one by one (seven, no less), following our budding scientist where she may lead us.

There really isn't much to draw for this kind of game, but you have to compensate for this lack of pencil work with extra brainwork. As always, there are still a few things you can do that should ease your brain's burden a bit.

Without further ado, get ready to mix it up!

Keys to the Game

No more than two experiments can ever be performed. Rule 1 states that, once mixed, the products of a done experiment are off limits. That means our aspiring scientist will either stop after one experiment or she'll also combine the remaining two flasks before hanging up the lab coat. Realizing this makes the game much more manageable.

The rules account for all six possible ways of combining two flasks. Since mixed flasks cannot be remixed, there are only six ways to combine two flasks, and Rules 2–5 take care of these.

As mentioned earlier, there isn't much to draw, but jotting down a condensed version of the rules can help keep things organized:

$$
\begin{array}{cccc}
1 & 2 & 3 & 4 \\
R & B & G & O
\end{array}
$$

$$
\begin{array}{ll}
1 + 2 = R & 3 + 4 = B \\
2 + 3 = O & 1 + 4 = G \\
1 + 3 = B & 2 + 4 = G
\end{array}
$$

Question Tally

Seven questions: All Ifs!

Battle Plan

All seven questions are Ifs but four of them deal with only one experiment while the remaining three deal with two. Therefore, the most efficient approach is to do all the ones with only one experiment first, before tackling the three that are more complex:

- #1, #3, #4, and #6 first.
- #2, #5, and #7 last.

Answers and Explanations

1. D   2. C   3. B   4. A   5. E   6. E   7. D

Question Order: 1, 3, 4, 6, 2, 5, 7

1. D

This is an unusual Acceptability; one whose format makes the question a bit more challenging. We've actually noted the six possible experiment results already. What we did *not* do is list the end results for each of the remaining flasks. Might as well start at the beginning. Consult the rules and use your pencil to jot down your notes:

1 + 2 = red. 3 remains green and 4 remains orange. "Red, green, orange" is not a choice. 1 + 3 = blue. 2 remains blue and 4 remains orange. "Blue, blue, orange" is not a choice. 1 + 4 = green. 2 remains blue and 3 remains green. "Green, green, blue" is not a choice.

Phew! Continuing:

2 + 3 = orange. 1 remains red and 4 remains orange. "Orange, orange, red" is not a choice. 2 + 4 = green. One remains red and 3 remains green. Oh, for the love of... Hurray! "Green, green, red" is choice (D). For the record, "Blue, blue, red," the product of combining 3 + 4 while leaving 1 and 2 as they were, would also have been an acceptable answer choice.

An Advanced test taker makes use of her pencil early in an abstract game with the intention of reaping the benefits later.

---

3. B

At this point, things get hairy. (I can hear you now, dear reader: "Whaddaya mean *at this point?!*") We're given a result and we have to work backwards from it.

Relax, this is actually cause for celebration: *We just wrote out all six results to a single experiment in question 1!* (See, I *knew* that was a good idea at the time!)

Of the choices, only (B) shows up in our scratch work.

4. A

Sort of a switch on question 3; here, exactly one flask contains blue after the single experiment. Once again, here's where working out all of the single experiment possibilities in question 1 really pays off. Among the six results, only one—"Green, green, blue"—meets the requirement of "exactly one blue." That's choice (A).

6. E

Similar to the two we just did, this question is asking for the flasks rather than the colors. As with questions 3 and 4, let's check our scratch work from question 1 to answer it.

With no oranges, we have three possible mixes: 1 + 4 (green, green, blue); 2 + 4 (green, green, red); and 3 + 4 (blue, blue, red). Since we're looking for what *must* have happened, we'll need the common thread among all three possibilities to get the correct answer. That's choice (E)—mixing flask 4 with something else.

2. C

Now we have *two* experiments to trace. This sounds like more than a sane person could keep track of but it's actually not that bad. Since done experiments can't be reused, there are actually only three possibilities here. Our scratch work for question 1 proved invaluable in the single-experiment questions, so working out the possibilities here should likewise make our lives easier in the remaining double-experiment questions in the set:

- 1 + 2 and 3 + 4 in either order result in red and blue, respectively.
- 1 + 3 and 2 + 4 in either order result in blue and green, respectively.
- 1 + 4 and 2 + 3 in either order result in green and orange, respectively.

"Blue, red" is choice (C).

5. E

This deceptively worded question *appears* to draw upon our scratch work for double experiments. However, it only wants to know the flasks eligible for mixing in the second experiment. In other words, we're looking for the two flasks experiment one *didn't touch* if that experiment resulted in a single orange.

Our scratch work from question 1 shows two possible ways to get "exactly one orange": 1 + 2 (red, green, orange) and 1 + 3 (blue, blue, orange). The former allows 3 + 4—choice (E)— to be mixed in experiment two.

An Advanced test taker recognizes questions that employ different wording, but actually mean the same thing or hinge on the same concept.

---

7. D

This question would indeed be tough had we not bothered to work out the scratch work earlier. Fortunately for us, we can simply refer to the results from question 2. "Exactly one orange" after two experiments is only possible from mixing 1 + 4 and 2 + 3. In those experiments, the remaining flask is green, which is choice (D).

What's Next?

Did you enjoy creating those diabolical concoctions? If so, you'll love the ones in the next game.

LOGIC GAME 10

Four apprentices—Louis, Madelyn, Nora, and Oliver—are initially assigned to projects Q, R, S, and T, respectively. During the year in which they are apprentices, two reassignments of apprentices to projects will be made, each time according to a different one of the following plans, which can be used in any order:
  Plan 1. The apprentice assigned to project Q switches projects with the apprentice assigned to project S and the apprentice assigned to project R switches projects with the apprentice assigned to project T.
  Plan 2. The apprentice assigned to project S switches projects with the apprentice assigned to project T.
  Plan 3. Louis and Madelyn switch projects with each other.

1. Which one of the following must be true after the second reassignment of apprentices to projects during the year if that reassignment assigns Nora to project T?

    (A)   Louis is assigned to project S.
    (B)   Madelyn is assigned to project R.
    (C)   Madelyn is assigned to project S.
    (D)   Oliver is assigned to project R.
    (E)   Oliver is assigned to project S.

2. Which one of the following could be true after only one reassignment during the year?

    (A)   Louis is assigned to project T.
    (B)   Nora is assigned to project R.
    (C)   Oliver is assigned to project Q.
    (D)   Louis and Nora each remain assigned to the same projects as before.
    (E)   Nora and Oliver each remain assigned to the same projects as before.

3. If at some time during the year, Louis is reassigned to project R, which one of the following could have been the assignment of apprentices to the projects immediately before the reassignment?

    (A)   Q: Louis; R: Madelyn; S: Oliver; T: Nora
    (B)   Q: Louis; R: Nora; S: Oliver; T: Madelyn
    (C)   Q: Nora; R: Madelyn; S: Louis; T: Oliver
    (D)   Q: Nora; R: Oliver; S: Louis; T: Madelyn
    (E)   Q: Oliver; R: Nora; S: Louis; T: Madelyn

4. Which one of the following is an acceptable assignment of apprentices to the projects after only one reassignment during the year?

    (A)   Q: Louis; R: Madelyn; S: Nora; T: Oliver
    (B)   Q: Madelyn; R: Louis; S: Nora; T: Oliver
    (C)   Q: Madelyn; R: Oliver; S: Nora; T: Louis
    (D)   Q: Nora; R: Louis; S: Oliver; T: Madelyn
    (E)   Q: Nora; R: Madelyn; S: Oliver; T: Louis

5. If the first reassignment is made according to plan 1, which one of the following must be true?

    (A)   Louis is assigned to project T as a result of the second reassignment.
    (B)   Madelyn is assigned to project Q as a result of the second reassignment.
    (C)   Madelyn is assigned to project T as a result of the second reassignment.
    (D)   Oliver is assigned to project S as a result of the second reassignment.
    (E)   Oliver is assigned to project T as a result of the second reassignment.

Logic Game 10: The Mysterious Apprentices

What Makes It Difficult?

Louis, Madelyn, Nora, and Oliver are embarking on some top-secret projects. In fact, they're *so* secret that we don't have enough information to make any deductions!

We're up against the same basic thing as in the previous game. Unfortunately, the questions are a good deal harder as they focus more on rewinding time than moving forward. With no deductions, we will once again have to brute force our way through the questions.

And so, the plot thickens (and with how *thin* it was in this game to begin with, that's not saying much)…

Keys to the Game

Anticipate the relevant issues that will be tested. Here, we need to focus on who's doing what for each of the three plans, and what reassignments make certain other reassignments possible.

Exactly two reassignments will be made. It's listed that way in the opening paragraph but it deserves mention due to the severe lack of information in this game. With only two reassignments, we can breathe a little easier knowing that the possibilities aren't *quite* limitless.

In Plans 2 and 3, two switch assignments, and two stay the same. In Plan 1, all four swap. Not a major revelation, but again, anything that we can latch onto that places some restrictions on the action should help us in the long run.

An Advanced test taker sees a Logic Game from all possible angles, noticing everything from big deductions down to small observations.

And with that, all we can do is sum up the rules:

Initial Setup:

Q	R	S	T
L	M	N	O

Plan 1: Q $\leftrightarrow$ S AND R $\leftrightarrow$ T
Plan 2: S $\leftrightarrow$ T
Plan 3: L $\leftrightarrow$ M

Question Tally

Five questions: three Ifs, one Could be True, one Acceptability.

Battle Plan

This one also involves either one or two "processes" (reassignments, in this case). As we saw in the previous game, the most efficient method of attack is to hit all of the questions that only deal with *one* reassignment before moving on to the more complex ones:

- #4 first.
- #5 second.
- #2 third.
- #1 fourth.
- #3 last.

Answers and Explanations

1. E　　**2. E**　　**3. A**　　**4. B**　　**5. A**

Question Order: 4, 5, 2, 1, 3

4. B

A standard Acceptability question. Since there are only three ways to do one reassignment and there are four more questions further down the queue, it doesn't hurt to take a moment to map out all three right now:

	Q	R	S	T
Initial:	L	M	N	O
Plan 1:	N	O	L	M
Plan 2:	L	M	O	N
Plan 3:	M	L	N	O

(B) is possible with Plan 3, so it is correct.

An Advanced test taker does the Acceptability question first regardless of its printed order.

---

5. A

Using our table from question 4, we see that a Plan 1 first reassignment results in NOLM. Each of the choices concerns the *second* reassignment, so what can we figure out about that? Since L has S and M has T, the second reassignment is actually identical *whether they use Plan 2 or Plan 3*! In either case, L gets T as a result—choice (A).

2. E

With our table from question 4, this one becomes a cinch. A quick scan reveals that only (E) can be true (if Plan 3 is implemented).

1. E

According to the table from question 4, the first reassignment can leave Nora in one of three places: *Q*, *T*, or *S*. Of the three, only *S* provides Nora with a path to *T* in one reassignment, so the order must be Plan 3 (she needs to stay at *S*) → Plan 2. In this case, Oliver would end up with *S*—choice (E).

3. A

This is the toughest one of the bunch (hence a great one to do last). The correct answer to this question must satisfy two requirements: It must be a valid first reassignment and it must grant Louis access to *R* in one future reassignment. A glance at our trusty question 4 table reveals that (B), (C), and (E) do not meet the first requirement. Between (A) and (D), the latter does not provide Louis with a way to reach *R*, so (A) is correct.

What's Next?

Need a vacation from creepy folks messing with time? Then try your hand at an assembly game. This is quite relaxing, with five islands to boot. Or so it seems at first . . .

LOGIC GAME 11

A lake contains exactly five islands—J, K, L, M, O—which are unconnected by bridges. Contractors will build a network of bridges that satisfies the following specifications:

Each bridge directly connects exactly two islands with each other, and no two bridges intersect.

No more than one bridge directly connects any two islands.

No island has more than three bridges that directly connect it with other islands.

J, K, and L are each directly connected by bridge with one or both of M and O.

J is directly connected by bridge with exactly two islands.

K is directly connected by bridge with exactly one island.

A bridge directly connects J with O, and a bridge directly connects M with O.

1. Which one of the following is a complete and accurate list of the islands any one of which could be directly connected by bridge with L?

    (A)   J, K
    (B)   J, M
    (C)   J, O
    (D)   J, M, O
    (E)   J, K, M, O

2. Which one of the following could be true about the completed network of bridges?

    (A)   J is directly connected by bridge both with L and with M.
    (B)   K is directly connected by bridge both with M and with O.
    (C)   L is directly connected by bridge both with J and with M.
    (D)   M is directly connected by bridge with J, with K, and with L.
    (E)   O is directly connected by bridge with K, with L, and with M.

3. If a bridge directly connects K with O, then which one of the following could be true?

    (A)   No bridge directly connects L with M.
    (B)   A bridge directly connects J with L.
    (C)   A bridge directly connects L with O.
    (D)   There are exactly three bridges directly connecting L with other islands.
    (E)   There are exactly two bridges directly connecting O with other islands.

4. If a bridge directly connects L with M and a bridge directly connects L with O, then which one of the following must be true?

    (A)   A bridge directly connects J with M.
    (B)   A bridge directly connects K with M.
    (C)   A bridge directly connects K with O.
    (D)   There are exactly two bridges directly connecting L with other islands.
    (E)   There are exactly two bridges directly connecting M with other islands.

5. If no island that is directly connected by bridge with M is also directly connected by bridge with O, then there must be a bridge directly connecting

    (A)   J with L
    (B)   J with M
    (C)   K with O
    (D)   L with M
    (E)   L with O

Logic Game 11: Island Bridges

What Makes It Difficult?

Assembly games will often have sketches that are quite elaborate, so there's generally a lot of information to keep track of, and this game is no different. In assemblies, possible sketches are key as there generally aren't too many. Simply getting over the weirdness and working them out is often more than half the battle. While, on average, assembly games do tend to take longer to set up than most, the extra work invested also means that their question sets tend to be quicker to plow through as well.

With more rules than bridges, and nearly every rule containing a cryptic numerical restriction, simply keeping everything straight in this game can be challenge enough. Fortunately, if you calmed down long enough to organize everything, you'll notice that this game allows quite a few more deductions than our time warps did.

Break out the bathing suits. We're going for a swim in the lake!

Keys to the Game

O has either 2 or 3 bridges. Rule 7 guarantees two while Rule 3 allows a possible third.

K's only connection is with either M or O—a combination of Rules 4 and 6.

O is a Key Player that allows us to set up limited options. With two of O's connections laid out on the pavement, we can deduce the following two sketches:

Option I

```
   J     K/L
    \   /
      O
      /
K/L —— M
```

Needs J–L or J–M
L–M is possible

Option II

```
   J
  / \
 L   O
  \ /
   M
   |
   K
```

L–O is possible

An Advanced test taker scopes out all of the possibilities in games that are heavily invested in numerical restrictions.

Question Tally

Five questions: one Complete & Accurate List, one Could be True, three Ifs.

Battle Plan

With two fairly complete Options, there's really no harm in simply doing these in order.

Answers and Explanations

1. D   **2. C**   **3. B**   **4. B**   **5. A**

Question Order: 1–5

1. D

No bridge is allowed more than three connections (Rule 3), so (E) is out. In Option II, L is currently connected to both J and M, and a further connection to O is also possible. That's (D).

2. C

Funny how we were *just* speaking of L connecting to both J and M as that happens to be the answer to this question as well!

For the record: (A) J is already connected to O (Rule 7) and is only allowed one additional connection (Rule 5); (B) K can only have one connection (Rule 6); (D) along with Rule 7, this would give M four connections, which violates Rule 3.

3. B

This puts us in Option I with the following sketch:

For J to have two connections, it must connect to either L or M as well. The former is choice (B).

4. B

The premise here places us in Option II with the following sketch:

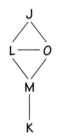

A scan of the choices reveals that only (B) works.

5. A

Option II satisfies the premise, so let's begin there. A glance of this Option allows us to eliminate (B), (C), and (E) as not necessarily true. As for the remaining two choices, we can break (D) with the following version of Option I:

(A), however, must be true in every sketch.

An Advanced test taker exhausts all of his previous work before making more sketches.

What's Next?

Are lakes not your thing? Our final game in this chapter is a bit more . . . up in the air.

LOGIC GAME 12

Each nonstop flight offered by Zephyr Airlines departs from one and arrives at another of five cities: Honolulu, Montreal, Philadelphia, Toronto, and Vancouver. Any two cities are said to be connected with each other if Zephyr offers nonstop flights between them. Each city is connected with at least one other city. The following conditions govern Zephyr's nonstop flights:

Montreal is connected with exactly one other city.
Honolulu is not connected with Toronto.
Any city that is connected with Honolulu is also connected with Toronto.
If Philadelphia is connected with Toronto, then Philadelphia is not connected with Vancouver.

1. Which one of the following could be a complete and accurate list of Zephyr Airlines' connected cities?

   (A) Honolulu and Vancouver; Montreal and Toronto; Philadelphia and Vancouver; Toronto and Vancouver
   (B) Honolulu and Vancouver; Montreal and Philadelphia; Montreal and Toronto; Philadelphia and Toronto; Toronto and Vancouver
   (C) Honolulu and Philadelphia; Honolulu and Montreal; Philadelphia and Toronto; Toronto and Vancouver
   (D) Honolulu and Philadelphia; Montreal and Toronto; Philadelphia and Toronto; Philadelphia and Vancouver; Toronto and Vancouver
   (E) Honolulu and Philadelphia; Honolulu and Toronto; Montreal and Philadelphia; Philadelphia and Vancouver

2. If exactly three cities are each connected with Philadelphia, then which one of the following could be a pair of connected cities?

   (A) Honolulu and Montreal
   (B) Honolulu and Vancouver
   (C) Montreal and Toronto
   (D) Montreal and Vancouver
   (E) Philadelphia and Vancouver

3. Which one of the following is a pair of cities that CANNOT be connected?

   (A) Honolulu and Montreal
   (B) Honolulu and Philadelphia
   (C) Montreal and Philadelphia
   (D) Montreal and Vancouver
   (E) Philadelphia and Toronto

4. Which one of the following could be true?

   (A) Montreal and Philadelphia are connected with each other, but neither is connected with any other city.
   (B) Montreal and Toronto are connected with each other, but neither is connected with any other city.
   (C) Philadelphia and Toronto are connected with each other, but neither is connected with any other city.
   (D) Philadelphia and Vancouver are connected with each other, but neither is connected with any other city.
   (E) Toronto and Vancouver are connected with each other, but neither is connected with any other city.

5. If Toronto is the only city that is connected with Philadelphia, then which one of the following could be true?

   (A) Exactly one city is connected with Toronto.
   (B) Exactly one city is connected with Vancouver.
   (C) Exactly two cities are each connected with Honolulu.
   (D) Exactly two cities are each connected with Toronto.
   (E) Exactly four cities are each connected with Toronto.

6. At most how many pairs of cities could be connected?

   (A) four
   (B) five
   (C) six
   (D) seven
   (E) eight

7. If four of the cities are each connected with the remaining city, then the cities in which one of the following pairs must be connected with each other?

   (A) Honolulu and Montreal
   (B) Honolulu and Philadelphia
   (C) Honolulu and Vancouver
   (D) Montreal and Philadelphia
   (E) Montreal and Toronto

Logic Game 12: Zephyr Airlines

What Makes It Difficult?

We expect airports to be confusing places that can seem rather chaotic and Zephyr Airlines certainly doesn't disappoint in that department. Like the previous assembly game, the key to this one is to work out some possible sketches to make the game more concrete. Unlike the previous game, however, this one does not provide us with the plethora of exact numerical restrictions that made the former game manageable.

With only four rules and half of them involving negatives, this game feels a lot more "open." Rules 3 and 4 use formal logic, though the careless test taker could easily miss this fact in the former as it doesn't employ the word "if." Rule 1 tries to be helpful with an exact number, but unfortunately, it's too little, too late for it to do any good.

Get ready for takeoff.

Keys to the Game

M—H isn't possible. Anything that connects to Honolulu connects to Toronto (Rule 3). Since Montreal is only allowed one connection, it cannot connect to Honolulu.

Anything not connected to T is also not connected to H. This is the contrapositive of Rule 3.

P cannot connect to both T and V. This is the translation of Rule 4.

P cannot connect to both H and V. Connecting to Honolulu means connecting to Toronto (Rule 3). Combine that with Rule 4 and this is the result.

H is the most restricted city on the list. While the remaining cities are each allowed three or four connections, Honolulu is only allowed two—it cannot connect to Montreal (Rule 1) and it cannot connect to Toronto (Rule 2), so it can only connect to either Philadelphia, Vancouver, or both. This allows us to set up the following limited options.

Incorporating all of this information, our final sketches look like so:

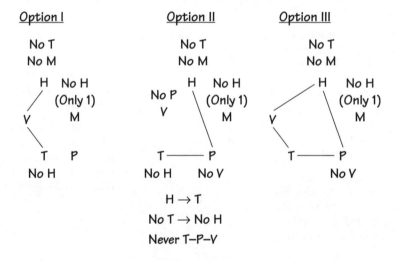

An Advanced test taker focuses on the most restricted entities when Key Players aren't present.

Question Tally

Seven questions: one Acceptability, three Ifs, one Cannot be True, one Could be True, one Must be True.

Battle Plan

We've got a full assortment of questions in this one. None of the Ifs look particularly nasty, so the standard plan of attack will work:

- #1 first.
- #2, #5, and #7 second.
- #3, #4, and #6 last.

Answers and Explanations

1. A   2. B   3. A   4. A   5. D   6. B   7. C

Question Order: 1, 2, 5, 7, 3, 4, 6

1. A

(B) gives Montreal two connections, which violates Rule 1. (E) violates Rule 2 by linking H and T. (C) can be eliminated with Rule 3, as Montreal cannot connect to Honolulu. Finally, Rule 4 is enough to throw out (D) as T—P—V is not allowed. That leaves (A), the correct answer.

2. B

The abstract if clause, "Exactly three cities are connected with Philadelphia," demands that you pose the question: "Which three?" Rule 4 prohibits T—P—V, so the three must be Montreal, Honolulu, and one of either Vancouver or Toronto. We're not done yet: Rule 3 states that a connection to Honolulu requires a connection to Toronto, so Philadelphia *must* be connected to Montreal, Honolulu, and Toronto. That allows us to throw out (A), (C), and (D) because of Rule 1 and (E) because of Rule 4.

5. D

Philadelphia's only connection is to Toronto, so we're limited to Option I:

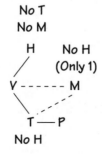

Montreal still needs a connection and it can connect to either Vancouver or Toronto (as shown by the dotted lines). (D) works if the latter is true.

7. C

Begin by asking yourself, "Which city can connect to four others?" Rule 1 drops Montreal, Rule 2 eliminates Honolulu and Toronto, and Rule 3 axes Philadelphia. So the lucky city must be Vancouver. And with Vancouver connected to every other city, (C) must work.

3. A

With three options and a sketch from question 5, the best way to approach this is to simply check your previous work. All three Options have "No H" next to Montreal, so (A) must be correct.

For the record: (B) is possible in Option III, (C) is possible in any of the three Options, (D) and (E) are both possible in question 5's sketch.

4. A

(A) is possible in Option I. The remaining choices are all impossible as each leaves Honolulu stranded.

An Advanced test taker is confident enough in his abilities to *not* slog through the wrong choices after the correct one has been found.

---

6. B

A quick glance at our Options reveals that the maximum number of connections must happen in Option III. This sketch features four connections so far. Montreal still needs one, which brings the count up to five. After Montreal's connection, no further connections are possible, so (B) is correct.

What's Next?

You've now seen examples of Sequencing, Matching, Distribution, Selection, Process, and Mapping game actions playing out individually in various games. Now let's turn to chapter 4 and see what happens when these actions are combined *within* single games.

CHAPTER FOUR

Volatile Mixtures

The plot thickens, as we move now from single-action games to multiple-action—or Hybrid—games.

Hybrid, or Mixture, game
Performing two or more of the other actions.

What does that mean, exactly? Well, remember "Shelving Books" in chapter 2, the game in which we had to distribute six books among three shelves? Not a simple task, was it? Well, now imagine that we also had to determine which books were paperback and which were hardcover. That certainly complicates matters, doesn't it? Or how about chapter 2's "Bus Riders"? Instead of there being just enough seats for all the passengers (how often does *that* happen in real life, anyway?), what if we had to first select the six lucky riders who get seats out of a pool of ten eligible passengers? That would, annoyingly, add a selection element to the game's basic sequencing action.

And that's essentially what these Hybrid games do: add one game action on top of another. They're complicated because they require us to handle many things at once. As the games in previous chapters aptly illustrate, managing a single game action can be daunting enough; now we have to become jugglers.

So, what can you do? A few pointers:

- Keep your focus as you scope out the various challenges presented by Hybrid games. It's easy to get distracted.
- Think in terms of active verbs when decoding the game introductions. For example, say to yourself: "My job is to *select*; to *match*; to *order*"—and so on.
- Determine which action if any, is the primary driver of each game. In one game, sequencing may dominate, while a grouping element may be secondary. In another game, these may be reversed.
- When answering individual questions, focus on the action that's tested. Even when multiple game actions are present, some questions focus on only one.

Enough said—let's get at 'em.

LOGIC GAME 13

Eight people—Jack, Karen, Laura, Mark, Nick, Owen, Peggy, and Ruth—will be placed on two four-person teams—X and Y—for a relay race that is run in four successive legs: first, second, third, and fourth. The teams race concurrently. Each team member runs exactly one of the legs, one team member per leg, according to the following conditions:

Jack is on the same team as Karen.
Karen is not on the same team as Nick.
Ruth runs an earlier leg of the race than Peggy runs, whether or not they are on the same team as each other.
Mark and Nick are both on team Y.
Neither Jack nor Mark runs third.
Karen and Laura both run second.
Owen runs fourth.

1. Which one of the following must be true?

    (A) If Jack and Owen are assigned to the same team as each other, Jack runs first.
    (B) If Jack and Peggy are assigned to the same team as each other, Jack runs fourth.
    (C) If Jack and Ruth are assigned to the same team as each other, Ruth runs third.
    (D) If Mark and Owen are assigned to the same team as each other, Mark runs fourth.
    (E) If Mark and Ruth are assigned to the same team as each other, Ruth runs third.

2. If Ruth is assigned to team X, which one of the following is a complete and accurate list of the legs that she could run?

    (A) first
    (B) second
    (C) first, second
    (D) first, third
    (E) second, third

3. If Owen and Ruth are assigned to the same team as each other, which one of the following must be true?

    (A) Mark runs fourth.
    (B) Nick runs first.
    (C) Nick runs fourth.
    (D) Peggy runs first.
    (E) Peggy runs fourth.

4. Any of the following can be true EXCEPT:

    (A) Jack runs first.
    (B) Mark runs fourth.
    (C) Nick runs first.
    (D) Nick and Peggy both run third.
    (E) Owen and Peggy both run fourth.

5. If Ruth and Peggy are assigned to the same team as each other, which one of the following must be true?

    (A) Jack runs first.
    (B) Mark runs fourth.
    (C) Nick runs third.
    (D) Peggy runs third.
    (E) Ruth runs first.

6. Any of the following can be true EXCEPT:

    (A) Jack runs fourth.
    (B) Nick runs fourth.
    (C) Peggy runs fourth.
    (D) Ruth runs first.
    (E) Ruth runs third.

7. If Peggy runs third on the same team to which Jack is assigned, which one of the following must be true?

    (A) Jack runs the first leg on the team to which he is assigned.
    (B) Ruth runs the first leg on the team to which she is assigned.
    (C) Owen runs on the same team as Jack.
    (D) Owen runs on the same team as Mark.
    (E) Ruth runs on the same team as Mark.

Logic Game 13: Four-Legged Race

What Makes It Difficult?

Our first game is a fairly common Hybrid variety, a mixture of sequencing and distribution. Eight people need to be distributed between two four-person teams for a relay race. Complicating this is the fact that the race has four legs. So we need to worry about not only who goes on which team, but also standard sequencing concerns such as who runs before and who runs after *within* teams.

There are as many rules as questions and, while most of them *look* concrete for a straight distribution game, the sequencing element makes every one of them less concrete than it seems. Rule 3 is particularly troublesome as it places Ruth before Peggy *whether they're on the same team or not.*

The question set is fairly difficult, containing two of the "can be true EXCEPT" variety that don't provide any additional information as well as a "must be true" that's five questions rolled into one in place of the normal Acceptability question that we look forward to seeing. As is typical of all mixture games, every question contains elements of both actions, which greatly complicates things. And now . . .

On your mark, get set, go!

Keys to the Game

J is on team X. This must be true since Nick is on team Y (Rule 4), Jack is with Karen (Rule 1), and Karen is not with Nick (Rule 2).

L is on team Y. Karen is with Jack (Rule 1) and Jack is on team X, so Laura, who runs the second leg with Karen, must be on team Y.

Not much more can be done but what we *did* figure out allows us to draw the following sketch:

```
              (J + 2)      (MN + 1)
              Team X       Team Y
              _____  1   _____

              ___K___  2   ___L___

      No J    _____  3   _____  No M

                       4
              _____      _____
                     ↘  0  ↗
                      R...P
```

You *could* spend your time working out countless "what ifs" about the arrangement of runners and legs, but doing so is pointless as there are far too many possibilities to make that feasible.

An Advanced test taker does *not* waste time plotting out *every* possibility in a game that has too many.

Question Tally

Seven questions: one Must be True, four Ifs, two Can be True EXCEPT.

Battle Plan

A quick look at the choices reveals that our "Must be True" is actually a "five-If" question and question #2 wants some sort of complete and accurate list. Since these tend to require more information than normal Ifs, they are best done *after* the other Ifs in the set. Our order is as follows:

- #3, #5, and #7 first.
- #2 second.
- #1 third.
- #4 and #6 last.

Five-If question

This is a nasty question that contains an If clause in each of its five choices. The question stem to a five-If tends to masquerade as an innocent looking non-If.

Answers and Explanations

1. A   2. D   3. E   4. C   5. C   6. B   7. B

Question Order: 3, 5, 7, 2, 1, 4, 6

3. E

If Owen and Ruth are on the same team, which team is that? Well, there's no room for both of them on team Y, so they must be teammates on team X in the following way:

	(J + 2) Team X		(MN + 1) Team Y
	J	1	M
	K	2	L
	R	3	N
	O	4	P

Rule 7 forces Owen to run fourth for team X. Jack can't run third (Rule 5), so the only leg open to him is first. So Ruth is third on team X and Rule 3 places Peggy fourth on team Y—choice (E).

5. C

As we saw in question 3, team Y isn't accepting more than one new member, so Ruth and Peggy running on the same team places them on team X in one of the following ways:

(J + 2)		(MN + 1)		(J + 2)		(MN + 1)
Team X		Team Y		Team X		Team Y
J	1	M		R	1	M
K	2	L		K	2	L
R	3	N		P	3	N
P	4	O		J	4	O

In both cases, Nick runs third. That's choice (C).

An Advanced test taker is not afraid to plot out multiple options when necessary and does so quickly and confidently.

---

7. B

Jack is on team X, so Peggy running third on his team places her on X as well. Before sketching anything out, note that this condition had already been met in the second sketch for question 5. Using that sketch, we can rule out (A), (C), and (E). To decide between the remaining two choices, try to "break" one of them with a sketch. If, for example, we *separated* Owen and Mark, the sketch could work like so:

(J + 2)		(MN + 1)
Team X		Team Y
J	1	R
K	2	L
P	3	N
O	4	M

That does work, so (D) is out as well. That leaves (B) and it is indeed correct: With leg 2 on both teams already occupied and Peggy running third, Rule 3 *forces* Ruth to run first.

2. D

Ruth, Ruth, where on team X art thou? With four previous sketches, we shouldn't have to do much work, if any, to determine that. In question 5, she could be either first or third. The only choice that contains both is (D).

1. A

This is a dreaded five-If question. However, armed with no fewer than *four* previous sketches, this beast is easily defanged: Question 7's sketch eliminates (B) and (E) while question 5's second sketch eliminates (C) and (D). That's what I'm talking about! We're left with (A) and we hardly did a thing!

An Advanced test taker is adept at eliminating choices in "must be true" questions by finding exceptions to assertions in the wrong choices.

---

4. C

Translate the EXCEPT to turn this into a "must be false." Time for a scavenger hunt: Question 7's sketch throws out (A), (B), and (D). Question 5's first sketch removes (E). We're left with (C), the correct answer.

6. B

Another "must be false" in disguise. And the hunt resumes: (A), (C), (D), and (E) can all be eliminated by the two sketches to question 5, leaving (B) as correct. And the hunt ends just as quickly as it started! (Yawn . . . wasn't this supposed to be a *challenge*?)

What's Next?

As you can see, there's a lot going on in these mixture games, but the upside is that they usually provide fertile ground for more deductions. So keep your eyes open for opportunities to combine the rules. "Four-Legged Race" combines a sequence with a distribution aspect. The following game, "Dog Show," combines a basic linear sequencing arrangement with a matching element.

LOGIC GAME 14

Exactly six dogs—P, Q, R, S, T, and U—are entered in a dog show. The judge of the show awards exactly four ribbons, one for each of first, second, third, and fourth places, to four of the dogs. The information that follows is all that is available about the six dogs:

Each dog is either a greyhound or a Labrador, but not both.

> Two of the six dogs are female and four are male.
> The judge awards ribbons to both female dogs, exactly one of which is a Labrador.
> Exactly one Labrador wins a ribbon.
> Dogs P and R place ahead of dog S, and dog S places ahead of dogs Q and T.
> Dogs P and R are greyhounds.
> Dogs S and U are Labradors.

1. Which one of the following is a complete and accurate list of the dogs that can be greyhounds?

    (A) P, Q
    (B) P, R
    (C) P, Q, R
    (D) P, R, T
    (E) P, Q, R, T

2. Which one of the following statements CANNOT be true?

    (A) A female greyhound wins the second place ribbon.
    (B) A female Labrador wins the second place ribbon.
    (C) A female Labrador wins the third place ribbon.
    (D) A male greyhound wins the fourth place ribbon.
    (E) A female greyhound wins the fourth place ribbon.

3. Which one of the following dogs must be male?

    (A) dog P
    (B) dog R
    (C) dog S
    (D) dog T
    (E) dog U

4. Which one of the following statements can be false?

    (A) Dog P places ahead of dog R.
    (B) Dog P places ahead of dog T.
    (C) Dog R places ahead of dog U.
    (D) Dog R places ahead of dog T.
    (E) Dog S places ahead of dog U.

5. If dog Q is female, which one of the following statements can be false?

    (A) Dog P is male.
    (B) Dog R is male.
    (C) Dog Q wins the fourth place ribbon.
    (D) Dog Q is a greyhound.
    (E) Dog T is a greyhound.

6. If dog T wins the fourth place ribbon, then which one of the following statements must be true?

    (A) Dog P is male.
    (B) Dog Q is male.
    (C) Dog T is male.
    (D) Dog Q is a Labrador.
    (E) Dog T is a Labrador.

7. Which one of the following statements could be true?

    (A) Dog P does not win a ribbon.
    (B) Dog R does not win a ribbon.
    (C) Dog S does not win a ribbon.
    (D) Dog T wins a ribbon.
    (E) Dog U wins a ribbon.

Logic Games 14: Dog Show

What Makes It Difficult?

The sequencing element isn't so bad here—only six dogs ranked in order. But the matching part is a little involved, what with two breeds and two genders to sort through. We have to keep tabs on two things about the six dogs, and combining all that with the 1–6 sequencing element makes for a somewhat complicated mixture.

Surprisingly, the rules aren't too bad. We're told upfront that there are only two breeds to consider and we're also given the exact numbers for the male/female element. As an added bonus, none of the rules are in the dreaded formal logic format that seems to plague just about every difficult game out there.

Unfortunately, the generosity of the test makers ends there. With so much about this game that's up in the air, you would expect to find plenty of hypothetical "if-then" questions but you only get two out of seven. The remaining questions all demand information without giving you anything, so expect the success of the game to depend heavily on your ability to spot key deductions.

Now, let the show begin!

Keys to the Game

No male Labradors win ribbons. This is the combination of Rules 3 and 4.

Both losers are male. Since both females win ribbons, the fifth and sixth place dogs must both be male.

Dog S is the female Labrador who wins the third place ribbon. This one takes quite a bit of detective work. Rule 5 places Dog S ahead of at least two other dogs (Q and T). Only one Lab wins and U is also a Lab (Rule 7), so U must be one of the loser males. Therefore, S is actually ahead of Q, T, and U. P and R must sequence before S, so S must be third. If you noticed this, give yourself a well-deserved pat on the back!

Either of Q or T is the other loser. Only one dog after S wins, so one of Q or T (the two remaining dogs) must be our final loser.

The dogs in first, second, and fourth place are all greyhounds. Since the female Lab winner is third, and only one Lab wins (Rule 4), the other three winners must be greyhounds.

Using all of these wonderful deductions, we can make the following sketch:

	Winners				Losers	
	1	2	3	4	5	6
Dog	P/R	P/R	S	Q/T	___	___
Breed	grey	grey	Lab	grey	___	___
Gender	___	___	f	___	m	m

U is a Lab.
There is only 1 more female.

An Advanced test taker nails down all that she can during the setup stage.

Question Tally

Seven questions: one Complete & Accurate List, one Cannot be True, one Must be True, one Can be False, two Ifs, one Could be True.

Battle Plan

With no Acceptability questions and one of nearly every type of non-If possible, the question set is basically screaming, "I've got more deductions than some Logic Games *sections!*" Good thing you found plenty (you *did* find them, right?) In any case, we can never have *too* much ammo, so good strategy dictates that we should still begin with the sketch-producing Ifs:

- #5 and #6 first.
- #2, #3, #4, and #7 second.
- #1 last.

Answers and Explanations

1. E   2. B   3. E   4. A   5. E   6. B   7. D

Question Order: 5, 6, 2, 3, 4, 7, 1

5. E

If dog Q is female it must be fourth since both females win (Rule 3):

	Winners				Losers	
	1	2	3	4	5	6
Dog	P/R	P/R	S	Q	T/U	T/U
Breed	grey	grey	Lab	grey	___	___
Gender	m	m	f	f	m	m

With only two females, P and R are both male and both T and U must be the losers. A quick scan of the choices reveals that only (E) can be false.

6. B

If T wins fourth, we have:

	Winners					Losers	
	1	2	3	4		5	6
Dog	P/R	P/R	S	T		Q/U	Q/U
Breed	grey	grey	Lab	grey			
Gender			f			m	m

So the losers are Q and U. Since both losers are male, Q must be male—choice (B).

2. B

The bad news is that we only have two sketches moving into this cannot be true. The good news is that our Master Sketch is fairly complete: A quick scan through the choices reveals that (B) is rendered impossible by the Master Sketch.

3. E

If you've been making the right deductions, the correct answer to a non-If "must be true" should *always* be in your Master Sketch. Why is that, you ask? Well, consider the definition of the word "deduction." Now consider what this type of question is asking for. Notice anything similar?

For this question, the only dogs that *have to* be male are the two losers (almost sounds like a curse, doesn't it?) Since U is a Lab and he's not the Lab that wins (poor guy . . .), (E) must be correct.

4. A

This question is a cinch as our Master Sketch quickly reveals that (A) can be false. For the record: P and R place ahead of S, and S places ahead of Q and T (Rule 5), so (B) and (D) are set in stone. Since S places ahead of at least two dogs and there are only two losers, S must be the winning Lab and U the losing Lab (Rules 4 and 7). Winners naturally place ahead of losers, so (C) and (E) are out as well.

7. D

Check your previous work. Of the choices, (D) is true in question 6's sketch. The other four choices are rendered impossible by the Master Sketch.

An Advanced test taker is comfortable with all four "truth values" (could be true, could be false, must be true, must be false) in Logic Games and can quickly test each one.

---

1. E

Our Master Sketch comes to the rescue once more: P and R are definitely greyhounds while either of Q or T (or both) can be as well. That's choice (E).

What's Next?

Are you getting the hang of these mixture types? As involved as these first two mixtures were, each was still only a mixture of two actions. That, however, will change in the remaining games for this chapter.

Next up is a game that's fairly similar to "Dog Show" in that it also contains sequencing and matching. Unfortunately (or fortunately) that's where the similarities end as this game manages to squeeze in a distribution element as well. And as you'll see, that can make a world of difference.

LOGIC GAME 15

A zoo's reptile house has a straight row of exactly five consecutive habitats—numbered 1 through 5 from left to right—for housing exactly seven reptiles—four snakes and three lizards. Five of the reptiles are female and two are male. The reptiles must be housed as follows:

No habitat houses more than two reptiles.

No habitat houses both a snake and a lizard.

No female snake is housed in a habitat that is immediately next to a habitat housing a male lizard.

1. Which one of the following could be a complete and accurate matching of habitats to reptiles?

   (A)   1: two female snakes; 2: one male snake; 3: one female lizard; 4: one male snake, one female lizard; 5: one female lizard

   (B)   1: empty; 2: two female snakes; 3: two female lizards; 4: two male snakes; 5: one female lizard

   (C)   1: one female snake, one male snake; 2: two female snakes; 3: one male lizard; 4: one female lizard; 5: one female lizard

   (D)   1: two male snakes; 2: empty; 3: one female lizard; 4: one female lizard; 5: two female snakes, one female lizard

   (E)   1: one female snake, one male snake; 2: one female snake, one male snake; 3: one male lizard; 4: one female lizard; 5: one female lizard

2. If habitat 2 contains at least one female snake and habitat 4 contains two male lizards, then which one of the following could be true?

   (A)   Habitat 3 contains two reptiles.
   (B)   Habitat 5 contains two reptiles.
   (C)   Habitat 1 contains a female lizard.
   (D)   Habitat 2 contains a female lizard.
   (E)   Habitat 5 contains a female lizard.

3. Which one of the following must be true?

   (A)   At least one female reptile is alone in a habitat.
   (B)   At least one male reptile is alone in a habitat.
   (C)   At least one lizard is alone in a habitat.
   (D)   At least one lizard is male.
   (E)   At least one snake is male.

4. Which one of the following CANNOT be the complete housing arrangement for habitats 1 and 2?

   (A)   1: one female snake, one male snake; 2: one male snake
   (B)   1: one male lizard; 2: one male snake
   (C)   1: two female lizards; 2: one female snake
   (D)   1: one male snake; 2: empty
   (E)   1: empty; 2: one female lizard

5. If habitat 3 is empty, and no snake is housed in a habitat that is immediately next to a habitat containing a snake, then which one of the following could be false?

   (A)   All snakes are housed in even-numbered habitats.
   (B)   None of the lizards is male.
   (C)   No snake is alone in a habitat.
   (D)   No lizard is housed in a habitat that is immediately next to a habitat containing a lizard.
   (E)   Exactly one habitat contains exactly one reptile.

6. If all snakes are female and each of the lizards has a habitat to itself, then which one of the following habitats CANNOT contain any snakes?

   (A)   habitat 1
   (B)   habitat 2
   (C)   habitat 3
   (D)   habitat 4
   (E)   habitat 5

Logic Game 15: Lizards and Snakes

What Makes It Difficult?

This one *seems* like a sequencing/matching mixture at first, but seven reptiles to five habitats means a distribution element as well. The sequencing element is pretty standard but the matching aspect has us juggling snakes versus lizards and male versus female. Fortunately, the opening paragraph gives the exact numbers of each. You *did* notice that, right?

An Advanced test taker knows that the opening paragraph to a tough Logic Game is just as good a place for additional rules as the indented list that follows.

The rules don't appear to be too helpful. There are only three, and every one of them begins with the word "no" (so much for maintaining a positive attitude throughout this test!) Rule 3 seems particularly restrictive (a good thing), yet we can't really make use of that restrictiveness from the onset (not as good of a thing.)

Time to get these restless reptiles into some proper homes!

Keys to the Game

The habitats are either three singles with two doubles or one single with three doubles. This comes straight from Rule 1. With no more than two per habitat, these are the only possible combinations.

An Advanced test taker turns vague numerical restrictions into concrete numbers.

At least two of the snakes are female. With four snakes and only two males in the snake/lizard lot, at most two of the snakes can be male.

At least one of the lizards is female. Similar to the reasoning in the previous key, with three total lizards, at least one must be female.

Our final sketch:

	1	2	3	4	5
Reptile 1	___	___	___	___	___
Reptile 2	___	___	___	___	___

Never SL   S S S S L L L
No fS next to mL   f f f f f m m
At least 2 fS
At least 1 fL

Question Tally

Six questions: one Acceptability, one Partial Acceptability, three Ifs, one Must be True.

Battle Plan

Apply the standard battle plan with one exception: The partial acceptability should be treated as a could be true as it asks for a very *small* part of the sketch, which makes things difficult.

- #1 first.
- #2, #5, and #6 second.
- #3 third.
- #4 last.

Answers and Explanations

1. B   2. E   3. C   4. D   5. A   6. C

Question Order: 1, 2, 5, 6, 3, 4

1. B

We start with an always-welcome acceptability question, so we'll apply the familiar method of using the rules to knock off choices. And the violators are: (D) has three reptiles in habitat 5 (Rule 1); (A) has lizards shacking up with snakes in habitat 4 (Rule 2); (C) and (E) both have female snakes next to male lizards (Rule 3). That leaves (B), our acceptable sketch.

2. E

The stem here gives us a load of information to build into a little picture. Habitat 4 has two male lizards, and since there are only two males to start with, all the other reptiles must be female. So we have four female snakes (one of which is placed in habitat 2 by the stem) and a female lizard. So who goes where? The female snakes can't go in habitats 3, 4, or 5, since the stem puts the male lizards in habitat 4 (Rule 3). So the four female snakes must go in habitats 1 and 2, two in each, and the female lizard can go in either 3 or 5:

	1	2	3	4	5
Reptile 1	fS	fS	___	mL	___
Reptile 2	fS	fS	___	mL	___

fL

Of the choices, only (E) is possible.

5. A

There are four snakes, at most two in any habitat, so if habitat 3 is empty and snakes aren't next to each other, where could the snakes go? Two of them will have to go in one of 1 and 2 and two of them will have to go in one of 4 and 5:

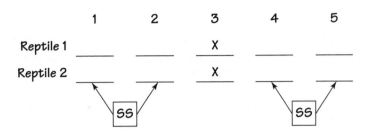

(A) *could* work but need not to as the snakes can take up residence in 1 and 5, so it is correct.

Notice how much work it takes to knock off the *wrong* choices. (B) must be true as any male lizards would need to live next to two *male* snakes (Rule 3). But we only have two males in total, so both lizards must be female. With habitat 3 condemned, our snakes must shack up two to a pad to leave room for the three lizards, each of which neighbors a snake habitat, so (C) and (D) must be true. And since we have two habitats for three lizards, the numbers *must* work out to two and one, which makes (E) true. Phew!

An Advanced test taker doesn't squander her time checking wrong choices after the correct one has been found.

---

6. C

If each of the lizards has a habitat to itself, then the four snakes must shack up two to a habitat to avoid mixing lizards and snakes. Since all the snakes are female, two of the lizards must be male (and living alone) and the remaining one must be female (and living alone). The female snakes can't live next to the male lizards, so our lone female lizard must keep the peace in the neighborhood. There are two possible sketches:

	1	2	3	4	5			1	2	3	4	5
Reptile 1	fS	fS	fL	mL	mL		Reptile 1	mL	mL	fL	fS	fS
Reptile 2	fS	fS					Reptile 2				fS	fS

In either case, habitat 3 *must* be the female lizard, so (C) is correct.

3. C

With an odd number of lizards and Rule 3 preventing lizard-snake co-ops, there *must* be at least one lizard living alone, so (C) is correct. As for the wrong choices: (B) and (E) can be thrown out with question 2's sketch; the remaining two choices can be dismissed with the following sketches, respectively:

	1	2	3	4	5			1	2	3	4	5
Reptile 1	fL	fS		mL	mL		Reptile 1	mS	mS	fS	fL	fL
Reptile 2	fL	fS		fL			Reptile 2	fS				fL

4. D

This question is nasty. Even with *seven* sketches (don't forget the Acceptability!), we barely get any help: one of question 3's sketches throws out (A). With no other source of help, we have no choice but to use brute force of the remaining choices:

(B) With one male lizard in 1 and one male snake in 2, our sketch might go like this:

	1	2	3	4	5
Reptile 1	mL	mS	fS	fS	fL
Reptile 2			fS	fS	

(C) With two female lizards in 1 and one female snake in 2, our sketch might go like this:

	1	2	3	4	5
Reptile 1	fL	fS	fS	mS	mS
Reptile 2	fL		fS		

(D) With one male snake in 1 and nothing in 2, our sketch might go like this:

	1	2	3	4	5
Reptile 1	mS				
Reptile 2					

What happened? Don't worry; the ink in your book didn't rub off. There's just no legal way to place the remaining six entities in this sketch and here's why: With only one snake in the first two habitats, we have three snakes and three lizards in the last three habitats. But we can only place two in each habitat, which forces a lizard-snake co-op and that would violate Rule 2. With the correct answer in hand, you should move on to the next game. For the record:

(E) With habitat 1 empty and one female lizard in 2, our sketch might go like this:

	1	2	3	4	5
Reptile 1		fL	fL	fS	mS
Reptile 2			fL	fS	mS

An Advanced test taker has the will and the means to apply brute force when necessary.

What's Next?

As you can see, games with few rules tend to yield few concrete deductions, which in turn make them tough. This isn't always the case—the next game has *many* rules and few concrete deductions!

LOGIC GAME 16

Exactly six of seven jugglers—G, H, K, L, N, P, and Q—are each assigned to exactly one of three positions—front, middle, and rear—on one of two teams—team 1 and team 2. For each team, exactly one juggler must be assigned to each position according to the following conditions:

If either G or H or both are assigned to teams, they are assigned to front positions.

If assigned to a team, K is assigned to a middle position.

If assigned to a team, L is assigned to team 1.

Neither P nor K is on the same team as N.

P is not on the same team as Q.

If H is on team 2, then Q is assigned to the middle position on team 1.

1. Which one of the following is an acceptable list of assignments of jugglers to team 2?

   (A)   front: Q; middle: K; rear: N
   (B)   front: H; middle: P; rear: K
   (C)   front: H; middle: L; rear: N
   (D)   front: G; middle: Q; rear: P
   (E)   front: G; middle: Q; rear: N

2. If H is assigned to team 2, which one of the following is an acceptable assignment of jugglers to team 1?

   (A)   front: G; middle: K; rear: L
   (B)   front: G; middle: K; rear: N
   (C)   front: L; middle: K; rear: P
   (D)   front: L; middle: Q; rear: G
   (E)   front: L; middle: Q; rear: N

3. Which one of the following is an acceptable list of assignments of jugglers to team 1?

   (A)   front: G; middle: K; rear: L
   (B)   front: G; middle: K; rear: P
   (C)   front: L; middle: K; rear: Q
   (D)   front: Q; middle: K; rear: P
   (E)   front: Q; middle: L; rear: N

4. If G is assigned to team 1, which one of the following is a pair of jugglers who could also be assigned to team 1?

   (A)   H and N
   (B)   K and L
   (C)   K and P
   (D)   L and N
   (E)   L and Q

5. If G is assigned to team 1 and K is assigned to team 2, which one of the following must be assigned the rear position on team 2?

   (A)   H
   (B)   L
   (C)   N
   (D)   P
   (E)   Q

Logic Game 16: Jugglers' Positions

What Makes It Difficult?

This mixture centers around jugglers but, to get things started, we'll be doing quite a bit of juggling of our own: We need to *select* six of the seven jugglers, *distribute* these lucky six into two teams, then *match* each team member to one of three positions. And that's the easy part.

While the game *does* have plenty of rules (6), two of them are negatives and the remaining four are formal logic. The sheer amount of formal logic would normally allow us to nail *some* things down but the selection element of this game stops us dead in our tracks: We can't deduce much when we don't even know which jugglers will be in play.

A glance at the questions reveals that things are about to get much worse. There are only five, and three of them have a partial acceptability element. While any kind of acceptability is usually a good thing, it's a nightmare when selection is part of the mix.

Hope you've brushed up on your juggling skills. You'll need them to keep things moving along.

Keys to the Game

G or H or both takes a front slot. With only one juggler not selected, at least one of the two jugglers in Rule 1 must be used.

If both middle positions are already occupied, K cannot be chosen—the contrapositive of Rule 2.

If team 1 is already full, L cannot be chosen—the contrapositive of Rule 3.

If Q is not in the middle of team 1, H cannot be on team 2—the contrapositive of Rule 6.

Here's what we've got:

GHKLNPQ

Team 1		Team 2
_____	Front	_____
_____	Middle	_____
_____	Rear	_____

At least one front slot has G or H.
Never NP; NK; PQ

$$K \rightarrow middle$$
$$No\ middle \rightarrow No\ K$$
$$L \rightarrow Team\ 1$$
$$Team\ 1\ Full \rightarrow No\ L$$
$$H\ Team\ 2 \rightarrow Q_{middle}\ Team\ 1$$
$$No\ Q_{middle}\ Team\ 1 \rightarrow No\ H\ Team\ 2$$

Question Tally

Five questions: two Partial Acceptability, three Ifs.

Battle Plan

No one question stands out as significantly easier or harder than any other, so apply our standard plan of attack:

- #1 and #3 first.
- #2, #4, and #5 last.

Answers and Explanations

1. E   2. E   3. E   4. E   5. D

Question Order: 1, 3, 2, 4, 5

1. E

This is an Acceptability question, so use the rules to throw out invalid choices but remember that the correct choice must also allow for a valid three-juggler team 1. (B) violates Rule 2 by assigning K to a rear position. (C) violates Rule 3 by putting L on team 2. (A) puts K and N together (Rule 4) and (D) puts P and Q together (Rule 5), so nix these as well. That leaves (E), which allows a number of valid combinations for team 1 (H_{front} K_{middle} L_{rear} is one).

3. E

Here is another Acceptability question, but this time we only have one direct rule violator: (D) forgets to mind his P's and Q's again by putting them together to violate Rule 5. With that out of the way, we'll need to check each remaining choice for a valid team 2:

(A) leaves H N P Q for team 2. Since we do not have Q in the middle position of team 1, H must sit out. Unfortunately, that forces P and Q together (Rule 5), so (A) does not allow for a valid team 2.

(B) leaves H L N Q for team 2. H needs to sit out but L cannot be on team 2, so (B) does not allow for a valid team 2.

(C) leaves G H N P for team 2. H sitting out again forces N and P together (Rule 4), so (C) does not allow for a valid team 2.

This leaves (E), which *does* work: With H sitting out one last time, G K P can indeed form a team with G_{front} K_{middle} and P_{rear}.

2. E

This is an Acceptability question with an If clause. With H on team 2, Rule 6 triggers and Q must take team 1's middle spot. That eliminates (A), (B), and (C). Of the remaining choices, (D) violates Rule 1 by assigning G to a rear position, so (E) is correct.

4. E

A rather vague If, but help for this one comes in an unexpected way: (B) and (C) showed up in question 3's *invalid* team 1 choices (rearranging the entities in question 3's choices wouldn't help as G *needs* to be in the front and K *needs* to be in a middle position), so we can eliminate them here as well. (A) directly violates Rule 1 and can be thrown out as well.

Between the remaining two choices, (D) leaves H K P Q for team 2. H needs to sit out due to Q not being on team 1 (Rule 6) and P and Q cannot go together (Rule 5), so (D) is wrong and (E) is correct—G L Q allows Q_{middle} for team 1 and H_{front} K_{middle} P_{rear} for team 2.

An Advanced test taker does not doubt himself over rare anomalies such as "four E's in a row."

---

5. D

The question places G on team 1 and K on team 2. Hmm… now where have we seen *that* before… That's right, the correct answer to the previous question! In question 4, we needed to place P in the rear of team 2. That's choice (D).

An Advanced test taker is aware not only of the logic *within* a question but also of the logic *across* questions.

What's Next?

All right then—we're four-fifths of the way through this Logic Games section, and if you've gotten this far you're probably ready for the final four killer games.

CHAPTER FIVE

Huh...?

The title of this chapter reflects the response most test takers have upon encountering the kind of games you're about to see: "Games That Make You Reconsider Your Decision to Go to Law School."

So far, in chapters 2–4, you've done battle with individual Sequencing, Matching, Distribution, Selection, Process, and Mapping games, as well as Hybrid games that combine these game actions in various ways. What more is there, you ask? What can possibly be even harder than these first 16 games?

Well, the games in this chapter all involve and combine these same types of game actions, but they do so in particularly novel (read: "brutal") ways. As usual, we'll touch on the specific difficulties of each in the individual game explanations. For now, suffice it to say that these final four games represent the toughest of the tough, the scariest of the scary—to put it bluntly, the nastiest possible material you may encounter on the LSAT Logic Games section.

Good luck.

LOGIC GAME 17

A crew of up to five workers is to install a partition in at most three days. The crew completes five tasks in this order: framing, wall boarding, taping, sanding, priming.

The crew is selected from the following list, which specifies exactly the tasks each person can do:

George: taping
Helena: sanding, priming
Inga: framing, priming
Kelly: framing, sanding
Leanda: wall boarding, taping
Maricita: sanding
Olaf: wall boarding, priming

The following conditions must apply:

At least one task is done each day.
Taping and priming are done on different days.
Each crew member does at least one task during the installation, but no more than one task a day.
Each task is done by exactly one worker, completed the day it is started and before the next task begins.

1. Which one of the following could be a complete and accurate list of the members of the crew?

    (A) George, Helena, Inga, Kelly
    (B) George, Helena, Kelly, Leanda
    (C) Helena, Inga, Kelly, Olaf
    (D) Helena, Inga, Maricita, Olaf
    (E) George, Helena, Leanda, Maricita, Olaf

2. If the installation takes three days, and if the same two crew members work on the first and third days, then which one of the following could be the pair of crew members who work on those two days?

    (A) Helena and Inga
    (B) Inga and Kelly
    (C) Inga and Leanda
    (D) Kelly and Olaf
    (E) Leanda and Olaf

3. Each of the following could be a complete and accurate list of the members of the crew EXCEPT:

    (A) Helena, Inga, Kelly, Maricita
    (B) Inga, Kelly, Leanda, Olaf
    (C) George, Helena, Inga, Leanda
    (D) Inga, Leanda, Maricita, Olaf
    (E) Kelly, Leanda, Maricita, Olaf

4. If the installation takes three days, and if the sanding is done on the third day, then which one of the following could be a list of all the crew members who work on the second day?

    (A) Inga
    (B) Kelly
    (C) Olaf
    (D) George and Helena
    (E) Leanda and Olaf

5. Which one of the following could be a pair of members of the crew both of whom work on the same days as each other and each of whom perform two tasks?

    (A) George and Maricita
    (B) Helena and Kelly
    (C) Inga and Leanda
    (D) Kelly and Leanda
    (E) Leanda and Olaf

Logic Game 17: Installation Crew

What Makes It Difficult?

We've got a fairly standard mixture here—*select* crew members, *match* them to tasks, then *schedule* them over the course of one or more days. "How's that any harder than the last two games?" you may ask. Well, there's just *one* teeny difference between this mixture and the ones in the previous chapter— we have *no idea* as to how many people or days this job will take! Along with a pool of seven differently abled potential crew members, that just about sums up the difficulty of this game in a nutshell.

Welcome to the final games chapter. Please remove your jaws from the ground before proceeding.

Keys to the Game

The job will take either two or three days. You can arrive at this by combining the "at most three days" from the opening paragraph with the implications of Rule 2.

The crew tolerates neither freeloaders nor overachievers. Rule 3 requires everyone chosen to do something with a limit of one thing on any given day.

Tasks are performed solo with no spillover—the implications of Rule 4, which makes our lives a bit easier.

Rearrange the given information to make it more useful. Since the test maker was nice enough to make the order of the *tasks* concrete, why not rearrange our ability table to match? Instead of sticking with the indented monstrosity, reorganize it like so:

Framing	Wall boarding	Taping	Sanding	Priming
I	L	G	H	I
K	O	L	K	K

An Advanced test taker is adept at converting confusing data into game-breaking information by focusing on what *is* concrete.

Question Tally

Five questions: one Acceptability, two Ifs, one Acceptability EXCEPT, one Could be True.

Battle Plan

In such a tough game, it's even more important not to rush into battle without thinking first. Since the parameters to the game are so vague, be sure to attack the Acceptability questions first before wading into the remainder of the pack.

- #1 and #3 first.
- #2 and #4 second.
- #5 last.

Answers and Explanations

1. B   2. D   3. A   4. E   5. D

Question Order: 1, 3, 2, 4, 5

1. B

An acceptable crew must be capable of tackling every one of the five tasks, so check them one at a time: (E) is missing a framer, (A) is missing a wall boarder, while (C) and (D) both need someone to do the taping. That leaves (B), the correct answer.

3. A

This is a slightly tougher Acceptability question as we do not know which rule the correct choice will violate. Fortunately, you won't have to search long as (A) is missing both Leanda and Olaf, our expert wall boarders.

An Advanced test taker uses the Acceptability questions in a difficult game to cement his understanding of its inner workings further before moving on to tackle the tougher questions in the set.

---

2. D

With two crew members working on each of the first and third days, the tasks must be divided like this:

	Day 1		Day 2	Day 3	
Framing	Wall boarding		Taping	Sanding	Priming
I	L		G	H	H
K	O		L	K	I

Our pair of hardworking crew members for days 1 and 3 must be able to handle framing, wall boarding, sanding, and priming. Only (D) can do all four.

4. E

With sanding on the third day, there are two possible ways to distribute the five tasks: Either wall boarding is on the first day (question 2's sketch) or it's on the second day. The sketch to question 2 axes (A), (B), and (C), so wall boarding must be on the first day:

Day 1	Day 2		Day 3	
Framing	Wall boarding	Taping	Sanding	Priming
I	L	G	H	H
K	O	L	K	I

Helena cannot be on day 2 in this sketch, so the answer is (E).

5. D

This last question is more of a Reading Comprehension puzzler than anything else. Once you unpack the stem, the solution is rather simple. The stem is asking for a pair of people who can share two traits: working two tasks each and working the same two days. The first trait is more concrete: While it's ambiguous which workers work on which days, we do know who can do each task, so let's focus on that aspect first. Two people performing two tasks each means we need a pair that can handle four of the five tasks between them, and (A), (B), and (E) fall on this count alone. As for the remaining two choices, Inga and Leanda from choice (C) *can* perform a total of four tasks, but to have them work on the same two days, they would have to frame (Inga) and wall board (Leanda) on the first day, followed by taping and priming on the next, which violates Rule 2. This leaves (D), which does indeed work: Kelly frames and Leanda wall boards on day 1, then Leanda tapes and Kelly sands on day 2.

> An Advanced test taker has the ability to see past the wording the test makers give him, and recognize the more specific and helpful implications of that wording.

What's Next?

Wasn't expecting such a (relatively) harmless game to be such a beast, were you? The next game also carries a familiar feel to it. And like the game we just finished, there's *also* one teeny difference between it and its earlier cousins . . .

LOGIC GAME 18

Within a tennis league each of five teams occupies one of five positions, numbered 1 through 5 in order of rank, with number 1 as the highest position. The teams are initially in the order R, J, S, M, L, with R in position 1. Teams change positions only when a lower-positioned team defeats a higher-positioned team. The rules are as follows:

Matches are played alternately in odd-position rounds and in even-position rounds.

In an odd-position round, teams in positions 3 and 5 play against teams positioned immediately above them.

In an even-position round, teams in positions 2 and 4 play against teams positioned immediately above them.

When a lower-positioned team defeats a higher-positioned team, the two teams switch positions after the round is completed.

1. Which one of the following could be the order of teams, from position 1 through position 5 respectively, after exactly one round of even-position matches if no odd-position round has yet been played?

   (A) J, R, M, L, S
   (B) J, R, S, L, M
   (C) R, J, M, L, S
   (D) R, J, M, S, L
   (E) R, S, J, L, M

2. If exactly two rounds of matches have been played, beginning with an odd-position round, and if the lower-positioned teams have won every match in those two rounds, then each of the following must be true EXCEPT:

   (A) L is one position higher than J.
   (B) R is one position higher than L.
   (C) S is one position higher than R.
   (D) J is in position 4.
   (E) M is in position 3.

3. Which one of the following could be true after exactly two rounds of matches have been played?

   (A) J has won two matches.
   (B) L has lost two matches.
   (C) R has won two matches.
   (D) L's only match was played against J.
   (E) M played against S in two matches.

4. If after exactly three rounds of matches M is in position 4, and J and L have won all of their matches, then which one of the following can be true?

   (A) J is in position 2.
   (B) J is in position 3.
   (C) L is in position 2.
   (D) R is in position 1.
   (E) S is in position 3.

5. If after exactly three rounds M has won three matches and the rankings of the other four teams relative to each other remain the same, then which one of the following must be in position 3?

   (A) J
   (B) L
   (C) M
   (D) R
   (E) S

6. If after exactly three rounds the teams, in order from first to fifth position, are R, J, L, S, and M, then which one of the following could be the order, from first to fifth position, of the teams after the second round?

   (A) J, R, M, S, L
   (B) J, L, S, M, R
   (C) R, J, S, L, M
   (D) R, L, M, S, J
   (E) R, M, L, S, J

Logic Game 18: Tennis Tournament

What Makes It Difficult?

This time warp is pretty similar to the two in chapter 3 but there *is* one important difference: The process isn't limited to a certain number of rounds. That means it can potentially require you to fast forward and/or rewind through *multiple* rounds in succession! (Not bad, your jaw didn't fall quite as far this time...)

To complicate things, we have odd rounds, even rounds, and a conditional swapping of entities in the rules. The questions don't look any better as *five* of the six involve multiple rounds of play. All in all, a difficult game that's quite likely to be extremely time-consuming.

Excited? It's time to serve or be served.

Keys to the Game

The odd and even rounds alternate. Rule 1 is great news as it greatly reduces the complexity that this game might otherwise have had.

Stay focused on key issues governing the game. What happens in each type of round? How do players switch positions?

Turn abstract rules into concrete thoughts. Even though most Process games do not allow for a Master Sketch, this one does and you should take a moment to create it before attacking the questions:

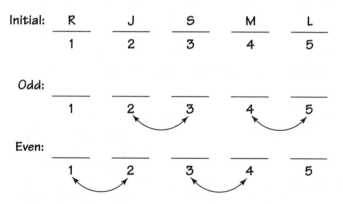

An Advanced test taker recognizes that even highly abstract games may have concrete elements.

Question Tally

Six questions: one Acceptability, four Ifs, one Could be True.

Battle Plan

With the exception of the lone Acceptability, every question in this set involves multiple rounds of play, so we might as well follow the standard order of attack:

- #1 first.
- #2, #4, #5, and #6 second.
- #3 last.

Answers and Explanations

1. D   2. E   3. A   4. C   5. A   6. C

Question Order: 1, 2, 4, 5, 6, 3

1. D

This Acceptability appears daunting at first but is actually surprisingly . . . easy. An even round as the first round in the tournament means everyone but L, who is initially ranked fifth, will play (and possibly swap positions). Only choice (D) keeps L in fifth place, so it must be correct.

With the warm-up out of the way, let's move on to the *real* questions.

An Advanced test taker is often rewarded with a "gimme" just for figuring out the mechanics of a really difficult game.

---

2. E

Tons of information here, so let's work with it. There have been two rounds of matches, we started with an odd-positioned round, and the lower-ranked team has won every match. That allows us to create the following sketch:

Initial: R	J	S	M	L
1	2	3	4	5
Odd: R	S	J	L	M
1	2	3	4	5
Even: S	R	L	J	M
1	2	3	4	5

Of the choices, the only one that isn't true is (E), since M ends up fifth.

4. C

This is where things get nasty. We know that three rounds have been played but we don't know whether the opening round was odd or even, so we'll have to sketch *both* of them out (to keep the number of sketches down to a manageable number, we'll assume that the higher-ranked player always wins unless the lower-ranked player is either J or L):

Initial:	R	J	S	M	L	Initial:	R	J	S	M	L
	1	2	3	4	5		1	2	3	4	5

Odd:	R	J	S	L	M	Even:	J	R	S	M	L
	1	2	3	4	5		1	2	3	4	5

Even:	J	R	L	S	M	Odd:	J	R	S	L	M
	1	2	3	4	5		1	2	3	4	5

Odd:	J	L	R	M	S	Even:	J	R	L	S	M
	1	2	3	4	5		1	2	3	4	5

It seems that beginning with an even round does not allow M to end up in fourth position given those restrictions, so the tournament in question must have opened with an odd round. Of the choices, only (C) can be true.

5. A

Another three-rounder that doesn't give us the opening round! Fortunately, M has just been so utterly *destroying* the competition (watch out, Maria Sharapova!) that all of her opponents have been too stunned to swap positions. And there's more good news: Before you break down and create both sketches, note that this one is a "must be true" *and* that it's asking for the entity in one specific spot. Since a "must be true" must happen in *every* sketch that meets its requirements, making only one sketch should answer this. Since we've been favoring the odd opening, let's use the even opening this time to balance our available scratch work somewhat:

Initial:	R	J	S	M	L
	1	2	3	4	5

Even:	R	J	M	S	L
	1	2	3	4	5

Odd:	R	M	J	S	L
	1	2	3	4	5

Even:	M	R	J	S	L
	1	2	3	4	5

So J ends up third, which is (A).

6. C

"Not *another* three-rounder...!" Hang on, this one is different and in a good way: We have the results from the third round and are asked for the results of the round before it. What do we know about the mechanics of this tournament? *No player can move more than one rank in either direction per round!* With that in mind, there is no need to sketch anything: (A) violates this principle by moving L two to the right; (B) violates this principle by moving R four to the right; (D) violates this principle by moving M two to the left; and (E) violates this principle by moving J three to the right. We're left with (C), which must be correct!

An Advanced test taker makes use of the underlying principle in really tough games to crack that game's most difficult questions in record time.

---

3. A

And finally, we reach the could be true at the end of our queue. A glance at question 4's first sketch reveals that (A) is indeed possible. Note that "won two matches" is not the same as "moved up in ranking twice."

What's Next?

Did you enjoy your game of tennis or was that too much of a racket for you? Don't worry, we've got two more for you to enjoy. The good news is that, like this game, the *next* one is also similar to a previous game except for some *teeny* differences that makes it just a *tad* harder than its predecessor. What's the bad news? The predecessor I'm referring to is the game we just finished . . .

LOGIC GAME 19

The population of a small country is organized into five clans—N, O, P, S, and T. Each year exactly three of the five clans participate in the annual harvest ceremonies. The rules specifying the order of participation of the clans in the ceremonies are as follows:

Each clan must participate at least once in any two consecutive years.

No clan participates for three consecutive years.

Participation takes place in cycles, with each cycle ending when each of the five clans has participated three times. Only then does a new cycle begin.

No clan participates more than three times within any cycle.

1. If the clans participating in the first year of a given cycle are N, O, and P, which one of the following could be the clans participating in the second year of that cycle?

    (A)   N, O, S
    (B)   N, O, T
    (C)   N, P, S
    (D)   O, P, T
    (E)   O, S, T

2. Which one of the following can be true about the clans' participation in the ceremonies?

    (A)   N participates in the first, second, and third years.
    (B)   N participates in the second, third, and fourth years.
    (C)   Both O and S participate in the first and third years.
    (D)   Both N and S participate in the first, third, and fifth years.
    (E)   Both S and T participate in the second, third, and fifth years.

3. Any cycle for the clans' participation in the ceremonies must be completed at the end of exactly how many years?

    (A)   five
    (B)   six
    (C)   seven
    (D)   eight
    (E)   nine

4. Which one of the following must be true about the three clans that participate in the ceremonies in the first year?

    (A)   At most two of them participate together in the third year.
    (B)   At least two of them participate together in the second year.
    (C)   All three of them participate together in the fourth year.
    (D)   All three of them participate together in the fifth year.
    (E)   None of them participates in the third year.

5. If, in a particular cycle, N, O, and S participate in the ceremonies in the first year, which one of the following must be true?

    (A)   N participates in the second and third years.
    (B)   O participates in the third and fourth years.
    (C)   N and O both participate in the third year
    (D)   P and T both participate in the fifth year.
    (E)   S and T both participate in the fifth year.

6. If, in a particular cycle, N, O, and T participate in the first year and if O and P participate in the fourth year, any of the following could be a clan that participates in the third year EXCEPT:

    (A)   N
    (B)   O
    (C)   P
    (D)   S
    (E)   T

7. If, in a particular cycle, N, O, and S participate in the ceremonies in the first year and O, S, and T participate in the third year, then which one of the following could be the clans that participate in the fifth year?

    (A)   N, O, P
    (B)   N, O, S
    (C)   N, P, S
    (D)   O, P, S
    (E)   P, S, T

Logic Game 19: Clan Ceremonies

What Makes It Difficult?

Like the previous game, we've got a Time Warp with no set length. Unlike the previous game, we don't have the "starting position" and the rules concerning placement aren't nearly as clear either.

The questions are no less scary: One quick glance at some of the choices reveals that the process could possibly continue for *five* years! With *seven* questions and lots of hypothetical ones, this is one crazy clan ceremony.

If you've made it this far into the book, however, you probably expected no less (and a lot more, actually)…

Keys to the Game

There are *exactly* three participations each year. This concrete rule can easily be missed as it's buried in the opening paragraph. It's a significant one, too, as we'll see shortly.

An Advanced test taker reads the opening paragraph carefully so as not to miss anything of importance.

A cycle is five years. This critical deduction is absolutely necessary for efficient handling of the game. Since each of the five clans participates three times in a cycle and there are exactly three participations each year, a cycle must be five years long. Doubly important is the fact that deductions generally aren't expected in Time Warps.

The two clans that did *not* participate on a given year must do so on the following year. This is essentially the gist of Rule 1.

The loophole closer can actually do more harm than good. This can easily be misinterpreted to mean that a clan can participate *up to three times* within a cycle.

An Advanced test taker takes the time needed to understand the rules properly so as not to blunder when attacking the questions.

See, the game's not so bad. And like its predecessor, this one has a sketch as well:

Clans: N O P S T

1	2	3	4	5
___	___	___	___	___
___	___	___	___	___
___	___	___	___	___

Question Tally

Seven questions: four Ifs, one Can be True, two Must be True.

Battle Plan

While none of the questions seem particularly inviting at first, #3 *does* seem like a good place to start due to its relative simplicity. On the flipside, #5 seems the most vague (every other If is specific about what it is asking for) so our modified plan of attack should be:

- #3 first.
- #1, #6, and #7 second.
- #5 third.
- #2 and #4 last.

Answers and Explanations

1. E   2. C   3. A   4. A   5. D   6. C   7. E

Question Order: 3, 1, 6, 7, 5, 2, 4

3. A

Here's the freebie in this set. The number of years in a cycle is a critical deduction and this question rewards you for making it. Five clans, three participations each, and exactly three per year means a cycle is five years.

An Advanced test taker always makes a beeline for any obvious freebies before moving on to tackle the tougher stuff.

---

1. E

With NOP participating in the first year, we have:

	1	2	3	4	5
	N	S	___	___	___
	O	T	___	___	___
	P	___	___	___	___

Since all five clans must participate in any two-year period (Rule 1), year 2 must include S and T. Only (E) does, so it is correct.

6. C

Inserting the given information into our sketch gives us:

1	2	3	4	5
N	S	___	O	___
O	P	___	P	___
T	___	___	___	___

With NOT in the first year, the two definite for year 2 are S and P. Since P is also in year 4, it cannot participate in the third year (Rule 2). That's (C).

7. E

Lots of good information, so get it all into your sketch before proceeding:

1	2	3	4	5
N	T	O	N	T
O	P	S	P	O/S
S	N	T	O/S	P

With NOS in year 1, P and T must both be in year 2. OST in year 3 means that the duplicate in year 2 is N (since N would otherwise be missing from the year 2 to year 3 span). OST in year 3 also means that year 4 must have N and P. For the four remaining spots, we still need to place a P, an O, an S, and a T. T and P can't go in year 4 as the former would break Rule 2, while the latter would have clan P participating twice in the same year, so both go in year 5. Finally, O and S go in the final two spots in either order.

Back to the question at hand: the fifth year must include P and T, which only (E) does. While we didn't have to work out *every* spot in this sketch to answer *this* question, the fact that previous full sketches are nonexistent in this abstract game makes it a good idea to do so.

An Advanced test taker will fully work out a hypothetical sketch if there's a chance that it may help her in a later question.

---

5. D

This question seemed intimidating when we were crafting our Battle Plan but is much more manageable after all the other Ifs. The question wants a must be true and its premise is compatible with question 7's. A quick scan of question 7's sketch reveals that only (D) *must* happen.

2. C

Once again, our previous work comes to the rescue. Question 7's sketch proves that (C) is indeed possible.

4. A

The amazing question 7 sketch helps us through one more question: In that one sketch, (A) is the only one that works.

What's Next?

With a ceremonial schedule like *that*, how do those crazy clans keep it straight? But that is, after all, what we'd expect from the toughest of the tough. Next up is our final Logic Game, and of course it wouldn't be right if we didn't end with another real killer. What's it like, you ask? Well, it's kind of hard to put into words . . .

LOGIC GAME 20

In a game, "words" (real or nonsensical) consist of any combination of at least four letters of the English alphabet. Any "sentence" consists of exactly five words and satisfies the following conditions:

The five words are written from left to right on a single line in alphabetical order.

The sentence is started by any word, and each successive word is formed by applying exactly one of three operations to the word immediately to its left: delete one letter; add one letter; replace one letter with another letter.

At most three of the five words begin with the same letter as one another.

Except for the leftmost word, each word is formed by a different operation from that which formed the word immediately to its left.

1. Which one of the following could be a sentence in the word game?

    (A) bzeak bleak leak peak pea
    (B) crbek creek reek seek sxeek
    (C) dteam gleam glean lean mean
    (D) feed freed reed seed seeg
    (E) food fool fools fopls opls

2. The last letter of the alphabet that the first word of a sentence in the word game can begin with is

    (A) t
    (B) w
    (C) x
    (D) y
    (E) z

3. If the first word in a sentence is "blender" and the third word is "slender," then the second word can be

    (A) bender
    (B) gender
    (C) lender
    (D) sender
    (E) tender

4. If the first word in a sentence consists of nine letters, then the minimum number of letters that the fourth word can contain is

    (A) four
    (B) five
    (C) six
    (D) seven
    (E) eight

5. If "clean" is the first word in a sentence and "learn" is another word in the sentence, then which one of the following is a complete and accurate list of the positions each of which could be the position in which "learn" occurs in the sentence?

    (A) second
    (B) third
    (C) fourth, fifth
    (D) second, third, fourth
    (E) third, fourth, fifth

6. If the first word in a sentence consists of four letters, then the maximum number of letters that the fifth word in this sentence could contain is

    (A) four
    (B) five
    (C) six
    (D) seven
    (E) eight

Logic Game 20: Word!

What Makes It Difficult?

What *doesn't* make it difficult? We trust that you found enough to give you a real headache in this one to safely skip this formality and move right on to the keys of the game.

Keys to the Game

Get a grasp of the unusual game action. As unusual as the game is, it consists of a game action you've seen before. The "sentence" may be laid out in a line but each word in it depends on its predecessor, which is essentially a process element.

An Advanced test taker breaks down even an "oddball" game into its most familiar elements.

The first word can be anything. Since only the latter words have operations performed on them, the first word can be any combination of four or more letters.

Three types of operations can be performed. New words are formed by adding a letter, dropping a letter, or replacing a letter in the previous word.

No operation may be used twice in a row—the translation of Rule 4.

There's no real way to sketch anything, so we'll simply have to hit the questions as they come.

An Advanced test taker makes sure she understands how complicated rules work before wading into the questions.

Question Tally

Six questions: one Acceptability, one Must be True, four Ifs.

Battle Plan

None of the questions seem much worse than any of the others, so our standard plan of attack applies:

- #1 first.
- #3–#6 second.
- #2 last.

Answers and Explanations

1. B   2. D   3. C   4. D   5. E   6. C

Question Order: 1, 3, 4, 5, 6, 2

1. B

(A) violates the requirement in the opening paragraph by having a word with only three letters. Rule 3 eliminates (E) for having four words that start with an F. Rule 4 axes both (C) and (D) because each uses the letter replacement operation twice in a row—"dteam" to "gleam" to "glean" in (C) and "reed" to "seed" to "seeg" in (D). That leaves (B) as correct.

An Advanced test taker doesn't lose sight of rules buried in the opening paragraph.

---

3. C

The correct answer to this question must meet two requirements: It needs to be a word that can be derived from "blender" *and* it needs to be a word that "slender" can be derived from. (B), (D), and (E) fail the first test. Of the remaining two, only "lender" can become "slender" (by adding a letter), so (C) is correct.

An Advanced test taker makes a complex question more manageable by taking its steps one at a time.

---

4. D

This is a math question that's not as hard as it looks. To go from the first word to the fourth word, we must perform a total of three operations. Can all three be "drop a letter"? Unfortunately, Rule 4 prohibits that. However, as long as the middle operation is "change a letter" (it *could* be "add a letter" but that would be counterproductive here) the first and third operations could both be "drop a letter." Our nine-letter word would thus become a seven-letter word. That's (D).

5. E

Translation: If we start with "clean," where can we get "learn" (it's *really* not as philosophical as it sounds)? At minimum, we need to drop the "c" and add an "r", so second is impossible but third is definitely possible. This eliminates (A), (C), and (D). To knock out the remaining wrong choice, simply test either the fourth or fifth word. One possible sentence that places "learn" in the fourth spot is "clean, glean, lean, learn, yearn." Fourth works, so (E) is correct.

6. C

This question is very similar to question 4, so let's handle it the same way: There are four operations from the first word to the fifth word. Since no two consecutive operations can be the same (Rule 4), we can have at most two "add a letter" operations. With two "add a letter" and two "replace a letter" operations, our four-letter word becomes a six-letter word. That's (C).

2. D

With no actual sketches in this game, it's no wonder that we get no help for this final question. The question hinges on Rules 1 and 3: Words must be in alphabetical order, and no more than three can start with the same letter. Starting from the end, let's test out Z first: Can Z be the first letter of the first word? No, the most we can have are three words beginning with Z, and there's nowhere to go but down from there. If the first word begins with Z, it's inevitable that somewhere along the chain, the alphabetical order will be broken. What about Y? This does work—YABC, YABCD, YBCD, ZBCD, ZBCDX is one example.

An Advanced test taker has time to test the tougher questions because she uses her time efficiently on the easier ones.

---

section two

LOGICAL REASONING

CHAPTER SIX

The Logical Reasoning Challenge

1. Many people do not understand themselves, nor do they try to gain self-understanding. These people might try to understand others, but these attempts are sure to fail, because without self-understanding it is impossible to understand others. It is clear from this that anyone who lacks self-understanding will be incapable of understanding others.

The reasoning in this argument is flawed because the argument…

Do you like to point out the unwarranted assumptions in the arguments of others? Do you like to hone in on logical flaws like a detective, and analyze precisely how arguments could be made better or worse? If so, then LSAT Logical Reasoning is for you. And since it accounts for not one but two of the four scored sections of the LSAT, pointing out the error in people's ways has never been more rewarding!

So win arguments! Prove people wrong! Amaze your friends! Be the life of the party! Get a score of 180 on the LSAT! . . . Just a few of the many and varied uses of the ability to master the subtle art of Logical Reasoning.

Disclaimer: Hacking through the bogus arguments of others and/or demonstrating superior logical acumen in everyday conversation will NOT make you the most popular person in town.

The purpose of this chapter is to help you hone your critical thinking skills through practice on some of the toughest Logical Reasoning material around. The following offers some guidelines on how to get the most out of the Logical Reasoning material in this book.

USING THE LOGICAL REASONING QUESTIONS IN THIS BOOK

This section is broken up into a number of chapters each detailing various difficulties commonly encountered in LSAT Logical Reasoning. It is designed to allow you to learn as you go and to apply your learning to subsequent questions as you progress through the section.

- First, we introduce you to the five major categories of difficult Logical Reasoning questions.

- Then we offer in-depth practice with tough questions in each of these five major categories.

- After that, nine other common but often difficult Logical Reasoning features or structural elements are presented, each highlighted by an example.

- Finally, 40 additional questions representative of all the elements and forms discussed are served up for your practicing pleasure.

Instructions are provided throughout intended to lead you through the various sections. Here are a few general pointers to keep in mind when tackling all Logical Reasoning questions, but especially challenging questions like the ones you're about to see:

Keep your eye out for the author's evidence, conclusion, and any assumptions relied upon in the argument. The wordiness and logical subtlety of the questions that follow often cause test takers to lose sight of what's actually being said, and it's nearly impossible to answer questions like these correctly when one is foggy about the specifics. The conclusion is the "what" of the matter; the evidence is the reasons "why" the author feels entitled to make that particular claim; and assumptions are any missing premises that are nonetheless needed in order for the conclusion to stand.

Paraphrase the text. We include the same advice later on for the longer Reading Comprehension passages. You can get a leg up on tough text by simplifying the passage's ideas and translating them into your own words.

Observe timing guidelines. On the real test, 24–26 questions in 35 minutes works out roughly to a minute and a quarter per question. Try to answer the questions in this section in about that time, but you can certainly cut yourself a little slack considering the high level of difficulty of the questions in this section.

Familiarize yourself with the common Logical Reasoning concepts tested. Review the logical elements and structures discussed throughout the chapter, and look to recognize which of them are present in each Logical Reasoning question you encounter in this book as well as in any other questions you practice with during your LSAT preparation. While the specific subject matter (names, places, scenarios, etc.) changes from question to question and test to test, the underlying logical patterns remain incredibly consistent. Get to know them.

Oh and don't worry about the whole "self-understanding" thing. The author was just talking in circles anyway . . .

CHAPTER SEVEN

Types of Challenging Logical Reasoning Questions

You should already be aware that common Logical Reasoning questions ask about:
- Assumptions
- Strengthening/Weakening an argument
- Logical flaws
- Inferences
- Principles
- Parallel reasoning

Less common questions ask about:
- Methods of argument
- Paradoxes
- Points at issue between two different arguments
- Roles of statements in an argument

A few of these are inherently difficult question types, but most of them can be easy or difficult depending on other factors that we'll be analyzing for you in the next few chapters.

In this chapter, we'll take a brief look at the five categories of difficult Logical Reasoning questions: Formal Logic, Parallel Reasoning, Inference, Principle, and Just Plain Tough. Chapter 8 will provide you with additional, in-depth practice with these categories, but first you need to familiarize yourself with the types of tough Logical Reasoning questions you're likely to see on Test Day.

FORMAL LOGIC

Formal Logic questions
These involve formal logic elements like inference or assumption, or use words and phrases like *if/then, only if, all, some, none, no, unless, most, every, always,* and *never.*

When a stimulus contains these words, translations and deductions are often possible, which in a way brings us into Logic Games territory. For some, this is good news. For others, the appearance of such Logic Games elements on the Logical Reasoning sections is an unmitigated disaster.

Let's try a Formal Logic example.

1. Only an expert in some branch of psychology could understand why Patrick is behaving irrationally. But no expert is certain of being able to solve someone else's problem. Patrick wants to devise a solution to his own behavioral problem.

   Which one of the following conclusions can be validly drawn from the passage?

   (A)   Patrick does not understand why he is behaving in this way.
   (B)   Patrick is not an expert in psychology.
   (C)   Patrick is not certain of being able to devise a solution to his own behavioral problem.
   (D)   Unless Charles is an expert in some branch of psychology, Charles should not offer a solution to Patrick's behavioral problem.
   (E)   If Charles is certain of being able to solve Patrick's behavioral problem, then Charles does not understand why Patrick is behaving in this way.

Explanation: Psychological Expert

E

The first two sentences are actually strict formal statements: Experts are the *only ones* who can understand Patrick's behavior, and experts are *unable* to be certain of solving his problems. If Charles *is* certain of being able to solve Patrick's problem, then he can't possibly be an expert (sentence 2). And if he's not an expert, then he can't possibly understand Patrick's behavior (sentence 1).

(A), (B) Nothing allows us to conclude that Patrick isn't an expert in psychology. He may be, in which case he'd have a shot at understanding his own bizarre behavior.

(C) Patrick wants to devise a solution, but we can't infer whether he feels certain of doing so, because the "certainty rule" applies only to people attempting to solve other people's problems.

(D) contradicts the passage. Since experts are the ones who can't be certain of solving the behavior problem, being an expert would be a strike against Charles's offering a viable solution.

PARALLEL REASONING

Parallel Reasoning is a perennial LSAT question type. Since time immemorial (well, at least since the early '90s) there have been two Parallel Reasoning questions on every LSAT Logical Reasoning section (occasionally just one, but almost always two per section). So on Test Day you can just about count on seeing four questions that ask you to find the choice that mirrors the logic of a stimulus. Test takers generally find these difficult because they're fairly lengthy and involved, and each choice tells a different story, making it hard to focus on the underlying logic of the original.

Parallel Reasoning questions
These identify an argument that uses the same kind of evidence to draw the same kind of conclusion.

Question 2 is a Parallel Reasoning question.

2. My father likes turnips, but not potatoes, which he says are tasteless. So it is not true that whoever likes potatoes likes turnips.

    The flawed reasoning in the argument above most closely resembles that in which one of the following?

    (A) This book is not a paperback, but it is expensive. So it is not true that some paperbacks are expensive.
    (B) Although this recently published work of fiction has more than 75 pages, it is not a novel. Thus, it is not the case that all novels have more than 75 pages.
    (C) All ornate buildings were constructed before the twentieth century. This house is ornate, so it must be true that it was built before the twentieth century.
    (D) Erica enjoys studying physics, but not pure mathematics, which she says is boring. So it is not true that whoever enjoys studying physics enjoys studying pure mathematics.
    (E) People who do their own oil changes are car fanatics. My next-door neighbors are car fanatics, so it follows that they do their own oil changes.

Explanation: Potatoes & Turnips

B

When you're asked for a parallel flaw, you can reject any choice that is proper logic, and any choice demonstrating a different flaw.

Father likes turnips but not potatoes. So how can one deduce, based on father, anything about people who *like* potatoes? One can't. In the same way, (B)'s first sentence is about a non-novel, yet (B) goes on to draw a conclusion about novels. Note that if the terms in the stimulus's "So" sentence and (B)'s "Thus" sentence were reversed, each argument would be repaired. That the same repair works for both makes it even more certain that they're parallel.

(A) is great but for the word "some," which has no parallel in the stimulus. (C) is proper logic: One can deduce that this house is pre-1900 based on the evidence.

(D) in superficially similar form to the stimulus, but (D) is actually proper logic: Erica *is*, as (D) argues, an exception to the rule that all who love physics love pure math.

(E) 's conclusion just reverses its two terms; that's a logical error but not the same one as in the original.

INFERENCE

Inference questions require you to walk the fine line between *must* and *could*: Lots of things *can* generally be true but only one choice *has* to be, such as in the following example.

3. Researchers have discovered that caffeine can be as physically addictive as other psychoactive substances. Some people find that they become unusually depressed, drowsy, or even irritable if they do not have their customary dose of caffeine. This is significant because as many people consume caffeine as consume any one of the other addictive psychoactive substances.

   Which one of the following can be logically concluded from the information above?

   (A) There is no psychoactive substance to which more people are physically addicted than are addicted to caffeine.
   (B) A physical addiction to a particular psychoactive substance will typically give rise to diverse psychological symptoms.
   (C) Not all substances to which people can become physically addicted are psychoactive.
   (D) If one is physically addicted to a psychoactive substance, one will become unusually depressed when one is no longer ingesting that substance.
   (E) If alcohol is a physically addictive psychoactive substance, there are **not** more people who consume alcohol than consume caffeine.

Explanation: Caffeine Addiction

E

(E) is a straightforward inference from the last sentence. We're told that "as many people consume" caffeine as consume any "other physically addictive psychoactive substance." So assuming, as (E) does, that alcohol qualifies as one such "other" substance, there may be the same number of consumers of caffeine as of alcohol, but the latter cannot possibly outnumber the former.

The stimulus leaves the door open for many psychoactive substances more physically addictive than caffeine, contrary to (A). (B) goes too far in making an inference about that which is "typical" of addictive substances, since all of the symptomatic evidence concerns caffeine alone. The distinction that (C) proposes between psychoactive and nonpsychoactive substances couldn't be further from the author's mind, so it cannot be part of a proper inference. And (D) gets into the area of what happens when an addictive substance is suspended, but that issue too never comes up during the brief discussion.

Inference questions
Inference questions ask for a necessary, but unstated, conclusion.

PRINCIPLE

Principle questions are among the most difficult questions in the Logical Reasoning sections. These questions ask you either to extract a principle from a certain scenario or to apply a given principle in a situation. Recognizing principles from and applying principles to specific situations are, of course, very lawyer-like things to do, so it's not surprising that the test makers want to test this skill. Most Principle questions come with difficult choices, and this one is no exception.

4. The publisher of a best-selling self-help book had, in some promotional material, claimed that it showed readers how to become exceptionally successful. Of course, everyone knows that no book can deliver to the many what, by definition, must remain limited to the few: exceptional success. Thus, although it is clear that the publisher knowingly made a false claim, doing so should not be considered unethical in this case.

Which one of the following principles, if valid, most strongly supports the reasoning above?

(A) Knowingly making a false claim is unethical only if it is reasonable for people to accept the claim as true.

(B) Knowingly making a false claim is unethical if those making it derive a gain at the expense of those acting as if the claim were true.

(C) Knowingly making a false claim is unethical in only those cases in which those who accept the claim as true suffer a hardship greater than the gain they were anticipating.

(D) Knowingly making a false claim is unethical only if there is a possibility that someone will act as if the claim might be true.

(E) Knowingly making a false claim is unethical in at least those cases in which for someone else to discover that the claim is false, that person must have acted as if the claim were true.

Explanation: Ethical Lies

A

A "principle that supports the reasoning" will show why it is permissible to reach such a conclusion from the kind of evidence provided. The author concludes that the publisher was not acting unethically, even though the publisher made a false claim. Normally, we tend to think that publishing false claims is unethical, so what else is going on? The only other fact that we're told is that while the claim is false, *everyone knows* that it is false. The implication is that while deception may be unethical, there's nothing wrong with making a false claim that is obviously false. So if (A) is a governing principle, and making a false claim is unethical only if it is *reasonable* to accept the claim as true, then the publisher is off the hook, since it can't be reasonable to believe something that is obviously false. Incidentally, you may well have disagreed with the author as to whether the claim really was false. After all, the author didn't promise to make *everyone* exceptionally successful, the promise was only to readers. But that doesn't matter to the structure of the argument, or the principle that would support the author's reasoning.

(B), if anything, would *undermine* the reasoning in the stimulus, since the publisher presumably had something to gain by making the false claim. But in any case, no one accepts this claim, so the publisher isn't in any position to gain anything from this crowd.

(C) There's no mention of the *degree* of hardship suffered by anyone, so that question isn't relevant to the author's reasoning. Also, as in (B), no one accepts this claim, so no one suffers a hardship by virtue of accepting the claim.

(D) Even if the phrase "everyone knows" is taken extremely literally, (D) might not support the argument, because it's at least possible that people act contrary to the knowledge they have. As applied here, it's possible that some people act as if the claim is true, even though they know in their heart of hearts that the claim is false.

(E) sets minimum standards for ethical behavior, so (E) couldn't support the author's conclusion that the publisher's actions were OK. Further, since the claim is "obviously" false, this isn't a case where discovering that something is false requires one to act as if it is true. So (E) doesn't apply here.

JUST PLAIN TOUGH

Not every difficult Logical Reasoning question is distinguished by a common logical feature—some are "just plain tough." These are akin to the Supercharged Standards of the Logic Games section, and foreshadow the "Just Plain Tough" Reading Comprehension passages you'll see later on. These general killers come in all varieties: standard question types like Assumption, Inference, and Strengthen/Weaken an argument, as well as less common types such as Paradox questions like the example below. If you're shooting for that elusive 180, you simply have to be prepared to face down the tough stuff no matter what form it takes.

Give this tough question a shot:

5. Environmental scientist: It is true that over the past ten years, there has been a sixfold increase in government funding for the preservation of wetlands, while the total area of wetlands needing such preservation has increased only twofold (although this area was already large ten years ago). Even when inflation is taken into account, the amount of funding now is at least three times what it was ten years ago. Nevertheless, the current amount of government funding for the preservation of wetlands is inadequate and should be augmented.

Which one of the following, if true, most helps to reconcile the environmental scientist's conclusion with the evidence cited above?

(A) The governmental agency responsible for administering wetland-preservation funds has been consistently mismanaged and run inefficiently over the past ten years.

(B) Over the past ten years, the salaries of scientists employed by the government to work on the preservation of wetlands have increased at a rate higher than the inflation rate.

(C) Research over the past ten years has enabled scientists today to identify wetlands in need of preservation well before the areas are at serious risk of destruction.

(D) More people today, scientists and nonscientists alike, are working to preserve all natural resources, including wetlands.

(E) Unlike today, funding for the preservation of wetlands was almost nonexistent ten years ago.

Explanation: Wetland Funds

E

The author's conclusion (signaled by the contrast structural clue "Nevertheless") is that funding for preservation of wetlands should be increased despite the fact that funding has grown much more quickly in the past than the area of wetlands needing such protection. To reconcile this conclusion to the evidence cited, we need to find an answer choice that explains why funding is still inadequate despite the fact that it has been increasing more quickly than the total area of wetlands needing protection. (E) clears up the mystery: If funding was almost nonexistent ten years ago, as choice (E) states, then it is quite possible that even though it has increased sixfold, it is still inadequate. If (E) is true, the conclusion seems reasonable despite the discrepancy in growth rates cited in the evidence.

(A) might explain why spending for preservation of wetlands has risen so dramatically in the last ten years (the money has been wasted), but would not provide us with a reason why funding should be augmented in the future. In fact, one could argue that if the money is being spent inefficiently, then it's best to spend that money in areas where it can be used to achieve more substantial results.

(B) may explain one of the reasons why the government is spending more to preserve wetlands now than it was ten years ago, but it does not explain why we should spend even more to preserve wetlands in the future. Raising scientists' salaries does not justify even more spending, especially considering that the funding has increased so much over the last ten years. Nothing in this answer choice gives us a reason to believe that current funding is inadequate and should be increased.

(C) If anything, the fact that scientists can identify wetlands in need of restoration earlier would reduce the need for drastic, desperate measures.

(D) mentions all natural resources while the stimulus only mentions wetlands.

> An Advanced test taker rephrases a paradox as a question and looks for the answer choice that answers it.

NOW TRY THESE . . .

Next, try your hand at the following five questions. Each question represents one of the categories just discussed. See if you can pick out the logical element operating in each.

6. Quasars—celestial objects so far away that their light takes at least 500 million years to reach Earth—have been seen since 1963. For anything that far away to appear from Earth the way quasars do, it would have to burn steadily at a rate that produces more light than 90 billion suns would produce. But nothing that burns at a rate that produces that much light could exist for more than about 100 million years.

   If the statements above are true, which one of the following must also be true on the basis of them?

   (A) Instruments in use before 1963 were not sensitive enough to permit quasars to be seen.
   (B) Light from quasars first began reaching Earth in 1963.
   (C) Anything that from Earth appears as bright as a quasar does must produce more light than would be produced by 90 billion suns.
   (D) Nothing that is as far from Earth as quasars are can continue to exist for more than about 100 million years.
   (E) No quasar that has ever been seen from Earth exists any longer.

7. Medical research findings are customarily not made public prior to their publication in a medical journal that has had them reviewed by a panel of experts in a process called peer review. It is claimed that this practice delays public access to potentially beneficial information that, in extreme instances, could save lives. Yet prepublication peer review is the only way to prevent erroneous and therefore potentially harmful information from reaching a public that is ill equipped to evaluate medical claims on its own. Therefore, waiting until a medical journal has published the research findings that have passed peer review is the price that must be paid to protect the public from making decisions based on possibly substandard research.

   The argument assumes that

   (A) unless medical research findings are brought to peer review by a medical journal, peer review will not occur
   (B) anyone who does not serve on a medical review panel does not have the necessary knowledge and expertise to evaluate medical research findings
   (C) the general public does not have access to the medical journals in which research findings are published
   (D) all medical research findings are subjected to prepublication peer review
   (E) peer review panels are sometimes subject to political and professional pressures that can make their judgments less than impartial

8. People cannot be morally responsible for things over which they have no control. Therefore, they should not be held morally responsible for any inevitable consequences of such things, either. Determining whether adults have any control over the treatment they are receiving can be difficult. Hence in some cases it can be difficult to know whether adults bear any moral responsibility for the way they are treated. Everyone, however, sometimes acts in ways that are an inevitable consequence of treatment received as an infant, and infants clearly cannot control, and so are not morally responsible for, the treatment they receive.

   Anyone making the claims above would be logically committed to which one of the following further claims?

   (A) An infant should never be held morally responsible for an action that infant has performed.
   (B) There are certain commonly performed actions for which no one performing those actions should ever be held morally responsible.
   (C) Adults who claim that they have no control over the treatment they are receiving should often be held at least partially responsible for being so treated.
   (D) If a given action is within a certain person's control that person should be held morally responsible for the consequences of that action.
   (E) No adult should be held morally responsible for every action he or she performs.

9. Someone's benefiting from having done harm to another person is morally justifiable only if the person who was harmed knew that what was done could cause that harm but consented to its being done anyway.

   Which one of the following judgments most closely conforms to the principle above?

   (A) Attempting to avoid being kept after school as punishment for breaking a window, Sonia falsely claimed that her brother had broken it; Sonia's action was morally unjustifiable since it resulted in both children being kept after school for something only Sonia had done.

   (B) Since Ned would not have won the prize for best model airplane if Penny's brother had not inadvertently damaged her entry while playing with it, Ned is morally unjustified in accepting his prize.

   (C) Wesley, a doctor, persuaded Max to take part in a medical experiment in which a new drug was being tested; since Wesley failed to warn Max about the serious side effects of the drug and the drug proved to have no other effects, Wesley was morally unjustified in using the results obtained from Max in his report.

   (D) Because Roger's mother suffered severe complications as a result of donating a kidney to him for a lifesaving kidney transplant, it was morally unjustifiable for Roger to receive the transplant, even though his mother, herself a doctor, had been eager for the transplant to be performed.

   (E) For James, who was convicted of having defrauded a large number of people out of their savings and wrote a book about his scheme while in prison, to be denied the profits from his book would be morally unjustifiable since he has already been punished for his crime.

10. Large inequalities in wealth always threaten the viability of true democracy, since wealth is the basis of political power, and true democracy depends on the equal distribution of political power among all citizens.

    The reasoning in which one of the following arguments most closely parallels the reasoning in the argument above?

    (A) Consumer culture and an emphasis on technological innovation are a dangerous combination, since together they are uncontrollable and lead to irrational excess.

    (B) If Sara went to the bookstore every time her pocket was full, Sara would never have enough money to cover her living expenses, since books are her love and they are getting very expensive.

    (C) It is very difficult to write a successful science fiction novel that is set in the past, since historical fiction depends on historical accuracy, whereas science fiction does not.

    (D) Honesty is important in maintaining friendships. But sometimes honesty can lead to arguments, so it is difficult to predict the effect a particular honest act will have on a friendship.

    (E) Repeated encroachments on one's leisure time by a demanding job interfere with the requirements of good health. The reason is that good health depends on regular moderate exercise, but adequate leisure time is essential to regular exercise.

ANSWERS AND EXPLANATIONS

Explanation: Quasars

6. E

Here's a rare Inference question that's vulnerable to pre-phrasing: Quasars burn so hot that they can't last for more than 100 million years, but light from quasars takes at least 500 million years to get here. Quasars have only been seen since 1963, and so any quasar light that anyone on Earth has seen has to be at least 500 million years old, and so, as (E) points out, that quasar itself cannot exist any more. By the time its light hits us, it's been dead for at least 400 million years.

(A) could be true, but we don't know why quasars weren't seen before.

(B) Light from quasars was noticed in 1963, but could have reached Earth before that.

(C) Quasars have to produce lots of light to appear the way they do given that they're so far away. But presumably objects that are much closer could appear as bright as a quasar. Quasars from 500 million light years away don't appear brighter than a camera flash from 12 inches away!—and it's doubtful that your trusty Kodak produces more light than 90 billion suns.

(D) For all we know, lots of things (like dead rock, for example) could exist for more than 100 million years, no matter where it is. It's the heat that puts the limit on a quasar's life, not the distance from Earth.

- Most of the time in Inference questions, you have to hit the choices without a strong idea of what the correct answer will look like. But sometimes you can see a natural combination of statements that leads to a deduction. When that happens, scan for your deduction.

Explanation: Peer Review

7. A

This is our Just Plain Tough representative.

Searching for the author's assumption in a long and dense argument like this one can be tough—*try underlining key evidence and conclusion if you're getting lost in dense text*. What's happening here? Well, medical findings aren't released to the public until after they've been published in a journal that has given them peer review. People claim that this delays access to potentially lifesaving information. Yet peer review is the only way to keep harmful information from reaching an unequipped public. Therefore, waiting until a journal has done peer review and has published the findings is the only way to protect the public from uninvestigated research.

So what's the author assuming? Well, she tells us that peer review is the only way that the information can be okayed, then concludes that the public has to wait until a medical journal has published the findings. But what if there's some other way that findings can undergo peer review? If this were true, then the author's conclusion would be invalidated. *Yes, that's the denial test, presented in a sneaky way.* So (A) must be a necessary assumption. (B)'s way off, since we have no reason to believe that there aren't plenty of people who would evaluate medical research findings who don't happen to be on medical review panels. (C) tries to lead you down an erroneous road— it's not that the public can't read the journals once they're published, it's that the public shouldn't be presented with potentially harmful information that hasn't been adequately reviewed. As for

(D), we have no reason to assume that all findings are subjected to peer review—maybe some never get that far, and are halted before they reach that stage. And (E) is way beyond the scope, since we needn't assume anything about the partiality of peer review panels.

> An Advanced test taker is wary of extreme answer choices. The right answer to an inference question doesn't intensify the argument.

Explanation: Moral Responsibility

8. E

Formal Logic is the name of the game here, if you hadn't guessed. This question is a good example of a Formal Logic question that requires you to combine many statements, which makes it among the most difficult and time-consuming questions on the exam.

> An Advanced test taker begins a tough Formal Logic question by scoping out the concrete information and using it to set off a chain of deductions.

One claim in the passage is that everyone will sometimes act in ways that are consequential to the treatment they received while an infant. Since the treatment was beyond that person's control, so are the consequential acts. Therefore, all adults will sometimes do things (relating to when they were infants) for which they should not be held morally responsible. If everyone can disavow themselves of responsibility of *at least one* action, then there is nobody who can be held responsible for *all* of his actions.

(A) Infants may perform actions that are *not* the consequence of treatment received. In those cases, the argument is silent as to responsibility.

(B) Similar to (A), this choice discusses the responsibility for actions that aren't necessarily out of the individual's control.

(C) The argument doesn't necessarily support this point, stating that in some cases, determining adult control over treatment received is difficult. Since nothing guides us as to when individuals who claim to lack control must take responsibility, this choice can't be fully resolved.

(D) The argument is limited to discussing responsibility for actions beyond the person's control. Nothing is said with respect to actions within control.

> An Advanced test taker uses every method at her disposal to increase her odds of getting the point.

Explanation: Justifiable Harm

9. C

We're given a principle of conduct, and asked for the real-life scenario that best matches up to it. The issue is, "When is it morally justified to benefit from harming someone else?" And the principle cites a two-part necessary condition, signaled as usual by "only if": the victim's awareness that the behavior could be harmful, and his/her consent. We must see that in the *absence* of such awareness and/or consent, the benefits accruing from the harm will not be morally justified. Having done that analysis, we can then proceed with confidence to the choices and see how they stack up:

(A) ignores the whole issue of awareness and consent, focusing instead on issues (false statements; *preventing* harm) that the principle never mentions. Besides, Sonia attempts to benefit, but does not—she gets stuck in detention anyway—so the morality test doesn't apply here; no one here benefits from harming another.

(B) brings in the concept of accidental behavior, and again ignores the awareness and consent issues.

(C) Here ya go. Max lacked awareness of the potential harm of the experimental drug. Thus a necessary condition for the moral justification in Wesley's using the results is lacking. He harmed Max without informing Max of the risks. Thus, according to the principle, it is not morally justified for Wesley to benefit from the harm he inflicted on Max, and so the judgment in (C) is right on the money. For the record:

(D) Roger's mother consented to the operation, and the wording seems to suggest that, as a doctor, she'd be aware of the risks. Since this situation meets the two criteria for moral justification, we cannot use the principle at hand to conclude that Roger was morally wrong to benefit from the transplant.

(E) argues that taking the profits from James is unjustifiable, but that can't be correct here: James is the one trying to benefit from having done harm, and the principle in the stimulus certainly wouldn't support it in this case (who, after all, consents to being defrauded?). Denying James the profits would be in line with the principle in the stimulus, but (E) says that denying James is UNjustifiable, which conflicts with the principle.

> An Advanced test taker always looks for a 1:1 matchup when tackling Principle questions.

Explanation: Democratic Wealth

10. E

Obviously this is our Parallel Reasoning question of the bunch, and as you'll see, there are generally two varieties: ones that ask you to mirror the logic of an argument, and ones that ask you to mirror the *flawed* logic of an argument. If the stem doesn't designate the reasoning in the original as flawed, then we can safely assume that the logic is valid and that the logic of the right answer will be valid in the same way.

Notice the Formal Logic element present here; in fact, it's extremely common to find Formal Logic constructions in Parallel Reasoning questions. When the statements are linked as closely as these, it's possible, and often helpful, to represent them algebraically.

Here's the argument, restated in variables: A problem with X (wealth) is bad for Y (democracy), since X is necessary for Z (political power), and Y (democracy) depends upon Z (political power). The same structure is found in choice (E): A problem with X (leisure time) is bad for Y (health), since X (leisure time) is necessary for Z (regular exercise), and Y (health) depends upon Z (regular exercise).

(A) X and Y are a bad combination, since together they lead to Z.

(B) If X, then Y, since Z.

(C) It's hard to do X with characteristic Y, since Y depends on Z, whereas X does not.

(D) X is important for Y, but since X can sometimes cause Z, the effect of X on Y is uncertain. The original argument did not have this element of uncertainty and, on that point alone, is not parallel to this choice.

An Advanced test taker sees a Parallel Reasoning problem for its structure rather than its content.

What's Next?

Need more practice with these types of Logical Reasoning questions? We've got just the thing for you—in the very next chapter.

CHAPTER EIGHT

A Closer Look

Now it's time to really dig in and drill on the common types of tough Logical Reasoning questions we touched upon in chapter 7. We'll begin with five straight Formal Logic challenges, then move on to Parallel Reasoning, Inference, Principle, and Just Plain Tough questions. Enjoy!

PRACTICE SET 1: FORMAL LOGIC

1. A recent survey showed that 50 percent of people polled believe that elected officials should resign if indicted for a crime, whereas 35 percent believe that elected officials should resign only if they are convicted of a crime. Therefore, more people believe that elected officials should resign if indicted than believe that they should resign if convicted.

    The reasoning above is flawed because it

    (A) draws a conclusion about the population in general based only on a sample of that population
    (B) confuses a sufficient condition with a required condition
    (C) is based on an ambiguity of one of its terms
    (D) draws a conclusion about a specific belief based on responses to queries about two different specific beliefs
    (E) contains premises that cannot all be true

2. A poor farmer was fond of telling his children: "In this world, you are either rich or poor, and you are either honest or dishonest. All poor farmers are honest. Therefore, all rich farmers are dishonest."

    The farmer's conclusion is properly drawn if the argument assumes that

    (A) every honest farmer is poor
    (B) every honest person is a farmer
    (C) everyone who is dishonest is a rich farmer
    (D) everyone who is poor is honest
    (E) every poor person is a farmer

3. Columnist: Almost anyone can be an expert, for there are no official guidelines determining what an expert must know. Anybody who manages to convince some people of his or her qualifications in an area—whatever those may be—is an expert.

    The columnist's conclusion follows logically if which one of the following is assumed?

    (A) Almost anyone can convince some people of his or her qualifications in some area.
    (B) Some experts convince everyone of their qualifications in almost every area.
    (C) Convincing certain people that one is qualified in an area requires that one actually be qualified in that area.
    (D) Every expert has convinced some people of his or her qualifications in some area.
    (E) Some people manage to convince almost everyone of their qualifications in one or more areas.

4. No one who lacks knowledge of a subject is competent to pass judgment on that subject. Since political know-how is a matter, not of adhering to technical rules, but of insight and style learned through apprenticeship and experience, only seasoned politicians are competent to judge whether a particular political policy is fair to all.

    A major weakness of the argument is that it

    (A) relies on a generalization about the characteristic that makes someone competent to pass judgment
    (B) fails to give specific examples to illustrate how political know-how can be acquired
    (C) uses the term "apprenticeship" to describe what is seldom a formalized relationship
    (D) equates political know-how with understanding the social implications of political policies
    (E) assumes that when inexperienced politicians set policy they are guided by the advice of more experienced politicians

5. No chordates are tracheophytes, and all members of Pteropsida are tracheophytes. So no members of Pteropsida belong to the family Hominidae.

    The conclusion above follows logically if which one of the following is assumed?

    (A) All members of the family Hominidae are tracheophytes.
    (B) All members of the family Hominidae are chordates.
    (C) All tracheophytes are members of Pteropsida.
    (D) No members of the family Hominidae are chordates.
    (E) No chordates are members of Pteropsida.

PRACTICE SET 1: ANSWERS AND EXPLANATIONS

Explanation: Official Resignation

1. B

Reading the question stem first alerts us to the fact that there is a flaw in this argument, so we know to look carefully for it as we read. Fifty percent of people believe that an official should resign *if* indicted for a crime. This means that half the people believe that *every* indicted official should resign. In other words, for these people, an official's indictment is *sufficient* to call for that official's resignation. Thirtyfive percent of people believe that an official should resign *only if* they are convicted, which means that these people believe that *only* convicted officials should resign. In other words, for these people, conviction is *required* for resignation. The author then concludes that more people believe that elected officials should resign if indicted than believe that they should resign if convicted. Granted, 50 percent is more than 35 percent, but the author has neglected an important distinction, the difference between "if" and "only if." Fifty percent of people believe that every indicted official should resign, but we aren't told what percentage of people believe that every convicted official should resign. We only know the percentage of people that believe that conviction is *necessary* for resignation—a different issue. For all we know, 100 percent of people believe that every convicted official should resign, it's just that 35 percent of people believe that no other factor should lead an official to resign. Thus, the author has confused necessity with sufficiency, and committed the flaw in (B).

(A) No, the author does not generalize to a whole population based on a sample. The author makes no generalizations at all.

(C) What ambiguity?

(D) The author does draw conclusions about the two beliefs cited in the poll, but there is not a separate, third belief that is the basis of the author's conclusion.

(E) It *is* possible that the premises can all be true, as described above.

An Advanced test taker simplifies an "only if" statement by turning it into a straightforward "if-then."

Explanation: Poor Rich Farmers

2. A

It's another formal argument in casual clothing for question 2, and there's a missing assumption for us to track down. What's our poor farmer saying? Everyone is either rich or poor. Also, everyone is either honest or dishonest. All poor farmers are honest. Therefore, all rich farmers are dishonest. Wait a minute—we've accounted for the fact that every farmer who is poor is also honest. But remember that just because all poor farmers are honest, it's doesn't necessarily mean that all honest farmers are poor. It's possible that there could be rich farmers who are honest. So, by concluding that all rich farmers are dishonest, the author is assuming that every farmer who is honest is also poor. Don't believe me? *Here it is again: When in doubt, try the denial test to check an assumption. If you negate the choice in question, and the argument still holds, then that choice is not correct. However, if the argument falls apart, then it's the answer we seek.* Well, if the opposite of (A) is true, if *not* every honest farmer is poor, and all people must be either poor or rich, then some honest farmers must be rich. That contradicts the author's stated conclusion that all rich farmers are dishonest, so (A) must be correct.

We needn't assume (B), that all honest people are farmers, since the author's conclusion pertains only to farmers, not to people in general. (C) also goes too far, since we needn't assume that all dishonest people are rich farmers in order to conclude that all rich farmers are dishonest. (D) brings in other people again, and we're just concerned with farmers—all poor *farmers* are honest, but that doesn't mean that all poor *people* are honest. *Always keep an eye on the scope of the subject matter.* And (E) does just the opposite, claiming that all poor people are farmers—we needn't assume that either.

Explanation: Expert

3. A

"Evidence" Keywords can help you locate conclusions, when you need to do so.

"Almost anyone can be an expert? How so? Why do you say that?" If that's what went through your head after reading sentence 1, good for you. That's critical reading. The word "for" is a synonym for "because," and everything following "for" is indeed evidence; it explains *why* almost anyone can be an expert. The term's definition is a loose one, we're told, so if you can persuade people that you're qualified in some area, then you're an expert. The mismatched terms here are "almost anyone" (in the conclusion) and "persuading people" in the evidence, and (A) matches them up. Consider: If (A) were false, if the ability to persuade people of one's qualifications were rare, then by the columnist's own logic, being an expert would be a rare thing. (A) has to be a necessary assumption, because if it's false then the conclusion is doomed.

(B) and (E) raise the notions of near-universal expertise and near-universal persuasiveness, respectively. But the columnist is only concerned with being seen as an expert in one area, not necessarily in many areas (B); and persuading *some* people is all that's called for, not necessarily many people (E). (C) counters the columnist's strong implication that actual qualifications need have nothing to do with expertise—it's one's persuasive abilities that count. On the other hand, contrary to (D) the columnist doesn't deny the possibility that some people are experts based on real expertise, irrespective of what they've gotten people to believe. To put it another way, the columnist is explaining that which is *sufficient to* earn the title of expert, but (D) takes it as *necessary* for expertise, and that's a very different thing.

An Advanced test taker notices small shifts in scope between the information in a stimulus and the focus of the corresponding choices.

Explanation: Political Know-How

4. D

Only veteran politicians are competent to judge whether a policy is fair, says the author, because competence in passing judgment on a subject requires knowledge of that subject, and only veteran politicians have political know-how. But is political know-how the same "subject" as policy fairness? Is political know-how the field of knowledge that deals with the social implications of legislation? The author seems to think so, but must he be right? That's the criticism that (D) makes: It's not obvious that political know-how is the same thing as understanding the social implications of policy, but the argument treats it as such.

(A) attacks the first statement, which is a premise, but the generalization that unknowledgeable people aren't competent to pass judgment is a very reasonable claim.

(B) Specific examples of how political know-how is acquired aren't necessary. Few of us would dispute the author's claim that it's acquired by watching, and working with, those who have it.

(C) isn't a weakness; the author simply uses "apprenticeship" metaphorically to imply that politicians learn the ropes from experienced politicians who already possess "know-how."

(E) isn't something that the author must be assuming, since the argument concerns who is *competent* to judge policy, not who actually does so and how.

Explanation: Family Members

5. B

Your work on a Formal Logic question should start with that which is most concrete.

The most concrete element of the entire situation is that the latter term of the conclusion—"no Pteropsidae are Hominidae"—is never mentioned in the evidence. The author must therefore be assuming something about Hominidae, so any choice failing to mention that term, namely (C) and (E), can be thrown out immediately. Let's build this systematically. The second clause says that every Pteropsida is a member of the tracheophytes group. Well, our conclusion is to separate the Pteropsidae from the Hominidae, and we'll do that if we can separate the Hominidae from the tracheophytes— that would accomplish the goal.

"Chordates"—a new term—are separated from the tracheophytes. No overlap there. So if we can prove that all Hominidae are part of the chordates group, consider what happens: Chordates and tracheophytes are totally separate; Hominidae are totally inside the former; and Pteropsidae are totally inside the latter. That confirms the conclusion. The choice that gives us what we want, then, is (B). Locating all Hominidae in a group (chordates) utterly distinct from tracheophytes achieves the desired goal.

(A) would put all Hominidae in a group—tracheophytes— that includes all Pteropsida. That puts the two groups in the conclusion in closer proximity rather than further apart. And (D) simply leaves Hominidae out of the chordate group, with no sense of where Hominidae are located.

An Advanced test taker meticulously analyzes formal logic statements and can identify what must, can, and cannot be true based on them.

PRACTICE SET 2: PARALLEL REASONING

Fail A → Bad B
Good A → Good B

E1 → eligible

1. Anyone who fails to answer a patient's questions cannot be a competent physician. That is why I feel confident about my physician's competence: she carefully answers every one of my questions, no matter how trivial.

   Which one of the following most closely parallels the flawed reasoning in the argument above?

   (A) Anyone who grows up in a large family is accustomed to making compromises. Meredith is accustomed to making compromises, so she might have grown up in a large family.

   (B) Anyone who is not in favor of this proposal is ill informed on the issue. Jeanne opposes the proposal, so she is ill informed on the issue.

   (C) No one who likes music misses a performance of the symphony. Paul likes music, yet last week he missed a performance of the symphony.

   (D) Anyone who works two or more jobs is unable to find a balance between professional and personal life. Maggie has only one job, so she can find a balance between her professional and personal life.

   (E) No one who is hot-tempered and strong-willed will succeed in this business. Jeremy is strong-willed, so he will not succeed in this business.

2. At the company picnic, all of the employees who participated in more than four of the scheduled events, and only those employees, were eligible for the raffle held at the end of the day. Since only a small proportion of the employees were eligible for the raffle, most of the employees must have participated in fewer than four of the scheduled events.

   Which one of the following arguments exhibits a flawed pattern of reasoning most like that exhibited by the argument above?

   (A) Only third- and fourth-year students are allowed to keep cars on campus. Since one quarter of the third-year students keep cars on campus and one half of the fourth-year students keep cars on campus, it must be that fewer third-year students than fourth-year students keep cars on campus.

   (B) Only those violin students who attended extra rehearsal sessions were eligible for selection as soloists. Since two of the violin students were selected as soloists, those two must have been the only violin students who attended the extra sessions.

   (C) The only students honored at a special banquet were the band members who made the dean's list last semester. Since most of the band members were honored, most of the band members must have made the dean's list.

   (D) All of the members of the service club who volunteered at the hospital last summer were biology majors. Since ten of the club members are biology majors, those ten members must have volunteered at the hospital last summer.

   (E) All of the swim team members who had decreased their racing times during the season were given awards that no other members were given. Since fewer than half the team members were given such awards, the racing times of more than half the team members must have increased during the season.

3. The museum's night security guard maintains that the thieves who stole the portrait did not enter the museum at any point at or above ground level. Therefore, the thieves must have gained access to the museum from below ground level.

   The flawed pattern of reasoning in the argument above is most similar to that in which one of the following?

   (A) The rules stipulate the participants in the contest be judged on both form and accuracy. The eventual winner was judged highest in neither category, so there must be a third criterion that judges were free to invoke.

   (B) The store's competitors claim that the store, in selling off the shirts at those prices, neither made any profit nor broke even. Consequently, the store's customers must have been able to buy shirts there at less than the store's cost.

   (C) If the census is to be believed, the percentage of men who are married is higher than the percentage of women who are married. Thus, the census must show a higher number of men than of women overall.

   (D) The product label establishes that this insecticide is safe for both humans and pets. Therefore, the insecticide must also be safe for such wild mammals as deer and rabbits.

   (E) As had generally been expected, not all questionnaires were sent in by the official deadline. It follows that plans must have been made for the processing of questionnaires received late.

4. Kostman's original painting of Rosati was not a very accurate portrait. Therefore, your reproduction of Kostman's painting of Rosati will not be a very accurate production of the painting.

   Which one of the following is most similar in its flawed reasoning to the flawed reasoning in the argument above?

   (A) George's speech was filled with half-truths and misquotes. So the tape recording made of it cannot be of good sound quality.

   (B) An artist who paints a picture of an ugly scene must necessarily paint an ugly picture, unless the picture is a distorted representation of the scene.

   (C) If a child's eyes resemble her mother's, then if the mother's eyes are brown the child's eyes also must be brown.

   (D) Jo imitated Layne. But Jo is different from Layne, so Jo could not have imitated Layne very well.

   (E) Harold's second novel is similar to his first. Therefore, his second novel must be enthralling, because his first novel won a prestigious literary prize.

5. The studies showing that increased consumption of fruits and vegetables may help decrease the incidence of some types of cancer do not distinguish between organically grown and nonorganically grown produce; they were conducted with produce at least some of which contained pesticide residues. The studies may also be taken as showing, therefore, that there is no increased health risk associated with eating fruits and vegetables containing pesticide residues.

   The pattern of flawed reasoning in which one of the following is most similar to the pattern of flawed reasoning in the argument above?

   (A) Research shows that the incidence of certain major illnesses, including heart disease and cancer, is decreased in communities that have a modern power plant. The fact that this tendency is present whether the power plant is nuclear or not shows that there is no increased health risk associated with living next to a nuclear power plant.

   (B) Research has shown that there is no long-term health risk associated with a diet consisting largely of foods high in saturated fat and cholesterol if such a diet is consumed by someone with a physically active lifestyle. So, exercise is a more useful strategy for achieving cardiological health than is dietary restriction.

   (C) Research has shown that young people who drive motorcycles and receive one full year of extensive driving instruction are in fact less likely to become involved in accidents than those who simply pass a driving test and drive cars. This shows that there is not an inherently greater risk associated with driving a motorcycle than with driving a car.

   (D) Research has shown that kitchen cutting boards retain significant numbers of microbes even after careful washing, but that after washing fewer microbes are found on wooden boards than on plastic boards. There is, therefore, no greater risk of contracting microbial illnesses associated with using wooden cutting boards than with using plastic cutting boards.

   (E) Research shows that there is no greater longterm health benefit associated with taking vitamin supplements than with a moderate increase in the intake of fruits and vegetables. Clearly, then, there is no long-term health risk associated with the failure to take vitamin supplements, so long as enough fruits and vegetables are consumed.

PRACTICE SET 2: ANSWERS AND EXPLANATIONS

Explanation: Competent Physicians

1. D

Were you able to spot the common logical flaw in this reasoning? Hopefully you recognized the author's confusion of necessary and sufficient conditions, and searched the choices looking for a similar mistake. It's helpful to translate the first sentence into if-then form: IF you don't answer questions, THEN you're not a competent doctor. So answering questions is *necessary* to being a good doctor. Fine. But then the author goes on to say that "Since my doctor answers my questions fully, she must be competent." Uh-oh!

The author mistakes a condition *necessary* for being a good doctor (answering questions) for one that's *sufficient* for being a good doctor. Being a good question answerer is required of good doctors, but that doesn't mean that's the *only* requirement—a doctor can answer questions well and still be a bad doctor for other reasons. So we're to find a situation in which necessity and sufficiency are confused in a similar manner. Check out the choices:

(A) Close, but no cigar: Being accustomed to making compromises is necessary to growing up in a large family. But being accustomed to making compromises doesn't *guarantee* that one grew up in a large family; others can certainly pick up this habit as well. So (A) seems to be in line with the original, but veers off at the last moment: (A) would exhibit the same necessary/sufficient confusion of the original if it concluded "therefore Meredith MUST have grown up in a large family." But the tentative nature of (A)'s conclusion has no parallel to the stimulus.

(B) is proper logic. Jeanne, like any other opponent of the issue, must be ill-informed. Not flawed, so not parallel.

(C) Paul's situation contradicts the first sentence, which said that all those who like music never miss a performance. He likes music, yet blew off the performance. Curious. We can characterize this scenario as "an exception to a general rule," which is not the action of the stimulus argument. There's no confusion of necessary and sufficient conditions in (C), so (C) is not parallel to the original.

(D) If someone works two or more jobs, that person cannot find a balance between career and personal life. Is there an element of necessity here? Yup: Working fewer than two jobs is a *necessary* requirement for balance. Maggie meets this condition—she has only one job. And just like in the original, the author of (D) treats this necessary condition as sufficient in concluding that Maggie *can* therefore achieve balance between career and personal life. Not necessarily! She's cleared this one hurdle, but for all we know working fewer than two jobs is not the *only* thing necessary to achieving such balance. Same confusion, same result—(D)'s the winner here.

(E) There's necessity here as well: It's *necessary* to be cool and easygoing (or however we wish to describe "not hot-tempered and strong-willed") to succeed. Jeremy fails to meet one of the conditions right off the bat (he *is* strong-willed), so (E) deviates already on this count. There can be no confusion of a necessary for a sufficient condition if Jeremy doesn't meet the necessary condition in the first place. (E) is flawed, sure: We cannot conclude from the mere fact of Jeremy's strong will that he won't succeed in the business, because we know nothing of his hot temper. This flaw, however, is far from the flaw in the original.

An Advanced test taker abstracts arguments, rephrasing them in general terms, particularly in Parallel Reasoning questions.

Explanation: Company Picnic

2. E

The stimulus is indeed flawed—but it comes so close to validity! The author only makes one little slipup towards the end. Did you catch it?

The argument begins O.K.: Everyone who competed in more than four scheduled events qualified for the raffle, and only a small percentage of the employees qualified. It follows that *most* of the employees, since they didn't qualify for the raffle, must have competed in *four events or fewer*. That seems at first glance to be a valid conclusion. But do you see where the stimulus goes wrong? By concluding that the majority competed in *fewer* than four, it neglects the possibility that many employees—perhaps a sizable majority—competed in *exactly* four events. In the same way, (E) concludes that because few swimmers got awards, and only those whose times decreased got awards, therefore most swimmers' times must have *increased*—ignoring the possibility that the times of most of the swimmers may simply have stayed the same.

(A) deals with a comparison between two types of students (3rd year vs. 4th year) and draws a comparative conclusion. Not so the original. (A)'s flaw, incidentally, is that it assumes that the numbers of 3rd and 4th year students must have been identical (only then could you conclude that more of the latter than the former keep cars on campus).

(B) is faulty, true (there may have been *many* more students who attended the extra sessions; it's just that two were chosen), but not in the same way as the original which, as described above, errs by pointing to two extremes without noting a third alternative.

(C) is the one choice here that amounts to proper logic. Its first sentence translates to "If a band member was honored, then s/he was on the dean's list." From that it would be valid to conclude that since most of the members were honored, most of the members were indeed on the dean's list. But of course we're looking for a *flawed* argument.

(D) more or less commits the "fallacy of affirming the consequent" when it essentially argues that "If a member volunteered, then she was a bio major; these ten were bio majors, hence they volunteered." That's a flaw, sure, but not the one committed in the original.

An Advanced test taker has a solid grasp on the nature of sets.

Explanation: Security Guard

3. B

Why must the thieves have entered through the basement (i.e. below ground level)? Because the security guard *says* they didn't come in on ground level or above. That is different from evidence *proving* that alternative means of entrance were not used. The essence of the logic is a flatly factual statement of a phenomenon that must have occurred, but a statement that is based on a subjective assessment that dismisses other alternatives. That describes (B) pretty well, as well as the stimulus, doesn't it? The competitors' "claim" about what cannot have happened is used to support a flat assertion about what *must* have happened.

(A), (E) The evidence in each choice is factual (the results of the judging in (A), and (E)'s statement about the late filers). But the stimulus evidence is a claim that some *party* is making, and an argument that lacks that element cannot be parallel to the original.

(C) The conditional "If the census is to be believed" has no parallel in the stimulus, nor does the movement from small groups (married men vs. married women) to large (all men vs. all women).

(D) is, yes, based on a claim that isn't factually proven. But we are looking for a claim that something could *not* have occurred as evidence for a conclusion about what must be the case. So the evidence in (D) falls short, and the conclusion that the product is safe for *other* creatures isn't like the stimulus conclusion either.

An Advanced test taker gets to the heart of the matter, recognizing which logical elements are most likely to be relevant to the right answer.

Explanation: Bad Copy

4. A

Finding a parallel flaw involves the same method as finding any parallel argument.

The value judgment that the listener's copy of Kostman's painting won't be accurate is based on the lack of accuracy in the original painting. The idea seems to be that the next generation must repeat the sins of the previous one, an idea repeated in (A). To choose (A) you don't even have to delve into the real problem with the logic—namely, the scope shift from evidence to conclusion—because the structure of all of the other choices deviates so wildly from the structure of the stimulus. (B)'s structure includes an "unless" exception nowhere paralleled in the stimulus. (C) offers two if clauses, not present in the original, and a shift from resemblance to identity that is also unique to (C). "But" in and of itself kills (D), since the original offers no counterpremises; and the fact that (E)'s conclusion is based on two pieces of evidence is enough to break any possible parallel with the stimulus.

An Advanced test taker knows that a Parallel argument must parallel *every* aspect of the original.

Explanation: Fruits & Veggies

5. A

For Parallel Logic, comparing conclusions can be a quick route to an otherwise subtle right answer. This one looks like a horror-show, but those who learned Kaplan's technique of comparing parts of arguments in order to discard violators acquired a quick and easy point here. The stimulus's conclusion, signaled by "therefore," is that there's no greater risk of . . . well, call it "a certain behavior." And only (A) mimics that. "No increased risk in living near a nuclear plant" parallels "No increased risk in eating produce with pesticide residues."

Consider the other choices' conclusions. (C) and (D) both conclude that there is no greater risk of *A than B*—a comparison that appears nowhere in the stimulus. (B), too, involves a comparison, and loses the sense of "no greater risk" to boot. (E) asserts that a behavior involves *no risk* (as opposed to "no greater risk"), and also adds a necessary condition ("so long as . . . ") not present in the original.

Irrespective of whatever else is going on in choices (B)–(E), then, all of them can be discarded because the conclusions don't match up.

An Advanced test taker spends only as much time as is necessary to eliminate a choice.

PRACTICE SET 3: INFERENCE

1. The number of North American children who are obese—that is, who have more body fat than do 85 percent of North American children their age—is steadily increasing, according to four major studies conducted over the past 15 years.

   If the finding reported above is correct, it can be properly concluded that

   (A) when four major studies all produce similar results, those studies must be accurate
   (B) North American children have been progressively less physically active over the past 15 years
   (C) the number of North American children who are not obese increased over the past 15 years
   (D) over the past 15 years, the number of North American children who are underweight has declined
   (E) the incidence of obesity in North American children tends to increase as the children grow older

2. In the past, the railroads in Ostronia were run as regional monopolies and operated with little regard for what customers wanted. In recent years, with improvements to the Ostronian national highway network, the railroad companies have faced heavy competition from long-distance trucking companies. But because of government subsidies that have permitted Ostronain railroad companies to operate even while incurring substantial losses, the companies continue to disregard customers' needs and desires.

   If the statements above are true, which one of the following must also be true on the basis of them?

   (A) If the government of Ostronia ceases to subsidize railroad companies, few of those companies will continue to operate.
   (B) Few companies in Ostronia that have received subsidies from the government have taken the needs and desires of their customers into account.
   (C) Without government subsidies, railroad companies in Ostronia would have to increase the prices they charge their customers.
   (D) The transportation system in Ostronia is no more efficient today than in was in the past.
   (E) In recent years, some companies in Ostronia that have had little regard for the desires of their customers have nonetheless survived.

3. Certain instruments used in veterinary surgery can be made either of stainless steel or of nylon. In a study of such instruments, 50 complete sterilizations of a set of nylon instruments required 3.4 times the amount of energy used to manufacture that set of instruments, whereas 50 complete sterilizations of a set of stainless steel instruments required 2.1 times the amount of energy required to manufacture that set of instruments.

   If the statements above are true, each of the following could be true EXCEPT:

   (A) The 50 complete sterilizations of the nylon instruments used more energy than did the 50 complete sterilizations of the stainless steel instruments.
   (B) More energy was required for each complete sterilization of the nylon instruments than was required to manufacture the nylon instruments.
   (C) More nylon instruments than stainless steel instruments were sterilized in the study.
   (D) More energy was used to produce the stainless steel instruments than was used to produce the nylon instruments.
   (E) The total cost of 50 complete sterilizations of the stainless steel instruments was greater than the cost of manufacturing the stainless steel instruments.

4. Decision makers tend to have distinctive styles. One such style is for the decision maker to seek the widest possible input from advisers and to explore alternatives while making up his or her mind. In fact, decision makers of this sort will often argue vigorously for a particular idea, emphasizing its strong points and downplaying its weaknesses, not because they actually believe in the idea but because they want to see if their real reservations about it are idiosyncratic or are held independently by their advisers.

    Which one of the following is most strongly supported by the statements above?

    (A) If certain decision makers' statements are quoted accurately and at length, the content of the quote could nonetheless be greatly at variance with the decision eventually made.

    (B) Certain decision makers do not know which ideas they do not really believe in until after they have presented a variety of ideas to their advisers.

    (C) If certain decision makers dismiss an idea out of hand, it must be because its weaknesses are more pronounced than any strong points it may have.

    (D) Certain decision makers proceed in a way that makes it likely that they will frequently decide in favor of ideas in which they do not believe.

    (E) If certain decision makers' advisers know the actual beliefs of those they advise, those advisers will give better advice than they would if they did not know those beliefs.

5. Curator: The decision to restore the cloak of the central figure in Veronese's painting from its present red to the green found underneath is fully justified. Reliable x-ray and chemical tests show that the red pigment was applied after the painting had been completed, and that the red paint was not mixed in Veronese's workshop. Hence it appears likely that an artist other than Veronese tampered with Veronese's painting after its completion.

    Art critic: But in a copy of Veronese's painting made shortly after Veronese died, the cloak is red. It is highly unlikely that a copyist would have made so major a change so soon after Veronese's death.

    The art critic's response to the curator would provide the strongest support for which one of the following conclusions?

    (A) The copy of Veronese's painting that was made soon after the painter's death is indistinguishable from the original.

    (B) No painting should be restored before the painting is tested with technologically sophisticated equipment.

    (C) The proposed restoration will fail to restore Veronese's painting to the appearance it had at the end of the artist's lifetime.

    (D) The value of an artist's work is not necessarily compromised when that work is tampered with by later artists.

    (E) Veronese did not originally intend the central figure's cloak to be green.

PRACTICE SET 3: ANSWERS AND EXPLANATIONS

Explanation: Obese Children

1. C

The stimulus states that the number of obese North American kids has increased over the last 15 years. The crux of the matter is the definition of "obese": "obese" technically refers to the fattest 15 *percent* of North American kids. With that standard, you'll always have the same percentage of kids labeled obese, regardless of actual amounts of body fat. Even if every child in North America were emaciated, according to this particular definition, the heaviest 15 percent of them would be labeled "obese." If a number representing 15 percent of all kids has increased, we know that the *total* number of kids must also have increased. So the other, non-obese, 85 percent of the group of kids must also have grown in number. Thus, since there are more obese kids nowadays, there must also be more non-obese kids. That's (C).

(A) is simply silly; we can't conclude that the agreement of four studies always signals truth.

(B) The question of "physical activity" is beyond the scope of the stimulus. Moreover, because the definition of obesity is based on a fixed percentage of kids, we don't even know if kids in general have become fatter than they were. Think about it: Even if all the kids *lost* weight, there would still technically be a group of kids who have more body fat than 85 percent of the children their age. (B) is totally unsupported.

(D) If the term "underweight" refers to a fixed statistical percentage (the way "obese" does), then the number of underweight kids must have *grown* along with the total number of kids. If, unlike obesity, being underweight isn't merely a matter of belonging to a certain percentage of the group of children, then we don't know what to say about (D). Either way, it can't be concluded from the information in the stimulus.

(E) can't be true, since kids are being compared to other kids their age. By the very definition of obesity, there'll always be 15 percent of kids of every age that are obese.

> An Advanced test taker knows that the way in which numbers and percentages are used or misused is key to answering many questions.

Explanation: Ostronian Railroads

2. E

The important—indeed the only—point to notice is that nothing has changed, that Ostronia's railroad companies have always treated customers like dirt and continue to do so, regardless of current economic difficulties. That's what (E) sums up pretty neatly. All the other choices distort stuff thrown in to distract us from that one key point.

(A) commits the "fallacy of denying the antecedent." Even though the subsidies do permit the railroads to operate, it doesn't follow that *not* having the subsidies will *not* permit them to operate.

*Abh phew was
dumb~ read
carefully*

(B) This argument is solely about the *railroad* subsidies, but (B)'s scope is companies *in general* that have gotten subsidy. No evidence is present to support any inference about the customer service history of those various firms.

(C) Another variation of denial of the antecedent, à la (A). We cannot be sure *what* would happen if and when the subsidies were removed, because all we know is what is happening with the subsidies in place. (C) takes the certain position that prices would have to go up if the subsidies were removed, but where's the evidence for that prediction? In fact, any number of other alternatives could come into play.

(D) Huge (and classic) scope shift here, from the argument's interest in the railroads' customer service history to (D)'s interest in their *efficiency*.

An Advanced test taker always pays attention to the scope of the argument, which helps him to axe easy and difficult choices alike.

Explanation: Sterile Instruments

3. B

If this one reminded you of a logic game, so much the better: Your LG skills serve you well here. First, note that the question asks for the one thing that *cannot* be true. Next, draw out the information the stimulus gives—and doesn't give. There are two sets of instruments; the same procedures are done to each; and the procedures yield similar results. It takes more energy to sterilize a set of these instruments than it does to manufacture them. But we don't know how many instruments make up each set, nor do we know exactly how much energy it takes to manufacture either set. It could take more to make nylon tools, or it could take more to make stainless steel, or it could take equal amounts of energy for both. We just don't know. Unfortunately there's no way to predict the answer here. It's just a matter of slogging through the choices until you find the right one.

(A) could be true. If the same amount of energy was required to manufacture both the nylon and the steel instruments, then sterilizing the nylon instruments would have been more energy consuming than sterilizing the steel. (B), however, can't be true, and yes, it takes a little math-thinking, but that's life. (*You could have skipped this choice and checked out the others*; if all of them can be true, then (B) must be correct whether or not you understand why.) If 50 complete sterilizations of the nylon instruments took 3.4 times the energy to make that set, then they should be able to do roughly 15 sterilizations with the same energy as manufacture. One complete sterilization, then, must have taken far less energy than the amount needed to manufacture. (C) could be true; as we noted above, we don't know how many types of instruments appear in each kit, so there could be more nylon instruments than steel. Since both kits were sterilized an equal number of times, more nylon instruments could have been sterilized. (D) absolutely could be true, since we don't know how much energy was required to produce either set. (E) is also quite possible. If materials are cheap, and energy is very expensive, then using far more energy to sterilize than manufacture steel instruments could make sterilizing them more expensive than making them in the first place.

An Advanced test taker doesn't hesitate to work out actual examples to clarify her understanding of a numerical concept.

Explanation: Decision Making Style

4. A

We're told that one type of decision maker will sometimes advocate a position just to see how others react to it rather than because of a commitment to that position. This supports (A), which states that the substance of what some decision makers say might not necessarily be consistent with the decisions they ultimately make.

(B) That some decision makers present contrary ideas (in order to test out what they actually believe in) implies that they, at least, do have an idea of how they feel *before* they approach their advisers.

(C) The passage is based on decision making through discussion, so the nature of the decision in this one is outside of the scope.

(D) Some decision makers may argue in favor of an idea they don't believe in for the purpose of confirming their suspicions, but this in no way suggests that they will end up settling for an idea in which they don't believe.

(E) The decision makers seek to test their beliefs by listening to others. If the advisers knew the actual beliefs of the decision makers in advance, this would probably skew their advice towards what they think the speaker wants to hear, and thus defeat the decision maker's purpose.

Explanation: Veronese's Painting

5. C

By asking for a conclusion supported by the art critic's response, this question essentially asks you to plant a big "Therefore" in front of each answer choice and choose the one that most logically follows from the critic's remarks. In response to the claim that the change from red to green is justified (which is the curator's main point), the critic points out counterevidence suggesting that Veronese's intended color was in fact red. The upshot, therefore—as (C) states—is that changing the color from red to green is not likely to restore the painting to its state during the painter's life. In the end, the restoration would not be "justified."

(A)'s sweeping assertion about the Veronese copy does not follow from the critic's limited evidence about one particular element of the copy—the cloak.

(B) Testing, whether sophisticated or crude, is outside the scope here. And the critic is concerned with the merits of one proposed Veronese restoration, not the merits of restoration in general.

(D) "Tampering"? The critic is talking about a Veronese *copy*. And that copy has nothing to do with "the value of" the original Veronese. Furthermore, the very specific topic and scope are the merits of one proposed change to a *Veronese* painting.

(E) Mentally inserting the word "Therefore" between the critic's statement and choice (E) should confirm why the latter is wrong. There's a big gap between the evidence about the post-mortem copy and (E)'s proposed conclusion about Veronese's "original intentions."

PRACTICE SET 4: PRINCIPLE

1. To perform an act that is morally wrong is to offend against humanity, and all offenses against humanity are equally bad. Because murder is morally wrong, it is just as bad to have murdered one person by setting off a bomb as it would have been to have murdered a hundred people by setting off that bomb.

   Which one of the following judgments conforms to the principles invoked above?

   (A) If lying is morally wrong, telling a lie is as bad as murdering someone.

   (B) Risking one's life to save the lives of a hundred people is morally no better than risking one's life to save one person.

   (C) If stealing is morally wrong, it is equally important to society to prevent people from stealing as it is to prevent them from committing murder.

   (D) Accidentally causing the death of a person is just as bad as murdering that person.

   (E) In a situation in which the life of one person can be saved only by killing another person, killing and not killing are equally bad.

2. An editorial in the Grandburg Daily Herald claims that Grandburg's voters would generally welcome the defeat of the political party now in control of the Grandburg City Council. The editorial bases its claim on a recent survey that found that 59 percent of Grandburg's registered voters think that the party will definitely be out of power after next year's city council elections.

   Which one of the following is a principle that, if established, would provide the strongest justification for the editorial's conclusion?

   (A) The way voters feel about a political party at a given time can reasonably be considered a reliable indicator of the way they will continue to feel about that party, barring unforeseeable political developments.

   (B) The results of surveys that gauge current voter sentiment toward a given political party can legitimately be used as the basis for making claims about the likely future prospects of that political party.

   (C) An increase in ill-feeling toward a political party that is in power can reasonably be expected to result in a corresponding increase in support for rival political parties.

   (D) The proportion of voters who expect a given political possibility to be realized can legitimately be assumed to approximate the proportion of voters who are in favor of that possibility being realized.

   (E) It can reasonably be assumed that registered voters who respond to a survey regarding the outcome of a future election will exercise their right to vote in that election.

3. To classify a work of art as truly great, it is necessary that the work have both originality and far-reaching influence upon the artistic community.

The principle above, if valid, most strongly supports which one of the following arguments?

(A) By breaking down traditional schemes of representation, Picasso redefined painting. It is this extreme originality that warrants his work being considered truly great.

(B) Some of the most original art being produced today is found in isolated communities, but because of this isolation these works have only minor influence, and hence cannot be considered truly great.

(C) Certain examples of the drumming practiced in parts of Africa's west coast employ a musical vocabulary that resists representation in Western notational schemes. This tremendous originality coupled with the profound impact these pieces are having on musicians everywhere, is enough to consider these works to be truly great.

(D) The piece of art in the lobby is clearly not classified as truly great, so it follows that it fails to be original.

(E) Since Bach's music is truly great, it not only has both originality and a major influence on musicians, it has broad popular appeal as well.

4. When the Pinecrest Animal Shelter, a charitable organization, was in danger of closing because it could not pay for important repairs, its directors appealed to the townspeople to donate money that would be earmarked to pay for those repairs. Since more funds were ultimately donated than were used for the repairs, the directors plan to donate the surplus funds to other animal shelters. But before doing so, the directors should obtain permission from those who made the donations.

Which one of the following principles, if valid, most helps to justify the position advocated above and yet places the least restriction on the allocation of funds by directors of charitable organizations?

(A) The directors of charitable organizations cannot allocate publicly solicited funds to any purposes for which the directors had not specifically earmarked the funds in advance.

(B) People who solicit charitable donations from the public for a specific cause should spend the funds only on that cause, or, if that becomes impossible, should dispose of the funds according to the expressed wishes of the donors.

(C) Directors of charitable organizations who solicit money from the public must return all the money received from an appeal if more money is received than can practicably be used for the purposes specified in the appeal.

(D) Donors of money to charitable organizations cannot delegate to the directors of those organizations the responsibility of allocating the funds received to various purposes consonant with the purposes of the organization as the directors of the organization see fit.

(E) People who contribute money to charitable organizations should be considered to be placing their trust in the directors of those organizations to use the money wisely according to whatever circumstance might arise.

5. Jack's aunt gave him her will, asking him to make it public when she died; he promised to do so. After her death, Jack looked at the will; it stipulated that all her money go to her friend George. Jack knew that if he made the will public, George would squander the money, benefiting neither George nor anyone else. Jack also knew that if he did not make the will public, the money would go to his own mother, who would use it to benefit herself and others, harming no one. After reflection, he decided not to make the will public.

Which one of the following principles, if valid, would require Jack to act as he did in the situation described?

(A) Duties to family members take priority over duties to people who are not family members.

(B) Violating a promise is impermissible whenever doing so would become known by others.

(C) One must choose an alternative that benefits some and harms no one over an alternative that harms some and benefits no one.

(D) When faced with alternatives it is obligatory to choose whichever one will benefit the greatest number of people.

(E) A promise becomes nonbinding when the person to whom the promise was made is no longer living.

PRACTICE SET 4: ANSWERS AND EXPLANATIONS

Explanation: Moral Wrongs

1. A

Anyone who read the question stem first would know to expect two things—the stimulus contains a "principle," and each choice contains a "judgment." Our job is to find the judgment amongst the choices that matches the principles in the stimulus. First, then, we need to understand the principles in the stimulus. If a morally wrong act offends humanity (a principle), and all offenses against humanity are equally bad (a second principle), then *all morally wrong acts are equally bad*. Now we can match the judgment in correct choice (A) to the principles in the passage: If lying is morally wrong and murder is morally wrong (the stimulus states that murder is morally wrong), these two acts must be equally bad because the first sentence states that all morally wrong acts are equally bad.

(B) and (D) Risking one's life to save lives is most likely a morally good act, while we don't know if accidentally killing someone is considered morally bad (for the sake of this question, at least). These two choices therefore fall outside the scope of the argument, which concerns only morally wrong acts.

(C) Outside the scope—"prevention" goes one step too far and is an issue that's neither dealt with in the principles in the stimulus nor in the judgments of the choices.

(E) In order for (E) to conform, we'd have to infer, on our own, that not saving a life in such a situation is a morally bad thing. This, however, would be unwarranted —the principles, taken together, simply state that any two things that are *known to be* morally bad can be considered equally bad. There's no room in this principle for our interpretation of the moral value of various acts in specific situations.

An Advanced test taker recognizes the kinds of wrong choices that appear again and again on the LSAT.

Explanation: Grandburg City Council

2. C

Did you notice that the editorial's evidence and conclusion are based on utterly different issues? The evidence talks about what the surveyed voters *think will happen*, but draws a conclusion about what voters *want*. Weird, but we are requested to justify this silly logic, and so we need a principle asserting that what voters predict is a reliable reflection of what they want. And that's (D), in a nutshell.

(A)'s focus is on the likelihood of a group's opinions not changing over time, an issue not raised by the editorial.

(B) supports the idea that a survey group's opinions might affect their prediction about what will happen, the very opposite of what's going on in the editorial.

(C)'s reference to *increased ill will* has no relation to what's said in the *Daily Herald*, and as in (B), this choice seems to think that the conclusion (rather than the evidence) is a prediction.

(E), in its focus on the relationship between survey respondents and ultimate voters, is quite removed from the editorial's content.

An Advanced test taker is always receptive to logical flaws . . . even in questions that do not normally feature them.

Explanation: Great Art

3. B

To be truly great, an art work must have both originality and far-reaching influence. These two elements are *necessary* for greatness: No work is great unless it is both original and influential. However, these conditions aren't *sufficient* for greatness: That is, an art work could have both characteristics and still not be a truly great work. We're looking for an argument that accords with the general principle in the stimulus, and this common distinction between necessity and sufficiency will help us to eliminate a few choices. As for the correct choice, there's no real good way to pre-phrase an answer here, so we'll just have to jump right into the choices.

(A) We're told that Picasso's work satisfies one of the conditions, but we're told nothing about the other. (A) thus ignores one half of the principle. But note that even if Picasso's work was both original and influential, that still wouldn't be sufficient to deem his art truly great.

(B) The argument in (B) is valid and accords perfectly with the principle: Here's a work of art that has one characteristic but not the other, which, according to the principle, *does* disqualify it from greatness. And that's exactly what the author of the argument in (B) concludes. Although original, some art does not have far-reaching influence, and therefore it can't be truly great.

(C), like (A), confuses necessity with sufficiency. (C) describes a work of art that satisfies both requirements, and then concludes that the art in question can be considered truly great. The principle in the stimulus asserts that possessing both characteristics (originality and influence) are necessary for greatness, but the argument in (C) functions as if all a work *needs* are these two things to be great. Not so: It puts the art work in the ballpark of greatness—it doesn't disqualify it, that is—but there may be other factors involved. Originality and influence aren't enough by themselves (they are necessary but not sufficient) to make art truly great; they do not *guarantee* greatness.

(D) Just because art is not truly great doesn't mean it can't be original. All truly great works have those qualities, but we don't know anything about works that aren't truly great.

(E) is a classic half right, half wrong answer choice. If all you read was the first two clauses, you'd think this is the right answer. Bach's work is truly great, and therefore it is original and has far reaching influence (good so far), but we *don't know that it must also therefore have broad popular appeal*. The stimulus doesn't discuss broad popular appeal and thus this part of (E) is outside the scope and not supported by the stimulus.

An Advanced test taker always recognizes Formal Logic—no matter how it shows up on the LSAT.

Explanation: The Closing of Pinecrest

4. B

Yuck. This one had "come back to me later" written all over it. The stem by itself lets us know we're in for a rough ride. We're looking for a principle that does two things: It must support the position; and it must place the least restriction on $ allocation. So what's the position? The directors raised money for a cause, but they raised more money than they needed for that cause. What should be done with the extra cash? The directors want to donate it to other animal shelters, which seems reasonable enough, but the author says that they ought to get the permission of the donors first. That's the "position" the correct choice will support. It was difficult to pre-phrase an exact answer, but you could have hit the answer choices looking for something that addresses the issue of what should be done with excess funds, and would support the notion that the directors needed to ask for permission before allocating the funds to similar causes. (B) does the job. It's on-point, since this is a situation in which spending money on the original cause is impossible.

(B) supports the position, since it limits the permissible uses of the money to the specific cause, requiring the directors to inform the donors if plans change. Finally, (B) supports the position without placing excess restrictions on money allocation. The only restrictions (B) places are those necessary to justify the position. As for the others:

(A) and (C) would place excess restrictions on the directors, and don't justify the position, either. If (A) were adopted, then the directors wouldn't be able to allocate any of the excess $ to other causes, even if the donors said it was OK, since those causes weren't specified in advance. That's pretty restrictive, and it conflicts with the position that it's OK to use the funds in other ways, as long as they get permission first. (C) has the same problem, requiring all the extra $ to be returned.

(D) doesn't apply, since the $ was raised for a specific purpose, and the directors weren't trying to get the power to use the extra $ as they saw fit. (D) would be relevant if the directors knew that more money would be raised, and *in advance* asked for the power to use the extra $ for consonant purposes as they saw fit. As is, (D) is off-point.

(E) doesn't support the position. If the directors can do whatever they want, why would they have to get permission first?

Explanation: Jack and George

5. D

This one is pretty nasty, but again, reading the stem carefully puts you on the right track. We're looking for a choice that would *require* Jack to act the way he did. What did he do? He didn't keep his promise to make the will public. If he had, then the money would have gone to George, who would have wasted it, helping no one. Since he didn't make the will public, the money goes to his kindly mother, who will use it to help herself and others. It's tough to form a precise pre-phrase here, but we're looking for something that forces one to give money where it will do the most good, even if one has promised to do otherwise. That's what (D) does. If the only consideration Jack ought to consider is the number of people that will benefit, then he ought to give the cash to Mom, who (along with others) will certainly benefit. If he gave the money to George, then no one would benefit, and the principle in (D) would be violated. (D) is thus the principle that requires Jack to act as he did.

If you had trouble with this question (and many did), you probably had trouble with the answer choices. They're subtle, but learning the ways in which wrong choices go astray is important for handling the toughest questions.

(A) If (A) governs the situation, Jack wouldn't know what to do, because he might have a duty to his aunt to keep his promise, and a duty to his mother to support her in her dotage. (A) would support choosing Mom over George, but there's another family member to whom Jack might owe a duty.

(B) First, Jack *did* violate a promise, so any choice discouraging promise-breaking won't support Jack's actions. Second, we don't know whether this action will be found out by others, so (B) doesn't apply here.

(C) is tough, but we don't know that giving the money to George will harm anyone. All we know is that it won't *help* anyone. So we don't know whether giving the money to George is an alternative that would "harm some and benefit no one."

(E) would excuse Jack from the promise he made, but wouldn't *require* him to give the money to Mom. After his promise became nonbinding, he could still have given the money to George anyway.

An Advanced test taker rolls with the punches. When he sees something a bit unusual, he relates it to something more familiar.

PRACTICE SET 5: JUST PLAIN TOUGH

1. Samples from the floor of a rock shelter in Pennsylvania were dated by analyzing the carbon they contained. The dates assigned to samples associated with human activities formed a consistent series, beginning with the present and going back in time, a series that was correlated with the depth from which the samples came. The oldest and deepest sample was dated at 19,650 years before the present, plus or minus 2,400 years. Skeptics, viewing that date as to early and inconsistent with the accepted date of human migration into North America, suggested that the samples could have been contaminated by dissolved "old carbon" carried by percolating groundwater from nearby coal deposits.

   Which of the following considerations, if true, argues most strongly against the suggestion of the skeptics?

   (A) No likely mechanism of contamination involving percolating groundwater would have affected the deeper samples from the site without affecting the uppermost sample.
   (B) Not every application of the carbon-dating procedure has led to results that have been generally acceptable to scientists.
   (C) There is no evidence that people were using coal for fuel at any time when the deepest layer might have been laid down.
   (D) No sample in the series, when retested by the carbon-dating procedure, was assigned an earlier date than that assigned to a sample from a layer above it.
   (E) No North American site besides the one in Pennsylvania has ever yielded a sample to which the carbon-dating procedure assigned a date that was comparably ancient.

2. X: Since many chemicals useful for agriculture and medicine derive from rare or endangered plant species, it is likely that many plant species that are now extinct could have provided us with substances that would have been a boon to humanity. Therefore, if we want to ensure that chemicals from plants are available for use in the future, we must make more serious efforts to preserve for all time our natural resources.

   Y: But living things are not our "resources." Yours is a selfish approach to conservation. We should rather strive to preserve living species because they deserve to survive, not because of the good they can do us.

   X's argument relies on which one of the following assumptions?

   (A) Medicine would now be more advanced than it is if there had been a serious conservation policy in the past.
   (B) All living things exist to serve humankind.
   (C) The use of rare and endangered plant species as a source for chemicals will not itself render those species extinct.
   (D) The only way to persuade people to preserve natural resources is to convince them that it is in their interest to do so.
   (E) Few, if any, plant species have been saved from extinction through human efforts.

3. Roxanne: To protect declining elephant herds from poachers seeking to obtain ivory, people concerned about such endangered species should buy no new ivory. The new ivory and old ivory markets are entirely independent, however, so purchasing antique ivory provides no incentive to poachers to obtain more new ivory. Therefore, only antique ivory—that which is at least 75 years old—can be bought in good conscience.

Salvador: Since current demand for antique ivory exceeds the supply, many people who are unconcerned about endangered species but would prefer to buy antique ivory are buying new ivory instead. People sharing your concern about endangered species, therefore, should refrain from buying any ivory at all—thereby ensuring that demand for new ivory will drop.

A point on which Roxanne's and Salvador's views differ is whether

(A) there are substances that can serve as satisfactory substitutes for ivory in its current uses

(B) decreased demand for antique ivory would cause a decrease in demand for new ivory

(C) people should take steps to avert a threat to the continued existence of elephant herds

(D) a widespread refusal to buy new ivory will have a substantial effect on the survival of elephants

(E) people concerned about endangered species should refuse to buy ivory objects that are less than 75 years old

Questions 4–5

The fishing industry cannot currently be relied upon to help the government count the seabirds killed by net fishing, since an accurate count might result in restriction of net fishing. The government should therefore institute a program under which tissue samples from the dead birds are examined to determine the amount of toxins in the fish eaten by the birds. The industry would then have a reason to turn in the bird carcasses, since the industry needs to know whether the fish it catches are contaminated with toxins.

4. Which one of the following, if true, most strengthens the argument?

(A) The seabirds that are killed by net fishing do not eat all of the species of fish caught by the fishing industry.

(B) The government has not in the past sought to determine whether fish were contaminated with toxins by examining tissue samples of seabirds.

(C) The government cannot gain an accurate count of the number of seabirds killed by net fishing unless the fishing industry cooperates.

(D) If the government knew that fish caught by the fishing industry were contaminated by toxins, the government would restrict net fishing.

(E) If net fishing were restricted by the government, then the fishing industry would become more inclined to reveal the number of seabirds killed by net fishing.

5. Which one of the following, if true, most strongly indicates that the government program would not by itself provide an accurate count of the seabirds killed by net fishing?

(A) The seabirds killed by net fishing might be contaminated with several different toxins even if the birds eat only one kind of fish.

(B) The fishing industry could learn whether the fish it catches are contaminated with toxins if only a few of the seabirds killed by the nets were examined.

(C) The government could gain valuable information about the source of toxins by examining tissue samples of the seabirds caught in the nets.

(D) The fish caught in a particular net might be contaminated with the same toxins as those in the seabirds caught in that net.

(E) The government would be willing to certify that the fish caught by the industry are not contaminated with toxins if tests done on the seabirds showed no contamination.

PRACTICE SET 5: ANSWERS AND EXPLANATIONS

Explanation: PA Rock Shelter

1. A

Before weakening the skeptics' suggestion we need to know what they're skeptical *about*, and it's the time line that has been posited between human activities and the carbon dating at each level of the Pennsylvania rock shelter. What's controversial here is the deepest carbon sample. If this *is* a time line of human activity, then the earliest humans must have inhabited the site approximately 20,000 years ago. It's *that* that the skeptics take issue with: since that dating conflicts with what has been believed about the arrival of humans in North America, they suggest that contamination is to blame, that the carbon simply seeped out of nearby coal deposits into the lowest level (and, thus, that the presence of carbon that deep has nothing to do with human activity at all).

Now, there is no *evidence* that carbon contamination occurred; it's simply a plausible alternative theory that the skeptics have cooked up because they don't like the one at hand (i.e. that humans lived in North America 20,000 years ago). So if we can render that alternative theory implausible, then we will have shut the skeptics up—and that's just what (A) does.

According to (A), if such carbon contamination *had* occurred, it could only have done so by contaminating the upper levels too, which would fly in the face of the excellent correlation between carbon samples and human activity above. (After all, since the uppermost layers have been dated to the present, they clearly have *not* been contaminated.) In other words, (A) says that in the absence of contamination evidence up above, it's totally unlikely that contamination could have occurred below—which, again, effectively silences the skeptics.

(B)'s suggestion of an occasional weakness in the carbon-dating technique doesn't necessarily affect *this* application of the technique.

(C) at best is irrelevant (human use of coal is not part of either the original theory or that of the skeptics), and at worst is an *au-contraire* choice, since the skeptics are trying to deny the presence of humans 20,000 years ago and (C) seems to support that denial.

(D) merely speaks to the accuracy of the carbon dating, but what is at issue are the inferences that can be drawn *from* it with regard to humanity.

(E) is certainly *au contraire*. This is in line with the skeptics' view that this Pennsylvania site's early carbon sampling is an anomaly, and not an effective challenge to earlier estimates of when humans appeared in North America.

An Advanced test taker sees all angles, and recognizes subtle nuances that others miss.

Explanation: Plant Preservation

2. C

X argues "to preserve for all time our natural resources" so that chemicals can be extracted from particular plants. If, however, using the plants for chemicals would actually eventually cause the plants' extinction, then the whole effort to conserve them will have been counterproductive. Since this negation of (C) causes the argument to fall apart, we can be confident that (C) is an assumption that's crucial to the argument.

(A), (E) We can reasonably infer that X might believe these to be true; however, that's not the same as saying that X's argument *relies* on these pieces of information—his or her argument would be unaffected by the absence of either.

(B) is too broad, as "all living things" includes humans and animals and all sorts of other groups that are outside the scope of the argument.

(D) The basis of X's argument *is* to show that it's in our best interest to preserve natural resources, but whether this is the *only* way to advocate this position is irrelevant.

An Advanced test taker quickly eliminates assumption choices that are simply too broad in their scope to be necessary to the argument in question.

Explanation: Ivory Purchase

3. B

On Point at Issue questions, it's often helpful to first identify the points on which the parties agree. Roxanne feels that the new and antique ivory markets are entirely independent, so buying antique ivory doesn't encourage poachers. Salvador describes a more complex situation in which buying antique ivory can deplete the antique ivory market, thus driving others to buy new, poached ivory. At issue, then, is whether buying antique ivory causes an increased demand for new ivory. Or, stated negatively, whether "decreased demand for antique ivory would cause a decrease in demand for new ivory" (B).

The issue of substitutes for ivory (A) is never mentioned by either party. Although they disagree on the steps to take, Roxanne and Salvador agree that steps should be taken to protect elephant herds (C). Neither Roxanne nor Salvador endorse buying new ivory, so they wouldn't disagree about (D) or (E).

An Advanced test taker knows that for a choice to be correct on a "point-at-issue" question, it must be a statement on which both speakers have taken clear—and contradictory—positions.

Explanation: Counting Fish

4. C

The stem tells us we'll be looking for a statement that strengthens the argument, so the first step, as always, is to break down the argument into evidence, conclusion, and assumptions. Smack dab in the middle of the stimulus, highlighted by the always reliable structural signal "therefore," the author tells us the conclusion: "The government should *therefore* institute a program" to test the toxin level in the fish eaten by the seabirds killed by net fishing. The evidence appears in the other two sentences—The fishing industry currently has no incentive to report the number of seabirds actually killed by net fishing (the first sentence), and, if the program is adopted, the industry will have a reason to turn in birds because the industry will get desirable information in return (the third sentence). In other words, under the program, the author envisions a win-win situation for the government and the fishing industry. Since the argument is essentially for the creation of the program, a strengthener must bolster the need for such a program of cooperation. (C) does this nicely: If the government can't reach its objective (an accurate count of seabirds killed by net fishing) without the cooperation of the fishing industry, a program providing an incentive for the fishing industry to help out, such as the one outlined, is essential.

(A), if anything, weakens the argument, by working against the fishing industry's incentive to cooperate. (A) makes any data that the government gives to the industry less valuable.

(B) is irrelevant; it really doesn't matter what the government has done in the past regarding tissue sampling. You might have thought that (B) weakens the argument, similar to (A), by reasoning that if (B) were true the government might, through inexperience, have difficulty administering the program—However, this reasoning is not supported by the stimulus. In any case, it's far from a strengthener.

(D) certainly doesn't support the idea of the program; the only effect it would have is to help destroy the incentive of the fishing industry to participate.

(E) brings up a hypothetical situation, and a result of it, that are totally irrelevant to the program itself; the point is not to find out how many seabirds are killed by a *reduced* amount of net fishing, but to find out how many are killed under current conditions.

5. B

In this long question stem we're asked to recognize a situation in which the program is *not* likely to achieve its desired result. In other words, we want to undermine the conclusion. The program relies on the fishing industry's incentive for cooperation. Under the program, the fishing industry must hand over the dead seabirds, which yields the information that the government needs—the total number of dead seabirds. The fishing industry, in return, receives valuable information about toxin levels in fish. However, if (B) is true, then the fishing industry can secure the info it wants without turning over *all* of the dead seabirds, which would stymie the intent of the program to provide an accurate count of seabirds killed by net fishing.

(A), (C), and (D) All of these choices deal with possible things the government may find *once the seabirds are turned in*, and thus all three of these choices discuss things that are beyond the scope of the argument. We're looking for something that will affect how many seabirds are turned in—remember that the government is concerned with getting an accurate count of the seabirds that died. In order to undermine the government program, we need an answer choice that would make it likely that the number of seabirds turned in *won't* reflect the actual number of seabirds killed by net fishing. None of the factors stated in these choices impacts on that issue at all.

(E), like (A), (C), and (D), has no bearing on the number of seabirds turned in. The only difference is that unlike the other wrong choices, the irrelevancy in this one centers on what the government may do in a specific situation, rather than what the government may learn about the nature of contamination.

> An Advanced test taker knows that the two most common ways to weaken an argument are by breaking down the argument's central assumption, and by asserting alternative possibilities relevant to the argument.

What's Next?

This concludes our in-depth look at the five major categories of tough LR questions. In the next chapter we'll look at the logical flaws and other structural formulations that present difficulties for LSAT test takers on the Logical Reasoning sections. The concept of "alternative explanation"— nicely highlighted here in "Counting Fish"—is among them.

CHAPTER NINE

Other Logical Reasoning Challenges

Aside from the major categories of tough Logical Reasoning questions discussed thus far, there are also a number of other logical elements that appear somewhat regularly on the LSAT and are notorious for giving test takers trouble. These logical features and question types often appear in conjunction with the major categories discussed in chapters 7 and 8—indeed, we've noted en route those questions that contain some of these logical nuances. But let's now have a better look at them as challenges to reckon with in their own right. Sink your teeth into the following questions, one at a time, focusing on the distinguishing features of each.

NECESSARY AND SUFFICIENT CONDITIONS

If I throw a baseball at the window, the window will break.

Considering the statement above, if I *don't* throw a baseball at the window, can we conclude that the window has *not* broken? No. While the baseball is enough to break the window—that is, is *sufficient* to break the window—nothing in the statement above indicates that the baseball is *necessary* to break the window. The window may break some other way, such as from a sonic boom, or from an egg thrown at it on Halloween.

Questions that test an understanding of the difference between necessary and sufficient conditions are perennial LSAT favorites. The question below is a complex Formal Logic question that's centered squarely on the notion of necessity vs. sufficiency.

1. Only computer scientists understand the architecture of personal computers, and only those who understand the architecture of personal computers appreciate the advances in technology made in the last decade. It follows that only those who appreciate these advances are computer scientists. Which one of the following most accurately describes a flaw in the reasoning in the argument?

    (A) The argument contains no stated or implied relationship between computer scientists and those who appreciate the advances in technology in the last decade.

    (B) The argument ignores the fact that some computer scientists may not appreciate the advances in technology made in the last decade.

    (C) The argument ignores the fact that computer scientists may appreciate other things besides the advances in technology made in the last decade.

    (D) The premises of the argument are stated in such a way that they exclude the possibility of drawing any logical conclusion.

    (E) The premises of the argument presuppose that everyone understands the architecture of personal computers.

Explanation: Computer Architecture

B

We hope you noticed the landslide of necessity going on here: Being a computer scientist is *necessary* to understanding the architecture of personal computers, which in turn is *necessary* to appreciate the technological advances made in the last decade.

> An Advanced test taker can translate complex Formal Logic constructions such as "only . . . are" into easy-to-work-with statements.

Combine both statements and being a computer scientist becomes *necessary* for the appreciation of said technological advances. But wait, the conclusion has it all wrong: It states that appreciating the advances is *necessary* to being a computer scientist! What the author fails to consider is that, just because being a computer scientist is *necessary*, that doesn't mean it's *sufficient* to guarantee appreciation. There can in fact be plenty of computer scientists out there who simply don't care. That's choice (B).

(A) and (D) are too extreme. There *is* an implied relationship, a valid conclusion to be drawn here. It's just that the author draws a different conclusion, and that's the flaw.

(C) is outside the scope. The question is whether computer scientists appreciate the advances in technology, not whether they appreciate other developments.

In (E), no such presupposition is made. In fact, the author states flat out that only computer scientists understand the architecture of personal computers, so that familiarity is relatively rare—unless for some bizarre reason everyone in the world is a computer scientist (what a world *that* would be . . .).

ALTERNATIVE EXPLANATIONS

Perhaps, when arguing in real life, you've used the "Oh yeah? But what about . . ." defense. We look for alternative explanations for situations all the time, to prove our own points or argue against others. On the LSAT, Alternative Explanations problems have much in common with Necessary vs. Sufficient problems: In the previous example, seeing the broken window alone with no knowledge of the crime and concluding that it must have been a thrown baseball (an *unwarranted assumption*) is the perfect setup for an Alternative Explanation, as there is more than one way to break a window. In fact, many arguments on the LSAT are flawed, or can be weakened, because their authors fail to see that a piece of evidence can lead to more than one possible conclusion, or that a situation or result can have more than one possible explanation. See if you can spot the relevant alternative that would weaken the argument below.

2. Party spokesperson: The opposition party's proposal to stimulate economic activity in the province by refunding $600 million in provincial taxes to taxpayers, who could be expected to spend the money, envisions an illusory benefit. Since the province's budget is required to be in balance, either new taxes would be needed to make up the shortfall, in which case the purpose of the refund would be defeated, or else workers for the province would be dismissed. So either the province's taxpayers or its workers, who are also residents of the province, will have the $600 million to spend, but there can be no resulting net increase in spending to stimulate the province's economy.

    The conclusion about whether there would be a resulting net increase in spending would not follow if the

    (A) taxpayers of the province would spend outside the province at least $300 million of any $600 million refunded to them
    (B) taxpayers of the province would receive any refund in partial payments during the year rather than in a lump sum
    (C) province could assess new taxes in a way that would avoid angering taxpayers
    (D) province could, instead of refunding the money, stimulate its economy by redirecting its spending to use the $600 million for construction projects creating jobs around the province
    (E) province could keep its workers and use them more effectively, with a resulting savings of $600 million in its out-of-province expenditures

Explanation: Provincial Tax Refund

E

We are looking for an answer choice that will weaken the spokesperson's position that there would not be a net spending increase in the province if the tax refund occurred. To counter the spokesperson's claim, the right answer will demonstrate that the tax refund won't necessarily be offset by measures such as increasing other taxes or firing some province employees. In other words, it will point out an alternative possibility. It was fairly difficult to form a more specific pre-phrase, but we hope you recognized it when you saw it: (E) explains how the refunded money can be offset by another method—using existing workers more effectively. In this scenario, the people get a tax refund that they can use to stimulate economic activity without any new taxes eating away at their extra income and with no workers losing their jobs. If increased efficiency would save as much as the tax refund gives out, then the province's budget would be balanced, and all of the problems raised by the spokesperson would be solved.

(A) *Au contraire*, in this situation even *less* money would be spent in the province. If taxpayers would spend half their tax refund outside the area, then the spokesperson's claim that there would be no net gain for the province sounds even more persuasive.

(B) is outside the scope. Whether the taxpayers receive the money in installments or in one lump sum has no bearing on how much they would spend.

(C) is also outside the scope. The only thing that matters is whether the taxpayers will be spending enough money in the province to compensate for the tax refund. Whether the measures required to compensate for the refund make the taxpayers *angry* is irrelevant to the question of how much they would spend.

(D) This proposal still leaves the province's budget with a deficit that must be recouped somehow. Simply using the $600 million to stimulate the economy rather than as a refund for the people changes the *method* of spending but wouldn't counter the spokesperson's argument. However the money is spent, it needs to be compensated for somehow, but (D) fails to explain how the province will make up for the increased spending.

SCOPE SHIFTS

Have you ever been in an argument in which you just know that your opponent is pulling a fast one, but you can't quite put your finger on the flaw in his argument? Perhaps, somewhere along the way, he subtly changed the direction of the argument. This is a classic argumentative technique; in fact, one that the LSAT test makers are quite fond of. In a number of Logical Reasoning questions, the author introduces a subtle distinction that slightly alters or shifts the scope or focus of the argument, as in the following example:

3. We learn to use most of the machines in our lives through written instructions, without knowledge of the machines' inner workings, because most machines are specifically designed for use by nonexperts. So, in general, attaining technological expertise would prepare students for tomorrow's job market no better than would a more traditional education stressing verbal and quantitative skills. The argument depends on assuming which one of the following?

(A) Fewer people receive a traditional education stressing verbal and quantitative skills now than did 20 years ago.

(B) Facility in operating machines designed for use by nonexperts is almost never enhanced by expert knowledge of the machines' inner workings.

(C) Most jobs in tomorrow's job market will not demand the ability to operate many machines that are designed for use only by experts.

(D) Students cannot attain technological expertise and also receive an education that does not neglect verbal and quantitative skills.

(E) When learning to use a machine, technological expertise is never more important than verbal and quantitative skills.

Did you catch the scope shift here in "Machines vs. Academia"?

Explanation: Machines vs. Academia

C

Arguments are most vulnerable when the author shifts the scope between evidence and conclusion. The author finds developing tech expertise for "tomorrow's job market" to be useless, no better than a traditional education, because most of our machines are designed to be used by non-experts. She has committed a scope shift here—from everyday machines to machines used in the workplace—and it's a shift that (C) must paper over if the argument is to work. Without (C), it's quite possible that the machines needed in tomorrow's job market will require exactly the kind of high-tech education that the author has blasted as unnecessary.

The numbers receiving one type of education or another (A) has nothing to do with the wisdom of one type or another. (B) merely reinforces the superfluity of expertise when it comes to today's machines, but it leaves the key scope shift unaddressed. This author wouldn't assume (D) because she denies the very *need* for tech expertise. And by focusing solely on learning, rather than operating, (E) falls outside the scope of the whole discussion.

CAUSATION

The great German philosopher, Friedrich Nietzsche, put it perfectly in his 1888 book *Twilight of Idols*:

> There is no more dangerous error than that of *mistaking the consequence for the cause*: I call it reason's intrinsic form of corruption.

LSAT test takers mistake cause and effect at their own risk. Some Logical Reasoning questions even contain precisely the same kind of reasoning as the example Nietzsche furnishes on the same page as the quote.

> Everyone knows the book of the celebrated Cornaro in which he recommends his meager diet as a recipe for a long and happy life—a virtuous one, too . . . I do not doubt that hardly any book . . . has done so much harm, has shortened so many lives, as this curiosity, which is

so well meant. The reason: mistaking the consequence for the cause. The worthy Italian saw in his diet the *cause* of his long life: while the prerequisite of long life, an extraordinarily slow metabolism, a small consumption, was the cause of his meager diet.

What Nietzsche is saying is that a meager diet didn't cause Cornaro to live long; a necessary condition of long life caused him to eat little. A perfectly LSAT-like example, right down to the name—we certainly wouldn't be surprised to find "Cornaro" in a Logic Game or as a contestant in a Logical Reasoning dialogue debate.

The LSAT test makers are fond of all kinds of causation problems. In some, one causal element is mistaken for another. In others, correlation is mistaken for causation, or occasionally, vice versa.

The following is one such example where correlation is mistaken for causation. See what you make of it.

4. Medical researcher: As expected, records covering the last four years of ten major hospitals indicate that babies born prematurely were more likely to have low birth weights and to suffer from health problems than were babies not born prematurely. These records also indicate that mothers who had received adequate prenatal care were less likely to have low birth weight babies than were mothers who had received inadequate prenatal care. Adequate prenatal care, therefore, significantly decreases the risk of low birth weight babies.

Which one of the following, if true, most weakens the medical researcher's argument?

(A) The hospital records indicate that many babies that are born with normal birth weights are born to mothers who had inadequate prenatal care.

(B) Mothers giving birth prematurely are routinely classified by hospitals as having received inadequate prenatal care when the record of that care is not available.

(C) The hospital records indicate that low birth weight babies were routinely classified as having been born prematurely.

(D) Some babies not born prematurely, whose mothers received adequate prenatal care, have low birth weights.

(E) Women who receive adequate prenatal care, are less likely to give birth prematurely than are women who do not receive adequate prenatal care.

Explanation: Prenatal Care

B

We have to weaken the medical researcher's argument, so as usual we have to identify the components of the argument. The conclusion is that adequate prenatal care significantly decreases the risk of low birth weight babies. The evidence for this is that hospital records show that mothers who had received adequate prenatal care were less likely to have low birth weight babies. The medical researcher also tells us that records show that babies born prematurely were more likely to have low birth weights than on-time babies. This is a classic correlation = causation argument: the author cites a high correlation between inadequate prenatal care and low birth weight babies, and then concludes that one must have caused the other. In most cases the best way to weaken these arguments is to find an alternative explanation, or to find a situation where the two are not correlated (you see X, but you don't see Y).

(B) tells us that mothers giving birth prematurely are classified by hospitals as having received inadequate prenatal care when there is no actual record of the care they received. Well, from the stimulus we know that babies born prematurely are more likely to have low birth weight. (B) tells us that in at least some of these cases, a mother who gave birth prematurely was classified as having received inadequate prenatal care, even though her *actual* care was unknown. This means the number of premature births, including those resulting in low birth weight babies, that are classified as having inadequate prenatal care is most likely *artificially high*. This casts doubt then on the accuracy of the evidence that mothers who are recorded as having received adequate prenatal care are at less risk of giving birth to low weight babies. If (B) is true, then the correlation cited in the stimulus is not as strong as the author believes, and the author's conclusion is in turn weakened. So (B) is correct.

(A), (D) The medical researcher merely argues that adequate care decreases the *risk* of low birth weight; so the medical researcher accepts that there will be exceptions to the general *rule*. There will be some normal weight babies from mothers who had inadequate care, as (A) suggests, and there will be some low birth weight babies from mothers with adequate care, as (D) indicates. Neither of these choices impacts on the medical researcher's conclusion. If someone says that eating right will help you live longer, they aren't saying that no one with a bad diet lives to be 100, and they aren't saying that eating right will guarantee that you'll live for a long time. They're just saying that a good diet will help. (C) sounds similar to (B) at first, but premature babies aren't the issue here. The connection between premature babies and low birth weight babies does not affect the relationship between prenatal care and low birth weight, and that's the argument we want to weaken.

(E) strengthens the argument. If adequate prenatal care makes you less likely to give birth prematurely, then that should also reduce your chance of giving birth to a low birth weight baby. (Remember the first piece of evidence tells us that babies born prematurely are more likely to have low birth weights.)

REPRESENTATION

Ahh… fried iguana. The wonderful aroma . . . the incredible texture . . . I just love the smell of iguana in the morning. In fact, since everyone I know agrees that it's wonderful, the rest of the world must love it, too! Don't you agree?

If fried iguana isn't *your* idea of a delicious snack, you might not be alone (as hard as *that* may be to believe). In fact, the elite LSAT test taker in you might argue that my acquaintances and I aren't *representative* (or normal) enough for our snacking preferences to apply to everyone else in the known world.

Disclaimer: The above is in no way representative of the snacking preferences of all Kaplan employees. No iguanas were fried in the making of this example.

When an LSAT question tries to pass information that's applicable to one group onto another, it often commits a *flaw of representation*—that is, the two groups in the problem will contain one or more important differences that make the former an invalid representation of the latter. See if you can spot the flaw of representation in the following problem:

5. Philosopher: Scientists talk about the pursuit of truth, but, like most people, they are selfinterested. Accordingly, the professional activities of most scientists are directed toward personal career enhancement, and only incidentally toward the pursuit of truth. Hence, the activities of the scientific community are largely directed toward enhancing the status of that community as a whole, and only incidentally toward the pursuit of truth.

The reasoning in the philosopher's argument is flawed because the argument

(A) improperly infers that each and every scientist has a certain characteristic from the premise that most scientists have that characteristic

(B) improperly draws an inference about the scientific community as a whole from a premise about individual scientists

(C) presumes, without giving justification, that the aim of personal career enhancement never advances the pursuit of truth

(D) illicitly takes advantage of an ambiguity in the meaning of "self-interested"

(E) improperly draws an inference about a cause from premises about its effects

Explanation: Selfish Science

B

"Reasoning . . . flawed" signals you that the argument by definition is unpersuasive.

The philosopher moves from the specific—indicting individual scientists for their self-aggrandizement—to the general, in his conclusion ("Hence") that the scientific community *as a whole* works toward self-aggrandizement. That is "groupthink" bigotry and overgeneralization, and (B) skewers the philosopher on it.

(A) gets the relationship exactly reversed. (C) is false because the author does believe that the scientific community pursues truth—albeit "only incidentally." There's no ambiguity (D) in the term "self-interest"; indeed, the author specifies that in a scientific context it means "one's self-enhancement." The only cause-and-effect (E) that the philosopher posits is that scientists' self-interest causes them to work primarily toward their own career, but the move to the conclusion is not a cause-and-effect, but rather (as (B) notes) an overgeneralization.

NUMBERS AND STATISTICS

The LSAT test makers just *love* their statistics. Perhaps that's because statistics are used these days—often fallaciously—to supposedly "prove" or justify just about anything. That makes numbers and statistics a particularly fertile ground for Logical Flaw and Weaken the Argument questions. The following is one such example.

6. Waste management companies, which collect waste for disposal in landfills and incineration plants, report that disposable plastics make up an ever-increasing percentage of the waste they handle. It is clear that attempts to decrease the amount of plastic that people throw away in the garbage are failing.

Which one of the following, if true, most seriously weakens the argument?

(A) Because plastics create harmful pollutants when burned, an increasing percentage of the plastics handled by waste management companies are being disposed of in landfills.

(B) Although many plastics are recyclable, most of the plastics disposed of by waste management companies are not.

(C) People are more likely to save and reuse plastic containers than containers made of heavier materials like glass or metal.

(E) An increasing proportion of the paper, glass, and metal cans that waste management companies used to handle is now being recycled.

(E) While the percentage of products using plastic packaging is increasing, the total amount of plastic being manufactured has remained unchanged.

Explanation: Waste Management

D

Whenever stimuli throw around percent increases or decreases, beware: Percent increases and decreases are not the same as changes in the actual numbers or amount. Here the author signals the conclusion with "it is clear": What is clear is that people are throwing away just as much plastic or even more than ever before. We know that because waste management companies are reporting that an "ever-increasing" percentage of the waste they handle is plastic. But percentages are deceiving; there may, for example, be a higher percentage of plastic in the waste, but if the total amount of waste is decreasing, then the actual amount of plastic waste may have remained stable or even decreased. Choice (D) gets at this: Waste handlers are receiving less of other types of waste; thus there is less overall waste; thus the increase in percent of plastic waste does not necessarily mean that people are throwing out as much as or more plastic waste.

Choice (A) sets up an opposition that doesn't exist in the stimulus. There's no difference between plastic incinerated and that sent to a landfill; it's all included in the plastic waste "handled" by the management companies. The point (B) raises—that some plastic isn't recyclable, and therefore ends up in the garbage—would strengthen rather than weaken this argument. (C) is irrelevant; whatever people do with plastic at home is not the issue. The question is whether they are putting more of it in the trash. Same thing with choice (D). The amount of plastic manufactured, or even an increase in the amount of plastic packaging, isn't necessarily connected to how that plastic ends up in the trash.

An Advanced test taker knows that the test makers are often testing her ability to distinguish between percentages and raw numbers.

CIRCULAR REASONING

Advertisement: If you plan to go to law school, you should take the Kaplan LSAT course because, all things considered, it is very much in the interest of all aspiring lawyers to enroll in and complete Kaplan's preparation program for the LSAT.

How do you like this reasoning? Now, while there are many good reasons to take the Kaplan LSAT course (excellent teachers, world-class materials, access to all released LSAT questions with explanations, killer software, etc.), not one is actually mentioned in the ad.

Disclaimer: Not an actual ad. The Kaplan Marketing department is far more on the ball than this.

In fact, the hypothetical ad above says nothing; or, more precisely, *its conclusion says nothing different from its evidence.* And that's the essence of what's known as "Circular Reasoning," a type of flawed logic that shows up occasionally on the LSAT. The argument in the ad above essentially boils downs to "future law students should take Kaplan's LSAT course because future law students should take Kaplan's LSAT course." Of course, the language is dressed up a bit, and on the LSAT these can actually be quite tricky. Practice recognizing Circular Reasoning with the following example.

7. Cotrell is, at best, able to write magazine articles of average quality. The most compelling pieces of evidence for this are those few of the numerous articles submitted by Cotrell that are superior, since Cotrell, who is incapable of writing an article that is better than average, must obviously have plagiarized superior ones.

The argument is most vulnerable to criticism on which one of the following grounds?

(A) It simply ignores the existence of potential counterevidence.
(B) It generalizes from atypical occurrences.
(C) It presupposes what it seeks to establish.
(D) It relies on the judgment of experts in a matter to which their expertise is irrelevant.
(E) It infers limits on ability from a few isolated lapses in performance.

Explanation: Cotrell's Articles

C

References to circular arguments, those that "presuppose what they seek to establish," are usually made in LSAT wrong answers, but once in a while a genuinely circular argument comes along. This argument assumes that Cotrell is a lousy writer in order to prove that he's a lousy writer, and that's what circular reasoning, choice (C), is. The author provides no independent evidence whatsoever as to the quality of Cotrell's writing. Indeed, there is actually counterevidence—the "superior" articles—that Cotrell is better than the author gives him credit for, but the author blithely ascribes them to someone else, again with no independent support.

(A) is a popular wrong answer, but since the author explicitly *acknowledges* that the counterevidence of the superior Cotrell articles exists, he cannot be said to "ignore" it. If anything, the author takes the bad Cotrell writing from which he is reasoning as *typical* rather than atypical (B). No outside expertise (D) is cited or even alluded to, and (E) is a total 180: Rather, the author infers limited ability *despite* what he sees as occasional examples of *high* performance.

An Advanced test taker knows that valid evidence for an argument must *add something different* to that argument.

THE "ODD MAN OUT"

Next up in our potpourri of tough questions are questions that ask you to locate the one choice that *doesn't* satisfy a particular requirement; in other words, to find the "odd man out." These are difficult because the right answer may do the opposite of what's required, or may simply be irrelevant to the situation at hand. At the same time, the wrong choices are *all* relevant, and sometimes look and sound the same, lulling us into a state of mind in which every choice, including the bogus right answer, sounds reasonable. Finally, some test takers simply blow past the word "EXCEPT" or "NOT" in the question stem, and blow the question on that account.

8. Professor Robinson: A large meteorite impact crater in a certain region was thought to be the clue to explaining the mass extinction of plant and animal species that occurred at the end of the Mesozoic era. However, the crystalline structure of rocks recovered at the site indicates that the impact that formed this crater was not the culprit. When molten rocks crystallize, they display the polarity of Earth's magnetic field at that time. But the recrystallized rocks recovered at the site display normal magnetic polarity, even though Earth's magnetic field was reversed at the time of the mass extinction.

   Each of the following is an assumption on which Professor Robinson's argument depends EXCEPT:

   (A) The crater indicates an impact of more than sufficient size to have caused the mass extinction.
   (B) The recovered rocks recrystallized shortly after they melted.
   (C) No other event caused the rocks to melt after the impact formed the crater.
   (D) The recovered rocks melted as a result of the impact that formed the crater.
   (E) The mass extinction would have occurred soon after the impact that supposedly caused it.

Explanation: Impact Crater

A

The question stem tells us to find the one choice that is NOT assumed by the argument, which means that the four wrong choices must all be necessary assumptions. It's hard to imagine one argument relying on so many assumptions, but as we'll see, the four valid assumptions are all offshoots of one major assumption. Let's take a look at the argument. The professor's conclusion is that the meteorite impact didn't cause the mass extinction, as was once thought. The evidence for his conclusion is that the meteor impact site has the wrong polarity—the polarity of rocks recovered at the site is regular but the Earth's polarity was reversed when the plants and animals disappeared. Notice that the author says only that these rocks were "recovered at the site"—he gives no evidence that they were formed by the impact in question or that they even date from the same time period as the impact. The general assumption from which all the others spring is that there is a *connection* between these crystallized rocks and the supposed effects of the meteorite impact. If there *is* such a connection, then it is valid to use the polarity evidence to discount the old theory. Since we're looking for the odd man out, the statement that is NOT assumed, the best strategy is to evaluate the choices, looking for this connection between the rocks and the impact. (A) provides evidence that the impact could have caused the mass extinction. Remember however, that the professor argues that the impact was *not* the cause, so this information need not be assumed by the author. There's nothing here on the connection between the rocks and the impact that's necessary for the argument to be complete.

The rest of the choices, however, are valid assumptions because they *are* necessary if the rock-polarity evidence is to lead to the professor's conclusion:

(B) If the rocks did not recrystallize quickly, they may not necessarily reflect the polarity of the earth when the meteor hit and the rocks melted. The rocks would instead reflect the polarity at the time they did recrystallize, which could have been much later.

(C) and (D) further "solidify" the necessary connection: If the rocks had melted some time after the meteor's impact, then they would reflect the polarity of the earth when they recrystallized, no matter when that may have been. If it was long after, then the polarity evidence could be meaningless. So it's important to the professor's theory that the rocks melted as a result of the impact, and that they did not melt and recrystallize as a result of some *other* event sometime after the meteorite impact.

(E) also shores up the time element: If the mass extinction occurred *long* after the meteor hit that caused it (the denial of (E)), then it's possible that the earth's magnetic field changed in the interim, which would account for the discrepancy in polarities. The professor *relies* on this discrepancy to make his case. If we explain it away—which is what happens when we deny (E)—then his argument is damaged, which is why (E) must also be assumed.

TOUGH CHOICES

We've covered all kinds of tough Logical Reasoning questions, but we would be remiss to overlook questions that are difficult simply because they contain tough choices. Tough choices are especially prevalent in Method of Argument and Principle question types—both of which often include choices with general, somewhat abstract descriptions of what's going on in the passage—but there's really nothing stopping tough choices from showing up in any question type. Some of the questions you've seen already contain tough choices, and there's more to come later on. As for the question below, there's nothing inherently difficult about the story told in the stimulus, but the choices are a different matter altogether.

9. Politician: Nobody can deny that homelessness is a problem yet there seems to be little agreement on how to solve it. One thing, however is clear: Ignoring the problem will not make it go away. Only if the government steps in and provides the homeless with housing will this problem disappear, and this necessitates increased taxation. For this reason, we should raise taxes.

Which one of the following principles, if valid, most supports
the politician's argument?

(A)   Only if a measure is required to solve a problem should
      it be adopted.
(B)   Only if a measure is sufficient to solve a problem should
      it be adopted.
(C)   If a measure is required to solve a problem, then it
      should be adopted.
(D)   If a measure is sufficient to solve a problem, then it
      should be adopted.
(E)   If a measure is sufficient to solve a problem, any steps
      necessitated by that measure should be adopted.

Explanation: Raising Taxes

C

The argument in need of support by a principle ends with a succinct conclusion: "We should raise taxes." Why should we do so? Look at the words surrounding the evidence: "Only if..."; "and this necessitates...." They tell us that, on the topic of homelessness, the politician thinks that the problem can't be solved without government subsidized housing, and that such housing can't exist without higher taxes. In other words, since each of these is a necessary part of the solution, the author recommends setting the process in motion by raising taxes. This is explicitly the pattern of correct choice (C): If a measure (such as raising taxes) is required to solve a problem (yes it is, because higher taxes are *needed* to create the necessary government housing), then one must go for it.

That's pretty straightforward. The real challenge—and the real opportunity for learning—is an understanding of why the wrong choices are wrong.

(A), because it mentions "Only if" and "required," and because it precedes (C) on the list, is the most tempting wrong answer. But (A) has it exactly backwards, which you'll see if you engage in the proper translation. "Only Y are X," you may recall, translates to "All X are Y." So (A) is equivalent to "If a measure is adopted, it must have been required to solve a problem." That doesn't help us here! We need an if/then statement that leads to the conclusion that we should raise taxes; not one that tells us what will result if taxes are raised. We've said many times that the terms of an if/then statement cannot be arbitrarily or irresponsibly switched, and here's one instance where they have been.

(B), (D), and (E) are all wrong because they concern *sufficiency*, which is not a part of the politician's thinking. He never argues or implies that raising taxes, and the resulting government housing, are *enough* to solve the homelessness problem—just that the solution is impossible *without* such housing. Still troubled? Consider how differently the paragraph would be written if the politician's message were, "Simply raise taxes and build that housing, and watch that homelessness problem disappear." But that's not what he writes at all; indeed, the melancholy note on which the paragraph begins implies that the full solution is far from clear.

What's Next?

You've now heard about five major categories and nine subcategories of the most difficult LSAT Logical Reasoning material. What do you need to reinforce this learning and to match your wits against the conquests presented? More questions, of course. Onward to chapter 10.

CHAPTER TEN

Putting It All Together

By now, you should have a very definite idea of the many kinds of challenges presented in LSAT Logical Reasoning. While we've broken down these challenges into major and minor categories, roughly based on their prevalence on the test, the truth is that difficult questions are often combinations of the various logical elements you've just encountered. In other words, the logical elements and question types presented in chapters 7, 8, and 9 may, and often do, overlap in a single question. And just as in Hybrid Logic Games, the existence of multiple logical elements within questions complicates matters significantly.

In this chapter, you'll get practice with plenty of complex Logical Reasoning questions. Not every question contains more than one logical element, but many do, and we cite in the explanations the distinguishing logical or structural characteristics of each. We've arranged the questions in small groups so that you can learn as you go along and get practice recognizing the logical patterns that recur throughout the Logical Reasoning sections of the test.

PRACTICE SET 1

1. There is relatively little room for growth in the overall carpet market, which is tied to the size of the population. Most who purchase carpet do so only once or twice, first in their twenties or thirties, and then perhaps again in their fifties or sixties. Thus as the population ages, companies producing carpet will be able to gain market share in the carpet market only through purchasing competitors, and not through more aggressive marketing.

   Which one of the following, if true, casts the most doubt on the conclusion above?

   (A) Most of the major carpet producers market other floor coverings as well.
   (B) Most established carpet producers market several different brand names and varieties, and there is no remaining niche in the market for new brands to fill.
   (C) Two of the three mergers in the industry's last ten years led to a decline in profits and revenues for the newly merged companies.
   (D) Price reductions, achieved by cost-cutting in production, by some of the dominant firms in the carpet market are causing other producers to leave the market altogether.
   (E) The carpet market is unlike most markets in that consumers are becoming increasingly resistant to new patterns and styles.

2. A patient complained of feeling constantly fatigued. It was determined that the patient averaged only four to six hours of sleep per night, and this was determined to contribute to the patient's condition. However, the patient was not advised to sleep more.

   Which one of the following, if true, most helps to resolve the apparent discrepancy in the information above?

   (A) The shorter one's sleep time, the easier it is to awaken from sleeping.
   (B) The first two hours of sleep do the most to alleviate fatigue.
   (C) Some people required less sleep than the eight hours required by the average person.
   (D) Most people who suffer from nightmares experience them in the last hour of sleep before waking.
   (E) Worry about satisfying the need for sufficient sleep can make it more difficult to sleep.

Question 3–4

Whenever she considers voting in an election to select one candidate for a position and there is at least one issue important to her, Kay uses the following principle in choosing which course of action to take: it is acceptable for me to vote for a candidate whose opinions differ from mine on at least one issue important to me whenever I disagree with each of the other candidates on even more such issues; it is otherwise unacceptable to vote for that candidate. In the upcoming mayoral election, the three candidates are Legrand, Medina, and Norton. There is only one issue important to Kay, and only Medina shares her opinion on that issue.

3. If the statements in the passage are true, which one of the following must also be true about Kay's course of action in any election to select one candidate for a position?

   (A) If there are no issues important to her, it is unacceptable for her to vote for any candidate in the election.
   (B) If she agrees with each of the candidates on most of the issues important to her, it is unacceptable for her to vote for any candidate in the election.
   (C) If she agrees with a particular candidate on only one issue important to her, it is unacceptable for her to vote for that candidate.
   (D) If she disagrees with each of the candidates on exactly three issues important to her, it is unacceptable for her to vote for any candidate in the election.
   (E) If there are more issues important to her on which she disagrees with a particular candidate than there are such issues on which she agrees with that candidate, it is unacceptable for her to vote for that candidate.

4. According to the principle stated in the passage, in the upcoming mayoral election

   (A) it is acceptable for Kay to vote for either Medina or Legrand, but it is unacceptable for her to vote for Norton
   (B) the only unacceptable courses of action are for Kay to vote for Norton and for her to vote for Legrand
   (C) it is unacceptable for Kay to vote for any of the candidates
   (D) the only unacceptable course of action is for Kay to vote for Medina
   (E) it is acceptable for Kay to vote for any of the candidates

PRACTICE SET 1: ANSWERS AND EXPLANATIONS

Explanation: Carpet Share

Distinguishing Features: Alternative Explanation

1. D

Conclusion: Carpet manufacturers can only gain additional market share by acquiring competitors. (D) weakens this by showing an alternative way to increase market share: If some of the producers disappeared from the market, their customers could be snatched up by the surviving companies, thus increasing the survivors' market share.

(A) The scope of this argument is limited to market share in the carpet industry. Any mention of any other products is outside the scope.

(B), (E) These choices tends to strengthen the notion raised in the first sentence, namely that there's relatively little room for growth in the market.

(C) The argument states that purchasing competitors is the *only way* to gain market share; however, this doesn't *guarantee* that doing so will lead to success. It therefore has no bearing on the argument.

> An Advanced test taker does not carelessly choose a strengthener when asked for a weakener, or vice versa.

Explanation: Sleepless

Distinguishing Feature: Paradox

2. E

"Apparent discrepancy" means a seeming contradiction that you have to sort out.

You'd think that a fatigued person who wasn't sleeping very much—and whose lack of sleep was contributing to the fatigue—would be told to get some sleep, but that is not the recommendation, and we need a choice that explains why. Your search may have led you to (E) by elimination. "Awakening" (A) and "nightmares" (D) aren't part of the guy's problem, and while some may need less than 8 hours (C), who knows whether he's one of them? (B) might have been tempting if you reasoned that based on (B), the doctors would seek the patient's remedy in the first 2 sleep hours and not bother about the later hours. But that reasoning focuses on *solving* the patient's fatigue problem, whereas the question focuses on *avoiding* a particular solution.

That's really the key to understanding (E). Regardless of what is positively done to help the guy's fatigue problem, (E) explains why the doctors would avoid directing him to sleep more: Any worry over his inability to follow the "prescription" would likely only make things worse.

> An Advanced test taker knows that in explanation questions, his task is to reconcile, not to change, the facts presented in the stimulus.

Explanation: Voting Principles

Distinguishing Features: Formal Logic, Principle, Inference

3. D

The structure here is interesting: A long (8-line) sentence articulates a somewhat complex principle that Kay follows at election time. Then we get two short sentences revealing concrete facts about a particular mayoral election. Well, a quick scan of the two questions reveals that the first one is about the principle alone, while the second combines it all, so we'd better start by understanding the principle fully—and the scope proves to be central.

Given that an election is being held to select one candidate and that at least one issue is important to Kay (lines 1–3), the principle is really exploring the following specific and limited question: "When may I, Kay, in good conscience vote for someone *with whom I disagree?*" (Note lines 5–6 of the stimulus: "a candidate whose opinions differ from mine on at least one issue." Note, too, that the principle never discusses candidates with whom Kay's in total agreement. Presumably she has no dilemma about voting for any of *them*.) In short, Kay has set up a litmus test of sorts, for situations when she is considering voting for a candidate with whom she has "at least one" major area of disagreement.

Here's how you should have understood the protocol: Given that Kay is not in 100 percent agreement with any one candidate, she feels that it's O.K. to vote for someone she disagrees with (let's call him Candidate X) *as long as she has more areas of disagreement with the other candidates.* That's lines 6–7—see how that works? In other words, if her disagreements with the other candidates outnumber her disagreements with Candidate X, she feels it's O.K. to vote for X. Otherwise—no way.

Good enough. Now, before we add on the information about this election, let's attack Q. 22, which involves only the principle itself. The right answer is an inference—that which "must also be true"—so we're not going to try to pre-phrase an answer. Let's just start with the briefest choices, which happen to be the first three, and see which of the five follows logically:

(A) need not be true because it fails to meet one of the preconditions under which the principle will apply—namely, that this be an election in which "at least one issue [is] important to Kay." We have no idea what protocol she follows (staying home? voting at random? voting by party?) when *no* issues are important to her.

(B) is incomplete. O.K., so Kay agrees with each candidate on "most of the [major] issues." That's not good enough. We cannot use the principle to draw a conclusion until her *dis*agreements with each are enumerated. If she disagrees with one candidate on fewer major issues than the others, then the principle says she may vote for that candidate. If not, not. So (B) doesn't tell us enough to infer whether its conclusion must be true or not.

(C) is incomplete, too. Kay *may* vote for a candidate with whom she has but a single area of agreement, so long as she has more *dis*agreements on major issues with the other candidates. (C), like (B), fails to enlighten us about the relative numbers of disagreements—the linchpin of her principle—so we cannot draw its conclusion for sure.

(D), on the other hand, *does* enumerate those disagreements, and allows us to draw its conclusion. If Kay has the same number of disagreements with each candidate—which under (D), she does— then she's stuck. The principle says that she can only vote for any one of them if she has *more* major disagreements with the others. But here the number of disagreements with each candidate is the same. So (D) is right: By virtue of the principle she cannot properly vote for any of them.

(E)'s comparison may seem relevant but is really bogus. We are not asked by the principle to compare the numbers of agreements and disagreements between Kay and a *single candidate*. Again, the principle kicks in and gives us guidance only when Kay's disagreements with each of the candidates are compared.

Use the skills you develop throughout your preparation anywhere they may apply. Notice how this is very much like a mini Logic Game—the principle is simply the rule that Kay follows, and we're looking for a choice that must be true based on that rule. Sometimes in games we even get choices worded as if-thens, just like here. Most similar to games is the precision with which we must work—the difference between "more disagreements" and "equal number of disagreements" allows us to recognize (D) as the choice that must be true.

An Advanced test taker uses her Formal Logic skills to provide shortcuts in tough inference questions.

---

4. B

Now, how does the principle apply in the current election? There's only one issue that Kay cares about, and of the three mayoral candidates, she agrees with only Medina on that issue. By definition, then, she has more disagreements—i.e., one—with Legrand and Norton. What options are open to her? Well, she certainly may, if she chooses, vote for Medina, since there's nothing in the principle that blocks her voting for a candidate with whom she agrees. And she may, if she chooses, stay home and vote "with her feet"—for no one. The only things she cannot do—and correct choice (B) spells this out—is vote for either Legrand or Norton. Either vote is unacceptable, the principle says, because she disagrees with each and has *fewer* disagreements with another candidate (namely Medina).

(A) Legrand and Norton are logically identical in this situation—each is running, and each disagrees with Kay on one major issue—so there's no way, in terms of Kay's voting, that something could be true for Legrand but not for Norton. This is a classic example of what we've called "faulty comparison" or "faulty distinction." (C), (E) Contrary to (C), it *is* acceptable, as we've seen, for Kay to vote for Medina, but contrary to (E) she *cannot* vote for the two candidates with whom she disagrees.

(D) *Au contraire*, the only *acceptable* course is to vote for Medina (or, of course, to abstain altogether).

A basic rule of logic (and of life) is: "Everything not prohibited is permitted." A useful guideline for Logic Games, where we must allow for any possibilities that the rules don't restrict, it's also important to remember for Logical Reasoning as well. Here, Kay is *permitted* to vote for Medina, or not to vote at all, because there's nothing in her self-imposed code of conduct that *prohibits* either action. That same principle, of course, renders unacceptable a vote for Legrand or Norton.

An Advanced test taker boils down the principle as much as possible before attempting to find the choice that conforms.

PRACTICE SET 2

1. Some critics claim that it is unfair that so many great works of art are housed in huge metropolitan museums, since the populations served by these museums already have access to a wide variety of important artwork. But this criticism is in principle unwarranted because the limited number of masterpieces makes wider distribution of them impractical. Besides, if a masterpiece is to be fully appreciated, it must be seen alongside other works that provide a social and historical context for it.

Which one of the following, if established, could most logically serve as the principle appealed to in the argument countering the critics' claim?

(A) In providing facilities to the public, the goal should be to ensure that as many as possible of those people who could benefit from the facilities are able to do so.

(B) In providing facilities to the public, the goal should be to ensure that the greatest possible number of people gain the greatest benefit possible from them.

(C) It is unreasonable to enforce a redistribution of social goods that involves depriving some members of society of these goods in order to supply others.

(D) For it to be reasonable to criticize an arrangement as unfair, there must be a more equitable arrangement that is practically attainable.

(E) A work of art should be displayed in conditions resembling as closely as possible those in which the work was originally intended to be displayed.

2. Literary critic: The meaning of a literary work is not fixed but fluid, and therefore a number of equally valid interpretations of it may be offered. Interpretations primarily involve imposing meaning on a literary work rather than discovering meaning in it, so interpretations need not consider the writer's intentions. Thus, any interpretation of a literary work tells more about the critic than about the writer.

Which one of the following is an assumption required by the literary critic's argument?

(A) There are no criteria by which to distinguish the validity of different interpretations of literary works.

(B) A meaning imposed on a literary work reflects facts about the interpreter.

(C) A writer's intentions are relevant to a valid interpretation of the writer's work.

(D) The true intentions of the writer of a work of literature can never be known to a critic of that work.

(E) The deepest understanding of a literary work requires that one know the writer's history.

3. Art historian: Great works of art have often elicited outrage when first presented; in Europe, Stravinsky's *Rite of Spring* prompted a riot, and Manet's *Déjeuner sur l'herbe* elicited outrage and derision. So, since it is clear that art is often shocking, we should not hesitate to use public funds to support works of art that many people find shocking.

Which one of the following is an assumption that the art historian's argument requires in order for its conclusion to be properly drawn?

(A) Most art is shocking.

(B) Stravinsky and Manet received public funding for their art.

(C) Art used to be more shocking than it currently is.

(D) Public funds should support art.

(E) Anything that shocks is art.

4. Some statisticians claim that the surest way to increase the overall correctness of the total set of one's beliefs is: never change that set, except by rejecting a belief when given adequate evidence against it. However, if this were the only rule one followed, then whenever one were presented with any kind of evidence, one would have to either reject some of one's beliefs or else leave one's beliefs unchanged. But then, over time, one could only have fewer and fewer beliefs. Since we need many beliefs in order to survive, the statisticians' claim must be mistaken.

The argument is most vulnerable to criticism on the grounds that it

(A) presumes, without providing any justification, that the surest way of increasing the overall correctness of the total set of one's beliefs must not hinder one's ability to survive

(B) neglects the possibility that even while following the statisticians' rule, one might also accept new beliefs when presented with some kinds of evidence

(C) overlooks the possibility that some large sets of beliefs are more correct overall than are some small sets of beliefs

(D) takes for granted that one should accept some beliefs related to survival even when given adequate evidence against them

(E) takes for granted that the beliefs we need in order to have many beliefs must all be correct beliefs

PRACTICE SET 2: ANSWERS AND EXPLANATIONS

Explanation: Distributing Masterpieces

Distinguishing Features: Just Plain Tough, Principle

1. D

The difficulty here is that "the principle appealed to" isn't stated; it's implicit and, in fact, practically undetectable. You could stare at the stimulus for a long time without coming any closer to this particular principle, and so *sometimes, as here, the only thing to do is to go to the answer choices and look for something that rings a bell.*

First, however, *be sure that you have the argument down pat. In fact, in principle questions that involve two conflicting arguments, it's crucial that you understand both the argument whose principle you're asked to abstract, and the opposing argument.* The critics claim that the current practice of housing great works of art in huge city museums is unfair; the reason they give is that the people who go to these museums already have a lot of important artwork available to them. The counterargument objects to this criticism mainly because it would be impractical to try to distribute the few great works of art more widely, and also because masterpieces should be seen "in context." Now it's hard to detect a principle that covers both objections, but one thing you *should* grasp—the argument countering the critics is intended to show that they are wrong to characterize the current system as *unfair*. When you look at the answer choices you'll see that only one addresses this primary concern: (D), which covers the case nicely. The counterargument says that the critics are wrong to condemn the current arrangement as unfair because the alternative would be impractical and would not be as effective a way of showing the artworks. That's essentially what (D) says—it's only reasonable to criticize something as unfair if there's a better alternative.

Both (A) and (B) speak of providing benefits for as many people as possible—(B) is more extreme, speaking of the "greatest possible benefit" for the "greatest possible" number. The counterargument simply doesn't depend on such ideas—indeed both choices express principles we might expect to find the *critics* appealing to, since their basic complaint is that under the current system some people are missing out. (C) involves a "forced redistribution," which is immediately off the mark because no one is talking about "forcing" anyone to do anything. (E) is a trap, figuring that some of you will read "providing a social and historical context" to mean "showing something exactly as it was originally shown." That's not a reasonable reading, and besides, it ignores the main point of the argument, the question of practicality. Note that only (D) mentions the notion of unfairness: *When you're having trouble with principle questions, look* ∏ *for the choices that express key concepts and contain key terms that the other choices leave out.*

An Advanced test taker recognizes the validity of an answer choice when she sees it, even if the concept contained in the choice didn't occur to her up front.

Explanation: Literary Meaning

Distinguishing Feature: Scope Shift

2. B

An assumption is a statement that *must* be true for the argument to be valid.

The evidence states that interpretation involves imposing meaning on a work, rather than uncovering the meaning that the author intended. The argument than concludes that interpretations tell us more about the critic than the writer. This only follows if we allow that we can learn something about the critic from the interpretation she imposes on a work. (Otherwise, the critic could impose meanings all day long, and we still wouldn't know a thing about her.) This is nicely summed up in (B).

The argument never distinguishes valid and invalid interpretations (A), and we certainly don't need to accept any such statements for this argument to work. (C) adds the element of the author's intentions, but still deals primarily with the validity of interpretations, and so is not central to this argument. (D) is an over-generalization (critics can *never* know an author's intentions) and is not necessary to support the conclusion that interpretations tell us more about critics than authors. (E) introduces a new and irrelevant issue, the history of the writer.

An Advanced test taker recognizes statements that are too extreme to fit the scenario. He avoids choices that make overly generalized claims.

Explanation: Subscription Policy

Distinguishing Features: Formal Logic, Principle, Odd Man Out

3. D

Assumptions often emerge when a term creeps into the conclusion but isn't mentioned in the evidence. The conclusion is the first and only place where we hear about public funding of art. In order to conclude that public funds should fund shocking art, the author first must assume that public funds should fund art, period—which makes (D) correct. If (D) is false, then the entire argument is moot.

That "art is often shocking" doesn't imply that "most art is shocking" (A); often and most are not identical concepts. Stravinsky and Manet (B) make cameo appearances here solely to act as examples of creators of shocking art; as noted earlier, public funding isn't even mentioned until one sentence later. (C) raises a comparison with the past that is not so much as hinted at. As for (E), the author is concerned with the funding of art that shocks, not things that shock in general.

An Advanced test taker knows that understanding the passage on his own terms is the key to most questions.

Explanation: Overly Correct Beliefs

Distinguishing Features: Scope Shift, Just Plain Tough

4. A

When a stimulus is dense and lengthy, find the core argument right away.

Not until the last sentence do we really find out what the author's getting at. "Since" (evidence) we need many beliefs to survive, the statisticians' claim (implied "therefore") must be false. That claim, described at length earlier, is that one makes one's beliefs-set correct by eliminating the bad ones without taking on new ones. The author disputes this, implying that such a method could lead to death. But that doesn't make the statistician's claim *wrong*; it only suggests that it could have bad consequences. Consider the following parallel: "Bob says the surest way to make a lot of money is to work 20-hour days. But that would mean you'd be unhappy, so Bob is wrong." No, Bob may very well be right about how to make money; the evidence hasn't countered the claim at all. The speaker has assumed, with no evidence, that making money shouldn't conflict with one's happiness. In the same way our author has assumed, with no evidence, that having mostly correct beliefs shouldn't conflict with survival (A).

Note that (B), (C), and (E) cannot possibly be correct because none of them mentions survival, and the right answer must do so: The argument's flaw is that it introduces the idea of "survival" at the very end, with no connection to the rest of the logic. Beyond that, the statisticians' rule says not to take on new beliefs, so the author hasn't neglected the possibility that one could do so (B). (C) is an irrelevant comparison; it might be true that the author overlooks this possibility, but it has no direct bearing on the conclusion. (D) discusses "beliefs related to survival," a distortion of the two very different stimulus terms. (E) goes against the grain of the conclusion; the author never suggests, or takes for granted, that correct beliefs are better for survival than incorrect ones.

An Advanced test taker is sensitive to scope shifts.

PRACTICE SET 3

1. Reporter: A team of scientists has recently devised a new test that for the first time accurately diagnoses autism in children as young as 18 months old. When used to evaluate 16,000 children at their 18-month checkup, the test correctly diagnosed all 10 children later confirmed to be autistic, though it also wrongly identified 2 children as autistic. Autistic children can therefore now benefit much earlier in life than before from the treatments already available.

   Which one of the following is an assumption on which the reporter's argument depends?

   (A) No test intended for diagnosing autism at such an early age existed before the new test was devised.

   (B) A diagnostic test that sometimes falsely gives a positive diagnosis can still provide a reasonable basis for treatment decisions.

   (C) The new test can be used to evaluate all children, regardless of the level of development of their verbal skills.

   (D) Those children incorrectly identified as autistic will not be adversely affected by treatments aimed at helping autistic children.

   (E) There was no reliable evidence that autism could affect children so young until the advent of the new test.

2. Throughout European history famines have generally been followed by periods of rising wages, because when a labor force is diminished, workers are more valuable in accordance with the law of supply and demand. The Irish potato famine of the 1840s is an exception; it resulted in the death or emigration of half of Ireland's population, but there was no significant rise in the average wages in Ireland in the following decade.

   Which one of the following, if true, would LEAST contribute to an explanation of the exception to the generalization?

   (A) Improved medical care reduced the mortality rate among able-bodied adults in the decade following the famine to below prefamine levels.

   (B) Eviction policies of the landowners in Ireland were designed to force emigration of the elderly and infirm, who could not work, and to retain a high percentage of able-bodied workers.

   (C) Advances in technology increased the efficiency of industry and agriculture, and so allowed maintenance of economic output with less demand for labor.

   (D) The birth rate increased during the decade following the famine, and this compensated for much of the loss of population that was due to the famine.

   (E) England, which had political control of Ireland, legislated artificially low wages to provide English-owned industry and agriculture in Ireland with cheap labor.

3. Some planning committee members—those representing the construction industry—have significant financial interests in the committee's decisions. No one who is on the planning committee lives in the suburbs, although many of them work there.

   If the statements above are true, which one of the following must also be true?

   (A) No persons with significant financial interests in the planning committee's decisions are not in the construction industry.

   (B) No person who has significant financial interest in the planning committee's decisions lives in the suburbs.

   (C) Some persons with significant financial interests in the planning committee's decisions work in the suburbs.

   (D) Some planning committee members who represent the construction industry do not work in the suburbs.

   (E) Some persons with significant financial interests in the planning committee's decisions do not live in the suburbs.

4. All known deposits of the mineral tanzanite are in Tanzania. Therefore, because Ashley collects only tanzanite stones, she is unlikely ever to collect a stone not originally from Tanzania.

    Which one of the following is most similar in its reasoning to the argument above?

    (A) The lagoon on Scrag Island is home to many frogs. Since the owls on Scrag Island eat nothing but frogs from the island, the owls will probably never eat many frogs that live outside the lagoon.

    (B) Every frog ever seen on Scrag Island lives in the lagoon. The frogs on the island are eaten only by the owls on the island, and hence the owls may never eat an animal that lives outside the lagoon.

    (C) Frogs are the only animals known to live in the lagoon on Scrag Island. The diet of the owls on Scrag Island consists of nothing but frogs from the island. Therefore, the owls are unlikely ever to eat an animal that lives outside the lagoon.

    (D) The only frogs yet discovered on Scrag Island live in the lagoon. The diet of all the owls on Scrag Island consists entirely of frogs on the island, so the owls will probably never eat an animal that lives outside the lagoon.

    (E) Each frog on Scrag Island lives in the lagoon. No owl on Scrag Island is known to eat anything but frogs on the island. It follows that no owl on Scrag Island will eat anything that lives outside the lagoon.

PRACTICE SET 3: ANSWERS AND EXPLANATIONS

Explanation: Early Autism

Distinguishing Feature: Representation, Necessary Condition

1. B

Identify conclusion and evidence for Assumption questions, and try to predict an answer that links the two. Use the Kaplan Denial Test when you can't predict an answer or when your prediction doesn't appear in the choices.

The author concludes that autistic children can now be treated earlier than they could before the new test, and as evidence notes that the new test "accurately diagnoses autism" by identifying every autistic child in the large sample, even though it generated two false positive results. For this to be true, the false positives must not be a compelling reason to reject the new test; thus (B) is correct.

(A) is a tricky one because the word "intended" slips under many test takers' radar. This statement isn't crucial to the author's line of reasoning because there could have been tests "intended" for diagnosis that simply did not produce accurate results the way the new test does. The whole issue of intent is outside the scope. (C) is extreme because the word "all" broadens the scope beyond those autistic children the author discusses. This choice also brings in the issue of children's verbal skills, which is outside the scope. (D) may be desirable, but is not necessary to uphold the author's argument that autistic children can benefit. Keep your eyes on the prize: for Assumption questions, stay focused on the task of linking conclusion to evidence. An answer that only discusses the evidence is almost certainly wrong on this question type.

(E) Whether we had evidence of the disorder in children this young isn't relevant to whether children this young can benefit from treatment now that we do have a useful test.

> An Advanced test taker reads the answer choices extremely carefully and notices even the subtlest inaccuracy.

Explanation: Potato Famine Woes

Distinguishing Feature: Just Plain Tough, Odd Man Out

2. D

The logical progression here is from famine to decreased population to increased wages, thanks to supply and demand. The Irish potato famine is offered as an exception to this generalization. (D), however, doesn't help to explain the exception: Even if the birth rate increased in the years that followed, that would have no immediate effect on the work force—at least not in the following decade. We would therefore still expect a decreased work force and a rise in average wages.

(A), (B) If the labor force didn't decrease, then it's easy to explain the lack of wage increases following the famine. If (A) were true, then it's plausible that the post-famine work force stabilized more quickly than in other famine situations. (B) explains how the famine may have had a massive effect on the overall population, but not nearly the same effect on the work force.

(C) Back to supply and demand: If technology reduced the demand for labor, then that could explain how a smaller labor force would still be unable to command the higher wages than were otherwise typical in postfamine situations.

(E) Such governmental control resulting in artificially low wages could, in itself, explain this particular exception to the generalization.

An Advanced test taker identifies the issues involved in complex discrepancy questions, and then searches for a choice that addresses those issues.

Explanation: Construction Committee

Distinguishing Features: Formal Logic, Tough Choices, Inference

3. E

Two sentences here, one beginning with the word "Some," the other with "No one." Add to that an Inference stem and answer choices that begin with either "No" or "Some" and the result is unmistakable—this is classic formal logic. It's possible to combine the statements, just like we do in Logic Games, in order to deduce what must be true. The two most helpful terms in the short stimulus are "some" and "no one"—the former we understand to mean "at least one," while the latter excludes all members of a group from a particular situation. "Many" is simply not as helpful, because we have no way of telling which people this "many" refers to. So it's a good strategy to look to combine the first sentence with the first part of the second sentence. Were you able to do this? If so, you should have had no trouble scanning for the correct answer. If not, try it now before reading on. Okay: The first sentence tells us that at least one planner/construction rep (nothing wrong with shortening the terms to that) has an interest in the decisions. But no planner lives in the suburbs, so if we combine these facts, we can say conclusively that there must be at least one non-suburbanite (the planner from above) who has an interest in the decisions. That's the same as saying that some (at least one) persons interested in the decision don't live in the suburbs, choice (E). You may have noticed another deduction: It must be true that some construction reps don't live in the suburbs, since the planners in question, none of whom live in the suburbs, are "those representing the construction industry."

(A) Getting rid of the double negative, (A) translates into "all persons with significant interest in the decisions are in the construction industry." This need not be true—nothing forbids non-construction industry members outside of the committee from having major interest in the committee's decisions. (A) requires a strategically-inserted "only" in the first sentence in order to be true.

(B) No one on the committee itself lives in the suburbs, sure, but, as with (A), nothing prevents people *not* on the committee from having a financial interest in the committee's decisions. And who knows where those people live?—it could be anywhere, suburbs included. Again, it would take an "only" somewhere in the first sentence to make (B) work.

(C), (D) As mentioned above, this notion of "many" working in the suburbs is vague—which ones are they? We simply don't know, which is what creates the possibility that both (C) and (D) are false. In (C), it's possible that the "many" planners working in the suburbs don't coincide at all with the "some" who have a significant financial interest in the decisions. If these latter folks were the only ones interested in the decisions, then (C) would be false. Likewise for (D): Nothing prevents *all* of the planner/construction reps from working in the suburbs. Again, this all comes back to the ambiguity in this context of the word "many."

An Advanced test taker uses his Logic Games skills in Logical Reasoning Formal Logic questions.

Explanation: Ashley in Tanzania

Distinguishing Features: Parallel Reasoning, Formal Logic, Tough Choices

4. D

Comparisons are the key to Parallel Logic questions, even the toughest ones.

The choices are subtly similar, and even all deal with the same terms (frogs, Scrag Island, a lagoon, owls, and their eating habits). Despite these difficulties, or perhaps because of them, careful comparisons allow us to whittle down the choices relatively quickly.

Comparing conclusions knocks out only two choices (as opposed to four in question 21), but let's take what we can get! The stimulus conclusion, "a certain thing is unlikely to occur," is repeated in (A), (C), and (D), so they must stay in the running. But (B)'s "owls may never eat" is much weaker than the stimulus' "unlikely ever to collect," and (E)'s "no owl...will eat anything" goes too far in the other direction. Of the remaining choices, (A) may be easiest to throw out because its main evidence—the first sentence—contains a reference to "home to many frogs," something that has no parallel in the stimulus.

(C) vs. (D) is the toughest call, and with good reason: They only differ in terms of their first sentences. (Both go on to say that the owls eat only island frogs, and both conclude that the owls probably will never eat any animal living outside the lagoon.) When the first sentences of (C) and (D) are compared to the stimulus, we can see that the former goes afield.

(D)'s "All yet-discovered frogs on that island live in the lagoon" directly parallels "All known deposits are in Tanzania." But (C)'s first sentence translates to "All animals known to live in the lagoon are frogs." If the stimulus and (D) begin *All A are B*, (C) begins *All B are A*. When the dust settles, then, only (D) is left standing.

An Advanced test taker always begins with the most concrete part of a difficult Parallel Reasoning question.

PRACTICE SET 4

1. No projects that involve historical restorations were granted building permits this month. Since some of the current projects of the firm of Stein and Sapin are historical restorations, at least some of Stein and Sapin's projects were not granted building permits this month.

   The pattern of reasoning in the argument above is most similar to that in which one of the following?

   (A) None of the doctors working at City Hospital were trained abroad. So, although some hospitals require doctors trained abroad to pass an extra qualifying exam, until now, at least, this has not been an issue for City Hospital.

   (B) None of the news reports from the economic summit meeting have been encouraging. Since some other recent economic reports have showed positive trends, however, at least some of the economic news is encouraging at this time.

   (C) None of the new members of the orchestra have completed their paperwork. Since only those people who have completed their paperwork can be paid this week, at least some of the new members of the orchestra are likely to be paid late.

   (D) Several films directed by Hannah Barker were released this season, but none of the films released this season were enthusiastically reviewed. Therefore, at least some of Hannah Barker's films have not received enthusiastic reviews.

   (E) Some of the city's most beautiful parks are not larger than a few acres, and some of the parks only a few acres in size are among the city's oldest. Therefore, some of the city's most beautiful parks are also its oldest parks.

2. A recent study of 6,403 people showed that those treated with the drug pravastatin, one of the effects of which is to reduce cholesterol, had about one-third fewer nonfatal heart attacks and one-third fewer deaths from coronary disease than did those not taking the drug. This result is consistent with other studies, which show that those who have heart disease often have higher than average cholesterol levels. This shows that lowering cholesterol levels reduces the risk of heart disease.

   The argument's reasoning is flawed because the argument

   (A) neglects the possibility that pravastatin may have severe side effects

   (B) fails to consider that pravastatin may reduce the risk of heart disease but not as a consequence of its lowering cholesterol levels

   (C) relies on past findings, rather than drawing its principal conclusion from the data found in the specific study cited

   (D) draws a conclusion regarding the effects of lowering cholesterol levels on heart disease, when in fact the conclusion should focus on the relation between pravastatin and cholesterol levels

   (E) fails to consider what percentage of the general population might be taking pravastatin

Questions 3–4

There are about 75 brands of microwave popcorn on the market; altogether, they account for a little over half of the money from sales of microwave food products. It takes three minutes to pop corn in the microwave, compared to seven minutes to pop corn conventionally. Yet by weight, microwave popcorn typically costs over five times as much as conventional popcorn. Judging by the popularity of microwave popcorn, many people are willing to pay a high price for just a little additional convenience.

3. If the statements in the passage are true, which one of the following must also be true?

(A) No single brand of microwave popcorn accounts for a large share of microwave food product sales.

(B) There are more brands of microwave popcorn on the market than there are of any other microwave food product.

(C) By volume, more microwave popcorn is sold than is conventional popcorn.

(D) More money is spent on microwave food products that take three minutes or less to cook than on microwave food products that take longer to cook.

(E) Of the total number of microwave food products on the market, most are microwave popcorn products.

4. Which one of the following statements, if true, would call into question the conclusion in the passage?

(A) More than 50 percent of popcorn purchasers buy conventional popcorn rather than microwave popcorn.

(B) Most people who prefer microwave popcorn do so because it is less fattening than popcorn that is popped conventionally in oil.

(C) The price of microwave popcorn reflects its packaging more than it reflects the quality of the *popcorn contained in the package.

(D) The ratio of unpopped kernels to popped kernels is generally the same whether popcorn is popped in a microwave or conventionally in oil.

(E) Because microwave popcorn contains additives not contained in conventional popcorn, microwave popcorn weighs more than an equal volume of conventional popcorn.

PRACTICE SET 4: ANSWERS AND EXPLANATIONS

Explanation: Stein and Sapin Permits

Distinguishing Features: Parallel Reasoning, Formal Logic

1. D

A parallel logic question easily reducible to simple algebra. No *A* (no historical restoration projects) are *B* (got permits this month). Some *C* (this firm's projects) are *A* (restorations). Therefore some *C* (the firm's projects) are not *B* (didn't get permits). In the credited answer, *A* is "films released this season," *B* is "Barker's films," and *C* is "got enthusiastic reviews," the only difference being that answer choice (D) reverses the order in which the evidence is mentioned.

(A) No A are B. Some C are D. Therefore—um—up till now, B hasn't been an issue for E. Ah, forget it.

(B) No A are B. Some C are not B. Therefore some D are B.

(C) No A are B. Only B are C. Therefore some A are not C. Close but no cigar.

(E) fails to give us a "No A are B" statement at all, so we can throw this one out with no further ado.

An Advanced test taker meticulously analyzes Parallel Reasoning answer choices, and immediately tosses the ones that deviate from the original.

Explanation: The Effects of Pravastatin

Distinguishing Features: Causation

2. B

Try to predict an answer to faulty logic questions before proceeding to the choices.

Pravastatin reduces heart attacks and reduces cholesterol. But the author of this stimulus assumes that the drug reduces heart attacks *by reducing cholesterol*. In other words, it confuses correlation with causation, and (B), by focusing on the issue of consequence, gets this exactly right.

(A) deals with side effects and (E) with whether the drug is used widely or narrowly, both of which are well outside the scope. (C) is not a flaw, since the past findings provide additional evidence for the conclusion. (D) suggests the conclusion should focus on pravastatin and cholesterol levels, but that relationship is declared as part of the evidence (lines 2–3); why should the author make any more effort to draw a conclusion about that relationship?

An Advanced test taker is comfortable with the difference between correlation and causation.

> An Advanced test taker uses his knowledge of the argument's scope to determine the relevance of each answer choice.

Explanation: Microwave Popcorn

Distinguishing Features: Numbers and Statistics, Alternative Explanation, Inference

3. D

The right answer here is fairly intuitive, even straightforward. The tricky thing, as always, is wading through the wrong choices without getting distracted and seduced by an impostor. Microwave popcorn accounts for over half of the revenues derived from sales of all microwave food products. Microwaveable popcorn cooks in three minutes or less. Put two and two together, and presto: More money is spent on microwaveable food that prepares in three minutes or less than is spent on microwaveable food that takes more time than that. Stated another way: Since microwave popcorn alone accounts for a majority of the money spent on microwaveable food, and since the microwave popcorn prepares in three minutes or less, (D) must be true.

(A) We're given no information about the relative market share of the different brands of popcorn, so we can't infer (A). For all we know, one particular brand of microwave popcorn accounts for the lion's share of microwaveable popcorn sales, and by extension captures a large share of total microwave food sales.

(B) Nothing allows us to infer this; there could be 1,000 brands of microwaveable soup.

(C) The stimulus compares the two types of popcorn in terms of cost and preparation time, but never in terms of actual sales by volume.

(E) No; popcorn accounts for a majority of the *dollars* spent on microwaveable foods, but popcorn needn't represent a majority of all microwave food products.

> An Advanced test taker sticks to the facts—just as important as understanding what we can tell from the facts is knowing what we *cannot* tell from them.

4. B

The author concludes in the last sentence that people are willing to pay more for the convenience of microwave popcorn—presumably, the faster popping time compared to conventional popcorn. But once again, we see an author overlooking the possibility of other factors. If, as (B) has it, most people buy microwaveable popcorn because it's less fattening, then it's not necessarily true that they're willing to pay more money for the convenience of having their popcorn quickly. They might pay the premium price only to avoid the fat in conventional popcorn.

(A) So what? Even if fewer than 50 percent of consumers buy microwave popcorn, that could still be plenty of people, and the conclusion is stated in terms of "*many* people."

(C) The reason microwaveable popcorn costs so much is irrelevant; the point is that many people pay that extra cost, and the issue to be addressed is why they do so.

(D) We've seen irrelevant distinctions in wrong answer choices; here we have an irrelevant similarity. But what does this do to weaken the claim in the last sentence? Nothing. (If we were told that conventional popcorn results in five times as many unpopped kernels compared to microwave popcorn, then we'd have a possible weakener, but even then only as long as we assume that consumers don't like unpopped kernels.)

(E) tells us that microwaveable popcorn differs from conventional popcorn in that it contains additives, but instead of going on to tell us that people want the additives, it merely tells us that microwaveable corn is heavier. Is this heaviness attractive to consumers? Will they pay more for it? We have no idea.

An Advanced test taker thinks of "alternatives and assumptions" when faced with weakening an argument.

PRACTICE SET 5

Questions 1–2

Proposals for extending the United States school year to bring it more in line with its European and Japanese counterparts are often met with the objection that curtailing the schools' three-month summer vacation would violate an established United States tradition dating from the nineteenth century. However, this objection misses its mark. True, in the nineteenth century the majority of schools closed for three months every summer, but only because they were in rural areas where successful harvests depended on children's labor. If any policy could be justified by those appeals to tradition, it would be the policy of determining the length of the school year according to the needs of the economy.

1. Which one of the following principles, if accepted, would provide the strongest justification for the conclusion?

   (A) That a given social policy has traditionally been in force justifies maintaining that policy only if doing so does not conflict with more pressing social needs.

   (B) Appeals to its own traditions cannot excuse a country from the obligation to bring its practices in line with the legitimate expectations of the rest of the world.

   (C) Because appeals to tradition often serve to mask the real interests at issue, such appeals should be disregarded.

   (D) Traditional principles should be discarded when they no longer serve the needs of the economy.

   (E) The actual tradition embodied in a given practice can be accurately identified only by reference to the reasons that originally prompted that practice.

2. The argument counters the objection by

   (A) providing evidence to show that the objection relies on a misunderstanding about the amount of time each year United States schools traditionally have been closed

   (B) calling into question the relevance of information about historical practices to current disputes about proposed social change

   (C) arguing for an alternative understanding of the nature of the United States tradition regarding the length of the school year

   (D) showing that those who oppose extending the school year have no genuine concern for tradition

   (E) demonstrating that tradition justifies bringing the United States school year in line with that of the rest of the industrialized world

3. Government official: Clearly, censorship exists if we, as citizens, are not allowed to communicate what we are ready to communicate at our own expense or if other citizens are not permitted access to our communications at their own expense. Public unwillingness to provide funds for certain kinds of scientific, scholarly, or artistic activities cannot, therefore, be described as censorship.

   The flawed reasoning in the government official's argument is most parallel to that in which one of the following?

   (A) All actions that cause unnecessary harm to others are unjust; so if a just action causes harm to others, that action must be necessary.

   (B) Since there is more to good manners than simply using polite forms of address, it is not possible to say on first meeting a person whether or not that person has good manners.

   (C) Acrophobia, usually defined as a morbid fear of heights, can also mean a morbid fear of sharp objects. Since both fears have the same name, they undoubtedly have the same origin.

   (D) There is no doubt that a deed is heroic if the doer risks his or her own life to benefit another person. Thus an action is not heroic if the only thing it endangers is the reputation of the doer.

   (E) Perception of beauty in an object is determined by past and present influences on the mind of the beholder. Thus no object can be called beautiful, since not everyone will see beauty in it.

4. A television manufacturing plant has a total of
    1,000 workers, though an average of 10 are absent
    on any given day for various reasons. On days when
    exactly 10 workers are absent, the plant produces
    televisions at its normal rate. Thus, it is reasonable
    to assume that the plant could fire 10 workers
    without any loss in production.

    The argument is most vulnerable to criticism on the
    grounds that it

    (A) ignores the possibility that if 10 workers were
         fired, each of the remaining workers would
         produce more televisions than previously
    (B) fails to show that the absentee rate would
         drop if 10 workers were fired
    (C) takes for granted that the normal rate of
         production can be attained only when no
         more than the average number of workers
         are absent
    (D) overlooks the possibility that certain workers
         are crucial to the production of televisions
    (E) takes for granted that the rate of production
         is not affected by the number of workers
         employed at the plant

PRACTICE SET 5: ANSWERS AND EXPLANATIONS

Explanation: Traditional Education

Distinguishing Features: Principle, Just Plain Tough

1. E

First, a proposal is mentioned: to extend the U.S. school year in the Japanese and European manner. Then an objection is cited: Ditching summer vacation would violate a long tradition. Finally, the conclusion— the "objection misses its mark"—and the evidence: the "tradition" began because farmers needed kids to be free to work during the summer. The *real* tradition to follow, the author says, would be to follow the needs of the economy in scheduling school (which in turn might warrant changing the school year, as is being proposed). The principle that backs up this logic is going to focus on the reasons underlying a tradition (i.e. the reason that the objection "misses its mark"), and that's (E), which firmly distinguishes between a tradition itself and the reasons for the tradition in the first place. Following (E) to the letter would mandate going beyond the sheer three-month summer vacation to the reason it was first instituted, which in turn would support the author's view that the proposal wouldn't defy tradition in the way that the opponents claim.

(A) encourages the changing of policies and traditions that conflict with more pressing needs. But the author's point is that, correctly understood, lengthening the school year wouldn't really violate a tradition at all. In the same way, (B), (C), and (D) all intend to attack, or at least to limit, the importance of tradition, but the author is trying to show that a policy change (eliminating summer vacation) is not out of line with tradition—the *real* tradition as she explains it in the paragraph. The anti-traditionalist sentiment of all four wrong choices hurts, rather than helps, the author's mission here.

An Advanced test taker always pays close attention to an author's topic and scope.

---

2. C

"What is tradition?" That's the author's question. She argues that it should be understood differently, based not upon the specific practice (three months of vacation) but rather upon its *intent* (economic need). (C) paraphrases this nicely.

(A) The author accepts that schools are shut down for three months. That's not in dispute.

(B) *Au contraire*, the author expressly *uses* historical practices in formulating her approach to the problem under discussion.

(D) The author isn't really attacking her opponents personally, as (D) implies. At most, she is asserting not that they don't care about tradition but that they have misunderstood it.

(E) sort of sounds like the author's approval of the proposal. But "the rest of the industrialized world" goes way beyond simply "Japan and Europe." And she stops short of "demonstrating" that tradition would demand revoking summer vacation. To do so, she'd have to provide evidence as to the economic need for summer school, but she doesn't.

An Advanced test taker sees the LSAT as an integrated whole, and brings all her skills to bear on every question.

Explanation: Censorship

Distinguishing Features: Parallel Flaw, Formal Logic, Necessary and Sufficient Conditions

3. D

The conclusion, signaled by "therefore," is that to the author, a certain type of activity does not qualify as "censorship." If you scan the choices for their conclusions, only (D)'s fits that description: To (D)'s author, a certain type of activity does not qualify as "heroic." Can it be that simple? Yep. You needn't go further in your analysis and recognize the fuller structure, when you know that only one choice is possible. For the record, note that (D) and the stimulus share the same logical fallacy—assuming that an activity *sufficient* for a definition (lack of communication = censorship; risk of life for another's benefit = heroism) is at the same time *necessary* for that definition.

(A) This choice properly deduces the contrapositive from an if/then statement: "If an action causes unnecessary harm, then it's unjust; since a just action causes harm, it must be necessary."

(B) Whereas in the initial argument there's a confusion between necessity and sufficiency, this choice makes the proper distinction. It shows that a condition necessary for a result (determination of good manners) is not necessarily sufficient for that result.

(C) The flaw in this argument is the assumption that two things that have one property in common (their name) must, therefore, have others in common as well. This assumption is not necessarily true. While a flawed argument, it is a different flaw from the one which we are seeking.

(E) This argument defines beauty as a subjective term and argues against use of the term since different people will reach different conclusions. Again, this structure is different from the argument for which we need to find a parallel.

An Advanced test taker looks for shortcuts to even the toughest problems on the LSAT.

Explanation: Firing Absentees

Distinguishing Features: Numbers and Statistics, Representation

4. B

Beware of too-precise math in arguments (especially in Logical Flaw questions).

On the face of it, the 10 fired workers are indeed superfluous. After all, given that 10 people are absent per day on average, it does appear as if 990 workers are every bit as productive as the full 1,000. The difference, of course, is that the 10 absentees are an average; they certainly aren't going to be the exact 10 workers who get fired. Once the work force was cut to 990 there'd be no reason to believe that the absentee rate would change, so now the work force would be down to 980 on an average day, and that may be the figure at which productivity suffers. (Moreover, notwithstanding the average, there could be many more absentees than 10 on a given day. Now how certain is productivity? Now how smart was it to let 10 people go?) (B) points to the huge hole in the argument, and to the fuzziness at the heart of seemingly impeccable math.

(A) If increased productivity after the firings is a realistic possibility, then it would be smart, not folly, to let the 10 go.

(C) The author does not cite that there be no more than 10 absentees as a necessary condition of productivity. By recommending 10 layoffs he does seem to have that number "10" fixed in his head, but he doesn't seem worried about a possibly larger or smaller number.

(D) True, the author doesn't seem to consider that some workers may be critical to making the product, and if the wrong 10 people are let go there could be trouble. But (D) doesn't pick up on the essential problem with the math. (And if the *right* 10 people are dismissed, then (D) is irrelevant.)

(E) The author doesn't take it for granted: He makes it a central part of his calculation.

An Advanced test taker is suspicious whenever she sees in an argument raw numbers side by side with rates, percentages, or probabilities.

PRACTICE SET 6

1. Of every 100 burglar alarms police answer, 99 are false alarms. This situation causes an enormous and dangerous drain on increasingly scarce public resources. Each false alarm wastes an average of 45 minutes of police time. As a result police are consistently taken away from responding to other legitimate calls for service, and a disproportionate share of police service goes to alarm system users, who are mostly businesses and affluent homeowners. However, burglar alarm systems, unlike car alarm systems, are effective in deterring burglaries, so the only acceptable solution is to fine burglar alarm system owners the cost of 45 minutes of police time for each false alarm their systems generate.

   The statement that burglar alarm systems, unlike car alarm systems, are effective in deterring burglaries plays which one of the following roles in the argument?

   (A) It justifies placing more restrictions on owners of burglar alarms than on owners of car alarms.
   (B) It provides background information needed to make plausible the claim that the number of burglar alarms police are called on to answer is great enough to be a drain on public resources.
   (C) It provides a basis for excluding as unacceptable one obvious alternative to the proposal of fining owners of burglar alarm systems for false alarms.
   (D) It gives a reason why police might be more inclined to respond to burglar alarms than to car alarms.
   (E) It explains why a disproportionate number of the burglar alarms responded to by police come from alarm systems owned by businesses.

2. Mary, a veterinary student, has been assigned an experiment in mammalian physiology that would require her to take a healthy, anesthetized dog and subject it to a drastic blood loss in order to observe the physiological consequences of shock. The dog would neither regain consciousness nor survive the experiment. Mary decides not to do this assignment.

   Mary's decision most closely accords with which one of the following principles?

   (A) All other things being equal, gratuitously causing any animal to suffer pain is unjustified.
   (B) Taking the life of an animal is not justifiable unless doing so would immediately assist in saving several animal lives or in protecting the health of a person.
   (C) The only sufficient justification for experimenting on animals is that future animal suffering is thereby prevented.
   (D) Practicing veterinarians have a professional obligation to strive to prevent the unnecessary death of an animal except in cases of severely ill or injured animals whose prospects for recovery are dim.
   (E) No one is ever justified in acting with the sole intention of causing the death of a living thing, be it animal or human.

3. Ethicist: A society is just when, and only when, first, each person has an equal right to basic liberties, and second, inequalities in the distribution of income and wealth are not tolerated unless these inequalities are to everyone's advantage and are attached to jobs open to everyone.

Which one of the following judgments most closely conforms to the principle described above?

(A) Society S guarantees everyone an equal right to basic liberties, while allowing inequalities in the distribution of income and wealth that are to the advantage of everyone. Further, the jobs to which these inequalities are attached are open to most people. Thus, society S is just.

(B) Society S gives everyone an equal right to basic liberties, but at the expense of creating inequalities in the distribution of income and wealth. Thus, society S is not just.

(C) Society S allows inequalities in the distribution of income and wealth, although everyone benefits, and these inequalities are attached to jobs that are open to everyone. Thus, society S is just.

(D) Society S distributes income and wealth to everyone equally, but at the expense of creating inequalities in the right to basic liberties. Thus, society S is not just.

(E) Society S gives everyone an equal right to basic liberties, and although there is an inequality in the distribution of income and wealth, the jobs to which these inequalities are attached are open to all. Thus, society S is just.

4. The Scorpio Miser with its special high-efficiency engine costs more to buy than the standard Scorpio sports car. At current fuel prices, a buyer choosing the Miser would have to drive it 60,000 miles to make up the difference in purchase price through savings on fuel. It follows that, if fuel prices fell, it would take fewer miles to reach the break-even point.

Which one of the following arguments contains an error of reasoning similar to that in the argument above?

(A) The true annual rate of earnings on an interest-bearing account is the annual rate of interest less the annual rate of inflation. Consequently, if the rate of inflation drops, the rate of interest can be reduced by an equal amount without there being a change in the true rate of earnings.

(B) For retail food stores, the Polar freezer, unlike the Arctic freezer, provides a consistent temperature that allows the store to carry premium frozen foods. Though the Polar freezer uses more electricity, there is a bigger profit on premium foods. Thus, if electricity rates fell, a lower volume of premium-food sales could justify choosing the Polar freezer.

(C) With the Roadmaker, a crew can repave a mile of decayed road in less time than with the competing model, which is, however, much less expensive. Reduced staffing levels made possible by the Roadmaker eventually compensate for its higher price. Therefore, the Roadmaker is especially advantageous where average wages are low.

(D) The improved strain of the Northland apple tree bears fruit younger and lives longer than the standard strain. The standard strain does grow larger at maturity, but to allow for this, standard trees must be spaced farther apart. Therefore, new plantings should all be of the improved strain.

(E) Stocks pay dividends, which vary from year to year depending on profits made. Bonds pay interest, which remains constant from year to year. Therefore, since the interest earned on bonds does not decrease when economic conditions decline, investors interested in a reliable income should choose bonds.

PRACTICE SET 6: ANSWERS AND EXPLANATIONS

Explanation: False Alarm

Distinguishing Feature: Numbers and Statistics, Alternative Explanation

1. C

The argument begins by going after burglar alarm systems, and those who use them, hard: Almost all burglar alarms are false alarms, they take up dwindling police resources, and an unfair share of police attention goes to alarm system users. Then, just before the conclusion, the author slips in this statement: Burglar alarm systems, unlike car alarm systems, do work. What's the point of saying this?, asks question 20. The danger here is getting hung up on *car alarms*, and thinking they must figure in the argument somehow, but that was only a parenthetical remark. What the statement is saying here is simply that *burglar alarm systems work*. So, after a long diatribe about the bad points of the systems, the argument brings up a crucial point in their favor. Then comes the conclusion that the *only* acceptable solution is to fine the offending systems owners. The statement that burglar alarm systems work, then, is meant to lead to the conclusion that the only thing to do is to fine the owners. But those alarms are such a pain in the butt, what if they didn't work? Well then, maybe the obvious conclusion would be to ban them altogether. So (C) accurately describes the role the statement plays: It gives a reason for not doing anything drastic, like banning alarms or refusing to answer them.

(A) doesn't work at all—burglar alarms are being compared *favorably* to car alarms. As for (B), the statement doesn't suggest anything about the number of burglar alarms; anyway, that's a reference to sentence 1. *Just as in Reading Comprehension, Logical Reasoning answers can be wrong because they come from "the wrong part of the passage."* (D) fits right in with the *rest* of the stimulus, explaining why burglar alarm systems are a drain on police resources, but the statement in question is going *against* the bulk of the paragraph. If you find that hard to see, look at the structural clues again—the statement is preceded by a nice big "however." *In questions that ask what role a statement plays in an argument, take especially careful note of structuralclues—words like "however" and "although."* Finally, contrary to (E), the statement has nothing to do with businesses vs. homeowners.

An Advanced test taker can quickly identify the purpose of a statement because she is used to reading for purpose at all times.

Explanation: To Kill a Dog

Distinguishing Feature: Principle

2. B

The general principle that justifies vet student Mary's refusal to carry out the experiment is (B). It provides only two possible exceptions (immediately saving a person, or saving several animals) to a flat injunction against taking an animal's life, and neither of those exceptions pertains to this particular case, so the principle stands: Mary is right in not participating in taking this dog's life.

(A) wouldn't support her decision, since the dog is anesthetized; it wouldn't feel any pain. Moreover, if there were pain involved, such pain wouldn't necessarily qualify as "gratuitous," since there would be at least one positive result, namely Mary's increased knowledge.

(C) The experiment is designed to make Mary a more knowledgeable vet, and that increased knowledge might very well prevent some animal suffering in future. Thus, by (C)'s own terms, Mary might be wrong in refusing to participate.

(D) rules out most unnecessary death, but who's to say that this dog's death isn't "necessary" in order for Mary to become a competent vet? Moreover, Mary isn't a practicing vet, she's a student, so this one is clearly outside the scope.

(E) isn't applicable because the "sole intention" of the experiment isn't to kill the dog. It's also designed to teach Mary about the physiological consequences of shock.

An Advanced test taker recognizes that principle questions are similar to inference questions—the right answers are strictly consistent with the information in the original argument.

Explanation: Just Society

Distinguishing Feature: Formal Logic, Principle, Just Plain Tough

3. D

This Principle question seems to test your patience more than anything else, but it's actually a test of your formal logic skills. We get a formal principle, or law, with a "when and only when" condition, which is the same as "if and only if." Your understanding of that phrase is what's being tested here. Each of the choices ends with a judgment, and we have to select the justified one.

"If and only if" means that you're being given conditions that are both necessary and sufficient for a result. It covers all circumstances: If the conditions are met the result occurs; if they *aren't* met the result *doesn't* occur. This may confuse you at the moment, but it's really pretty straightforward. Let's see it at work in this example. Two conditions are labeled "1st" and "2nd," and the result is a "just society." What the rule is saying is, if both the 1st and 2nd conditions are met (and never mind for the moment what those conditions are), then a society is just. However: We can be sure that if either of the conditions is *not* met, then a society is *not* just. It's all or nothing.

How does this analysis help us? Let's put each choice, starting with its judgment, up against the principle. The moment we see a condition deviate from the desired judgment, that choice will bite the dust. And we know that four of the five choices will have some sort of disjunction between the judgment and the conditions, so we'll proceed with confidence:

(A) Here society S is just, and the 1st condition is met: Everyone there does have equal rights to basic liberties. But the 2nd one is *not* met. It says that the only way economic inequalities will be tolerated is when everyone benefits from them—specifically, those inequalities must be "to everyone's advantage and . . . attached to jobs open to everyone." (A) does offer inequalities, but the jobs attached to them are merely open to "most people." That falls short of the principle. (A)'s society, by the rule's definition, is therefore *not* just.

(B) fails to tell us whether the society's economic inequalities are to everyone's advantage or if they provide jobs that are open to all. Without knowing this, it is premature to declare such a society unjust.

(C)'s judgment is also premature, because (C) mentions nothing about whether its society offers everyone equal rights to basic liberties. Without knowing about that, we cannot be sure about the justness of the society (C) describes.

(D) In this society, people do not have equal rights to basic liberties, and we can conclude from this alone that the judgment that this society is not just is correct. Equal rights to basic liberties is the first stated necessary condition for a just society; thus, any society with unequal access to basic liberties is emphatically *not* just. (D) has its society pegged right.

(E) Having seen that (D) is right, we *know* that (E) goes bad; it's just a question of how. If it's read quickly, (E) seems so good: Its society (which (E) calls just) does give equal rights to basic liberties, and its economic inequalities *are* attached to jobs open to all. However: Are those inequalities "to everyone's advantage"? (E) fails to say; and we cannot be sure that this society is just unless we know that its inequalities are, indeed, to everyone's advantage. Similar to the judgments in (B) and (C), (E)'s judgment cannot be evaluated because we still lack a key piece of information.

An Advanced test taker is familiar with translating all kinds of Formal Logic statements—from basic "if-then" statements to complex ones like "if and only if."

Explanation: The Scorpio Miser

Distinguishing Features: Parallel Flaw

4. C

The Miser costs more than the Scorpio sports car, but if you drive it 60,000 miles, the author claims, the money you'll save on gas makes up for the extra money you paid when you bought the car. Evidently, the Miser gets more miles per gallon than the Scorpio: After 60,000 miles, you'll have bought fewer gallons of gas, and the savings on these gallons will equal your initial extra investment in the purchase price. Here's the flub: The author argues that if fuel prices fall, you'll recover your initial investment *faster*. But, actually, the opposite is true; your savings are nothing other than the money you *don't* spend on gas. So the less gas costs, the less you save per mile driven, and thus the *more* you have to drive before you break even. So we want a choice that also concludes the exact opposite of the truth. That's (C): The Roadmaker costs more initially (as did the Miser); the other model's drawback is that you need to employ more people (the Scorpio sports car required more gas). (C) concludes that where wages are low (i.e. where the competing model's drawback is *less* important), the Roadmaker is more advantageous. Not at all; the Roadmaker *saves* on wages, so it's especially advantageous compared to the competing model when wages are high, just as the gas-saving Miser is more advantageous when gas is expensive.

(A) isn't flawed. Since the true rate of earnings is interest minus inflation, you *can* lower interest when inflation drops and still get the same true rate of earnings, provided both drop by the same amount.

(B) is also reasonable. The Polar uses more electricity (its drawback) but allows one to stock high profit items (its plus). If the cost of electricity falls, then you can offset the extra cost of electricity with fewer sales of high profit items. Unlike the stimulus, (B) diminishes the Polar's drawback, not its advantage.

(D) compares two strains of apples and then recommends always going with the improved strain.

(D) lacks the important idea that after some particular time, one product surpasses another. There's also no mention of the improved strain being more advantageous when something or other is the case. But the most blatant difference, which should have helped you to cross this one off quickly, is the inclusion of a *recommendation*, an element absent from the original stimulus.

(E) does the same thing as (D)—it includes a recommendation, so it's no good for that reason alone. Moreover, the logic is perfectly reasonable, which kills it as well.

An Advanced test taker does not allow the length of a question to overwhelm him, but rather looks for ways to cut the text down to size.

PRACTICE SET 7

1. Several carefully conducted studies showed that 75 percent of strict vegetarians reached age 50 without developing serious heart disease. We can conclude from this that avoiding meat increases one's chances of avoiding serious heart disease. Therefore, people who want to reduce the risk of serious heart disease should not eat meat.

    The flawed pattern of reasoning exhibited by which one of the following is most similar to that exhibited by the argument above?

    (A) The majority of people who regularly drive over the speed limit will become involved in traffic accidents. To avoid harm to people who do not drive over the speed limit, we should hire more police officers to enforce the speed laws.

    (B) Studies have shown that cigarette smokers have a greater chance of incurring heart disease than people who do not smoke. Since cigarette smoking increases one's chances of incurring heart disease, people who want to try to avoid heart disease should give up cigarette smoking.

    (C) The majority of people who regularly drink coffee experience dental problems in the latter part of their lives. Since there is this correlation between drinking coffee and incurring dental problems, the government should make coffee less accessible to the general public.

    (D) Studies show that people who do not exercise regularly have a shorter life expectancy than those who exercise regularly. To help increase their patients' life expectancy, doctors should recommend regular exercise to their patients.

    (E) Most people who exercise regularly are able to handle stress. This shows that exercising regularly decreases one's chances of being overwhelmed by stress. So people who want to be able to handle stress should regularly engage in exercise.

2. The number of aircraft collisions on the ground is increasing because of the substantial increase in the number of flights operated by the airlines. Many of the fatalities that occur in such collisions are caused not by the collision itself, but by an inherent flaw in the cabin design of most aircraft, in which seats, by restricting access to emergency exits, impede escape. Therefore, to reduce the total number of fatalities that result annually from such collisions, the airlines should be required to remove all seats that restrict access to emergency exits.

    Which one of the following proposals, if implemented together with the proposal made in the passage, would improve the prospects for achieving the stated objective of reducing fatalities?

    (A) The airlines should be required, when buying new planes, to buy only planes with unrestricted access to emergency exits.

    (B) The airlines should not be permitted to increase further the number of flights in order to offset the decrease in the number of seats on each aircraft.

    (C) Airport authorities should be required to streamline their passenger check-in procedures to accommodate the increased number of passengers served by the airlines.

    (D) Airport authorities should be required to refine security precautions by making them less conspicuous without making them less effective.

    (E) The airlines should not be allowed to increase the ticket price for each passenger to offset the decrease in the number of seats on each aircraft.

3. On the basis of the available evidence, Antarctica has generally been thought to have been covered by ice for at least the past 14 million years. Recently, however, three-million-year-old fossils of a kind previously found only in ocean-floor sediments were discovered under the ice sheet covering central Antarctica. About three million years ago, therefore, the Antarctic ice sheet must temporarily have melted. After all, either severe climatic warming or volcanic activity in Antarctica's mountains could have melted the ice sheet, thus raising sea levels and submerging the continent.

The reasoning in the argument is most vulnerable to which one of the following criticisms?

(A) That a given position is widely believed to be true is taken to show that the position in question must, in fact, be true.

(B) That either of two things could independently have produced a given effect is taken to show that those two things could not have operated in conjunction to produce that effect.

(C) Establishing that a certain event occurred is confused with having established the cause of that event.

(D) A claim that has a very general application is based entirely on evidence from a narrowly restricted range of cases.

(E) An inconsistency that, as presented, has more than one possible resolution is treated as though only one resolution is possible.

4. In recent years the climate has been generally cool in northern Asia. But during periods when the average daily temperature and humidity in northern Asia were slightly higher than their normal levels the yields of most crops grown there increased significantly. In the next century, the increased average daily temperature and humidity attained during those periods are expected to become the norm. Yet scientists predict that the yearly yields of most of the region's crops will decrease during the next century.

Which one of the following, if true, most helps to resolve the apparent paradox in the information above?

(A) Crop yields in southern Asia are expected to remain constant even after the average daily temperature and humidity there increase from recent levels.

(B) Any increases in temperature and humidity would be accompanied by higher levels of atmospheric carbon dioxide, which is vital to plant respiration.

(C) The climate in northern Asia has generally been too cool and dry in recent years for populations of many crop insect pests to become established.

(D) In many parts of Asia, the increased annual precipitation that would result from warmer and wetter climates would cause most edible plant species to flourish.

(E) The recent climate of northern Asia prevents many crops from being farmed there during the winter.

PRACTICE SET 7: ANSWERS AND EXPLANATIONS

Explanation: Vegetarian Heart Disease

Distinguishing Features: Parallel Flaw, Representation, Numbers and Statistics

1. A

This is one of the tougher ones, partly because the choices are all long and dense and remarkably similar, and partly just because it's a logic question ("support the view that"). The key is recognizing that the view we need to support—"that language has an essential correspondence to . . . things"—is the *first* of the two theories described (lines 18–21) in paragraph 2. In this view, language is fixed and precise. This means that you need to search for a choice indicating language to be "solid and reliable," and you don't have to search for long, because (A) does the job. That two *independently*-developed languages categorize objects in the very same way supports the notion that there's something unchanging and definite about the relationship between words and objects; even two totally independent languages both pick up on the same things.

(B) Close but no cigar. Close to (A), in fact; darned close. But if one of the two similar languages derived from the other, as (B) suggests, then we can't infer from them that language has a *universal* dimension. The linguistic categories common to both of (B)'s languages could be unique to them, with no relationship to those in other languages, in which case the *second* hypothesis wins support.

(C), even more so than (B), connects the linguistic categories within *one* unique language and leaves out its correspondence with other languages.

(D) Highlighting "sentence structure" seems a little narrow for a passage about general theories of language. But worse than that is the way in which (D) narrows its attention to societies that have scientific sophistication, because that starts to smack of the *second* theory's concept of "agreed-upon conventions." Maybe those very sharp societies have linguistic agreement that differs totally from that which is found in the more backward ones—thus weakening, rather than supporting, the idea in question. To put it another way, theory 1 would gain more credence if the sentence structure in *all* societies, regardless of how advanced they were, was similar or identical. But that brings us back to (A), doesn't it?

(E) is outside of the scope. What speakers of a language *believe* their language to do or be is irrelevant to whether language does, in fact, have a universal dimension.

An Advanced test taker is not fooled by Parallel Reasoning choices written about the same subject matter as the original.

Explanation: Aircraft Collision

Distinguishing Features: Necessary and Sufficient Condition, Just Plain Tough

2. B

We're faced with a peculiar question stem here: We're looking for a proposal that would work *together with* the passage's proposal and improve its prospects for reducing fatalities. The correct answer should help ensure that clearing away seats to provide better exit access actually will decrease fatalities. (B) does the job because it deals with the *other factor* mentioned in the stimulus—that the increase in collisions was caused by an increase in flights. If (B) weren't to be implemented, if airlines *did* increase the number of flights, then there would be a danger that the number of collisions would increase as well, and thus that the total number of fatalities would *not* decrease, even though each individual collision might be safer. (B) eliminates this possible reason for an increase in collisions, and gives the stimulus proposal a better chance to work.

Of the other choices, only (A) is tempting—it says that any new planes bought must already meet the proposal's safety requirements. However, (A) doesn't really *add* anything to the passage's proposal. According to that proposal, *whatever* type of airplane the airlines buy, they'll have to clear access to the exits before using the planes—it might save time and money to buy airplanes in which this was already done, but it wouldn't help save lives. Also, we don't know how many (if any) new airplanes the airlines intend to buy— if they buy many, they run the risk that (B) tries to avoid, that of overcrowding. (A) may have been tempting, but you should have rejected it after reading (B)—a good illustration of why *you should read all the answer choices carefully in Logical Reasoning.* The other choices are wide misses. (C) and (E) talk about check-in procedures and ticket prices, which have nothing to do with passenger safety. (D) talks about "security precautions," a *little* nearer the mark, but it only vaguely speaks of "defining" them more clearly, not of making them more effective; in any case, security precautions weren't mentioned in the passage. Even if you couldn't decide between (A) and (B), you should have found it easy to eliminate the others—if worst comes to worst *be ready to eliminate obviously wrong choices to improve your odds of guessing correctly.*

An Advanced test taker notes the scope of the argument, and immediately discounts choices that violate it.

Explanation: Antarctic Fossil

Distinguishing Features: Tough Choices, Alternative Explanation

3. E

You should try to predict a logical flaw before proceeding into the choices.

The only evidence that the ice sheet *must* have melted 3,000,000 years ago is that a bunch of fossils of that age, usually only found on the ocean floor, were found in the sheet. But you need not be a paleontologist to figure that there are a lot of ways, short of the ice sheet melting, in which those fossils could have appeared there. That such fossils were "previously found only in" one place doesn't mean that they can't be found all over the earth. The creatures could have slipped through a hole in the otherwise solid ice sheet and frozen as fossils there. All you have to predict is that the right answer will say, *Not enough evidence to support the cause and effect,* and you can choose

(E) with confidence. (E) rightly deems the fossils an "inconsistency" and condemns the reasoning on the proper grounds.

(A) implies that the author is attempting to go along with the "general belief" when in fact he's seeking to prove an exception to it. (B) comes out of the "After all" sentence, and misreads it; either/or's are not mutually exclusive, so sentence 4 cannot be read as if warming and volcanic activity must be inconsistent, as (B) charges. The author establishes nothing—that's what (E) points out—so the confusion between event and cause mentioned by (C) has no connection with the argument as written. And the problem with the reasoning isn't that the fossil counterevidence is too narrow (D), it's that the counterevidence can be used to draw many other conclusions than the one drawn.

An Advanced test taker understands a logical mechanism such as causation to the point of knowing perfectly well when that mechanism is not employed.

Explanation: Asian Harvest

Distinguishing Features: Paradox, Tough Choices

4. C

The word "paradox" in the stem tells us to keep our eyes peeled for a surprising result or finding, which in this case comes to us in the form of a prediction: Why would the scientists predict that crop yields will *decrease* during the next century when it appears that the beneficial factors for crop growth (increased temperature and humidity) will become the norm? One would expect, under such conditions, for the yields to increase. Thus the paradox. It's difficult to pre-phrase an exact solution to the paradox, but we can pre-phrase the general notion that some other factor caused by the increased heat and humidity may adversely affect the crop yield. (C) follows from this idea: if (C) is true, and the cool and dry climate has kept pests away, then increased heat and humidity may very well increase the likelihood that pests will thrive, and thus take a bite out of crop yields. Under these circumstances, the scientists' prediction is more understandable, and thus what seemed to be a paradox is resolved.

(A) What happens in *southern* Asia has no bearing on this argument unless a relevant connection can be made between southern and northern Asia. The stimulus gives us no basis for inferring such a connection, so (A) offers no help in resolving the paradox.

(B) To the contrary. (B) only deepens the mystery since it provides a situation whereby the expected climate changes would *increase* crop yields, contrary to the scientists' prediction.

(D), if anything, reinforces the paradox by providing further evidence that the crop yields should increase in the next century. However, "many parts of Asia" is fairly vague, and may not include northern Asia, and "edible plant species" may only be a subset of crops in general. (D), while possibly an *au contraire* choice, is mostly outside the scope of the argument.

(E) Scope shift! The issue is how much the yield will increase or decrease, not the season in which the crops are farmed.

An Advanced test taker pre-phrases answers as much as possible, but knows when it's best to let the choices do some of the work for her.

PRACTICE SET 8

1. Nursing schools cannot attract a greater number of able applicants than they currently do unless the problems of low wages and high-stress working conditions in the nursing profession are solved. If the pool of able applicants to nursing school does not increase beyond the current level, either the profession will have to lower its entrance standards, or there will soon be an acute shortage of nurses. It is not certain, however, that lowering entrance standards will avert a shortage. It is clear that with either a shortage of nurses or lowered entrance standards for the profession, the current high quality of health care cannot be maintained.

Which one of the following can be properly inferred from the passage?

(A) If the nursing profession solves the problems of low wages and high-stress working conditions, it will attract able applicants in greater numbers than it currently does.

(B) The nursing profession will have to lower its entrance standards if the pool of able applicants to nursing school does not increase beyond the current level.

(C) If the nursing profession solves the problems of low wages and high-stress working conditions, high quality health care will be maintained.

(D) If the nursing profession fails to solve the problems of low wages and high-stress working conditions, there will soon be an acute shortage of nurses.

(E) The current high quality of health care will not be maintained if the problems of low wages and high-stress working conditions in the nursing profession are not solved.

2. Some environmentalists question the prudence of exploiting features of the environment, arguing that there are no economic benefits to be gained from forests, mountains, or wetlands that no longer exist. Many environmentalists claim that because nature has intrinsic value it would be wrong to destroy such features of the environment, even if the economic costs of doing so were outweighed by the economic costs of not doing so.

Which one of the following can be logically inferred from the passage?

(A) It is economically imprudent to exploit features of the environment.

(B) Some environmentalists appeal to a noneconomic justification in questioning the defensibility of exploiting features of the environment.

(C) Most environmentalists appeal to economic reasons in questioning the defensibility of exploiting features of the environment.

(D) Many environmentalists provide only a noneconomic justification in questioning the defensibility of exploiting features of the environment.

(E) Even if there is no economic reason for protecting the environment, there is a sound noneconomic justification for doing so.

Questions 3–4

Historian: There is no direct evidence that timber was traded between the ancient nations of Poran and Nayal, but the fact that a law setting tariffs on timber imports from Poran was enacted during the third Nayalese dynasty does suggest that during that period a timber trade was conducted.

Critic: Your reasoning is flawed. During its third dynasty, Nayal may well have imported timber from Poran, but certainly on today's statute books there remain many laws regulating activities that were once common but in which people no longer engage.

3. The critic's response to the historian's reasoning does which one of the following?

    (A) It implies an analogy between the present and the past.
    (B) It identifies a general principle that the historian's reasoning violates.
    (C) It distinguishes between what has been established as a certainty and what has been established as a possibility.
    (D) It establishes explicit criteria that must be used in evaluating indirect evidence.
    (E) It points out the dissimilar roles that law plays in societies that are distinct from one another.

4. The critic's response to the historian is flawed because it

    (A) produces evidence that is consistent with there not having been any timber trade between Poran and Nayal during the third Nayalese dynasty
    (B) cites current laws without indicating whether the laws cited are relevant to the timber trade
    (C) fails to recognize that the historian's conclusion was based on indirect evidence rather than direct evidence
    (D) takes no account of the difference between a law's enactment at a particular time and a law's existence as part of a legal code at a particular time
    (E) accepts without question the assumption about the purpose of laws that underlies the historian's argument

PRACTICE SET 8: ANSWERS AND EXPLANATIONS

Explanation: Nursing Admissions

Distinguishing Feature: Formal Logic, Inference, Just Plain Tough

1. E

This formal logic stimulus is made up of a string of conditional statements. Nursing schools can't attract more able applicants unless two problems are solved (low wages and bad conditions). It stands to reason then that if these two problems are NOT solved, as posited in correct choice (E), then the schools will NOT attract a greater number of able applicants. Add that to what follows: If the applicant pool doesn't increase (and we just saw that in choice (E) it doesn't), then either one of two things will happen: lower admissions standards or a shortage of nurses. Finally, we're told that if either one of *these* things happens (as must be the case according to (E)), then the current high quality of health care cannot be maintained. It takes a few steps, but (E) is inferable from the stimulus.

(A) and (C) both confuse the necessary condition in the first sentence for a sufficient one. (A) interprets "the number of applicants will not increase unless the problems are solved" to mean "if the problems are solved the number of able applicants *will* increase," while (C) takes it one step further to guarantee the maintenance of high quality health care.

(B) and (D) both fail on the grounds that a nonincrease in applicants can mean *either* a lowering of standards *or* a shortage of nurses. For (B), no increase doesn't necessarily mean lower standards; it could mean shortage. In (D), failing to solve the problems will prevent an increase, but this need not lead to shortage—it could lead to lower standards only.

> An Advanced test taker uses any skills gained in her LSAT preparation wherever they may apply on the rest of the test.

Explanation: Environmental Exploits

Distinguishing Features: Inference

2. B

Instead of offering an argument of his own, our stimulus author is reporting two arguments made by others on the topic of exploiting (in the sense of "making use of") aspects of our earth. "Some" environmentalists (sentence 1) believe that exploiting our resources may not make sense because you can't benefit economically from resources that have disappeared. "Many" of them (sentence 2) argue that exploitation is wrong because it's wrong to destroy the "intrinsic value" of nature, irrespective of the cost:benefits ratio. We can't tell whether there's any overlap between those two groups of environmentalists—that is, whether any of them hold both views (which is certainly plausible). But we can be sure that at least the members of the group in sentence 2 argue against exploitation on non-economic grounds; and they are the "some" mentioned in correct choice (B).

(A), (E) Each of these choices relies on the author's having taken a firm position on the issue. (A) would be inferable if the author agreed with the environmentalists of sentence 1, while (E) is in line with an advocate of sentence 2's position. But in fact our author takes no position at all, and it would therefore be premature to infer these hard and fast judgments simply from the author's presentation of the two opinions.

An Advanced test taker understands that on the LSAT, the word "some" strictly means "one or more."

An Advanced test taker has a keen eye and ear for distortions of the original text.

(C) is discardable because nothing in the stimulus brings up the concept of "most" environmentalists. We can infer that there are people who hold each of the positions mentioned, and as we've said it's possible that some hold both. But what are the views of the majority? No way to tell.

(D) is similarly too precise on the number breakdown, implying that there must be some environmentalists who hold only the view cited in sentence 2 and who disagree with the sentence 1 position. But no such environmentalists need exist, let alone "many" of them.

Explanation: Timber Trade

Distinguishing Features: Just Plain Tough, Alternative Explanation, Scope Shift.

3. A

Two points hinge on a dispute between an historian and a critic, and the first point is awarded for correctly recognizing the way in which the critic makes her argument. First the historian's argument: During the third Nayalese dynasty, a law taxing timber imports from Poran was enacted. So, although we have no actual evidence of the timber trade, we do have evidence that a law concerning timber trade was put into effect, which *suggests* the existence of a timber trade. The critic finds this reasoning flawed. She grants that the historian's conclusion may well be true—Nayal may indeed have imported timber from Poran—but this conclusion isn't supported by the evidence: It ignores the fact that many laws now exist governing activities that people no longer engage in. Her point, then, is that the historian's argument is flawed because it overlooks the possibility that any given law (specifically, the ancient Nayalese law) may be out of date and thus not truly reflect the activity of a particular era. In suggesting that evidence regarding today's statute books is relevant to the argument concerning ancient Poran and Nayal, the author is, as (A) has it, implying an analogy between present and past. Specifically, she implies that modern day laws and ancient laws are alike in that both can outlive their usefulness.

(B) The critic doesn't identify any principles at all, preferring to point to the specific example of a few outdated laws.

(C) is actually a better description of the historian's argument. He's the one who explains that the timber trade is established as a possibility, but not a certainty. The critic's response merely *recognizes* that this trade is a possibility and then goes on to attack the significance that the historian attaches to the Nayalese law.

(D) The critic attacks the historian's "indirect" evidence by implying that similar evidence in the modern period wouldn't necessarily support the same kind of conclusion. But she never offers a list of things that such indirect evidence could be checked against in order to prove its validity. In short, the critic never mentions any specific criteria.

(E) The critic uses an example of modern law to make a point about the old Nayalese law; thus, she isn't pointing out dissimilarities in laws—in fact, just the opposite.

4. D

Now to pick up the second point related to this debate; we're asked for the flaw in the critic's response. The historian's argument rests on the evidence that the Nayalese law was *enacted* in the third dynasty. So he's banking on the notion that a law regulating a nonexistent trade wouldn't be enacted, which seems to make sense. The critic shifts the scope away from "enacted" to "exists"— she argues that just because a law is on the books doesn't mean that it's up-to-date, current. But this is an unfair response, because "enacted," a word that the critic evidently missed, rules out this possible objection. It's highly unlikely that a law would be out of date at the time it was enacted. In order to truly weaken the historian's argument, the critic would need to offer examples of laws that were irrelevant when they were first put into effect. Her mistake is therefore to overlook the fact that the historian's evidence concerns the *enactment* of a law, not its mere *existence*, choice (D).

(A) The critic's evidence *doesn't* contradict the possibility of no timber trade between the ancient nations, and thus she *does* provide evidence consistent with this possibility. However, this is not a flaw in her reasoning. It's perfectly acceptable for this to be the case; we would almost expect her evidence to lean in that direction. Moreover, the critic's response attacks the historian's reasoning, not his conclusion that timber was probably traded.

(B) The current laws cited are intended to illustrate outdated laws, not outdated *timber* laws. They need not have anything to do with the timber trade because the author is citing these laws only to show that laws in general (and that would include ancient Nayalese tariffs) can be outdated.

(C) The distinction between direct and indirect evidence is not lost on the critic. She attacks the historian's reference to the Nayalese tariff, which is pretty clearly stated as indirect evidence. The critic's flaw is that she misses or misinterprets a concept *contained* in this indirect evidence ("enactment"), not that she fails to recognize the evidence as indirect.

(E) The critic doesn't accept the historian's assumption, but rather misunderstands it. The critic thinks the historian is assuming that the existence of a law at a particular time indicates that the activity it regulates also exists at that time. As we've seen, however, the historian is assuming only that the *enactment* of a law at some time indicates the existence of the activity it regulates at that time.

An Advanced test taker knows that the classic Logical Flaws can crop up almost anywhere in the Logical Reasoning section of the LSAT.

PRACTICE SET 9

1. Sharks have a higher ratio of cartilage mass to body mass than any other organism. They also have a greater resistance to cancer than any other organism. Shark cartilage contains a substance that inhibits tumor growth by stopping the development of a new blood network. In the past 20 years, none of the responses among terminal cancer patients to various therapeutic measures has been more positive than the response among those who consumed shark cartilage.

   If the claims made above are true, then each of the following could be true EXCEPT:

   (A) No organism resists cancer better than sharks do, but some resist cancer as well as sharks.

   (B) The organism most susceptible to cancer has a higher percentage of cartilage than some organisms that are less susceptible to cancer.

   (C) The substance in shark cartilage that inhibits tumor growth is found in most organisms.

   (D) In the past 20 years many terminal cancer patients have improved dramatically following many sorts of therapy.

   (E) Some organisms have immune systems more efficient than a shark's immune system.

2. The senator has long held to the general principle that no true work of art is obscene, and thus that there is no conflict between the need to encourage free artistic expression and the need to protect the sensibilities of the public from obscenity. When well-known works generally viewed as obscene are cited as possible counterexamples, the senator justifies accepting the principle by saying that if these works really are obscene then they cannot be works of art.

   The senator's reasoning contains which one of the following errors?

   (A) It seeks to persuade by emotional rather than intellectual means.

   (B) It contains an implicit contradiction.

   (C) It relies on an assertion of the senator's authority.

   (D) It assumes what it seeks to establish.

   (E) It attempts to justify a position by appeal to an irrelevant consideration.

Questions 3–4

Marcus: For most ethical dilemmas the journalist is likely to face, traditional journalistic ethics is clear, adequate, and essentially correct. For example, when journalists have uncovered newsworthy information, they should go to press with it as soon as possible. No delay motivated by the journalists' personal or professional interests is permissible.

Anita: Well, Marcus, of course interesting and important information should be brought before the public— that is a journalist's job. But in the typical case, where a journalist has some information but is in a quandary about whether it is yet important or "newsworthy," this guidance is inadequate.

3. The point made by Anita's statements is most accurately expressed by which one of the following?

   (A) Marcus' claim that traditional journalistic ethics is clear for most ethical dilemmas in journalism is incorrect.

   (B) A typical case illustrates that Marcus is wrong in claiming that traditional journalistic ethics is essentially correct for most ethical dilemmas in journalism.

   (C) The ethical principle that Marcus cites does not help the journalist in a typical kind of situation in which a decision needs to be made.

   (D) There are common situations in which a journalist must make a decision and in which no principle of journalistic ethics can be of help.

   (E) Traditional journalistic ethics amounts to no more than an unnecessarily convoluted description of the journalist's job.

4. In order to conclude properly from Anita's statements that Marcus' general claim about traditional journalistic ethics is incorrect, it would have to be assumed that

   (A) whether a piece of information is or is not newsworthy can raise ethical dilemmas for journalists

   (B) there are circumstances in which it would be ethically wrong for a journalist to go to press with legitimately acquired, newsworthy information

   (C) the most serious professional dilemmas that a journalist is likely to face are not ethical dilemmas

   (D) there are no ethical dilemmas that a journalist is likely to face that would not be conclusively resolved by an adequate system of journalistic ethics

   (E) for a system of journalistic ethics to be adequate it must be able to provide guidance in every case in which a journalist must make a professional decision

PRACTICE SET 9: ANSWERS AND EXPLANATIONS

Explanation: Shark Cartilage

Distinguishing Features: Inference Odd Man Out

1. A

This is an excellent question for reinforcing your understanding of the concept of consistency vs. inconsistency. We are looking for the one choice that cannot be true, meaning that the other four can be true—meaning that those four are *consistent* with the text.

(A) Happily, we don't have to search for long. (A)'s statement that "some [organisms] resist cancer as well as sharks" is flatly contradictory to sentence 2's claim that sharks "have a greater resistance to cancer than *any other* organism" (emphasis ours). That sentence and (A) cannot both be true. So (A) is what we want.

(B) The organism that is most susceptible to cancer (which could be any organism except the shark) may very well have a higher percentage of cartilage than some other organisms. The stimulus deals only with sharks, while (B) is so general that it can refer to virtually any organisms.

(C) Since sentence 3 doesn't assert that *only* shark cartilage contains this tumor-inhibiting substance, it may very well be true that many or indeed *most* creatures possess it, but that other factors cause those other organisms to have a greater cancer risk than does the shark.

(D) Sentence 4 asserts that no response to cancer therapy among terminal patients has been more positive than shark cartilage, which must mean that other therapies have been less positive. But it still could be true that those responses to other therapies have been "dramatic"—albeit less dramatic than the shark cartilage results. So (D) offers no contradiction to the stimulus.

(E) The concept of "immune system" is never mentioned in the stimulus, so it could easily be true that the shark's immune system is inferior to those found in other organisms. This doesn't contradict the claim that sharks have the greatest cancer resistance of all organisms, since we're not told, and cannot infer, what causes either the disease *or* the sharks' superior resistance to this one particular disease.

> An Advanced test taker is familiar with the ways in which the terms "consistent" and "inconsistent" are used on the LSAT.

Explanation: Obscene Art

Distinguishing Features: Circular Reasoning

2. D

The senator's position—that no work of art can be obscene, and hence that the world of art has nothing to do with protecting the public—is attacked by means of counterexamples, works of art that people call obscene. His response? "[I]f [they] really are obscene then they cannot be works of art." But that statement is just the contrapositive of the meaning of his original remark. "No work of art can be obscene" means "IF a work of art, THEN not obscene." Reverse and negate both terms and you get the senator's statement in the last sentence. So what's wrong with the reasoning? The senator provides no independent evidence as to the nature of obscenity and the nature of art—he defends the original principle by invoking its contrapositive, that is, its logical equivalent. So he is guilty of "circular reasoning" or, as (D) puts it, assuming the truth of that which he is trying to prove.

(A) The senator uses no emotional language or appeal. He is trying to persuade by logic, but he fails because he begs the question by restating his conclusion as if it offered more support. That's what (D) is saying.

(B) *Au contraire*, his points are logically equivalent (as mentioned above, contrapositives of one another)—not contradictory.

(C) would be true if he alleged (however absurdly) "Art is not obscene because I am a senator and what I say goes." There is, of course, no such assertion of authority here.

(E) Again, his appeal is to his own conclusion; he veers off not into the irrelevant, but into the redundant.

An Advanced test taker is quick to spot Circular Arguments.

Explanation: Ethical Journalism

Distinguishing Features: Just Plain Tough, Scope Shift

3. C

Anita strikes at the root of Marcus' argument. He has denied that there's any problem in applying traditional journalistic ethics to journalists' typical ethical dilemmas—just print whatever's newsworthy. Anita, somewhat condescendingly, points out that Marcus's formula basically begs the question, that it simply sidesteps the typical quandary in which journalists find themselves: figuring out what is newsworthy and what isn't. Her point is that Marcus' "traditional journalistic" ethical principle will leave journalists high and dry in most dilemmas. That's exactly what (C) says—when it comes down to helping a journalist make one of his or her key decisions ("in a typical kind of situation in which a decision has to be made" as (C) says so elegantly), Marcus' principle is useless.

Anita doesn't say that traditional journalistic ethics is *unclear,* as (A) would have it; she says that the version given by Marcus is inadequate. (B) is probably the most tempting wrong choice. However, (B) implies that Anita has used an example to demonstrate the failure of Marcus' principle, but actually she merely defines what the journalist's dilemma typically is, and shows how Marcus' principle is inadequate in such cases. Note, too, that (B) accuses Anita of denying that the traditional ethics are *correct*—but in point of fact Anita denies that *Marcus'* version of traditional journalistic ethics is *adequate.* As both (A) and (B) illustrate, *taking careful note of the vocabulary used in dialogue questions makes it easier to choose between close alternatives.* As for (D), Anita only attacks Marcus' principle, she never claims that *no* principle can be useful. Finally, (E) is correct to a degree—Anita does imply that Marcus has simply described a journalist's job when he says that journalists should publish important information. However, this isn't her point, it's something she says on the *way* to her point, which is that his ethical principle isn't of much use.

4. A

This question asks us to tighten Anita's argument. We want a necessary assumption that, together with Anita's statements, would prove that Marcus' claim about traditional journalistic ethics is wrong. *In cases like this the first step is always to pinpoint the claim being disputed.* Marcus claimed that the traditional ethics is clear, adequate, and essentially correct, for *most ethical dilemmas.* Anita's reply is that where a decision needs to be made about whether a story is *newsworthy,* traditional journalistic ethics are inadequate. Well, in order for this reply to disprove Marcus' contention *we need to connect the terms used by the two protagonists.* One would have to assume something like choice (A), that the question about whether something is or isn't newsworthy can raise ethical dilemmas for journalists. Otherwise, Anita's reply would be irrelevant. You may have overlooked this subtle assumption when reading Anita's argument and doing question 18, but you should have recognized it when you started reading the answer choices.

(B) is a tough one. Remember that Anita attacked traditional journalistic ethics as useless to a journalist in deciding whether information is newsworthy. (B) says that *even if* an item is newsworthy it may be unethical to publish it—which works *against* Anita's statements, rather than with them, by suggesting that the question of whether or not information is newsworthy is actually extraneous to the question of whether or not it ought to be printed. (B) says that the ethical dilemma does not have to do with newsworthiness, but lies elsewhere. (C) is beside the point; as we saw, Marcus' claim had to do with ethical dilemmas only. And in order to disprove Marcus' claim that traditional journalistic ethics is adequate for *most* ethical dilemmas, one need not assume either (D), that an adequate system of journalistic ethics would conclusively resolve *any* dilemma a journalist was likely to face, or (E), that an adequate system of journalistic ethics would provide guidance in every situation. Remember, we're looking for what *must* be assumed, not just a statement that sounds consistent with Anita's point of view.

An Advanced test taker knows that an apparent scope shift can often be bridged by an assumption.

PRACTICE SET 10

Questions 1–2

Dr. Schilling: Those who advocate replacing my country's private health insurance system with. nationalized health insurance because of the rising costs of medical care fail to consider the high human costs that consumers pay in countries with nationalized insurance: Access to high-technology medicine is restricted. Kidney transplants and open-heart surgery-familiar life-saving procedures are rationed. People are denied their right to treatments they want and need.

Dr. Laforte: Your country's reliance on private health insurance denies access even to basic, conventional medicine to the many people who cannot afford adequate health coverage.With nationalized insurance, rich and poor have equal access to life-saving medical procedures, and people's right to decent medical treatment regardless of income is not violated.

1. Dr. Schilling's and Dr. Laforte's statements provide the most support for holding that they would disagree about the truth of which one of the following?

    (A) People's rights are violated less when they are denied an available medical treatment they need because they lack the means to pay for it than when they are denied such treatment on noneconomic grounds.

    (B) Where health insurance is provided by private insurance companies, people who are wealthy generally receive better health care than do people who are unable to afford health insurance.

    (C) In countries that rely primarily on private health insurance to pay for medical costs, most people who would benefit from a kidney transplant receive one.

    (D) In countries with nationalized health insurance, no one who needs a familiar medical treatment in order to stay alive is denied that treatment.

    (E) Anyone who wants a particular medical treatment has a right to receive that treatment.

2. In responding to Dr. Schilling, Dr. Laforte employs which one of the following argumentative strategies?

    (A) showing that the objections raised by Dr. Schilling have no bearing on the question of which of the two systems under consideration is the superior system

    (B) calling into question Dr. Schilling's status as an authority on the issue of whether consumers' access to medical treatments is restricted in countries with nationalized health insurance

    (C) producing counterexamples to Dr. Schilling's claims that nationalized health insurance schemes extract high human costs from consumers

    (D) demonstrating that Dr. Schilling's reasoning is persuasive only because of his ambiguous use of the key word "consumer"

    (E) showing that the force of Dr. Schilling's criticism depends on construing the key notion of access in a particular limited way

Questions 3–4

Monica: The sculpture commissioned for our town plaza has been scorned by the public ever since it went up. But since the people in our town do not know very much about contemporary art, the unpopularity of the work says nothing about its artistic merit and thus gives no reason for removing it.

Hector: You may be right about what the sculpture's popularity means about its artistic merit. However, a work of art that was commissioned for a public space ought to benefit the public, and popular opinion is ultimately the only way of determining what the public feels is to its benefit. Thus, if public opinion of this sculpture is what you say, then it certainly ought to be removed.

3. Monica's and Hector's statements commit them to disagreeing about which one of the following principles?

   (A) Public opinion of a work of art is an important consideration in determining the work's artistic merit.
   (B) Works of art commissioned for public spaces ought at least to have sufficient artistic merit to benefit the public.
   (C) The only reason for removing a work of art commissioned for a public space would be that the balance of public opinion is against the work.
   (D) The sculpture cannot benefit the public by remaining in the town plaza unless the sculpture has artistic merit.
   (E) In determining whether the sculpture should remain in the town plaza, the artistic merit of the sculpture should be a central consideration.

4. The argument Hector makes in responding to Monica depends on the assumption that

   (A) no matter what the public's opinion is on an issue affecting the public good, that public opinion ought to be acted on, even though the opinion may not be a knowledgeable one
   (B) Monica's assessment of the public's opinion of the sculpture is accurate
   (C) if the sculpture had artistic merit, then even a public that was not knowledgeable about modern art would not scorn the sculpture
   (D) works of art commissioned for public spaces ought not to be expected to have artistic merit
   (E) if the public feels that it does not benefit from the sculpture, this shows that the public does not in fact benefit from the sculpture

PRACTICE SET 10: ANSWERS AND EXPLANATIONS

Explanation: Private Health Insurance

Distinguishing Features: Tough Choices, Just Plain Tough

1. A

Schilling gripes that national health insurance hurts consumers by rationing high-technology treatments. Laforte responds that medical treatment is also restricted where health insurance is private: People without the money for insurance are denied access even to conventional medicine. Both arguments concern consumer access to medicine. Schilling and Laforte would disagree over choice (A), which says that it's less of a violation of people's rights when they can't get treatment because they can't pay (as happens in private health insurance systems) than it is when people are denied treatment for noneconomic reasons (such as the rationing that occurs with nationalized insurance). Schilling rails against the nationalized system because people are denied treatments because of restricted access; that is, denied on noneconomic grounds. He would therefore agree with (A). Laforte, on the other hand, argues against the private system because some people can't afford it, which means that she would disagree with (A).

(B) is basically the reason Laforte doesn't like private health insurance. Schilling never disputes this—he just feels that it's less of a drawback than the rationing that results from national health insurance.

(C) Laforte would probably disagree with this; according to her, in the private system, many people can't even afford basic conventional medical procedures. However, we can't determine Schilling's stance on this: While he believes private health insurance provides better access to kidney transplants than does national health insurance, we can't infer that he believes that *most* people who would benefit from a kidney transplant actually get one.

(D) Schilling's last sentence indicates that he would disagree with this statement. However, Laforte's position relative to this statement is ambiguous: She argues that under the national system, rich and poor would have *equal access* to procedures and everyone would be granted the right to *decent* medical treatment. But she doesn't counter Schilling's assertion that access to high-tech medicine is restricted in the nationalized system, so we can't conclude that she would believe that no one in countries with nationalized insurance is *ever* denied a familiar life-saving procedure.

(E) is too vague. Both talk about life-saving procedures, decent treatments that people *need*. Perhaps both disputants believe there are limits to a person's right to receive *any* treatment he or she wants. We just don't know.

> An Advanced test taker fights through long, tough choices to locate the idea that he prephrased, or the choice that holds up best under close scrutiny.

2. E

"Don't talk to me about access," responds Laforte. "In your private system, many people can't even *afford* basic care." Laforte essentially redefines the notion of access to mean who can afford health care, as opposed to Schilling's notion that access means the availability of certain high-tech procedures. So as (E) says, Laforte's response turns on a rejection of Schilling's notion of "access." Laforte attacks Schilling for considering "access" only for those who need high-tech care; she expands the notion of access and shows that some in private insurance systems completely lack access. Thus, "access" to care isn't necessarily an advantage of private insurance—it depends on what *sort* of access you're talking about.

(A) Laforte certainly doesn't accuse Schilling of presenting an irrelevant argument; her argument centers on "access" and patient's rights, just as his does.

(B) has her questioning Schilling's authority, but she never attacks him personally. Her response centers on drawbacks inherent in private health insurance, specifically lack of access to that care.

(C) No, she never produces counterexamples. Instead, she shows that private insurance *also* extracts high costs, costs that she argues are higher than those demanded by national health insurance.

(D) No, Laforte doesn't attack Schilling's use of the word "consumer" by calling it "ambiguous." She simply points out that the realm of consumers includes those who lack insurance in private systems, but Laforte certainly doesn't accuse Schilling of playing with the word.

An Advanced test taker asks herself, "What *kind* of evidence do I have?" when faced with a Method of Argument question.

Explanation: Community Sculpture

Distinguishing Features: Principle, Scope Shift, Just Plain Tough, Tough Choices

3. E

We have to start by identifying the topic and scope. The topic, of course, is the town plaza sculpture, "scorned by the public." Someone apparently wants to get rid of it, because Monica is moved to assert that the work's unpopularity is "no reason to remove it." Why not? Because the public is ignorant of modern art, and hence their disdain says nothing about the work's artistic merit. We should leave Monica's remarks with the impression that when it comes to removing this sculpture, it is artistic merit, not public reaction, that is for her the viable criterion. Hector begins by conceding a point to Monica. Yes, he says, the unpopularity may not mean that the sculpture lacks merit. But "it certainly ought to be removed" if Monica is right about public opinion, because to Hector, the people's views are the only way to determine whether a public work of art is meeting the necessary criterion of "benefiting the public." So to Hector, public opinion *is* a viable criterion for the sculpture's removal, and in the end artistic merit is irrelevant. This directly contradicts Monica's view that artistic merit must be taken into account; and hence (E) is the principle on which the two disagree. Monica would utterly agree with (E), while Hector would take respectful exception.

(A) is a contention that Monica flatly rejects—she thinks that the ignorant public's view is irrelevant to a work's merit—but Hector *doesn't disagree* with Monica on this, as evidenced by his first sentence. He departs from her on the issue of what should be considered in a sculpture's removal. If anything, then, we'd have to say that both speakers would be in unison in their disagreement with the principle in (A)—hardly the basis of a point at issue.

(B) You can reject (B) because it mashes together two concepts—artistic merit and public benefit—in a way foreign to both Monica's and Hector's remarks.

(C) Monica, who thinks that public opinion should have no role in deciding whether the statute goes or stays, would surely disagree with (C), *but so might Hector:* For all we know he may believe that other criteria—perhaps different aspects of "public benefit," such as environmental impact—might conceivably be applied to the question. This is not a clear-cut area of disagreement, as (E) is.

(D), like (B), ties together "artistic merit" and "public benefit" in a way that neither speaker does. Monica, for instance, never mentions the issue of public benefit at all, so we have no idea how she feels about it.

4. E

Here we need only concern ourselves with Hector in a classic assumption question. His conclusion is that if the public opposes the sculpture it should be removed, and his evidence has to do with the relationship between public opinion and public benefit. Note that Hector indulges in a bit of a scope shift in his long second sentence (long sentences are where scope shifts often occur). He first asserts that a public artwork ought to *benefit the public,* and then goes on to say that checking the public pulse is the only way to determine *what the public feels is to its benefit* . . . Must those two things be identical? Of course not; there might be a huge difference between "public benefit" and that which the public *believes* to be beneficial. But Hector must assume that there is no difference, because he proceeds right from the public's disdain for the statue to a call for its removal. He acknowledges no possibility that public benefit might be separate from the public's view of what benefits itself. So he must be assuming (E). If (E) were false, then there might be other ways (other than checking the public pulse, that is) to determine the actual benefit of a particular sculpture, and Hector's recommendation might be voided.

(A) goes way beyond the narrow issue of a public sculpture to cover *all* issues. Hector need not assume such a sweeping statement about the force of public opinion in order to make his argument about this one artwork.

(B) Hector's argument doesn't depend on Monica's being right about the public's opinion of the sculpture—his argument is saying that *even if* her evidence is correct, her conclusion doesn't follow.

(C), (D) The issue of artistic merit is raised only in sentence 1 as a concession to Monica's view of the relationship between popularity and merit. But his real argument begins after than concession, with the Keyword "However." Therefore, the issue of artistic merit is largely irrelevant to Hector's real argument. Period. Thus his logic can by no means hinge on whether artistic merit might change the public's scorn (C), or what the proper *expectation* about artistic merit ought to be (D).

section three

READING COMPREHENSION

CHAPTER ELEVEN

The Reading Comprehension Challenge

See Spot run.

According to the passage, Spot engaged in which one of the following activities?

(A)   growling
(B)   sleeping
(C)   digging
(D)   running
(E)   eating

Ever since you learned to read, you've been tested on your comprehension of written material, so it's no surprise that Reading Comprehension is the most familiar section in all of standardized testing. Medicine, business, archaeology, psychology, dentistry, teaching, law—the exams that stand at the entrance to study in these and most other fields all have one thing in common: a Reading Comprehension section. No matter what academic area you pursue, you have to make sense of dense, unfamiliar prose. And passages don't get much more dense, difficult, or unfamiliar than those on the LSAT.

As with all LSAT material, Reading Comp passages and question sets run the gamut from cake to killer, and naturally for the purposes of this book we've compiled for your test-taking pleasure a group of the densest, nastiest passages we could find. If you can ace these, it's safe to say you have absolutely nothing to fear from the Reading Comp section come Test Day.

The following offers some guidelines on how to get the most out of the passages in this book.

USING THE READING COMPREHENSION PASSAGES IN THIS BOOK

The Reading Comp passages in this book are broken up into four categories:

- Just Plain Tough
- Blinded by Science
- Philosophers' Corner
- Comparative Reading

The passages in chapter 14 (Philosopher's Corner) are particularly complex. You may wish to work through the other chapters first before tackling this chapter. And here are a few more general pointers that should help guide your attack:

Read for the author's purpose and main idea. It's easy to get bogged down in details, especially in difficult passages like the ones in this book. But if you keep the author's purpose—that is, the reason he or she wrote the passage—and main idea in mind, you'll be able to answer many general types of questions immediately, and will know where to find the answers to the others.

Pay attention to passage structure. Many questions ask about how the author strings ideas together to present his or her overall point, or how certain elements function in relation to the passage as a whole. Paying attention to passage structure as you read will give you a leg up on these questions.

Paraphrase the text. You'll be able to process and apply the information in any passage, including these toughies, if you simplify the passage's ideas and translate them into your own words.

An Advanced test taker cuts past impressive-sounding text and boils it down to basic ideas.

Observe timing guidelines. Four passages in 35 minutes allows for roughly eight and a half minutes per passage, but considering the difficulty level of the readings in this book, it's reasonable to allow a little extra time. Try, however, not to exceed nine to ten minutes per passage. If you can knock out tough ones like the ones in this book in that amount of time, you should have no problem finishing easier passages in less than the average time allowed per passage.

Read the explanations. Review the key points of each passage, comparing your own synopsis of the passage to ours. Notice whether you are consistently spotting the main idea and focusing on the relevant parts of the passages. As in the Logic Games and Logical Reasoning sections, the thought processes and habits of Advanced test takers are highlighted throughout the explanations. Try to make these habits your own.

Have fun. No doubt this advice is easier to take for Logic Games than for Reading Comp. However, it still behooves you to approach the Reading Comp section with enthusiasm and a good-natured appreciation for the challenges presented. Who knows, you may even come across some material that's *interesting* to you.

CHAPTER TWELVE

Just Plain Tough

Technical science and abstract philosophical passages often give test takers trouble, and you'll cut your teeth on examples of these soon enough. But it's important to remember that the difficulties of the Reading Comp section are not confined to these types alone. Passages from any other category commonly represented in LSAT Reading Comp—humanities, social science, law—can pose serious problems for the unsuspecting test taker.

The following four examples epitomize difficult passages that are neither scientific nor particularly philosophical in nature, but nonetheless present their own unique challenges. They are, as the title of this chapter states, just plain tough—and it's up to you to be tougher.

PASSAGE 1

A fake can be defined as an artwork intended to deceive. The motives of its creator are decisive, and the merit of the object itself is a separate issue. The question mark in the title of Mark Jones's *Fake? The*
(5) *Art of Deception* reveals the study's broader concerns. Indeed, it might equally be entitled *Original?*, and the text begins by noting a variety of possibilities somewhere between the two extremes. These include works by an artist's followers in the style of the master,
(10) deliberate archaism, copying for pedagogical purposes, and the production of commercial facsimiles.

The greater part of *Fake?* is devoted to a chronological survey suggesting that faking feeds on the many different motives people have for collecting
(15) art, and that, on the whole, the faking of art flourishes whenever art collecting flourishes. In imperial Rome there was a widespread interest in collecting earlier Greek art, and therefore, in faking it. No doubt many of the sculptures now exhibited as "Roman copies" were
(20) originally passed off as Greek. In medieval Europe, because art was celebrated more for its devotional uses than for its provenance or the ingenuity of its creators, the faking of art was virtually nonexistent. The modern age of faking again in the Italian Renaissance, with
(25) two linked developments: a passionate identification with the world of antiquity and a growing sense of individual artistic identity. A patron of the young Michelangelo prevailed upon the artist to make his sculpture *Sleeping Cupid* look as though it had been
(30) buried in the earth so that "it will be taken for antique, and you will sell it much better." Within a few years, however, beginning with his first masterpiece, the *Bacchus*, Michelangelo had shown his contemporaries that great art can assimilate and transcend what came
(35) before, resulting in a wholly original work. Soon his genius made him the object of imitators.

Fake? also reminds us that in certain cultures authenticity is a foreign concept. This is true of much African art, where the authenticity of an object is
(40) considered by collectors to depend on its function. As an illustration, the study compares two versions of a *chi wara* mask made by the Bambara people of Mali. One has pegs allowing it to be attached to a cap for its intended ceremonial purpose. The second, otherwise
(45) identical, lacks the pegs and is a replica made for sale. African carving is notoriously difficult to date, but even if the ritual mask is recent, made perhaps to replace a damaged predecessor, and the replica much older, only the ritual mask should be seen as authentic,
(50) for it is tied to the form's original function. That, at least, is the consensus of the so-called experts. One wonders whether the Bambaran artists would agree.

1. The passage can best be described as doing which one of the following?

    (A) reconciling varied points of view
    (B) chronicling the evolution of a phenomenon
    (C) exploring a complex question
    (D) advocating a new approach
    (E) rejecting an inadequate explanation

2. Which one of the following best expresses the author's main point?

    (A) The faking of art has occurred throughout history and in virtually every culture.
    (B) Whether a work of art is fake or not is less important than whether it has artistic merit.
    (C) It is possible to show that a work of art is fake, but the authenticity of a work cannot be proved conclusively.
    (D) A variety of circumstances make it difficult to determine whether a work of art can appropriately be called a fake.
    (E) Without an international market to support it, the faking of art would cease.

3. According to the passage, an artwork can be definitively classified as a fake if the person who created it

    (A) consciously adopted the artistic style of an influential mentor.
    (B) deliberately imitated a famous work of art as a learning exercise.
    (C) wanted other people to be fooled by its appearance.
    (D) made multiple, identical copies of the work available for sale.
    (E) made the work resemble the art of an earlier era.

4. The author provides a least one example of each of the following EXCEPT:

    (A) categories of art that are neither wholly fake nor wholly original.
    (B) cultures in which the faking or art flourished.
    (C) qualities that art collectors have prized in their acquisitions.
    (D) cultures in which the categories "fake" and "original" do not apply.
    (E) contemporary artists whose works have inspired fakes.

5. The author implies which one of the following about the artistic merits of fakes?

   (A) Because of the circumstances of its production, a fake cannot be said to have true artistic merit.
   (B) A fake can be said to have artistic merit only if the attempted deception is successful.
   (C) A fake may or may not have artistic merit in its own right, regardless of the circumstances of its production.
   (D) Whether a fake has artistic merit depends on whether its creator is accomplished as an artist.
   (E) The artistic merit of a fake depends on the merit of the original work that inspired the fake.

6. By the standard described in the last paragraph of the passage, which one of the following would be considered authentic?

   (A) an ancient Roman copy of an ancient Greek sculpture
   (B) a painting begun by a Renaissance master and finished by his assistants after his death
   (C) a print of a painting signed by the artist who painted the original
   (D) a faithful replica of a ceremonial crown that preserves all the details of, and is indistinguishable from, the original
   (E) a modern reconstruction of a medieval altarpiece designed to serve its traditional role in a service of worship

7. Which one of the following best describes how the last paragraph functions in the context of the passage?

   (A) It offers a tentative answer to a question posed by the author in the opening paragraph.
   (B) It summarizes an account provided in detail in the preceding paragraph.
   (C) It provides additional support for an argument advanced by the author in the preceding paragraph.
   (D) It examines another facet of a distinction developed in the preceding paragraphs.
   (E) It affirms the general principle enunciated at the beginning of the passage.

Passage 1: Fake Artwook

What Makes It Difficult?

Though this is a fairly short passage, its discussion of what constitutes a fake artwork lacks a strong author's point of view. It's easy to get caught up in the details, and the attempt to process every word of the passage ("celebrated more for its devotional uses than for its provenance") can make for slow going. Even the first paragraph, which normally reveals the topic and scope of the passage fairly clearly, mostly hints at the structure that will come. Remember to keep focused on the larger picture and don't loose sight of the task at hand; to understand the main idea, and to know where to come back to the passage to research more specific questions.

Key Points of the Passage

Purpose and Main Idea: The author's purpose is to review what Jones does in his book; in her phrase, she wants to "reveal the study's broader concerns." The main idea is simply that, as Jones illustrates, the issue of fake vs. original art is far more complicated than the mere question of "Was something faked?" The motive behind faking proves to be important, and in some cultures, function is key as well.

Paragraph Structure: Paragraph 1 begins by giving a necessary condition for fake art—that the motive of the copier be to deceive; the work's merit is a separate thing. The author immediately uses Mark Jones' book *Fake?* to carry further the idea that fakery isn't just a matter of making a copy: There are other relevant issues, motive being one big one. And indeed, the paragraph lists situations that fall "somewhere between the two extremes" of original on the one hand, and fake on the other. One can readily concede that neither copying a master's work, nor deliberately evoking the past, nor copying for teaching purposes, nor making facsimiles to be sold (close paraphrases of the four items in lines 8–11), meets the definition of "intended to deceive." They're not original; but they're not fake either, at least by lines 1–2's definition. So it is a knotty issue.

Paragraph 2, as lines 12–17 promise, distills the bulk of *Fake?: The Art Of Deception* into a tour of how and why art was faked, from ancient Rome (where a big market in ancient Greek stuff inspired much fakery), through the Middle Ages (an era too religious to countenance much artistic funny business), to the Renaissance (where fakery really came into its own, for the reasons laid out in lines 23–27). And all the way through, the alert critical reader should be thinking about each era in the light of lines 12–17's promise to focus on "the many different motives" at work in art collection and art fakery. Presumably Jones's book takes one to the present day, but our author has polished off her take on present-day fakery in paragraph 1 and so our chronological summary stops with the often-faked Michelangelo.

Paragraph 3 is really a side trip: The author's still on the topic of fake art, but the scope has shifted to a specific exception that is illustrated by a specific example from Jones's book. African art, we're told, illustrates that in some cultures, functionality is important to whether a copy is fake or not. She offers the two Bambara *chi wara* masks—identical but for the pegs that attach the mask to a cap during a ritual—as an example of an instance in which authenticity hinges on function.

Answers and Explanations

1. C   2. D   3. C   4. E   5. C   6. E   7. D

1. C

The question is simple: "What's the passage doing?" But the given choices are so brief that all five may look appealing. Your best bet is first to come up with your own statement of the purpose. The overall passage brings up, and discusses at length, issues about fake art raised by Jones's book. It is, therefore, an "exploration." And from paragraph 1, where you learn that much artwork can fall into an ambiguous middle ground between original and fake, to the very last sentence—a hint that even the artistic creators, the Bambara, might disagree with self-styled experts as to what is "fake"—the author never fails to reinforce the idea that the question of what constitutes fake art is a complex one. (C) is amply justified.

(A) describes a passage in which different people's points of view are brought together/synthesized. But this is Mark Jones's book as viewed by a very sympathetic author. Nothing to reconcile.

(B) Jones takes a chronological approach, says lines 12–13, but the passage's author does not.

(D) describes a passage in which the author tries to get us to accept a new—usually her own—vision. But this author is simply articulating aspects of Jones's vision.

(E) "Explanation" doesn't apply; "interpretation" would be better. But in any event, our author likes Jones's book very much. No rejection here.

2. D

Your pre-phrasing of the author's main point should have followed up on your Global thinking in question 1, and encompassed the idea—supported by Jones's work and explained approvingly by the author—that "fakery" goes well beyond the mere circumstances of a copy's creation. That's not word for word (D), but it's extremely close.

(A) The passage doesn't indicate enough about every past culture to know whether "virtually everyone" sees art fakery. Certainly medieval Europe did not (lines 20–23). And that fakery "flourishes whenever art collecting" does (lines 15–16) implies that the degree of art fakery varies from era to era and, therefore, from culture to culture.

(B) Artistic merit and the whole issue of fakery are separate issues, says paragraph 1, but that doesn't imply that one is "less important than" the other.

(C) According to lines 37–38, only in some cultures is authenticity something that cannot be proven.

(E) Not only is no such extreme prediction about art fakery supported by the text, but the tone of paragraph 2 implies that fakery will go on whenever art collecting does.

An Advanced test taker always predicts the passage's purpose and main idea before moving on to the questions, because she knows that odds are high at least one question will ask for these ideas.

---

3. C

You need look no further than lines 1–2 for this one. The necessary condition for fake art is that it be "an artwork intended to deceive," and (C) just provides a straightforward paraphrase of that idea.

(A), (D), and (E) are all mentioned in paragraph 1 as examples of "middle ground" situations in which the issue of fake vs. original is mighty blurry. None of them acts as a definition of fake art.

(B) Deliberate fooling is what characterizes fake art, not deliberate imitation. Deliberate imitation need not be fake—as paragraph 1 makes clear. It depends on the creator's motive…which comes back to (C).

An Advanced test taker knows that making a prediction and scanning for choices that match make short (and confident) work of the answer choices.

---

4. E

In this EXCEPT question, four of the choices play a role in the passage, which suggests that the right answer is probably outside of its scope.

You can review the text, or seek out the wrong choices, or search for the odd man out directly. In any case, the search is aided if you realize that paragraph 2's review of Jones's chronology stops at Michelangelo, and so you never find out about (E), names of any contemporary artists whose work has been faked. All of the others appear:

(A) Lines 8–11 list those categories.

(B) Ancient Rome and the Renaissance would be two such cultures.

(C) For example, lines 25–27 detail qualities that were prized during the Renaissance.

(D) African art (lines 37–38) is one culture in which the categories don't apply.

5. C

The only reference to artistic merit comes in paragraph 1, specifically lines 2–3, where you learn that "merit" and "fakery" are two wholly separate issues. Search for that sentiment and you find it squarely in (C).

(A) and (B) both try to interrelate the issues of merit and fakery, (A) arguing that they're mutually exclusive, (B) that they're correlated. Neither are correct: They are separate issues altogether—as (C) realizes.

(D) and (E) each mentions an element that the passage never alludes to, or even implies.

An Advanced test taker uses the clues in the question stem to research exactly where in the passage an answer choice should come from.

---

6. E

The author's definition of authenticity appears not once but twice in paragraph 3: Lines 39–40 and 49–50 both assert that the functionality of an object determines its authenticity. Among the choices, then, find an object "tied to the form's original function," and only (E)—a copied item "designed to serve its traditional role"—meets that definition. The other choices mention function not at all; even (D), which describes an object virtually identical to its original, falls short because you never hear that the ceremonial crown is meant to be used.

7. D

In our analysis of the Paragraph Structure, above, we called paragraph 3 a "side trip," a visit to a different kind of cultural milieu and a very different sense of how the issue of fakery applies there. (D) picks up on paragraph 3's shift of scope to "another facet" of the distinction between original and fake.

(A) The opening paragraph poses no question for paragraph 3, or any other, to answer.

(B), (C) What paragraph 3 has to offer, of course, is new to the passage, having no necessary relation to paragraph 2 except that both discuss an aspect of the general topic of fakery.

(E) Paragraph 3 has no real and definite link to paragraph 1, either.

What's Next?

Let's move on to our next tough passage. In this one we make the leap from artwork to another seemingly innocuous humanities topic, fairy tales.

PASSAGE 2

Fairy tales address themselves to two communities, each with its own interests and each in periodic conflict with the other: parents and children. Nearly every study of fairy tales has taken the perspective of the
(5) parent, constructing the meaning of the tales by using the reading strategies of an adult bent on identifying universally valid tenets of moral instruction for children.

For example, the plot of "Hansel and Gretel" is set
(10) in motion by hard-hearted parents who abandon their children in the woods. But for psychologist Bruno Bettelheim, the tale is really about children who learn to give up their unhealthy dependency on their parents. According to Bettelheim, this story—in which the
(15) children ultimately overpower a witch who has taken them prisoner for the crime of attempting to eat the witch's gingerbread house—forces its young audience to recognize the dangers of unrestrained greed. As dependent children, Bettelheim argues, Hansel and
(20) Gretel had been a burden to their parents, but on their return home with the witch's jewels, they become the family's support. Thus, says Bettelheim, does the story train its young listeners to become "mature children."

There are two ways of interpreting a story: one is a
(25) "superficial" reading that focuses on the tale's manifest content, and the other is a "deeper" reading that looks for latent meanings. Many adults who read fairy tales are drawn to this second kind of interpretation in order to avoid facing the unpleasant truths that can emerge
(30) from the tales when adults—even parents—are portrayed as capable of acting out of selfish motives themselves. What makes fairy tales attractive to Bettelheim and other psychologists is that they can be used as scenarios that position the child as a
(35) transgressor whose deserved punishment provides a lesson for unruly children. Stories that run counter to such orthodoxies about child-rearing are, to a large extent, suppressed by Bettelheim or "rewritten" through reinterpretation. Once we examine his
(40) interpretations closely, we see that his readings produce meanings that are very different from those constructed by readers with different cultural assumptions and expectations, who, unlike Bettelheim, do not find inflexible tenets of moral instruction in the
(45) tales.

Bettelheim interprets all fairy tales as driven by children's fantasies of desire and revenge, and in doing so suppresses the true nature of parental behavior ranging from abuse to indulgence. Fortunately, these
(50) characterizations of selfish children and innocent adults have been discredited to some extent by recent psychoanalytic literature. The need to deny adult evil has been a pervasive feature of our society, leading us to position children not only as the sole agents of evil
(55) but also as the objects of unending moral instruction, hence the idea that a literature targeted for them must stand in the service of pragmatic instrumentality rather than foster an unproductive form of playful pleasure.

1. Which one of the following most accurately states the main idea of the passage?

   (A) While originally written for children, fairy tales also contain a deeper significance for adults that psychologists such as Bettelheim have shown to be their true meaning.

   (B) The "superficial" reading of a fairy tale, which deals only with the tale's content, is actually more enlightening for children than the "deeper" reading preferred by psychologists such as Bettelheim.

   (C) Because the content of fairy tales has historically run counter to prevailing orthodoxies about child-rearing, psychologists such as Bettelheim sometimes reinterpret them to suit their own pedagogical needs.

   (D) The pervasive need to deny adult evil has led psychologists such as Bettelheim to erroneously view fairy tales solely as instruments of moral instruction for children.

   (E) Although dismissed as unproductive by psychologists such as Bettelheim, fairy tales offer children imaginative experiences that help them grow into morally responsible adults.

2. Based on the passage, which one of the following elements of "Hansel and Gretel" would most likely be de-emphasized in Bettelheim's interpretation of the tale?

   (A) Hansel and Gretel are abandoned by their hard-hearted parents.
   (B) Hansel and Gretel are imprisoned by the witch.
   (C) Hansel and Gretel overpower the witch.
   (D) Hansel and Gretel take the witch's jewels.
   (E) Hansel and Gretel bring the witch's jewels home to their parents.

3. Which one of the following is the most accurate description of the author's attitude toward Bettelheim's view of fairy tales?

    (A) concern that the view will undermine the ability of fairy tales to provide moral instruction

    (B) scorn toward the view's supposition that moral tenets can be universally valid

    (C) disapproval of the view's depiction of children as selfish and adults as innocent

    (D) anger toward the view's claim that children often improve as a result of deserved punishment

    (E) disappointment with the view's emphasis on the manifest content of a tale

4. The author of the passage would be most likely to agree with which one of the following statements?

    (A) Children who never attempt to look for the deeper meanings in fairy tales will miss out on one of the principal pleasures of reading such tales.

    (B) It is better if children discover fairy tales on their own than for an adult to suggest that they read the tales.

    (C) A child who is unruly will behave better after reading a fairy tale if the tale is suggested to them by another child.

    (D) Most children are too young to comprehend the deeper meanings contained in fairy tales.

    (E) Children should be allowed to enjoy literature that has no instructive purpose.

5. Which one of the following principles most likely underlies the author's characterization of literary interpretation?

    (A) Only those trained in literary interpretation can detect the latent meanings in stories.

    (B) Only adults are psychologically mature enough to find the latent meanings in stories.

    (C) Only one of the various meanings readers may find in a story is truly correct.

    (D) The meanings we see in stories are influenced by the assumptions and expectations we bring to the story.

    (E) The latent meanings a story contains are deliberately placed there by the author.

6. According to the author, recent psychoanalytic literature suggests that

    (A) the moral instruction children receive from fairy tales is detrimental to their emotional development

    (B) fewer adults are guilty of improper child rearing than had once been thought

    (C) the need to deny adult evil is a pervasive feature of all modern societies

    (D) the plots of many fairy tales are similar to children's revenge fantasies

    (E) the idea that children are typically selfish and adults innocent is of questionable validity

7. It can be inferred from the passage that Bettelheim believes that children are

    (A) uninterested in inflexible tenets of moral instruction

    (B) unfairly subjected to the moral beliefs of their parents

    (C) often aware of inappropriate parental behavior

    (D) capable of shedding undesirable personal qualities

    (E) basically playful and carefree

8. Which one of the following statements is least compatible with Bettelheim's views, as those views are described in the passage?

    (A) The imaginations of children do not draw clear distinctions between inanimate objects and living things.

    (B) Children must learn that their own needs and feelings are to be valued, even when these differ from those of their parents.

    (C) As their minds mature, children tend to experience the world in terms of the dynamics of the family into which they were born.

    (D) The more secure that children feel within the world, the less they need to hold onto infantile notions.

    (E) Children's ability to distinguish between stories and reality is not fully developed until puberty.

Passage 2: Fairy Tales

What Makes It Difficult?

This passage seems, at first glance, to be a straightforward one on a familiar topic, fairy tales. The text quickly becomes dense, however, introducing psychologist Bettelheim, and his theories of interpretation. The language is complex, and the second half of paragraph 3 presents several sentences that can bog down the unwary test taker who insists on trying to sort out all of the specifics.

Key Points of the Passage

Purpose and Main Idea: The author's purpose is to argue against Bettelheim's theory of fairy tales as tools for the moral instruction of disobedient children, and to suggest that fairy tales may really just be "an unproductive form of playful pleasure." Thus the author's main idea can be easily pre-phrased as, simply, "fairy tales should be viewed as playful fun for children, not a means of making them behave as adults wish."

Paragraph Structure: Paragraph 1 explains that there are two points of view about fairy tales, and elaborates upon the (more prevalent) first view, that parents seek to offer moral instruction through the use of fairy tales.

"For example" kicks off paragraph 2, and what "Hansel and Gretel" exemplifies is that parental perspective. The author cites Bettelheim's morally centered interpretation; note lines 22–23 and its clear indication that, to Bettelheim, "Hansel and Gretel" is instructional to its kiddie audience.

Paragraph 3 may seem to wander a bit as it highlights the "superficial" and "deeper" ways of reading a story, but one soon sees that the latter is at the heart of the parental/Bettelheim approach; lines 27–32 confirm this. The rest of the paragraph offers the author's critique of that approach. That is, the reason that parents (and Bettelheim) are drawn to interpretations in which erring children are "improved," is because they dislike seeing parents portrayed as villains—even though it's quite clear (cf. lines 9–11 and 29–32) that adult misdeeds are present in the stories.

The end of the paragraph says that the stories can provide "different meanings" from the moral/instructional, but it's left to paragraph 4 to explain those meanings (after pointing out that the Bettelheim view has been largely discredited.) It is wrong to deny adult evil, and to put all the onus on the child (as Bettelheim and his ilk would do). Moreover, a story can legitimately be enjoyed on its "superficial" level, for pleasure alone.

An Advanced test taker reads for multiple points of view and keeps each separate.

Answers and Explanations

1. D   2. A   3. C   4. E   5. D   6. E   7. D   8. B

1. D

The entire movement of the passage is toward the third and fourth paragraphs' denunciation of the parent-centric, morally instructive view of fairy tales—the Bettelheim view—and only (D) picks up on that critique.

(A) is a classic 180, praising rather than decrying the Bettelheim interpretation.

(B) Certainly the author prefers the "superficial" reading of fairy tales (i.e. for simple pleasure), but (B) drags in the old idea of children's enlightenment, precisely what the author wants us to get away from.

(C) takes one detail (lines 36–39) and blows it up into the main idea. The author goes far beyond (C), as correct choice (D) attests.

(E) pushes the "moral/instructional" line that the author deplores, and even goes so far awry as to imply that Bettelheim was opposed to that line.

2. A

Bettelheim's interest is in denying "the true nature of parental behavior," in "position[ing] the child as a transgressor." Only (A) focuses on the parents' malign role in the "Hansel and Gretel" story, so it would not be part of his reading. The other choices describe elements of the story that lead to Bettelheim's sense that it's a story of children becoming mature.

> An Advanced test taker remembers that inference questions require you to think about what "must be true" based on the passage.

3. C

All five of the choices' main nouns recognize that the author disagrees with Bettelheim, and you must seek the one that takes issue with his view of fairy tales as vehicles for improving errant children at the behest of blameless parents. (C) is right on.

(A) Since the author dislikes the use of fairy tales for moral instruction, the last thing s/he would be "concerned" about is an undermining of that usage.

(B) "Universally valid moral tenets" appears in line 7; it's not a phrase or an issue to which the author returns. Whether moral tenets are universal or various, what gets the author's goat is the use of fairy tales to convey them.

(D) implies that the author is interested in child rearing—specifically, the effects of punishment on behavior—rather than on the interpretation of literature.

(E) On the contrary, a tale's "manifest content"—the superficial elements that can be read simply for pleasure—is what's lacking from the Bettelheim view.

4. E

(A) is the latest in a wearying series of wrong answers that fail to notice that the author dislikes the so-called deeper meanings, and wants fairy tales to be read for pure pleasure.

(B) The challenge of getting kids to read falls outside the scope.

(C) Recommendations from peers fall outside the scope; and in any case the passage is concerned with interpretations of texts, not with whether fairy tales can or do actually improve children.

(D), like (A), implies that so-called "deeper meanings" are to be sought, when the author plainly means for them to be avoided.

(E) is all that's left, and it had better be correct. It is. It says simply what lines 56–58 said more wordily, that moral instruction need have no place in kids' reading diet.

5. D

Here's another question where prediction is probably useless. Your best bet is to attack the choices in turn and look for support for one of them in the text.

(A) is contradicted by the fact that Bettelheim and other psychologists (however misguidedly) are clearly able to detect "latent meanings" in fairy tales, even though there's no reason to believe that they are trained interpreters.

(B) If Bettelheim is right, children can do so as well. But even if he's wrong, the author doesn't take the position that (B) implies, that only adults should be messing with interpretative activities.

(C) is a 180, since the author explicitly (in lines 39–41) acknowledges the possibility of multiple meanings.

(D) puts in abstract terms what the author is arguing all along. For instance, it's the assumptions that Bettelheim et al. bring—that we should deny adult evil, and should see fairy tales as instructive—that shape their interpretation. (D) is strongly supported by the passage.

(E) Author intent is utterly irrelevant to the discussion of fairy tales, none of whose authors are ever mentioned.

6. E

"Recent psychoanalytic literature" is a Hot Words phrase that points directly to lines 51–52, where it's written that it's "fortunate" that Bettelheim's notions have been "discredited." Those notions—that all fairy tales are about "selfish children and innocent adults," lines 46–49—are summarized by (E).

(A) The author doesn't subscribe to the moral-improvement approach to fairy tales, let alone to the idea that the tales hurt when they're designed to help.

(B) If anything, the sense in paragraph 4 is that adults are guiltier than they've been characterized in the past.

(C) No, the "need to deny adult evil has been a pervasive feature of our society."

(D) reflects lines 46–49, and thus summarizes what recent psychoanalytic literature has rejected, not suggested.

An Advanced test taker uses Hot Words to help zero in on the correct answer choice.

---

7. D

Bettelheim must believe that children are behaviorally malleable (D), otherwise he wouldn't go to such pains to treat fairy tales as vehicles for such molding.

(A) Bettelheim seems interested in using fairy tales for moral instruction whether kids are interested in it or not.

(B) is a view sympathetic to kids against their parents, and hence at odds with Bettelheim's sense of things.

(C) Children's awareness or unawareness never enters the scope of the passage.

(E) If Bettelheim accepted this view of kids, he'd probably be less insistent on the moral uplift of literature and more likely to support the kind of reading that reflects carefree play.

8. B

Four of the five choices will sit easily with Bettelheim's view of the world. That doesn't mean that Bettelheim must necessarily agree with the four wrong answers, simply that they don't contradict his views. (And the likelihood is that the right answer, which contradicts Bettelheim, is probably something that our author would propound.) Attack the choices in order.

(A)'s idea that kids don't clearly distinguish living things and objects doesn't contradict any of Bettelheim's ideas, and may get slight support from the way in which Hansel and Gretel seem to see the witch's gingerbread house and jewels as extensions of human personality. In any case (A) is consistent with the idea that very young children can be molded through vivid stories.

(B), which celebrates children's self-image over parental priorities, runs counter to Bettelheim's notion of the "child as transgressor" who is in need of "unending moral instruction." Hence (B) is the right answer here.

(C) Bettelheim would have no problem with (C)'s family centric conception of child development; it would fit in nicely with the idea that parents are innocent and kids are to be molded by them.

(D) essentially defines the assumption that Bettelheim is making when he asserts that a story can apply "universally valid" moral tenets to train children into maturity.

(E), like (A) is consonant with the idea that very young children's behavior and moral sense can be molded through the use of fairy tales.

What's Next?

Had enough of humanities? The next two passages will come from social sciences, but that doesn't mean that they're a piece of cake.

PASSAGE 3

Recent investigations into the psychology of decision making have sparked interest among scholars seeking to understand why governments sometimes take gambles that appear theoretically unjustifiable on
(5) the basis of expected costs and benefits. Researchers have demonstrated some significant discrepancies between objective measurements of possible decision outcomes and the ways in which people subjectively value such possible results. Many of these
(10) discrepancies relate to the observation that a possible outcome perceived as a loss typically motivates more strongly than the prospect of an equivalent gain. Risk taking is thus a more common strategy for those who believe they will lose what they already possess than it
(15) is for those who wish to gain something they do not have.

Previously, the notion that rational decision makers prefer risk-avoiding choices was considered to apply generally, epitomized by the assumption of many
(20) economists that entrepreneurs and consumers will choose a risky venture over a sure thing only when the expected measurable value of the outcome is sufficiently high to compensate the decision maker for taking the risk. What is the minimum prize that would
(25) be required to make a gamble involving a 50 percent chance of losing $100 and a 50 percent chance of winning the prize acceptable? It is commonplace that the pleasure of winning a sum of money is much less intense than the pain of losing the same amount;
(30) accordingly, such a gamble would typically be accepted only when the possible gain greatly exceeds the possible loss. Research subjects do, in fact, commonly judge that a 50 percent chance to lose $100 is unacceptable unless it is combined with an equal
(35) chance to win more than $300. Nevertheless, the recent studies indicate that risk-accepting strategies are common when the alternative to a sure loss is a substantial chance of losing an even larger amount, coupled with some chance—even a small one—of
(40) losing nothing.

Such observations are quite salient to scholars of international conflict and crisis. For example, governments typically are cautious in foreign policy initiatives that entail risk, especially the risk of armed
(45) conflict. But nations also often take huge gambles to retrieve what they perceive to have been taken from them by other nations. This type of motivation, then, can lead states to take risks that far outweigh the objectively measurable value of the lost assets. For
(50) example, when Britain and Argentina entered into armed conflict in 1982 over possession of the Falkland Islands—or Malvinas, as they are called in Spanish— each viewed the islands as territory that had been taken from them by the other; thus each was willing to
(55) commit enormous resources—and risks—to recapturing them. In international affairs, it is vital that each actor in such a situation understand the other's subjective view of what is at stake.

1. Suppose that a country seizes a piece of territory with great mineral wealth that is claimed by a neighboring country, with a concomitant risk of failure involving moderate but easily tolerable harm in the long run. Given the information in the passage, the author would most likely say that

   (A) the country's actions are consistent with previously accepted views of the psychology of risk-taking

   (B) the new research findings indicate that the country from which the territory has been seized probably weighs the risk factors involved in the situation similarly to the way in which they are weighed by the aggressor nation

   (C) in spite of surface appearances to the contrary, the new research findings suggest that the objective value of the potential gain is overridden by the risks

   (D) the facts of the situation show that the government is motivated by factors other than objective calculation of the measurable risks and probable benefits

   (E) the country's leaders most likely subjectively perceive the territory as having been taken from their country in the past

2. The question in lines 24–27 functions primarily as

   (A) the introduction to a thought experiment whose results the author expects will vary widely among different people

   (B) a rhetorical question whose assumed answer is in conflict with the previously accepted view concerning risk-taking behavior

   (C) the basis for an illustration of how the previously accepted view concerning risk-taking behavior applies accurately to some types of situations

   (D) a suggestion that the discrepancies between subjective and objective valuations of possible decision outcomes are more illusive than real

   (E) a transitional device to smooth an otherwise abrupt switch from discussion of previous theories to discussion of some previously unaccepted research findings

3. It can most reasonably be inferred from the passage that the author would agree with which one of the following statements?

   (A) When states try to regain losses through risky conflict, they generally are misled by inadequate or inaccurate information as to the risks that they run in doing so.

   (B) Government decision makers subjectively evaluate the acceptability of risks involving national assets in much the same way that they would evaluate risks involving personal assets.

   (C) A new method for predicting and mediating international conflict has emerged from a synthesis of the fields of economics and psychology.

   (D) Truly rational decision making is a rare phenomenon in international crises and can, ironically, lead to severe consequences for those who engage in it.

   (E) Contrary to previous assumptions, people are more likely to take substantial risks when their subjective assessments of expected benefits match or exceed the objectively measured costs.

4. The passage can be most accurately described as

   (A) a psychological analysis of the motives involved in certain types of collective decision making in the presence of conflict

   (B) a presentation of a psychological hypothesis that is then subjected to a political test case

   (C) a suggestion that psychologists should incorporate the findings of political scientists into their research

   (D) an examination of some new psychological considerations regarding risk and their application to another field of inquiry

   (E) a summary of two possible avenues for understanding international crises and conflicts

5. The passage most clearly suggests that the author would agree with which one of the following statements?

   (A) Researchers have previously been too willing to accept the claims that subjects make about their preferred choices in risk-related decision problems.

   (B) There is inadequate research support for the hypothesis that except when a gamble is the only available means for averting an otherwise certain loss, people typically are averse to risk taking.

   (C) It can reasonably be argued that the risk that Britain accepted in its 1982 conflict with Argentina outweighed the potential objectively measurable benefit of that venture.

   (D) The new findings suggest that because of the subjective elements involved, governmental strategies concerning risks of loss in international crises will remain incomprehensible to outside observers.

   (E) Moderate risks in cases involving unavoidable losses are often taken on the basis of reasoning that diverges markedly from that which was studied in the recent investigations.

Passage 3: Risk-Taking

What Makes It Difficult?

This passage starts off with a thorny first sentence, and things don't get easier from there. The topic—the psychology of decision-making—will be unfamiliar to most students, and the language is extremely dense. The paragraphs are long, and the fact that there are numbers in the second paragraph can be intimidating (even though the LSAT will never require you to perform calculations with the numbers used).

If the passage looked difficult, the set of questions compounds the challenge. There are only five points to be gained here, but as much text to read in answering them as in many eight question sets. The mix of questions isn't cutting you any slack; only one global question and no detail questions. Finally, the first question has a question stem that's almost as long as full paragraph in itself! For most test-takers this passage can be put off until last and attacked only if there's time; but the Advanced test taker knows she needs to tackle all of the passages to be successful on Test Day.

Key Points of the Passage

Purpose and Main Idea: The author's purpose is to explain recent findings regarding governmental risk taking. The main idea is that this recent research reveals that governments are more likely to take a risk to keep what they have (or what they believe to be already theirs) than to gain something they do not possess. A careful reading of the first paragraph laid this out, and the rest of the passage develops the ideas; a critical reader should be reassured as she sees the rest of the passage follow what she expected to see.

Paragraph Structure: Paragraph 1 lays bare the broad themes of the passage. Research has been done recently into risky behavior, especially by government; they found "significant discrepancies," "loss motivates more strongly than gain." There's a conclusion keyword in line 13 that helps point out the ultimate results; "thus" those who believe they are losing something are more inclined to take a risk than are those who seek to gain something new.

Paragraph 2 discusses the earlier research that "previously" it was thought that all decision makers would avoid risk unless there was a large incentive to do otherwise. Then comes a large example with lots of math in it, but the critical reader can skim to line 35 and the keyword "nevertheless," and the current research that modifies earlier thinking as to when risk is acceptable.

Paragraph 3 applies this psychology, especially the latter kind, to the behavior of governments. Why, the author wonders, don't governments always act according to objective cost-benefit analyses? The new findings tell us that, objectivity notwithstanding and irrespective of straightforwardly computed costs and benefits, when we feel that we have a lot to lose, we may be willing to take a big risk after all. That newly arrived at idea—that by far the bigger inducement is the avoidance of loss, a "subjective" judgment—is by the end brought to bear on the behavior of nations.

Answers and Explanations

1. A   2. C   3. B   4. D   5. C

1. A

Work on question 1 may be facilitated by trying the other four questions first. In any event, the hypothetical situation advanced here almost precisely mirrors the thinking described in lines 19–24. The "great mineral wealth" represents the "high expected measurable value," and the 0"com pensat[ion]…for taking the risk" is explicitly cited as "moderate" and "easily tolerable." Question 1's country is clearly choosing a risky venture along the lines of the "previous assumption," as choice (A) describes.

There's no information about how the country whose territory is being seized (B) would react, nor do the new findings shed light on it—after all, the acted-upon country isn't the one taking any risks. (C) has it backward: To the seizing country, the risks are clearly outweighed by the expected objective value (that's why it seized the territory in the first place). As usual on the LSAT, "motivation" (D) is almost a sure sign of a wrong answer. Here, if the situation is taken on its face, the seizing government seems motivated only by calculation of risks and benefits. There's no evidence that the seized territory is perceived in the same way as the Falkland Islands were perceived by both Britain and Argentina (E)—for all we know, the seizing country's first claim on the territory begins right now.

2. C

At this point in the discussion (lines 24–27), the author is dealing with the commonly held view of when and how rational actors take risks—namely, once we have objectively assessed costs and benefits. The question about the gamble is objectively assessed, and answered in lines 32–35. As correct choice (C) has it, the discussion illustrates the idea that oftentimes we do take risks based on objective factors, as has long been believed.

(A) implies that the author is conducting future experiments rather than reporting on past ones. Since lines 24–27's question is explicitly answered (the answer is, "about $300"), it certainly is not rhetorical (B). (D) blows up the objectivity/subjectivity thing into a full-out "discrepancy" or disagreement, when in fact the author is saying that both come into play in the decision making of nations. (E) implies that the author is awkwardly shifting gears when in fact it's all rather elegantly laid out, and that the findings were previously "unaccepted," when in fact they were merely previously unknown.

An Advanced test taker predicts the answer to a function question, in order to avoid tempting wrong answer choices.

---

3. B

The passage is explicitly dealing only with "rational decision makers" (line 17), but (A) is describing an incomplete and chaotic process at odds with the text. (B) is the winner, connecting the new findings about individuals' risk taking (cf. the "research subjects" and their assessment of gambling risks, lines 32+) with the risk taking of governments (paragraph 3). The test taker is well advised to examine all five choices, but not with respect or reverence. Once you've found a winner, your expectation should be that the others are poor. Check to make sure that they are. (C) certainly is: This is not a new "method"; there's nothing about "prediction of conflict"; and the "synthesis of…economics and psychology" is both inaccurate and too grandiose (if anything, it's a synthesis of the objective and subjective factors that enter into the gambles we take). (D)'s apocalyptic tone has no support in the text, and since (as noted with regard to (A) above) the scope of the passage is solely rational thinking, (D) is very peculiar in stating that such decision making is "rare." Meanwhile, that which (E) describes—the assessment of costs and benefits—is an objective approach rather than a subjective one, and is in line with "previous assumptions," not "contrary" to them.

4. D

(D) has it all, picking up on both the focus of the recent research findings and the author's interest in their impact on the "other field of inquiry," that of governmental decision-making.

(A) is most notable for what it lacks: namely, any reference to new findings or the decision making of governments. Also, to say that researchers have analyzed psychology is not to say that a report (like this passage) on their findings is itself "a psychological analysis." (B)'s "political test case" is obviously meant to be the 1982 war, but (B) misrepresents that detail, which is included to illustrate the applicability of the recent findings and not to test whether those findings apply. (C) implies an advocacy purpose on the part of the author, which is (maybe) hinted at in the last sentence only, and if anything, the author wants political science to take psychology into account, not vice versa. (E), like other wrong choices we've seen, seems to think that there is some sort of conflict or dichotomy at the heart of the passage, when in fact both are cited as valid. In any case, the objective and subjective are ways of understanding how governments react to "crises and conflicts"; they're not a means of understanding the crises and conflicts themselves.

An Advanced test taker recognizes that any question asking about the passage as a whole is a Global.

---

5. C

(A) puzzlingly brings up an issue in which the author shows no interest, namely the relationship between researchers and their gullibility in terms of their test subjects. (B) makes a hash of such concepts as "risk taking" and "certain loss," and, in any case, the author is out to celebrate these new findings, not to carp on their "inadequacy." You had to figure that paragraph 3's concrete example would show up in a question somewhere, and here it is in the last question's correct choice (C). How Britain and Argentina felt about the islands in question (i.e. that each had had the islands wrested by the other) is, again, a "feeling," a subjective judgment, and it's cited precisely to show how feelings can trump a nation's objective good judgment; we can safely infer that the author would agree with (C).

On Test Day one would probably stop there, but we hope that you'd at least peek at (D) and (E) to confirm that they're as bad as they need to be, and indeed they both prove to be 180's. The new findings help us to understand why governments may choose to take illogical risks, thus rendering their logic more "comprehensible" to us outsiders rather than less so (D), and the reasoning that was recently investigated was clearly in line with observed governmental decision making, not "divergent from" it (E).

What's Next?

How's it going so far? Next up we present one more social-sciences passage before moving on to the more specialized and esoteric material. Do what you can with it and then check out the explanations.

PASSAGE 4

In explaining the foundations of the discipline known as historical sociology—the examination of history using the methods of sociology—historical sociologist Philip Abrams argues that, while people are

(5) made by society as much as society is made by people, sociologists' approach to the subject is usually to focus on only one of these forms of influence to the exclusion of the other. Abrams insists on the necessity for sociologists to move beyond these one-sided

(10) approaches to understand society as an entity constructed by individuals who are at the same time constructed by their society. Abrams refers to this continuous process as "structuring."

Abrams also sees history as the result of

(15) structuring. People, both individually and as members of collectives, make history. But our making of history is itself formed and informed not only by the historical conditions we inherit from the past, but also by the prior formation of our own identities and capacities,

(20) which are shaped by what Abrams calls "contingencies"—social phenomena over which we have varying degrees of control. Contingencies include such things as the social conditions under which we come of age, the condition of our household's

(25) economy, the ideologies available to help us make sense of our situation, and accidental circumstances. The ways in which contingencies affect our individual or group identities create a structure of forces within which we are able to act, and that partially determines

(30) the sorts of actions we are able to perform.

In Abrams's analysis, historical structuring, like social structuring, is manifold and unremitting. To understand it, historical sociologists must extract from it certain significant episodes, or events, that their

(35) methodology can then analyze and interpret. According to Abrams, these events are points at which action and contingency meet, points that represent a cross section of the specific social and individual forces in play at a given time. At such moments, individuals stand forth

(40) as agents of history not simply because they possess a unique ability to act, but also because in them we see the force of the specific social conditions that allowed their actions to come forth. Individuals can "make their mark" on history, yet in individuals one also finds the

(45) convergence of wider social forces. In order to capture the various facets of this mutual interaction, Abrams recommends a fourfold structure to which he believes the investigations of historical sociologists should conform: first, description of the event itself; second,

(50) discussion of the social context that helped bring the event about and gave it significance; third, summary of the life history of the individual agent in the event; and fourth, analysis of the consequences of the event both for history and for the individual.

1. Which one of the following most accurately states the central idea of the passage?

    (A) Abrams argues that historical sociology rejects the claims of sociologists who assert that the sociological concept of structuring cannot be applied to the interactions between individuals and history.

    (B) Abrams argues that historical sociology assumes that, despite the views of sociologists to the contrary, history influences the social contingencies that affect individuals.

    (C) Abrams argues that historical sociology demonstrates that, despite the views of sociologists to the contrary, social structures both influence and are influenced by the events of history.

    (D) Abrams describes historical sociology as a discipline that unites two approaches taken by sociologists to studying the formation of societies and applies the resulting combined approach to the study of history.

    (E) Abrams describes historical sociology as an attempt to compensate for the shortcomings of traditional historical methods by applying the methods established in sociology.

2. Given the passage's argument, which one of the following sentences most logically completes the last paragraph?

    (A) Only if they adhere to this structure, Abrams believes, can historical sociologists conclude with any certainty that the events that constitute the historical record are influenced by the actions of individuals.

    (B) Only if they adhere to this structure, Abrams believes, will historical sociologists be able to counter the standard sociological assumption that there is very little connection between history and individual agency.

    (C) Unless they can agree to adhere to this structure, Abrams believes, historical sociologists risk having their discipline treated as little more than an interesting but ultimately indefensible adjunct to history and sociology.

    (D) By adhering to this structure, Abrams believes, historical sociologists can shed light on issues that traditional sociologists have chosen to ignore in their one-sided approaches to the formation of societies.

    (E) By adhering to this structure, Abrams believes, historical sociologists will be able to better portray the complex connections between human agency and history.

3. The passage states that a contingency could be each of the following EXCEPT:

    (A) a social phenomenon
    (B) a form of historical structuring
    (C) an accidental circumstance
    (D) a condition controllable to some extent by an individual
    (E) a partial determinant of an individual's actions

4. Which one of the following is most analogous to the ideal work of a historical sociologist as outlined by Abrams?

    (A) In a report on the enactment of a bill into law, a journalist explains why the need for the bill arose, sketches the biography of the principal legislator who wrote the bill, and ponders the effect that the bill's enactment will have both on society and on the legislator's career.
    (B) In a consultation with a patient, a doctor reviews the patient's medical history, suggests possible reasons for the patient's current condition, and recommends steps that the patient should take in the future to ensure that the condition improves or at least does not get any worse.
    (C) In an analysis of a historical novel, a critic provides information to support the claim that details of the work's setting are accurate, explains why the subject of the novel was of particular interest to the author, and compares the novel with some of the author's other books set in the same period.
    (D) In a presentation to stockholders, a corporation's chief executive officer describes the corporation's most profitable activities during the past year, introduces the vice president largely responsible for those activities, and discusses new projects the vice president will initiate in the coming year.
    (E) In developing a film based on a historical event, a filmmaker conducts interviews with participants in the event, bases part of the film's screenplay on the interviews, and concludes the screenplay with a sequence of scenes speculating on the outcome of the event had certain details been different.

5. The primary function of the first paragraph of the passage is to

    (A) outline the merits of Abrams's conception of historical sociology
    (B) convey the details of Abrams's conception of historical sociology
    (C) anticipate challenges to Abrams's conception of historical sociology
    (D) examine the roles of key terms used in Abrams's conception of historical sociology
    (E) identify the basis of Abrams's conception of historical sociology

6. Based on the passage, which one of the following is the LEAST illustrative example of the effect of a contingency upon an individual?

    (A) the effect of the fact that a person experienced political injustice on that person's decision to work for political reform
    (B) the effect of the fact that a person was raised in an agricultural region on that person's decision to pursue a career in agriculture
    (C) the effect of the fact that a person lives in a particular community on that person's decision to visit friends in another community
    (D) the effect of the fact that a person's parents practiced a particular religion on that person's decision to practice that religion
    (E) the effect of the fact that a person grew up in financial hardship on that person's decision to help others in financial hardship

Passage 4: Historical Structuring

What Makes It Difficult?

Much of the difficulty in this passage occurs in the third paragraph. It's long and dense, and lacking in specific examples. Other than the four step process given at the end of the paragraph, there's a dearth of keywords to help you find your way through the text. And the author's viewpoint is lacking; he examines Abrams and Abrams' ideas from a scholarly point of view but never weighs in as to what he actually thinks about Abrams.

Take a look at the questions. There are only six, and three that are a bit unusual—question 2 asks you to logically complete the last paragraph, question 4 (almost as long as the whole passage) is a mouthful, and question 6 asks you to apply what's in the passage, but is also an EXCEPT question, adding to the time required to complete it.

Key Points of the Passage

Purpose and Main Idea: The author's purpose is to describe the methods and philosophies of Abrams; his main idea could be stated as "Abrams believes that in studying history, it is necessary to consider both the effect of society on people, and the effect of people on society."

Paragraph Structure: In paragraph 1, the author tells us that in the field of historical sociology, many scholars have focused almost exclusively on the nature by which people are shaped by society, while other scholars have considered instead how people shape societies. This leads to Abrams's view that historical sociologists should consider both of these related processes, which Abrams groups under the term "structuring."

In paragraph 2, we learn that Abrams also sees structuring at work in the making of history. In other words, people's actions are described and interpreted, and that is what we call history. Abrams's notion of structuring comes into play when we consider that the people who make history are themselves shaped by historical conditions. Abrams refers to these conditions and "contingencies," and they include factors such as economic and political conditions, ideas and belief systems to which one is exposed, and so on. All of these "conditions" of history influence the development of people, who in turn influence the development of history.

In paragraph 3, we find a description of the kind of events that Abrams considers ideal for analysis. These are the points when "action and contingency meet"—that is, these events allow us to see people taking action to change history, but also let us note the forces that shaped the people taking action. The passage closes with a description of a fourfold method that Abrams recommended for analyzing these key points. Savvy test takers won't get bogged down in lists of details like this fourfold method. If a question requires it, we can easily go back for the specifics. Note that nowhere do we get a clear notion of the author's ideas. The entire passage is a fairly neutral description of the methods and philosophies of Philip Abrams. For that reason, there are no inference questions about what the author might agree or disagree with.

An Advanced test taker recognizes that the author may not have a strong positive or negative opinion about his subject.

Answers and Explanations

1. D   2. E   3. B   4. A   5. E   6. C

1. D

When the entire passage centers on the viewpoint of one thinker, beware of answer choices that assume too much about what others in the field think.

Since the passage is so dense, this Main Idea question is especially challenging . In paragraph 1, we read that Abrams suggests combining two approaches employed by many scholars—studying how people influence society, and studying how society influences people. The other paragraphs investigate how these methods apply to the study of history. (D) includes both of these aspects.

(A) We have no indication that anyone has asserted that "structuring" cannot be applied to historical analysis, so we certainly can't say that Abrams is rejecting such an assertion.

(B) and (C) likewise assume without justification that someone is disagreeing with Abrams. We don't know that sociologists would disagree with the theories advanced in the passage, because the entire passage centers on Abrams' views.

(E) is too strong. Abrams argues for applying sociological methods to history, but we have no indication that he would describe traditional methods as possessing "shortcomings."

2. E

When you have narrowed the field down to two choices—like (E) and (D) here—read very carefully to find the chink in the armor of the wrong choice. The passage centers on the concept of "structuring"—the complex influence of people on history (and society), and vice versa. The final paragraph describes a fourfold structure for studying this interaction, so (E) follows well to sum up both the paragraph and the passage.

(A) is rather one-sided, and leaves out the critical concept of individuals being influenced by history.

(B) We know from the first paragraph that most historical sociologists believe that history shaped individuals or vice-versa, so we certainly can't say that these sociologists feel there is no connection.

(C) is far too defensive—we have no reason to believe that historical sociology is not recognized as legitimate in the academic world.

(D) is rather subtly wrong, but is wrong nonetheless. The phrase "chosen to ignore" makes (D) too extreme, since we don't have any evidence from the passage that previous sociologists have actually "ignored" any issues intentionally. Also, this answer choice seems to be pitting historical sociology against traditional sociology, while the fourfold structure that Abrams is advancing is intended more to improve historical—not sociological—analysis.

3. B

For Detail questions, use Hot Words like "Contingency" to guide you back to the right place in the passage to refresh your memory.

Structuring is the interaction of historical contingencies and conditions with individuals. The contingencies themselves are just part of the equation, and so cannot alone be described as "a form of historical structuring," as we see in (B).

(A) See line 21.

(C) See line 26.

(D) See lines 21–22.

(E) See line 29.

An Advanced test taker always refers to the text to answer a detail question.

---

4. A

Just as in Parallel Reasoning in the Logical Reasoning section, the correct answer on questions like this one will show an exact correspondence with the original structure.

What would be an ideal example of historical sociology, according to Abrams? It would follow the fourfold structure he outlines at the end of the passage. Each clause of (A) corresponds to one aspect of this structure: "A report on the enactment of the bill" = "description of the event itself." "Why the need for the bill arose" = "discussion of the social context." "Sketched a brief biography" = "summary of the life history of the individual agent." "Ponders the effect the bill will have both on society and on the legislator's career" = "analysis of the consequences of the event both for history and for the individual."

(B), (C), (D), and (E) all fail to show the neat one-to-one correspondence with the fourfold structure that we see in (A).

5. E

A quick scan of the answer choices can help you quickly see where they agree and disagree.

This reveals that all of the answer choices center on Abrams's conception of historical sociology. So, how does the first paragraph function in relation to this topic? It sets the stage, and tells us the basics of Abrams's theory of structuring, which in turn become the basis for Abrams's conception of historical sociology, as indicated by (E).

(A) Actually, the author of the passage never discusses the merits of the Abrams's concept, and never reveals whether he feels the system has merit at all.

(B) The details, if they are revealed at all, come in the second and third paragraphs, not the first.

(C) We never hear anything about how others might respond to Abrams's conception, so we certainly can't say that the author anticipates these challenges.

(D) Although we first hear the key term structuring in the first paragraph, we don't examine its role in historical sociology until the second and third paragraphs. The first paragraph simply defines the term.

6. C

When a question asks for the LEAST illustrative example, don't bend over backwards to make a choice fit. Here, the four incorrect choices will all be clear examples of how contingencies affect individuals.

First we need to refresh our memories about what contingencies are. They are social phenomena that shape individuals, such as one's upbringing, or the belief systems to which one is exposed. All of the answer choices discuss the effect of an individual's background on a decision made by that individual. (C) is unique because the decision in question is a fairly trivial one: "to visit friends in another community." How would one's living in a particular community affect one's decision to visit friends somewhere else? It's not at all clear, and we might well conclude it has very little effect at all. (C) is not at all a clear example of environment shaping a person's actions. (A), (B), (D), and (E) all illustrate situations in which a person's upbringing or environment could have helped shape major decisions in that person's life.

What's Next?

Still here? Good. In the next chapter we'll explore the wonderful world of science. You don't have to be Einstein to handle these.

CHAPTER THIRTEEN

Blinded by Science

This Reading Comprehension category could also be called "It's Not Brain Surgery—It's Rocket Science." Actually, neither brain surgery nor rocket science would be an unusual topic for the LSAT Reading Comp section. Nor, for that matter, would esoteric, mind-numbingly technical topics such as MRI technology, mitochondria, symbiotic stars, or plate tectonics—the very subjects of the passages that follow.

We at Kaplan designate these as "hard" science passages, not in the sense of being difficult (although they certainly are that), but rather to distinguish these technical science passages from "soft" science passages, which view scientific topics from other angles such as the history or social repercussions of scientific findings. There's not always a "hard" science passage on the test, but when they appear, they often give test takers fits—especially those coming to law from a nontechnical background such as humanities or social science. The key to successfully tackling science passages is to not allow yourself to be overwhelmed by the technical terms and processes described.

An Advanced test taker notes the location and purpose of details, but doesn't attempt to memorize or even fully understand those details unless a question specifically asks about them.

Focus on the author's purpose and main idea, using the mass of details to fill in the big picture rather than to learn everything about the topics presented. You should dig deeper only when a point is at stake. Follow these keys, and when someone asks you how hard the science passages are on the LSAT Reading Comp section, you'll be able to proudly state, "hey, it's not *brain surgery*"—even when it is.

PASSAGE 5

It is a fundamental tenet of geophysics that the Earth's magnetic field can exist in either of two polarity states: a "normal" state, in which north-seeking compass needles point to the
(5) geographic north, and a "reverse" state, in which they point to the geographic south. Geological evidence shows that periodically the field's polarity reverses, and that these reversals have been taking place at an increasing rate. Evidence also indicates
(10) that the field does not reverse instantaneously from one polarity state to another; rather, the process involves a transition period that typically spans a few thousand years.

Though this much is known, the underlying
(15) causes of the reversal phenomenon are not well understood. It is generally accepted that the magnetic field itself is generated by the motion of free electrons in the outer core, a slowly churning mass of molten metal sandwiched between the
(20) Earth's mantle (the region of the Earth's interior lying below the crust) and its solid inner core. In some way that is not completely understood, gravity and the Earth's rotation, acting on temperature and density differences within the
(25) outer core fluid, provide the driving forces behind the generation of the field. The reversal phenomenon may be triggered when something disturbs the heat circulation pattern of the outer core fluid, and with it the magnetic field.
(30) Several explanations for this phenomenon have been proposed. One proposal, the "heat-transfer hypothesis," is that the triggering process is intimately related to the way the outer core vents its heat into the mantle. For example, such heat
(35) transfer could create hotter (rising) or cooler (descending) blobs of material from the inner and outer boundaries of the fluid core, thereby perturbing the main heat-circulation pattern. A more controversial alternative proposal is the
(40) "asteroid-impact hypothesis." In this scenario an extended period of cold and darkness results from the impact of an asteroid large enough to send a great cloud of dust into the atmosphere. Following this climatic change, ocean temperatures drop and
(45) the polar ice caps grow, redistributing the Earth's seawater. This redistribution increases the rotational acceleration of the mantle, causing friction and turbulence near the outer core-mantle boundary and initiating a reversal of the magnetic field.
(50) How well do these hypotheses account for such observations as the long-term increase in the frequency of reversal? In support of the asteroid-impact model, it has been argued that the gradual cooling of the average ocean temperature
(55) would enable progressively smaller asteroid impacts (which are known to occur more frequently than larger impacts) to cool the Earth's climate

sufficiently to induce ice-cap growth and reversals. But theories that depend on extraterrestrial
(60) intervention seem less convincing than theories like the first, which account for the phenomenon solely by means of the thermodynamic state of the outer core and its effect on the mantle.

1. Which one of the following statements regarding the Earth's outer core is best supported by information presented in the passage?

   (A) Heat circulation in the outer core controls the growth and diminution of the polar ice caps.
   (B) Impact of asteroids on the Earth's surface alters the way in which the outer core vents its heat into the mantle.
   (C) Motion of electrons within the metallic fluid in the outer core produces the Earth's magnetic field.
   (D) Friction and turbulence near the boundary between the outer core and the mantle are typically caused by asteroid impacts.
   (E) Cessation of heat circulation within the outer core brings on multiple reversals in the Earth's magnetic field.

2. The author's objection to the second hypothesis discussed in the passage is most applicable to which one of the following explanations concerning the extinction of the dinosaurs?

   (A) The extinction of the dinosaurs was the result of gradual changes in the composition of the Earth's atmosphere that occurred over millions of years.
   (B) The dinosaurs became extinct when their food supply was disrupted following the emergence of mammals.
   (C) The dinosaurs succumbed to the new, colder environment brought about by a buildup of volcanic ash in the atmosphere.
   (D) After massively overpopulating the planet, dinosaurs disappeared due to widespread starvation and the rapid spread of disease.
   (E) After radical climatic changes resulted from the impact of a comet, dinosaurs disappeared from the Earth.

3. The author mentions the creation of blobs of different temperatures in the Earth's outer core (lines 34–38) primarily in order to

   (A) present a way in which the venting of heat from the outer core might disturb the heat-circulation pattern within the outer core

   (B) provide proof for the proposal that ventilation of heat from the outer core into the mantle triggers polarity reversal

   (C) give an example of the way in which heat circulates between the Earth's outer core and the Earth's exterior

   (D) describe how the outer core maintains its temperature by venting its excess heat into the Earth's mantle

   (E) argue in favor of the theory that heat circulation in the Earth's interior produces the magnetic field

4. Which one of the following statements regarding the polarity of the Earth's magnetic field is best supported by information in the passage?

   (A) Most, but not all, geophysicists agree that the Earth's magnetic field may exist in two distinct polarity states.

   (B) Changes in the polarity of the Earth's magnetic field have occurred more often in the recent past than in the distant past.

   (C) Heat transfer would cause reversals of the polarity of the Earth's magnetic field to occur more quickly than would asteroid impact.

   (D) Geophysicists' understanding of the reversal of the Earth's magnetic field has increased significantly since the introduction of the heat-transfer hypothesis.

   (E) Friction near the boundary of the inner and outer cores brings on reversal of the polarity of the geomagnetic field.

5. Which one of the following can be inferred regarding the two proposals discussed in the passage?

   (A) Since their introduction, they have sharply divided the scientific community.

   (B) Both were formulated in order to explain changes in the frequency of polarity reversal.

   (C) Although no firm conclusions regarding them have yet been reached, both have been extensively investigated.

   (D) They are not the only proposals scientists have put forth to explain the phenomenon of polarity reversal.

   (E) Both were introduced some time ago and have since fallen into disfavor among geophysicists.

6. The author mentions each of the following as possible contributing causes to reversals of the Earth's magnetic field EXCEPT:

   (A) changes in the way heat circulates within the outer core fluid

   (B) extended periods of colder temperatures on the Earth's surface

   (C) the creation of circulating blobs of outer core material of different temperatures

   (D) changes in circulation patterns in the Earth's oceans

   (E) clouding of the Earth's atmosphere by a large amount of dust

Passage 5: Polarity Reversals

What Makes It Difficult?

This passage is long and full of unfamiliar terms. It's not likely that many test takers are familiar with "density difference within the outer core fluid," or "rotational acceleration of the mantle." Trying to understand all of the technical details of the passage can really bog down even the most science-minded student, creating a trap for the unwary reader who doesn't know to focus on the keywords and read for structure. And this passage is rich with keywords; "Though this much is known...not well understood;" "Several explanations for this phenomenon have been proposed." Even focusing on these terms brings out that the author will discuss an aspect that is still mysterious, and give some possible explanations. A critical reader will then expect the author might pick one of these explanations as most likely, or say they are all lacking and propose another.

Key Points of the Passage

Purpose and Main Idea: The author's purpose is to discuss the process that results in reversals of the magnetic field's polarity, as well as two distinct hypotheses that try to explain these reversals; the closer the author gets to stating a main idea is that the "heat-transfer hypothesis" offers a better explanation than the "asteroid-impact hypothesis."

Paragraph Structure: Paragraph 1 introduces the topic and scope of the passage; the Earth's magnetic field, that the field can exist in one of two polarity states, and that this state reverses (and has been reversing at increasing rates).

Paragraph 2 provides a lot of scientific facts about the Earth's magnetic field, particularly facts about what is generally accepted, and what remains yet unknown.

Paragraph 3 indicates there are "several" possible explanations, and outlines both the "heat-transfer hypothesis" and the "asteroid-impact hypothesis" of polarity reversal.

In paragraph 4, the author asserts that the "heat-transfer hypothesis" is a more compelling explanation of polarity reversal, and gives a reason why (better to rely on theories that don't require extraterrestrial intervention).

Answers and Explanations

1. C   2. E   3. A   4. B   5. D   6. D

1. C

This choice is a nice paraphrase of lines 16–21, which state that the Earth's magnetic field is generated by the movement of free electrons in the hot metallic fluid that constitutes the Earth's outer core.

(A) distorts the "asteroid-impact hypothesis." According to this hypothesis, "heat circulation in the outer core" is affected by changes in the polar ice caps, not the other way around.

(B) combines elements of both the "heat-transfer hypothesis" and the "asteroid-impact hypothesis" into a statement that has no support in the text.

(D) is part of the "asteroid-impact hypothesis"—a hypothesis that may or may not turn out to be correct.

(E) also distorts information in the text, which says that reversals in magnetic field polarity may be related to changes in "the heat circulation pattern of the outer core fluid…" (lines 27–28).

2. E

In lines 59–63, the author's objection to the "asteroid-impact hypothesis" is that it depends on an "extraterrestrial intervention," which he finds less compelling than explanations that rest on terrestrial (or earthly) events. Of the choices, only (E) presents an extraterrestrial explanation—cometary impact—for the extinction of the dinosaurs. Choices (A)–(D) each present an "earthly" reason for the disappearance of the dinosaurs—the type of reason that the author favors when it comes to explaining earthly events, whether magnetic field reversals or species extinction.

3. A

The author mentions hotter and cooler blobs in the context of describing the "heat-transfer hypothesis." This hypothesis suggests that heat circulation patterns in the outer core are affected by the way in which heat is vented from the outer core.

(B) distorts information in the text, which makes it clear that magnetic field reversal is thought to be caused by a disturbance in heat circulation patterns in the outer core (lines 26–28. (C) is too vague. The author mentions the blobs only in the context of laying out a specific hypothesis about magnetic field reversal. (C) is also beyond the passage's scope: The text dwells on the Earth's interior, not its exterior. (D) focuses on the substance of the detail, rather than why the author included it in the text. (E) also distorts information in the text. According to lines 16–18, it is an accepted fact that the magnetic field itself is produced by the movement of free electrons in the outer core's fluid.

An Advanced test taker always keeps the author's purpose in mind when answering a function question.

---

4. B

Lines 8–9 say that geological evidence demonstrates that magnetic field reversals have been occurring with greater frequency in the recent past.

(A) Lines 1–3 state that "[i]t is a fundamental tenet of geophysics that the Earth's magnetic field can exist in either of two polarity states…" A fundamental tenet is something that is agreed upon by everyone in the discipline. Besides, there's no sense in the text that any geophysicists contest this fact.

(C) is beyond the scope of the text. This passage is about the "underlying causes" (lines 14–15) of magnetic field reversals, not about how fast they occur. The only point made about the speed of these reversals is that they occur over a period of thousands of years.

(D) The "heat-transfer hypothesis" is simply one possible explanation that geophysicists have come up with to account for a process that they don't fully understand. To say that it has enhanced their knowledge of magnetic field reversal is an overstatement.

(E) Magnetic field reversal is thought to result from changes in heat circulation patterns in the outer core, not from friction along the boundary of inner and outer cores.

5. D

Although this passage discusses just two hypotheses about magnetic field reversal, we're told that others exist. The last sentence of the text explicitly refers to "theories that depend on extraterrestrial intervention" and "theories like the first" (i.e., "earthly" theories).

(A) is beyond the scope of the text. We're not told what geophysicists in general think about these hypotheses, let alone whether "they have sharply divided the scientific community." All we can infer from the text is that there is some support for both hypotheses.

(B) These two hypotheses were formulated to address the "underlying causes" of magnetic field reversal. That they might also address the issue of reversal frequency is simply a by-product of their primary function.

(C) is a "half-right, half-wrong" choice. True, no firm conclusions about either hypothesis have yet been reached; but there's no information about the extent to which the two have been explored.

(E) is beyond the scope of the text. We aren't told precisely when either hypothesis was formulated. Moreover, both hypotheses have at least some support among geophysicists.

An Advanced test taker looks for the subtle reasons answer choices are wrong, and reads a choice carefully before selecting it.

---

6. D

Changes in oceanic circulation patterns aren't mentioned anywhere in the text as possible contributors to magnetic field reversals. The "asteroid-impact hypothesis" does speak of temperature drops in and redistribution of seawater, but these events are different from changes in oceanic circulation patterns.

(A) Geophysicists think that change in heat circulation in outer core fluid is the basic cause of magnetic field reversals. They part company, however, over what causes the change in heat circulation.

(B) and (E) are components of the "asteroid-impact hypothesis."

(C) is part of the "heat-transfer hypothesis."

What's Next?

Not so bad, huh? Well, of course, we're just getting started, and not surprisingly, things do get a bit worse. "NGF," the next passage in our little group of nightmares, raises the bar, both in the density of the material and in technical jargon. We'll get back to you in the explanation.

PASSAGE 6

The survival of nerve cells, as well as their performance of some specialized functions, is regulated by chemicals known as neurotrophic factors, which are produced in the bodies of animals,
(5) including humans. Rita Levi-Montalcini's discovery in the 1950s of the first of these agents, a hormonelike substance now known as NGF, was a crucial development in the history of biochemistry, which led to Levi-Montalcini sharing the Nobel Prize
(10) for medicine in 1986.

In the mid-1940s, Levi-Montalcini had begun by hypothesizing that many of the immature nerve cells produced in the development of an organism are normally programmed to die. In order to confirm this
(15) theory, she conducted research that in 1949 found that, when embryos are in the process of forming their nervous systems, they produce many more nerve cells than are finally required, the number that survives eventually adjusting itself to the volume of
(20) tissue to be supplied with nerves. A further phase of the experimentation, which led to Levi-Montalcini's identification of the substance that controls this process, began with her observation that the development of nerves in chick embryos could be
(25) stimulated by implanting a certain variety of mouse tumor in the embryos. She theorized that a chemical produced by the tumors was responsible for the observed nerve growth. To investigate this hypothesis, she used the then new technique of tissue culture, by
(30) which specific types of body cells can be made to grow outside the organism from which they are derived. Within twenty-four hours, her tissue cultures of chick embryo extracts developed dense halos of nerve tissue near the places in the culture where she
(35) had added the mouse tumor. Further research identified a specific substance contributed by the mouse tumors that was responsible for the effects Levi-Montalcini had observed: a protein that she named "nerve growth factor" (NGF).
(40) NGF was the first of many cell-growth factors to be found in the bodies of animals. Through Levi-Montalcini's work and other subsequent research, it has been determined that this substance is present in many tissues and biological fluids, and that it is
(45) especially concentrated in some organs. In developing organisms, nerve cells apparently receive this growth factor locally from the cells of muscles or other organs to which they will form connections for transmission of nerve impulses, and sometimes from
(50) supporting cells intermingled with the nerve tissue. NGF seems to play two roles, serving initially to direct the developing nerve processes toward the correct, specific "target" cells with which they must connect, and later being necessary for the continued
(55) survival of those nerve cells. During some periods of their development, the types of nerve cells that are affected by NGF—primarily cells outside the brain and spinal cord—die if the factor is not present or if they encounter anti-NGF antibodies.

1. Which one of the following most accurately expresses the main point of the passage?

   (A) Levi-Montalcini's discovery of neurotrophic factors as a result of research carried out in the 1940s was a major contribution to our understanding of the role of naturally occurring chemicals, especially NGF, in the development of chick embryos.

   (B) Levi-Montalcini's discovery of NGF, a neurotrophic factor that stimulates the development of some types of nerve tissue and whose presence or absence in surrounding cells helps determine whether particular nerve cells will survive, was a pivotal development in biochemistry.

   (C) NGF, which is necessary for the survival and proper functioning of nerve cells, was discovered by Levi-Montalcini in a series of experiments using the technique of tissue culture, which she devised in the 1940s.

   (D) Partly as a result of Levi-Montalcini's research, it has been found that NGF and other neurotrophic factors are produced only by tissues to which nerves are already connected and that the presence of these factors is necessary for the health and proper functioning of nervous systems.

   (E) NGF, a chemical that was discovered by Levi-Montalcini, directs the growth of nerve cells toward the cells with which they must connect and ensures the survival of those nerve cells throughout the life of the organism except when the organism produces anti-NGF antibodies.

2. Based on the passage, the author would be most likely to believe that Levi-Montalcini's discovery of NGF is noteworthy primarily because it

   (A) paved the way for more specific knowledge of the processes governing the development of the nervous system

   (B) demonstrated that a then new laboratory technique could yield important and unanticipated experimental results

   (C) confirmed the hypothesis that many of a developing organism's immature nerve cells are normally programmed to die

   (D) indicated that this substance stimulates observable biochemical reactions in the tissues of different species

   (E) identified a specific substance, produced by mouse tumors, that can be used to stimulate nerve cell growth

3. The primary function of the third paragraph of the passage in relation to the second paragraph is to

(A) indicate that conclusions referred to in the second paragraph, though essentially correct, require further verification

(B) indicate that conclusions referred to in the second paragraph have been undermined by subsequently obtained evidence

(C) indicate ways in which conclusions referred to in the second paragraph have been further corroborated and refined

(D) describe subsequent discoveries of substances analogous to the substance discussed in the second paragraph

(E) indicate that experimental procedures discussed in the second paragraph have been supplanted by more precise techniques described in the third paragraph

4. Information in the passage most strongly supports which one of the following?

(A) Nerve cells in excess of those that are needed by the organism in which they develop eventually produce anti-NGF antibodies to suppress the effects of NGF.

(B) Nerve cells that grow in the absence of NGF are less numerous than, but qualitatively identical to, those that grow in the presence of NGF.

(C) Few of the nerve cells that connect with target cells toward which NGF directs them are needed by the organism in which they develop.

(D) Some of the nerve cells that grow in the presence of NGF are eventually converted to other types of living tissue by neurotrophic factors.

(E) Some of the nerve cells that grow in an embryo do not connect with any particular target cells.

5. The passage describes a specific experiment that tested which one of the following hypotheses?

(A) A certain kind of mouse tumor produces a chemical that stimulates the growth of nerve cells.

(B) Developing embryos initially grow many more nerve cells than they will eventually require.

(C) In addition to NGF, there are several other important neurotrophic factors regulating cell survival and function.

(D) Certain organs contain NGF in concentrations much higher than in the surrounding tissue.

(E) Certain nerve cells are supplied with NGF by the muscle cells to which they are connected.

6. Which one of the following is most strongly supported by the information in the passage?

(A) Some of the effects that the author describes as occurring in Levi-Montalcini's culture of chick embryo extract were due to neurotrophic factors other than NGF.

(B) Although NGF was the first neurotrophic factor to be identified, some other such factors are now more thoroughly understood.

(C) In her research in the 1940s and 1950s, Levi-Montalcini identified other neurotrophic factors in addition to NGF.

(D) Some neurotrophic factors other than NGF perform functions that are not specifically identified in the passage.

(E) The effects of NGF that Levi-Montalcini noted in her chick embryo experiment are also caused by other neurotrophic factors not discussed in the passage.

Passage 6: NGF

What Makes It Difficult?

As is common for tough science passages, the real difficulty here comes from tough scientific concepts. Rest assured that when the author uses a term like "neurotrophic factors," it will either be defined for you or it won't be necessary for you to know the definition.

Difficult paragraph structure contributes to making this passage a toughie. The second paragraph is a long one, full of detail but detail that can be overwhelming to understand if one doesn't keep a laser sharp focus on keywords. And the set of six questions is a long set; even the global question is almost a full column long.

Key Points of the Passage

Purpose and Main Idea: The author's purpose is to describe what NGF is, how Levi-Montalcini discovered it, and its importance in biology. And the main idea is stated in the first paragraph; Levi-Montalcini's discovery of NGF was a crucial development in the history of biochemistry.

Paragraph Structure: Paragraph 1 describes nerve cells and their regulators, and tells you that the discovery of NGF (one particular regulator) was a "crucial" discovery, leading to a Nobel Prize.

Paragraph 2, in a nutshell, summarizes the process by which NGF was discovered. Levi-Montalcini had "begun hypothesizing," (line 12); she experimented "to confirm this theory," (line 15); the experiment continued into a further phase, did more research; this is the top-level view you'll need to get to answer the questions. Don't dwell on the specifics here!

Paragraph 3 extends Levi-Montalcini's work and tells how NGF is present in the body, and that it seems to play two roles. Again, be careful not to get caught up in understanding every detail right now. If questions ask, you'll come back; if they don't, who cares what the specifics of NGF's two roles are?

An Advanced test taker remembers the LSAT isn't testing her knowledge of science; anything she needs to know will be given to her in the passage.

Answers and Explanations

1. B   2. A   3. C   4. E   5. A   6. D

1. B

When answer choices are lengthy, remember that much of what's there may be correct. But the correct answer will be right in its entirety. Therefore, be bold in quickly identifying ways in which four of the choices go wrong, and remember: If there's nothing wrong with a choice, it must be the right answer.

The point is that, in a lengthy wrong choice, some of its prose will reflect the passage accurately, so you need to bore through the verbiage to find the categorical ways in which four of the choices go astray. Otherwise, you'll get bogged down in things that sound good even if you've already armed yourself with a prediction. Take (A), for instance. Levi-Montalcini did make a discovery, and it was a big deal, and it did involve research begun in the 1940s. All of that is right. But the passage doesn't say that Levi-Montalcini discovered "neurotrophic factors," only that she discovered the first of them, NGF. Moreover, as (A) is worded, her work is most noteworthy for what it taught us about chick embryos. Say what? Levi-Montalcini used chick embryos in her research, but her Nobel-winning findings clearly have impact on many animals beyond baby chicks—most notably, humans. Get the idea? By zeroing in on one or more categorical ways in which a lengthy choice goes wrong, you can quickly eliminate tricky but ultimately incorrect answers.

(B) The main clause is, "The discovery... was pivotal." Quite right; that reflects the one subjective statement in the entire passage, made in lines 5–10. Does the rest of (B) accurately reflect the passage? Yes, the appositive (the modifying phrase between commas) deftly sums up the "two roles" discussed in lines 51–59. And is there a sin of omission? No, everything important is summed up here. But perhaps you'll want to confirm that the remaining choices are bad before making your final selection.

(C) emphasizes NGF's role in keeping nerve cells alive (overlooking those cells' development), makes "tissue culture" (which was only introduced in line 29) central to Levi-Montalcini's work, and ascribes the devising of tissue culture to her. All of that is bogus.

(D) How NGF is produced is never described in the passage (it's all about how Levi-Montalcini found it, and what it does). Moreover, to say that NGF "is necessary for the health and proper functioning of nervous systems" goes much further than lines 54–55. And since the star of the passage is Levi-Montalcini, it seems odd to diminish her work as only "partly" responsible.

(E) gives short shrift to Levi-Montalcini's discovery process and its importance and hence to the first two-thirds of the passage. Meanwhile, its main clause focuses only on lines 51–59, and distorts them to boot (the final "except" clause is tossed in and turns the choice into gibberish). We're left with our initial impression that (B) is the one and only non-flawed answer.

An Advanced test taker makes sure to check every word in an answer choice, and knows one wrong word spoils an otherwise perfect answer choice.

---

2. A

The noteworthiness of the NGF discovery is mentioned in paragraph 1, but comes back again in paragraph 3, and we ought to review both. Neurotrophic factors like NGF certainly sound important as far as paragraph 1 goes, and their importance is reinforced later by references to: NGF's being "the first of many" (line 40); "subsequent research" (line 42) that has found NGF throughout the body; and the chemical's two roles (lines 51–59). All of that is summed up in (A). As the first discovered neurotrophic factor, NGF did "pave the way," and there's little doubt as to the "specificity" of the knowledge sketched out in paragraph 3.

(B) There's no sense that finding NGF was "unanticipated." Indeed, much of Levi-Montalcini's work seems to have confirmed hypotheses she already held.

(C) The normal programming of immature cells to die should have struck you as a rather marginal affair, hardly meriting the term "noteworthy," especially since the issue never comes up in paragraph 3. (C) just echoes Levi-Montalcini's initial hypothesis (lines 11–14), which was not the endpoint of her research but the beginning: figuring that the cells were programmed to die, she asked the question, "Why?," a quest that led her ultimately to NGF.

(D) This choice does not match up at all with the two roles played by NGF, at least on the strength of lines 51–59. This vague statement is unsupported by the passage.

(E) This choice blows up the importance of mouse tumors (NGF, remember, is found in many animals), and "can be used to stimulate" wrongly implies that NGF is some sort of applied substance, rather than one occurring naturally in animals' bodies.

3. C

Because paragraph 2, as our Roadmap reminds us, lays out a step-by-step process the net results of which are outlined one paragraph later, the right answer ought to at least reflect the idea of process—which makes (C) pretty much a certainty. Each of the wrong choices introduces at least one major distortion:

(A) No sense is given that anything in particular needs greater "verification."

(B) Nothing in paragraph 3, or anywhere else, "undermines" Levi-Montalcini's work.

(D) At best, "analogous substances" relates to the brief reference to "other factors" in line 40. At worst, it's irrelevant. This passage is all about NGF.

(E) No "supplanting" of previous work is ever alluded to.

4. E

(A) combines lines 15–20 and line 59 into one big fat distortion. The self-adjustment process mentioned in the former has no connection to the antibodies mentioned in the latter.

(B) makes an unwarranted comparison between two types of nerve cells, and the phrase "qualitatively identical" offers a level of precision not justified by anything in the text.

(C) 180: The sense offered in paragraph 3 is that NGF directs necessary cells to the place where they're needed.

(D) hints at a "conversion" or transformation that has no basis in the text. Besides, (D) implies that NGF and neurotrophic factors are different things, whereas the first is actually an example of the second.

(E) The only one left must be inferable, and it is. According to lines 45–50, nerve cells can receive NGF from "supporting cells" to which they are not "connected."

5. A

A couple of Levi-Montalcini's hypotheses are mentioned here and there. But if you circled the phrase "To investigate that hypothesis" (line 28) and saw that an experiment is described immediately afterward, you probably had little difficulty settling on (A), which describes the hypothesis in lines 26–28 that the subsequent experiment (lines 29–35) was designed to test.

(B) mentions a finding of Levi-Montalcini's (lines 15–18), not a hypothesis for which an experiment was designed.

(C) Lines 1–5 and lines 40–41 hint at other neurotrophic factors, but the passage falls far short of describing them, let alone presenting an experiment designed to confirm their existence.

(D) No reference to differing levels of NGF is made anywhere in the passage.

(E), like (B), offers a research finding (this one, a discovery not necessarily made by Levi-Montalcini, is mentioned in lines 45–49), but no experiment backing it up is described.

6. D

All five choices allude to the neurotrophic factors other than NGF—neurotrophic factors that are mentioned briefly early on, and again later, but that play no important role in the overall text. Let's take them in order:

(A) Neurotrophic factors other than NGF never come up in the discussion of Levi-Montalcini's work with chick embryos.

(B) A statement that's far from inferable. Yes, neurotrophic factors other than NGF are known, but who's to say that they're better comprehended? Besides, if longevity is relevant here, then logic suggests that NGF—discovered first—would be known best of all.

(C) There's no justification for attributing the other neurotrophic factors' discovery to Levi-Montalcini. As far as we know from the passage, Levi-Montalcini worked on NGF and nothing else.

(D) Here's the one and only verifiable fact about other neurotrophic factors. Lines 1–6 confirm that there are more of them than just NGF, and the first two lines strongly suggest that they have other "specialized functions" that the passage never describes. (D) is correct.

(E) is almost functionally identical to (A), and is every bit as wrong. As far as we know, Levi-Montalcini's chick embryo work involved NGF and nothing else.

An Advanced test taker makes sure an Inference answer doesn't just sound right, but is supported by the text.

What's Next?

So far we've looked at the very large (the earth's magnetic field) and the very small (neurotrophic factors). Next let's stop somewhere in the middle, and talk about fungi.

PASSAGE 7

A lichen consists of a fungus living in symbiosis (i.e., a mutually beneficial relationship) with an alga. Although most branches of the complex evolutionary family tree of fungi have been well established, the
(5) evolutionary origins of lichen-forming fungi have been a mystery. But a new DNA study has revealed the relationship of lichen-forming fungi to several previously known branches of the fungus family tree. The study reveals that, far from being oddities,
(10) lichen-forming fungi are close relatives of such common fungi as brewer's yeast, morel mushrooms, and the fungus that causes Dutch elm disease. This accounts for the visible similarity of certain lichens to more recognizable fungi such as mushrooms.

(15) In general, fungi present complications for the researcher. Fungi are usually parasitic or symbiotic, and researchers are often unsure whether they are examining fungal DNA or that of the associated organism. But lichen-forming fungi are especially
(20) difficult to study. They have few distinguishing characteristics of shape or structure, and they are unusually difficult to isolate from their partner algae, with which they have a particularly delicate symbiosis. In some cases the alga is wedged between
(25) layers of fungal tissue; in others, the fungus grows through the alga's cell walls in order to take nourishment, and the tissues of the two organisms are entirely enmeshed and inseparable. As a result, lichen-forming fungi have long been difficult to
(30) classify definitively within the fungus family. By default they were thus considered a separate grouping of fungi with an unknown evolutionary origin. But, using new analytical tools that allow them to isolate the DNA of fungi in parasitic or symbiotic
(35) relationships, researchers were able to establish the DNA sequence in a certain gene found in 75 species of fungi, including 10 species of lichen-forming fungi. Based on these analyses, the researchers found 5 branches on the fungus family tree to which
(40) varieties of lichen-forming fungi belong. Furthermore, the researchers stress that it is likely that as more types of lichen-forming fungi are analyzed, they will be found to belong to still more branches of the fungus family tree.

(45) One implication of the new research is that it provides evidence to help overturn the long-standing evolutionary assumption that parasitic interactions inevitably evolve over time to a greater benignity and eventually to symbiosis so that the parasites will not
(50) destroy their hosts. The addition of lichen-forming fungi to positions along branches of the fungus family tree indicates that this assumption does not hold for fungi. Fungi both harmful and benign can now be found both early and late in fungus
(55) evolutionary history. Given the new layout of the fungus family tree resulting from the lichen study, it appears that fungi can evolve toward mutualism and then just as easily turn back again toward parasitism.

1. Which one of the following most accurately states the main point of the passage?

   (A) New research suggests that fungi are not only parasitic but also symbiotic organisms.
   (B) New research has revealed that lichen-forming fungi constitute a distinct species of fungus.
   (C) New research into the evolutionary origins of lichen-forming fungi reveals them to be closely related to various species of algae.
   (D) New research has isolated the DNA of lichen-forming fungi and uncovered their relationship to the fungus family tree.
   (E) New research into the fungal component of lichens explains the visible similarities between lichens and fungi by means of their common evolutionary origins.

2. Which one of the following most accurately describes the author's purpose in the last paragraph of the passage?

   (A) to suggest that new research overturns the assumption that lichen-forming fungi are primarily symbiotic, rather than parasitic, organisms
   (B) to show that findings based on new research regarding fungus classification have implications that affect a long-standing assumption of evolutionary science
   (C) to explain the fundamental purposes of fungus classification in order to position this classification within the broader field of evolutionary science
   (D) to demonstrate that a fundamental assumption of evolutionary science is verified by new research regarding fungus classification
   (E) to explain how symbiotic relationships can evolve into purely parasitic ones

3. Which one of the following most accurately describes the organization of the passage?

    (A) explanation of the difficulty of classifying lichens; description of the DNA sequence of lichen-forming fungi; summary of the implications of this description

    (B) definition of lichens; discussion of new discoveries concerning lichens' evolutionary history; application of these findings in support of an evolutionary theory

    (C) definition of lichens; discussion of the difficulty in classifying their fungal components; resolution of this difficulty and implications of the resulting research

    (D) discussion of the symbiotic relationship that constitutes lichens; discussion of how new research can distinguish parasitic from symbiotic fungi; implications of this research

    (E) explanation of the symbiotic nature of lichens; discussion of the problems this poses for genetic researchers; delineation of the implications these problems have for evolutionary theory

4. According to the passage, the elimination of which one of the following obstacles enabled scientists to identify the evolutionary origins of lichen-forming fungi?

    (A) The DNA of lichen-forming fungi was not easy to separate from that of their associated algae.

    (B) Lichen-forming fungi are difficult to distinguish from several common fungi with which they are closely related.

    (C) Lichen-forming fungi were grouped separately from other fungi on the fungus family tree.

    (D) Lichen-forming fungi are far less common than more recognizable fungi such as mushrooms.

    (E) The DNA of lichen-forming fungi is significantly more complex than that of other fungi.

5. Which one of the following, if true, most weakens the author's criticism of the assumption that parasitic interactions generally evolve toward symbiosis?

    (A) Evolutionary theorists now postulate that symbiotic interactions generally evolve toward greater parasitism, rather than vice versa.

    (B) The evolutionary tree of fungi is somewhat more complex than that of similarly parasitic or symbiotic organisms.

    (C) The DNA of fungi involved in symbiotic interactions is far more difficult to isolate than that of fungi involved in parasitic interactions.

    (D) The placement of lichen-forming fungi as a separate group on the fungus family tree masked the fact that parasitic fungi sometimes evolved much later than symbiotic ones.

    (E) Branches of the fungus family tree that have evolved from symbiosis to parasitism usually die out shortly thereafter.

Passage 7: Lichen-Forming Fungi

What Makes It Difficult?

Common themes are emerging in these difficult science passages. Dense vocabulary, unfamiliar subject matter, and dense paragraph structure (as in the previous passage, paragraph 2 of this passage is killer) combine to raise the bar. This time the author has also included some numbers in lines 36–39, which can scare test takers with humanities backgrounds.

Only five points are to be gained from this passage, and none of them look to be short and quick. This would be a great passage to save for last for most test takers, but the Advanced test taker needs to get points on every passage, and take heart—of the five questions on this passage, two are global and one is a detail.

Key Points of the Passage

Purpose and Main Idea: The author's purpose is relatively straightforward; to explain what a new DNA study reveals about the mysteries of lichen-forming fungi. The main idea can be stated as what the DNA studies reveal—that fungi can evolve to mutualism and then back to parasitism. This is stated nicely for you in the last sentence; don't worry if the words are unfamiliar to you know. If you need to, you know you can look back through the passage to define them.

Paragraph Structure: Paragraph 1 is primarily concerned with defining terms, "lichen" and "symbiosis," and giving examples of fungi to help you become at least a little bit familiar with the subject matter.

Paragraph 2 divides neatly into two halves, lines 15–32 listing the problems of analyzing fungi and lines 32–44 outlining the relevant findings of the study introduced at line 6. Among the former is the difficulty that lies in figuring out which DNA is which because the fungi and partner algae are so intertwined; as for the latter, it's all pretty complicated for the layperson, but the gist we get is that scientists can now isolate the DNA and successfully relate the fungi to the larger fungi family.

Paragraph 3 blatantly announces its purpose at line 45 with "One implication of the new research …"; the gist here is that science used to assume that parasites inevitably evolve into symbionts, but this new study of fungi suggests that such assumption isn't necessarily correct.

Answers and Explanations

1. D   2. B   3. C   4. A   5. E

1. D

The correct answer here has to focus on the new DNA research's answers to the fungi mysteries, and only (D) does so. Even if you don't quite comprehend this "fungus family tree" information, notice how the other four choices are all seriously compromised:

(A) Line 16 provides the detail that fungi are usually parasitic or symbiotic, and it sounds like a long-understood fact—hardly the result of new DNA research.

(B) In fact, the new research suggests (lines 6–14) that the kind of fungus that forms lichen is actually closer to, rather than distinct from, other types of fungi.

(C) messes up the central relationship in the passage. Certain fungi live symbiotically with certain algae and form lichens, and their DNA are often confusingly intertwined; but that's far from (C)'s idea that these fungi are genetically related to algae.

(E) sounds convincing, but there's no support for its idea that the similarity of lichens and fungi is a mystery that needed solving. A lichen is a fungus, or rather a fungus/algae merger. Thus, this choice is a distortion of a detail from the last sentence of the first paragraph.

An Advanced test taker remembers to focus on topic and scope when answering global questions, especially when the passage is dense.

---

2. B

Line 45 alone tells us that paragraph 3 is all about the implications of the new research, and (B)—besides being the only choice that uses the word "implications"—correctly highlights the findings' challenge to a long-standing evolutionary assumption (lines 45–50). Meanwhile, the four wrong choices exemplify four of the most common wrong answer types, and that helps us.

(A) misstates the classical assumption that the new research challenges. It's not a parasitism-vs.-symbiosis issue per se, but rather an issue of the allegedly inevitable evolution from the latter to the former.

(C) Fungus classification's place in science is wrapped up in paragraph 1, long before paragraph 3 comes along.

(D) The new research doesn't "verify" a long-held assumption; it challenges one.

(E), like many other wrong answers in this set, contrasts parasites with symbionts, as if anything in the passage was fundamentally concerned with their distinction. (E) also represents a distortion: Although paragraph 3 states that parasites usually become symbionts, and the new research suggests that such movement can be reversed, nowhere does the paragraph explain how either evolution comes about.

3. C

We've broken down the passage into four key issues, which we could express as questions: What are lichens? Why are fungi hard to study? What does the new research tell us? How can it help in the future? Only (C) echoes this structure.

(A) goes awry right away: It's fungi that are tough to classify, not lichens. And the passage concludes with the implications of the new evidence, not of the DNA description.

(B) bypasses the extensive discussion (lines 15–32) of the difficulties of classifying fungi, and misstates the discoveries as concerning lichens rather than fungi specifically. Finally, the passage ends by questioning, rather than supporting, a long-held theory. How wrong can a wrong answer go? (B) shows us that the answer is "almost completely" wrong.

(D) Distinguishing parasitic and symbiotic fungi is in no sense the scope of the research described, so beyond all of (D)'s errors of omission (where's fungi classification?), it suffers from this one big error of commission.

(E) The passage begins by asserting (rather than "explaining") lichens' symbiotic nature, but even worse, it's not the symbiotic nature per se that "poses problems for researchers," as (B) would have it. Finally, it's the implications of the new research with which the passage closes.

An Advanced test taker relies on the Roadmap to answer organization questions.

---

4. A

The Hot Word "obstacles" allows us to zero in on the first half of paragraph 2, which, we've already decided, lays out the difficulties inherent in fungi identification. Rescanning lines 15–32 should yield (A) pretty quickly. Lines 21–28 explain at length the confusing interconnectedness of fungi and algae within lichen, and when a few lines later we hear that scientists were able to "isolate the DNA of fungi," it must mean that they found a way to peel the two apart. So (A) is an example of an obstacle that, once overcome, facilitated the research. Note the difference between (A) and the other choices in this regard.

(B) If this difficulty were eliminated—if science could separate lichen-forming fungi from other types—that still would leave the intertwined algae to contend with.

(C) Likewise, if this were overcome—if all of the fungi were grouped together—it still would be tough, if not impossible, to separate out the algae.

(D) If lichen-forming fungi were more common, again what impact would there be on lichen and (especially) on the algae DNA? None.

(E) Simpler DNA would have no effect at all. Once again, the big obstacle is the inability up until now to separate out the DNA of the fungi and the algae. Only (A) understands that.

5. E

The assumption that the author criticizes, of course, is the long-standing belief that, as a rule, parasites eventually become harmless and drift into symbiosis; the basis of his criticism is the discovery of harmful (i.e., non-benign) fungi late in the game, at a time when presumably the relationship should be turning symbiotic. To the author, this means that the reverse road—from symbiosis to parasitism—is actually every bit as possible. But if (E) is true, and the branches that have followed that "reverse road" actually die off quickly, then the movement from symbiosis to parasitism is likely to be just an aberration—and the conventional assumption is correct after all.

(A) Evidence of movements from symbiosis to parasitism actually support the author's viewpoint.

(B) The relative complexity of fungi's evolution relative to that of others has nothing to do with the movement of relationships from harmful to benign or vice versa.

(C) The implications at the heart of paragraph 3 take place after the relevant DNA has been isolated, so the difficulty of obtaining the DNA has nothing to do with the findings. (C) also presents an irrelevant comparison among the various difficulties of DNA isolation.

(D) focuses on some sort of masking that went on, making it difficult to discover that "sometimes" the parasitic fungi evolved first. But that masking has nothing to do with the findings themselves, and the earlier evolution is too vague, sketchy, and occasional to have any impact on the reasoning.

What's Next?

Three science passages down, and one to go. This next passage, "Hormones' Influence on Behavior," takes us back into the human body and the world of very small science. Have fun!

PASSAGE 8

Discussions of how hormones influence behavior have generally been limited to the effects of gonadal hormones on reproductive behavior and have emphasized the parsimonious arrangement whereby the
(5) same hormones involved in the biology of reproduction also influence sexual behavior. It has now become clear, however, that other hormones, in addition to their recognized influence on biological functions, can affect behavior. Specifically, peptide and steroid hormones
(10) involved in maintaining the physiological balance, or homeostasis, of body fluids also appear to play an important role in the control of water and salt consumption. The phenomenon of homeostasis in animals depends on various mechanisms that promote
(15) stability within the organism despite an inconstant external environment; the homeostasis of body fluids, whereby the osmolality (the concentration of solutes) of blood plasma is closely regulated, is achieved primarily through alterations in the intake and
(20) excretion of water and sodium, the two principal components of the fluid matrix that surrounds body cells. Appropriate compensatory responses are initiated when deviations from normal are quite small, thereby maintaining plasma osmolality within relatively narrow
(25) ranges.

In the osmoregulation of body fluids, the movement of water across cell membranes permits minor fluctuations in the concentration of solutes in extracellular fluid to be buffered by corresponding
(30) changes in the relatively larger volume of cellular water. Nevertheless, the concentration of solutes in extracellular fluid may at times become elevated or reduced by more than the allowed tolerances of one or two percent. It is then that complementary
(35) physiological and behavioral responses come into play to restore plasma osmolality to normal. Thus, for example, a decrease in plasma osmolality, such as that which occurs after the consumption of water in excess of need, leads to the excretion of surplus body water in
(40) the urine by inhibiting secretion from the pituitary gland of vasopressin, a peptide hormone that promotes water conservation in the kidneys. As might be expected, thirst also is inhibited then, to prevent further dilution of body fluids. Conversely, an increase in
(45) plasma osmolality, such as that which occurs after one eats salty foods or after body water evaporates without being replaced, stimulates the release of vasopressin, increasing the conservation of water and the excretion of solutes in urine. This process is accompanied by
(50) increased thirst, with the result of making plasma osmolality more dilute through the consumption of water. The threshold for thirst appears to be slightly higher than for vasopressin secretion, so that thirst is stimulated only after vasopressin has been released in
(55) amounts sufficient to produce maximal water retention by the kidneys—that is, only after osmotic dehydration exceeds the capacity of the animal to deal with it physiologically.

1. Which one of the following best states the main idea of the passage?

   (A) Both the solute concentration and the volume of an animal's blood plasma must be kept within relatively narrow ranges
   (B) Behavioral responses to changes in an animal's blood plasma can compensate for physiological malfunction, allowing the body to avoid dehydration
   (C) The effect of hormones on animal behavior and physiology has only recently been discovered
   (D) Behavioral and physiological responses to major changes in osmolality of an animal's blood plasma are hormonally influenced and complement one another
   (E) The mechanisms regulating reproduction are similar to those that regulate thirst and sodium appetite

2. The author of the passage cites the relationship between gonadal hormones and reproductive behavior in order to

   (A) review briefly the history of research into the relationships between gonadal and peptide hormones that has led to the present discussion
   (B) decry the fact that previous research has concentrated on the relatively minor issue of the relationships between hormones and behavior
   (C) establish the emphasis of earlier research into the connections between hormones and behavior before elaborating on the results described in the passage
   (D) introduce a commonly held misconception about the relationships between hormones and behavior before refuting it with the results described in the passage
   (E) summarize the main findings of recent research described in the passage before detailing the various procedures that led to those findings

3. It can be inferred from the passage that which one of the following is true of vasopressin?

    (A) The amount secreted depends on the level of steroid hormones in the blood.
    (B) The amount secreted is important for maintaining homeostasis in cases of both increased and decreased osmolality.
    (C) It works in conjunction with steroid hormones in increasing plasma volume.
    (D) It works in conjunction with steroid hormones in regulating sodium appetite.
    (E) It is secreted after an animal becomes thirsty, as a mechanism for diluting plasma osmolality.

4. The primary function of the passage as a whole is to

    (A) present new information
    (B) question standard assumptions
    (C) reinterpret earlier findings
    (D) advocate a novel theory
    (E) outline a new approach

5. According to the passage, all of the following typically occur in the homeostasis of blood-plasma osmolality EXCEPT:

    (A) Hunger is diminished.
    (B) Thirst is initiated.
    (C) Vasopressin is secreted.
    (D) Water is excreted.
    (E) Sodium is consumed.

6. According to the passage, the withholding of vasopressin fulfills which one of the following functions in the restoration of plasma osmolality to normal levels?

    (A) It increases thirst and stimulates sodium appetite.
    (B) It helps prevent further dilution of body fluids.
    (C) It increases the conservation of water in the kidneys.
    (D) It causes minor changes in plasma volume.
    (E) It helps stimulate the secretion of steroid hormones.

Passage 8: Hormones

What Makes It Difficult?

You've already seen how complicated science passages can contain unfamiliar vocabulary, but this passage might take the cake in that regard. Just the first paragraph feels like something ripped from a medical school textbook. The paragraph structure doesn't help either; these may be two of the longest, densest paragraphs in the history of LSAT science passages.

Some relief comes in the questions; there are only six but the last four look short and quick. This is a good reminder that when the LSAT throws a very difficult passage at you, at least some of the questions will be relatively easy.

An Advanced test taker looks for the quickest points first on even the toughest passage.

Key Points of the Passage

Purpose and Main Idea: The author's purpose is neatly given in lines 9–13; to explain how hormones don't just influence the balance of body fluids, but also how much water and salt we consume. The main idea follows closely from the purpose, "hormones play a role not only in our physiology but also in our behavior."

Paragraph Structure: Paragraph 1 begins by acknowledging what is known and setting up the distinction between regulation of the body and regulation of behavior. The author then departs from the discussion of hormones, focusing on defining and discussing homeostasis and osmolality.

Paragraph 2 describes the process of osmoregulation, and says that minor fluctuations of solutes are OK, but when they fall outside the acceptable range, hormones come into play. Lines 36–58 explain the process. The hormone vasopressin causes the kidneys to retain water. When osmolality is low, the inhibiting of vasopressin leads the body to get rid of extra water and, not surprisingly, reduces thirst. (If the body's trying to get rid of water, greater thirst would put it at cross purposes by causing more water consumption.) The keyword "Conversely" in line 44 helps. When osmolality increases, more vasopressin is secreted, causing the reverse process: Water is conserved, and a person gets thirsty. There's more, but it's not central to that principal contrast, which is designed to show how at least one hormone— vasopressin—affects both the physiology of plasma and the behavior of the human being.

Answers and Explanations

1. D   2. C   3. B   4. A   5. A   6. B

1. D

(D) has it all, the hormones, the plasma osmolality, and the simultaneous physiological and behavioral influence.

(A) cites a detail from lines 22–25, which is bad enough for a global answer, but (A) also fails to realize that the bulk of the passage deals with what happens when osmolality goes beyond "narrow ranges." (B) draws an unwarranted distinction between behavioral responses and physiological ones, and focuses too narrowly on dehydration. If (C) were the main idea the passage would have to be going backward in time, detailing the dearth of hormone knowledge in past years and explaining how hormones' influence came to be discovered now. The role played in the passage by reproduction (E) is simply to illustrate the most commonly understood instance of hormones influencing both physiology and behavior. Once the author cranks up the discussion of plasma osmolality, reproduction is left behind.

2. C

The only appearance of "gonadal hormones" is in the very first sentence, whose explanation of a specific hormonal influence connection to both biology and behavior opens the door to the broader issue in lines 6–9 and another specific, extended example. (C) properly characterizes the reference's introductory nature, with (C)'s "research into" paraphrasing the passage's "Discussions of."

(A) formulates an irrelevant comparison between gonadal and peptide hormones, two separate entities as far as the passage is concerned. The connection between hormones and behavior is of intense interest to the author, contrary to (B); and he's not "decrying" anything. (D) Is the idea that gonadal hormones influence sexual behavior. That's accepted. The rest of the passage doesn't so much "refute" that idea, as broaden it to include other types of human behavior. And the findings in lines 9–58 go beyond that which is known about gonadal hormones; the findings don't double back to that topic as (E) would have it.

An Advanced test taker uses Hot Words in the question stem to focus research.

---

3. B

Since vasopressin is inhibited or stimulated depending on whether osmolality is lower or higher, respectively, and since the whole process begins whenever homeostasis is threatened, (B) is readily inferable. (A), (C), and (D) all mention steroid hormones, which are only mentioned in passing back at line 9. Vasopressin is a peptide hormone (line 41), that we know; whether vasopressin also qualifies as a steroid, or works with a steroid, goes unmentioned in the text, so all three choices should be rejected promptly. (E) gets a key relationship backward, cf. lines 53–54: "thirst is stimulated only after vasopressin has been released…"

4. A

Keeping topic, scope, purpose, and main idea in mind—tough to do with answer choices only three or four words long—we seek a choice that is fairly objective in tone and that points to that which "has now become clear." Only (A) fits the bill.

No "questioning," "reinterpreting," or "advocating" is going on—that knocks out (B), (C), and (D); and if (E) read "outline recent findings," it'd be a good choice, but no "approach" is outlined or even suggested.

5. A

Since the four wrong choices all "typically occur" in osmolality homeostasis, we need a choice that either emphatically doesn't occur, or that is outside the scope. The latter is more likely here, since a variety of opposing things can happen in homeostasis: Vasopressin can be secreted (C) or inhibited; thirst can be increased (B) or decreased; the person can excrete water (D) or consume sodium (E) depending on whether the osmolality is rising or falling. But hunger never enters into the process, at least insofar as the passage is concerned, so (A) is what we want.

An Advanced test taker characterizes the correct answer choice in EXCEPT questions.

---

6. B

The Hot Words here are "withholding of vasopressin." A quick skim of paragraph 2 indicates that it occurs in lines 37–44, when osmolality decreases. Vasopressin is inhibited, which leads to excretion of surplus water and to inhibited thirst. (Which makes sense; the body is trying to get rid of excess water, and less thirst means less inducement to drink.) So (B) correctly describes the process.

(A) is the opposite of what happens when vasopressin is inhibited or withheld. (C) describes the hormone's normal role (lines 41–42), but when vasopressin is held back, the opposite of conservation occurs. Vasopressin doesn't come into play, as far as we're told, when "minor changes" (D) occur. And (E) drags in those steroid hormones again—a one-line reference (line 9) that appears in the passage largely to inspire wrong answers like this one.

CHAPTER FOURTEEN

Philosopher's Corner

Organicism vs the analytic method, or Dworkin's theory of judicial interpretation (the subjects of two of the upcoming passages), for example. These are themselves philosophical subjects, and not just complex, philosophical treatments of real-life, easy to grasp phenomena. As the author of the "Mathematics as Language" passage states: "The debate centers around whether language corresponds in some essential way to objects and behaviors, making knowledge a solid and reliable commodity; or, on the other hand, whether the relationship between language and things is purely a matter of agreed-upon conventions, making knowledge tenuous, relative, and inexact." Precisely. And therein lies the difficulty of dealing with inherently philosophical material: These are abstract (to many, even obscure) concepts. Many find these to be even harder than science passages. Despite the technical terms, processes, and mass of details used to describe a star or a cell, physical things are still easier for many to get their hands around than abstractions such as organicism or a theory of law.

So buckle up for these final few. It may turn out to be a bumpy ride.

PASSAGE 9

What it means to "explain" something in science often comes down to the application of mathematics. Some thinkers hold that mathematics is a kind of language—a systematic contrivance of signs, the
(5) criteria for the authority of which are internal coherence, elegance, and depth. The application of such a highly artificial system to the physical world, they claim, results in the creation of a kind of statement about the world. Accordingly, what matters in the
(10) sciences is finding a mathematical concept that attempts, as other language does, to accurately describe the functioning of some aspect of the world.

At the center of the issue of scientific knowledge can thus be found questions about the relationship
(15) between language and what it refers to. A discussion about the role played by language in the pursuit of knowledge has been going on among linguists for several decades. The debate centers around whether language corresponds in some essential way to objects
(20) and behaviors, making knowledge a solid and reliable commodity; or, on the other hand, whether the relationship between language and things is purely a matter of agreed-upon conventions, making knowledge tenuous, relative, and inexact.

(25) Lately the latter theory has been gaining wider acceptance. According to linguists who support this theory, the way language is used varies depending upon changes in accepted practices and theories among those who work in a particular discipline. These
(30) linguists argue that, in the pursuit of knowledge, a statement is true only when there are no promising alternatives that might lead one to question it. Certainly this characterization would seem to be applicable to the sciences. In science, a mathematical statement may be
(35) taken to account for every aspect of a phenomenon it is applied to, but, some would argue, there is nothing inherent in mathematical language that guarantees such a correspondence. Under this view, acceptance of a mathematical statement by the scientific community—
(40) by virtue of the statement's predictive power or methodological efficiency—transforms what is basically an analogy or metaphor into an explanation of the physical process in question, to be held as true until another, more compelling analogy takes its place.

(45) In pursuing the implications of this theory, linguists have reached the point at which they must ask: If words or sentences do not correspond in an essential way to life or to our ideas about life, then just what are they capable of telling us about the world? In science
(50) and mathematics, then, it would seem equally necessary to ask: If models of electrolytes or $E = mc^2$, say, do not correspond essentially to the physical world, then just what functions do they perform in the acquisition of scientific knowledge? But this question
(55) has yet to be significantly addressed in the sciences.

1. Which one of the following statements most accurately expresses the passage's main point?

   (A) Although scientists must rely on both language and mathematics in their pursuit of scientific knowledge, each is an imperfect tool for perceiving and interpreting aspects of the physical world.

   (B) The acquisition of scientific knowledge depends on an agreement among scientists to accept some mathematical statements as more precise than others while acknowledging that all mathematics is inexact.

   (C) If science is truly to progress, scientists must temporarily abandon the pursuit of new knowledge in favor of a systematic analysis of how the knowledge they already possess came to be accepted as true.

   (D) In order to better understand the acquisition of scientific knowledge, scientists must investigate mathematical statements' relationship to the world just as linguists study language's relationship to the world.

   (E) Without the debates among linguists that preceded them, it is unlikely that scientists would ever have begun to explore the essential role played by mathematics in the acquisition of scientific knowledge.

2. Which one of the following statements, if true, lends the most support to the view that language has an essential correspondence to the things it describes?

   (A) The categories of physical objects employed by one language correspond remarkably to the categories employed by another language that developed independently of the first.

   (B) The categories of physical objects employed by one language correspond remarkably to the categories employed by another language that derives from the first.

   (C) The categories of physical objects employed by speakers of a language correspond remarkably to the categories employed by other speakers of the same language.

   (D) The sentence structures of languages in scientifically sophisticated societies vary little from language to language.

   (E) Native speakers of many languages believe that the categories of physical objects employed by their language correspond to natural categories of objects in the world.

3. According to the passage, mathematics can be considered a language because it

   (A) conveys meaning in the same way that metaphors do
   (B) constitutes a systematic collection of signs
   (C) corresponds exactly to aspects of physical phenomena
   (D) confers explanatory power on scientific theories
   (E) relies on previously agreed-upon conventions

4. The primary purpose of the third paragraph is to

   (A) offer support for the view of linguists who believe that language has an essential correspondence to things
   (B) elaborate the position of linguists who believe that truth is merely a matter of convention
   (C) illustrate the differences between the essentialist and conventionalist positions in the linguists debate
   (D) demonstrate the similarity of the linguists' debate to a current debate among scientists about the nature of explanation
   (E) explain the theory that mathematical statements are a kind of language

5. Based on the passage, linguists who subscribe to the theory described in lines 21–24 would hold that the statement "The ball is red" is true because

   (A) speakers of English have accepted that "The ball is red" applies to the particular physical relationship being described
   (B) speakers of English do not accept that synonyms for "ball" and "red" express these concepts as elegantly
   (C) "The ball is red" corresponds essentially to every aspect of the particular physical relationship being described
   (D) "ball" and "red" actually refer to an entity and a property respectively
   (E) "ball" and "red" are mathematical concepts that attempt to accurately describe some particular physical relationship in the world

Passage 9: Mathematics as Language

What Makes It Difficult?

This passage couples two difficulty factors for most test takers, albeit two not usually seen together; abstract philosophy and math and science. Even the first sentence is a whopper—"what it means to 'explain' something . . . often comes down to the application of mathematics." What? Terminology like "methodological efficiency" ups the ante, as does the author's use of rhetorical questions and lack of a strong statement of main idea.

There are only five points to be gained on this passage, and the first two are long and question 5 is an unusual one, requiring the application of what's in the passage to another situation. Lets try to break this passage down into manageable pieces and make it more user-friendly.

Key Points of the Passage

Purpose and Main Idea: Focusing on the broadest of broad strokes here will really pay off. The gist of the author's purpose is to describe the debate over the nature of language, and then to touch upon the impact of that debate on how mathematics (the basis of scientific explanation) can be used and understood. And the main idea might summarize something like, "As linguists study how words or sentences tell us about the world, scientists should also study how mathematical concepts tell us about the physical world."

Paragraph Structure: Paragraph 1 is all about how mathematics is used as the "language" in which science is explained. Math meets the common definition of language, after all (lines 4–6), and thus "tells" scientists things when applied to "some aspect of the world" (line 12). The phrase "Some thinkers hold..." is the problem here, because those with LSAT experience are used to anticipating "But other thinkers believe otherwise," a contrast that never comes; lines 3–6 turn out to be a sentiment that the author flatly agrees with and uses as evidence. But that's a trap that should cause only momentary aggravation at worst. By the end of paragraph 1 we simply need to have gleaned the idea that "math is the language of science."

Paragraph 2 begins with a helpful sentence, helpful in that it cements for us the topic ("the issue of scientific knowledge") and scope ("At the center of the issue . . . [are] questions about the relationship between language and what it refers to.") Then we see a "Some argue X/Other argue Y" construct, and it hinges on the issue of whether the meaning of language is fixed, solid, and essential, or whether it's fluid and dependent upon common agreement. (Even on a superficial level one can begin to see the implications of this debate in terms of paragraph 1. If language is fluid, and if math is a language, then how can math be used with precision?)

Paragraph 3 also begins helpfully, in that the author announces himself squarely in the second, "fluid" camp. Language in most disciplines, we're told, depends on what's going on in the disciplines themselves and will vary over time. Why should scientific "language" be any different?, asks sentence 4, and the rest of the paragraph goes on to reply "It shouldn't and it isn't." The sense of the rest—and it is difficult, no doubt about it—is that math isn't so much a precise statement, as an imprecise metaphor or analogy that will work until a better one comes along. Unsure about exactly what he's talking about? Doesn't matter; we have the gist of it.

Paragraph 4 announces the change of scope right away: "the implications of this theory" (line 45). The author implies that in non-science fields, such as literature and history perhaps, a dilemma exists: If words have no fixed meaning, then what can we truly learn from spoken or written language? And by the same token, in science—where math, lest we forget, IS the "language"— what can we really learn from E = mc2, a seemingly precise "equation" which, according to the author's theory, isn't precise at all, but a bunch of vague metaphors that may change over time? (This is more or less what we speculated at the end of paragraph 2. See above.) Anyhow, the author concludes by intoning that science hasn't begun to explore those questions. Fortunately, we don't have to explore any of it any further. We just want the payoff (in points) of having mastered this thing.

An Advanced test taker recognizes the common constructs that authors use repeatedly in LSAT passages.

Answers and Explanations

1. D   2. A   3. B   4. B   5. A

1. D

(D) has it all. It gets the topic and scope right (the difficulty of using math to acquire and describe scientific knowledge), brings in the author's often-discussed parallel to the use of language in other disciplines, and even hints at the issue raised in paragraph 4's last sentence—the issue in which scientific inquiry has been deficient.

As usual, each of the wrong choices includes serious errors of omission and commission that should allow us to settle on (D) even if we are unsure about (D)'s strengths:

(A) According to the author, mathematics IS a language, but (A)'s claim that science must rely on both language and mathematics seems to imply that they are different. Moreover, from paragraph 1 on the author is scrupulous to restrict his main focus to math and science. "Language" is used to illuminate certain problems in scientific awareness.

(B)'s reference to some math being more precise than other math has no relationship to the passage's ideas. The contrast set up in paragraph 3 is clearly precision vs. imprecision.

(C) The future "progress" of science, as a concept, never appears in the text, nor is there any reference to "abandon[ing] the pursuit of new knowledge." And what "scientists must [do]" is deftly spelled out in (D); it has nothing to do with (C)'s talk of going back to past knowledge to decide how we figured it out originally—whatever that means.

(E) According to the last sentence of the passage, the question of the function of mathematics in the acquisition of knowledge "has yet to be significantly addressed." The author wouldn't congratulate linguists for beginning a discussion that hasn't happened.

2. A

This is one of the tougher ones, partly because the choices are all long and dense and remarkably similar, and partly just because it's a logic question ("support the view that"). The key is recognizing that the view we need to support—"that language has an essential correspondence to . . . things"—is the first of the two theories described (lines 18–21) in paragraph 2. In this view, language is fixed and precise. This means that you need to search for a choice indicating language to be "solid and reliable," and you don't have to search for long, because (A) does the job. That two independently developed languages categorize objects in the very same way supports the notion that there's something unchanging and definite about the relationship between words and objects; even two totally independent languages both pick up on the same things.

(B) Close but no cigar. Close to (A), in fact. But if one of the two similar languages derived from the other, as (B) suggests, then we can't infer from them that language has a universal dimension. The linguistic categories common to both of (B)'s languages could be unique to them, with no relationship to those in other languages, in which case the second hypothesis wins support.

(C), even more so than (B), connects the linguistic categories within one unique language and leaves out its correspondence with other languages.

(D) Highlighting "sentence structure" seems a little narrow for a passage about general theories of language. But worse than that is the way in which (D) narrows its attention to societies that have scientific sophistication, because that starts to smack of the second theory's concept of "agreed-upon conventions." Maybe those very sharp societies have linguistic agreement that differs totally from that which is found in the more backward ones—thus weakening, rather than supporting, the idea in question. To put it another way, theory 1 would gain more credence if the sentence structure in all societies, regardless of how advanced they were, was similar or identical. But that brings us back to (A).

(E) is outside of the scope. What speakers of a language believe their language to do or be is irrelevant to whether language does, in fact, have a universal dimension.

3. C

Even students driven daffy by the middle of the text will hopefully recall that the passage begins with the very definition for which question 24 asks, lines 3–4. (B) substitutes "collection" for "contrivance" but is otherwise verbatim.

(A), (E) In theory 2, language is metaphor (lines 38–44), relying on agreed-upon conventions (line 23). But does it define language? No one's agreed on that, even less on whether mathematics meets that criterion.

(C) is a concept from theory 1, not necessarily relevant to math and certainly not presented as a sheer definition of language.

(D) refers to the way mathematics is used in science, not to what makes math a language. The power to explain is the function and beauty of language but not, insofar as the passage is concerned anyway, its definition.

4. B

The first sentence of paragraph 3 makes it clear that the paragraph's topic is theory 2, the one described in lines 21–24, and if you're wondering whether the author strays from it, take note of the signposts: "According to linguists who support this view," (lines 26–27); "These linguists argue that" (lines 29–30); and "Under this view," (line 38). These Keyword phrases alone tell us that all along, paragraph 3 is embroidering the theory that language is fluid and a matter of convention— of course, (B)'s "elaborate" is more of an LSAT word than "embroider."

(A) evokes theory 1, not 2.

(C) is wrong in asserting that paragraph 3 is a compare/contrast vehicle between the two theories. In fact, theory 1 is left behind by the time we get to paragraph 3, and it's no wonder: Inferably, theory 1 poses fewer problems for the idea of math as language (if it's precise, it's precise, right?). The author's real interest is in whether language is in fact vague and changing, and that's why he devotes all of paragraph 3 (and paragraph 4) to that issue.

(D) According to the last sentence (lines 54–55) the debate in science has barely begun, so it's hard to see what (D) is talking about, let alone define paragraph 3 in (D)'s terms. What paragraph 3 does do is show that the same linguistic issues may apply in science as elsewhere, but that's the "elaboration" to which correct choice (B) refers.

(E) hearkens back to paragraph 1. By paragraph 3 we're exploring just what kind of language mathematics is.

5. A

An extrapolation question. There's nothing about balls, red or otherwise, in the passage; instead we have to apply the passage's ideas to this concrete example. But which ideas? The key is to check out lines 21–24 and recognize that we're talking theory 2 here—the one that believes language to be un-fixed, a matter of common agreement. To those holding this view, the English sentence "The ball is red" is true simply because all English speakers agree upon what "ball" and "red" mean. That's (A).

(B) The issue is why "The ball is red" is true, not whether there might or might not be better ways of saying it, e.g. "The sphere is scarlet."

(C) "Essential correspondence" is part of theory 1, not 2.

(D)'s entity vs. property distinction isn't a key element of either theory.

(E) "The ball is red" is a conventional-language sentence that is true for different reasons, depending on which theory one supports. That has nothing to do with mathematics, which is a parallel but totally different aspect of the passage.

An Advanced test taker isn't thrown by an unusual question stem; she focuses on what the question is asking and tackles it confidently.

What's Next?

The working in this one is fairly dense, but you won't find any relief from the wordiness and abstraction in the next passage.

PASSAGE 10

Scientists typically advocate the analytic method of studying complex systems: systems are divided into component parts that are investigated separately. But nineteenth-century critics of this method claimed
(5)   that when a system's parts are isolated, its complexity tends to be lost. To address the perceived weaknesses of the analytic method, these critics put forward a concept called organicism, which posited that the whole determines the nature of its parts and that the
(10)   parts of a whole are interdependent.

Organicism depended upon the theory of internal relations, which states that relations between entities are possible only within some whole that embraces them, and that entities are altered by the relationships
(15)   into which they enter. If an entity stands in a relationship with another entity, it has some property as a consequence. Without this relationship, and hence without the property, the entity would be different— and so would be another entity. Thus, the property is
(20)   one of the entity's defining characteristics. Each of an entity's relationships likewise determines a defining characteristic of the entity.

One problem with the theory of internal relations is that not all properties of an entity are defining
(25)   characteristics: numerous properties are accompanying characteristics—even if they are always present, their presence does not influence the entity's identity. Thus, even if it is admitted that every relationship into which an entity enters determines some characteristic of the
(30)   entity, it is not necessarily true that such characteristics will define the entity; it is possible for the entity to enter into a relationship yet remain essentially unchanged.

The ultimate difficulty with the theory of internal
(35)   relations is that it renders the acquisition of knowledge impossible. To truly know an entity, we must know all of its relationships; but because the entity is related to everything in each whole of which it is a part, these wholes must be known completely before the entity
(40)   can be known. This seems to be a prerequisite impossible to satisfy.

Organicists' criticism of the analytic method arose from their failure to fully comprehend the method. In rejecting the analytic method, organicists overlooked
(45)   the fact that before the proponents of the method analyzed the component parts of a system, they first determined both the laws applicable to the whole system and the initial conditions of the system; proponents of the method thus did not study parts of a
(50)   system in full isolation from the system as a whole. Since organicists failed to recognize this, they never advanced any argument to show that laws and initial conditions of complex systems cannot be discovered. Hence, organicists offered no valid reason for rejecting
(55)   the analytic method or for adopting organicism as a replacement for it.

1. Which one of the following most completely and accurately summarizes the argument of the passage?

    (A) By calling into question the possibility that complex systems can be studied in their entirety, organicists offered an alternative to the analytic method favored by nineteenth-century scientists.

    (B) Organicists did not offer a useful method of studying complex systems because they did not acknowledge that there are relationships into which an entity may enter that do not alter the entity's identity.

    (C) Organicism is flawed because it relies on a theory that both ignores the fact that not all characteristics of entities are defining and ultimately makes the acquisition of knowledge impossible.

    (D) Organicism does not offer a valid challenge to the analytic method both because it relies on faulty theory and because it is based on a misrepresentation of the analytic method.

    (E) In criticizing the analytic method, organicists neglected to disprove that scientists who employ the method are able to discover the laws and initial conditions of the systems they study.

2. According to the passage, organicists' chief objection to the analytic method was that the method

    (A) oversimplified systems by isolating their components

    (B) assumed that a system can be divided into component parts

    (C) ignored the laws applicable to the system as a whole

    (D) claimed that the parts of a system are more important than the system as a whole

    (E) denied the claim that entities enter into relationships

3. The passage offers information to help answer each of the following questions EXCEPT:

   (A) Why does the theory of internal relations appear to make the acquisition of knowledge impossible?

   (B) Why did the organicists propose replacing the analytic method?

   (C) What is the difference between a defining characteristic and an accompanying characteristic?

   (D) What did organicists claim are the effects of an entity's entering into a relationship with another entity?

   (E) What are some of the advantages of separating out the parts of a system for study?

4. The passage most strongly supports the ascription of which one of the following views to scientists who use the analytic method?

   (A) A complex system is best understood by studying its component parts in full isolation from the system as a whole.

   (B) The parts of a system should be studied with an awareness of the laws and initial conditions that govern the system.

   (C) It is not possible to determine the laws governing a system until the system's parts are separated from one another.

   (D) Because the parts of a system are interdependent, they cannot be studied separately without destroying the system's complexity.

   (E) Studying the parts of a system individually eliminates the need to determine which characteristics of the parts are defining characteristics.

5. Which one of the following is a principle upon which the author bases an argument against the theory of internal relations?

   (A) An adequate theory of complex systems must define the entities of which the system is composed.

   (B) An acceptable theory cannot have consequences that contradict its basic purpose.

   (C) An adequate method of study of complex systems should reveal the actual complexity of the systems it studies.

   (D) An acceptable theory must describe the laws and initial conditions of a complex system.

   (E) An acceptable method of studying complex systems should not study parts of the system in isolation from the system as a whole.

Passage 10: Organicism

What Makes It Difficult?

First, the good news. The passage has a nice, concise paragraph structure—five relatively short paragraphs should make for bite-size chunks of text. Now, the bad news; those bites are going to be a little hard to swallow. The passage gives lots of new terminology, and while you know on the LSAT that the test makers don't expect you to come in knowing what "organicism" or "the theory of internal relations" are, the definitions given aren't much more helpful. Organicism is the theory that "the whole determines the nature of its parts and that the parts of a whole are interdependent." That's not impossible to digest, but it's enough to make nearly any reader stop, think, and reread. Just don't let yourself do that five or ten times; if it doesn't make sense after the second read, mark it so that you know where the definition of organicism is and can come back to it if you need to.

An Advanced test taker doesn't let herself get bogged down in tough prose—detail-oriented OR overly abstract.

Key Points of the Passage

Purpose and Main Idea: The author's purpose is strongly hinted at in the topic sentences of the final three paragraphs: It is to argue that organicism fails as a replacement for the analytic method described in the first sentence. The main point involves the reasons why it fails: The theoretical basis for organicism, the theory of internal relations, has serious problems, and the organicists base their criticism upon a faulty understanding of the analytic method.

Paragraph Structure: Paragraph 1 sets the terms of the debate: Scientists typically use the analytic method to study complex systems, "but"—and this contrast Keyword always comes with a red flag—critics feel that isolating components for study (the modus operandi of the analytical method) detracts from understanding the system as a whole. Naturally, these critics propose a method that embraces the whole, and that sees a complex organism as made up of interrelated components whose nature is determined by relationships to each other and to the overall system. This method is called "organicism," and its supporters, "organicists."

No surprises in paragraph 2: The active reader expects at this point a description of organicism, and happily one is forthcoming. Organicism is based on the theory of "internal relations," which proposes that the relationships an entity enters into affect the very nature of the entity itself. This may seem a little abstract, but perhaps we can see it better in comparison to the analytic method that organicism was formulated to challenge: The analytic method favors studying the components of a system in isolation, whereas organicists believe that an entity can't be defined in isolation because its relationships to other entities are themselves properties of the entity. We're still awaiting the author's take on the situation—so far the discussion has been entirely factual. For all we know, it may remain that way.

But the first sentence of paragraph 3 kills that notion—here we're struck with the first signs of authorial opinion: "One problem with the theory of internal relations . . . " Seems like the author is turning on the organicists, and indeed, paragraph 3 discusses one hitch to the theory: Not every relationship an entity enters into changes the entity as the organicists suppose. This is because not every property is a "defining" property; some are "accompanying" properties. There's no sense getting bogged down with these terms—the point to take away from paragraph 3 is simply that it's possible for an entity's relationships not to affect its nature, which is a blow to the theory of internal relations on which organicism is based.

Paragraph 4 adds fuel to the fire, as the author presents us with the "ultimate" difficulty of internal relations. According to the theory, in order to know an entity, we have to know all its relations, since these relations supposedly define the entity's nature. But this, according to the author, is impossible—we can never fully know the essence of the many wholes to which an entity is related, and therefore we can never fully know any entity in the sense that the theory of internal relations posits. In other words, the author believes that the theory is based upon an impossible condition.

Paragraph 5 continues the burial of organicism, and again, the first sentence sets the tone: The organicists' critique of the analytical method was based on their failure to properly understand it. The author believes that they focused too heavily on the isolation element of the theory, assuming that components of systems would only be studied in isolation and out of context to the whole. This is wrong, says the author: Before even getting to that stage, practitioners of the analytic method study the laws of the whole system and the initial conditions of the system. Because they didn't recognize this, the organicists posed no counter-argument on this level. And as if the author's position wasn't clear enough by now, the final sentence restates the main point: For the reasons cited in paragraphs 3, 4, and 5, organicism failed in its bid to replace the analytic method.

Answers and Explanations

1. D   2. A   3. E   4. B   5. B

1. D

As suggested above, consider the passage as a whole before settling on the main point, for the author's disapproval of organicism doesn't surface until line 23. But disapprove he does, as evidenced by the topic sentences listed in the second bullet point above. Still, the choices require careful consideration—they all in some way question the efficacy of organicism, so we need to scrutinize each to find the one that matches up with the author's particular complaint. Let's consider them one by one.

(A) goes against the grain: Organicists are the ones who seem to call for the study of systems in their entirety. After all, they were the ones who felt that the analytic method of studying a system by isolating its components was flawed. Organicists believe that the whole determines the nature of the parts, and advocate a "holistic" approach, so (A) has it wrong when it says that they call into question the possibility of studying complex systems in their entirety.

(B) and (C) point to the author's criticism of organicism in the third and fourth paragraphs, but neither is inclusive enough to "completely and accurately summarize the argument." The weaknesses of organicism are mentioned to support a larger point; namely, that this method failed as a substitute for the analytic method. These choices ignore the analytic method entirely, and thus ignore the major issue of the confrontation between the two methodologies.

(D), however, hits on the issue missing from (B) and (C)—it addresses the debate between the analytic method and organicism, set out in paragraph 1 and definitively settled in the last line of paragraph 5. Organicism fails as a substitute for the analytic method—no description of the argument in this passage would be complete without this. (D) also includes the reasons for the failure of organicism, a nice touch that adequately covers the material in the final three paragraphs. While many of the wrong choices cover one part of the passage or another, only (D) is inclusive enough to describe the author's entire argument.

(E), like the other wrong choices, is too narrow to be the main point here. It refers exclusively to a criticism of organicism levied in paragraph 5 and so, like the others, fails to address the main issue of organicism's failure to supplant the analytic method.

> An Advanced test taker realizes test makers make questions harder by giving more plausible wrong answer choices. Read your choice carefully before finalizing it; rushing can lead into careless mistakes.

---

2. A

This one's a bit shorter, and thankfully, simpler. Your mental roadmap of the passage should lead you right to paragraph 1, the place where the debate between methods is introduced. What is the organicists' beef with the analytic method? It's right there in lines 4–6: "critics of this method (organicists) claimed that when a system's parts are isolated its complexity tends to be lost." (A) is a pretty close paraphrase of this, substituting "oversimplified" for loss of complexity, and "components" for "parts."

(B) Organicists don't question the general notion that a system can be broken down into parts—they question whether a complex system can be understood by studying those parts in isolation.

(C) distorts a detail from paragraph 5: The author criticizes the organicists for not recognizing that the analytic method folks determine the laws applicable to the system as a whole before analyzing its component parts.

(D) The analytic method makes no such claim, nor do the organicists accuse it of doing so. This choice distorts the issue of isolating parts. The analytic method is about studying parts in isolation, but there's no indication of any comparison of the importance of the parts relative to the whole.

(E) "Relationships" is an organicist conception. Nowhere are we told that the analytic method denies that entities enter into relationships (even though the method itself may suggest that such relationships, if they exist, are unimportant)—and the organicists never accuse the method of making this denial.

3. E

This question stem may have seemed a little odd, but a slight translation should make the task appear easier. In order to be able to answer a question contained in a choice, that question must relate to a definite issue or detail in the passage. So we're essentially asked here to find the choice that does not address some relevant issue in the passage, and you have enough practice with recognizing things that aren't relevant—simply look for something that's outside the scope, or that distorts the information in the passage. There's no way to pre-phrase here, so we'll simply have to test the choices:

(A) Paragraph 4 is nothing more than the answer to this question.

(B) Paragraph 1 gets the ball rolling with the organicists' reason for attempting to replace the analytic method.

(C) These terms should sound familiar, and in fact, this distinction is explicated precisely in paragraph 3.

(D) Paragraph 2 provides all the information you need to answer the question posed in this choice (and more information than most would ever want on the effects of relationships on entities).

(E) The terms may sound familiar, but the word "advantages" throws this one off: The analytic method involves separating out the parts of a system for study, but nowhere are we told the specific advantages of this approach. All we know about are the supposed disadvantages of this approach, put forth by the organicists. And although the author criticizes the organicists' critique of the analytic method, he doesn't do so by citing the advantages of isolating components, but rather by focusing on the deficiencies of organicism. (E) contains the question the passage cannot answer, and thus gets the point for 3.

An Advanced test taker notices "EXCEPT" in the question stem and eliminates the answer choices he would select as correct absent the "EXCEPT."

---

4. B

Next up we're asked to find a view that accords with the thinking of the analytic method scientists. Paragraph 1 contains the main thing we know about them—they believe in dividing systems into component parts for study. This is what has prompted the whole organicist reaction, so this would make a fine pre-phrase. However, no choice simply states this notion—in fact, most of the wrong choices distort this notion of isolation, as we'll see below. The answer comes from paragraph 5, where we find out that before the proponents of the analytic method isolated components for study, they first determined the initial conditions and the laws applicable to the whole. So (B), which essentially restates the information in lines 45–48, is right on the money.

(A) takes the isolation notion to an extreme, and in fact even contradicts lines 45–48: Because the analytic method folks make an attempt to understand the system as a whole, it certainly cannot be said that the method involves studying the parts "in full isolation."

(C) uses the terminology of the passage, but distorts the ideas. Determining the laws applicable to the system happens before the components can be studied. It therefore makes no sense to say that the proponents of the analytic method would believe that it is impossible to determine the system's governing laws until the parts are isolated.

(D) is a view that can be ascribed to the organicists, not the supporters of the analytic method.

(E) The notion of "defining characteristics" is brought up by the author in paragraph 3 as a defense against the organicists' critique of the analytic method.

5. B

Finally, we're asked to find a principle on which the author's critique of the theory of internal relations is based, which immediately tells us that paragraphs 3 and 4 are the ones in play here.

In those paragraphs, we find two complaints against the theory: "one problem" with the theory in paragraph 3, and the "ultimate difficulty" with the theory in paragraph 4. Not surprisingly, it is this major difficulty on which the correct principle is based. Internal relations entails a way to understand an entity by means of analyzing its relations to other entities. But the author thinks this is impossible—one cannot fully know the whole, so applying the theory "renders the acquisition of knowledge impossible." Therein lies the contradiction referred to in correct choice (B): The application of the theory leads to a violation of the theory's purpose. The purpose is to know the system, yet the application of the theory itself makes it impossible to know. According to (B), a theory based on such a contradiction cannot be acceptable, and that jibes perfectly with the author's second and "ultimate" criticism of the internal relations theory.

(A) The argument to divide and conquer is consistent with the analytic method, but isn't part of the author's attack on internal relations as that attack appears in paragraphs 3 and 4. If anything, the theory of internal relations is also consistent with the principle in (A)—in seeking to understand an entity's relationships, the theory attempts to provide a way for such a definition to occur.

(C) The issue of "complexity" is out of place here; it is the organicists who invoke a "loss of complexity" in their critique of the analytic method.

(D) is tricky in that it uses, but distorts, the ideas in the final paragraph. The author raises the issue of describing the laws and initial conditions of a system to point to a flaw in the organicists' overall approach—they didn't recognize that this was part of the analytic method. This is not, however, related specifically to the author's criticism of the theory of internal relations, which again, is located in paragraphs 3 and 4.

(E), like many previous wrong choices in this question set, mistakes the players in the passage. We're looking for support for the author's argument against the organicists' theory of internal relations, but instead this principle supports the organicists' critique of the analytic method as described in paragraph 1.

What's Next?

Perhaps not surprisingly, philosophical conjecture isn't limited to the natural sciences, but can often appear in social sciences passages. Time to move on to one such passage.

PASSAGE 11

Recently, a new school of economics called steady-state economics has seriously challenged neoclassical economics, the reigning school in Western economic decision making. According to the neoclassical model,
(5) an economy is a closed system involving only the circular flow of exchange value between producers and consumers. Therefore, no noneconomic constraints impinge upon the economy and growth has no limits. Indeed, some neoclassical economists argue that
(10) growth itself is crucial, because, they claim, the solutions to problems often associated with growth (income inequities, for example) can be found only in the capital that further growth creates.

Steady-state economists believe the neoclassical
(15) model to be unrealistic and hold that the economy is dependent on nature. Resources, they argue, enter the economy as raw material and exit as consumed products or waste; the greater the resources, the greater the size of the economy. According to these
(20) economists, nature's limited capacity to regenerate raw material and absorb waste suggests that there is an optimal size for the economy, and that growth beyond this ideal point would increase the cost to the environment at a faster rate than the benefit to
(25) producers and consumers, generating cycles that impoverish rather than enrich. Steady-state economists thus believe that the concept of an ever growing economy is dangerous, and that the only alternative is to maintain a state in which the economy remains in
(30) equilibrium with nature. Neoclassical economists, on the other hand, consider nature to be just one element of the economy rather than an outside constraint, believing that natural resources, if depleted, can be replaced with other elements—i.e., human-made
(35) resources—that will allow the economy to continue with its process of unlimited growth.

Some steady-state economists, pointing to the widening disparity between indices of actual growth (which simply count the total monetary value of goods
(40) and services) and the index of environmentally sustainable growth (which is based on personal consumption, factoring in depletion of raw materials and production costs), believe that Western economies have already exceeded their optimal size. In response
(45) to the warnings from neoclassical economists that checking economic growth only leads to economic stagnation, they argue that there are alternatives to growth that still accomplish what is required of any economy: the satisfaction of human wants. One of
(50) the alternatives is conservation. Conservation—for example, increasing the efficiency of resource use through means such as recycling—differs from growth in that it is qualitative, not quantitative, requiring improvement in resource management rather than an
(55) increase in the amount of resources. One measure of the success of a steady-state economy would be the degree to which it could implement alternatives to growth, such as conservation, without sacrificing the ability to satisfy the wants of producers and consumers.

1. Which one of the following most completely and accurately expresses the main point of the passage?

   (A) Neoclassical economists, who, unlike steady-state economists, hold that economic growth is not subject to outside constraints, believe that nature is just one element of the economy and that if natural resources in Western economies are depleted they can be replaced with human-made resources.

   (B) Some neoclassical economists, who, unlike steady-state economists, hold that growth is crucial to the health of economies, believe that the solutions to certain problems in Western economies can thus be found in the additional capital generated by unlimited growth.

   (C) Some steady-state economists, who, unlike neoclassical economists, hold that unlimited growth is neither possible nor desirable, believe that Western economies should limit economic growth by adopting conservation strategies, even if such strategies lead temporarily to economic stagnation.

   (D) Some steady-state economists, who, unlike neoclassical economists, hold that the optimal sizes of economies are limited by the availability of natural resources, believe that Western economies should limit economic growth and that, with alternatives like conservation, satisfaction of human wants need not be sacrificed.

   (E) Steady-state and neoclassical economists, who both hold that economies involve the circular flow of exchange value between producers and consumers, nevertheless differ over the most effective way of guaranteeing that a steady increase in this exchange value continues unimpeded in Western economies.

2. Based on the passage, neoclassical economists would likely hold that steady-state economists are wrong to believe each of the following EXCEPT:

   (A) The environment's ability to yield raw material is limited.
   (B) Natural resources are an external constraint on economies.
   (C) The concept of unlimited economic growth is dangerous.
   (D) Western economies have exceeded their optimal size.
   (E) Economies have certain optimal sizes.

3. According to the passage, steady-state economists believe that unlimited economic growth is dangerous because it

   (A) may deplete natural resources faster than other natural resources are discovered to replace them

   (B) may convert natural resources into products faster than more efficient resource use can compensate

   (C) may proliferate goods and services faster than it generates new markets for them

   (D) may create income inequities faster than it creates the capital needed to redress them

   (E) may increase the cost to the environment faster than it increases benefits to producers and consumers

4. A steady-state economist would be LEAST likely to endorse which one of the following as a means of helping a steady-state economy reduce growth without compromising its ability to satisfy human wants?

   (A) a manufacturer's commitment to recycle its product packaging

   (B) a manufacturer's decision to use a less expensive fuel in its production process

   (C) a manufacturer's implementation of a quality control process to reduce the output of defective products

   (D) a manufacturer's conversion from one type of production process to another with greater fuel efficiency

   (E) a manufacturer's reduction of output in order to eliminate an overproduction problem

5. Based on the passage, a steady-state economist is most likely to claim that a successful economy is one that satisfies which one of the following principles?

   (A) A successful economy uses human-made resources in addition to natural resources.

   (B) A successful economy satisfies human wants faster than it creates new ones.

   (C) A successful economy maintains an equilibrium with nature while still satisfying human wants.

   (D) A successful economy implements every possible means to prevent growth.

   (E) A successful economy satisfies the wants of producers and consumers by using resources to spur growth.

6. In the view of steady-state economists, which one of the following is a noneconomic constraint as referred to in line 7?

   (A) the total amount of human wants

   (B) the index of environmentally sustainable growth

   (C) the capacity of nature to absorb waste

   (D) the problems associated with economic growth

   (E) the possibility of economic stagnation

7. Which one of the following most accurately describes what the last paragraph does in the passage?

   (A) It contradicts the ways in which the two economic schools interpret certain data and gives a criterion for judging between them based on the basic goals of an economy.

   (B) It gives an example that illustrates the weakness of the new economic school and recommends an economic policy based on the basic goals of the prevailing economic school.

   (C) It introduces an objection to the new economic school and argues that the policies of the new economic school would be less successful than growth-oriented economic policies at achieving the basic goal an economy must meet.

   (D) It notes an objection to implementing the policies of the new economic school and identifies an additional policy that can help avoid that objection and still meet the goal an economy must meet.

   (E) It contrasts the policy of the prevailing economic school with the recommendation mentioned earlier of the new economic school and shows that they are based on differing views on the basic goal an economy must meet.

8. The passage suggests which one of the following about neoclassical economists?

   (A) They assume that natural resources are infinitely available.

   (B) They assume that human-made resources are infinitely available.

   (C) They assume that availability of resources places an upper limit on growth.

   (D) They assume that efficient management of resources is necessary to growth.

   (E) They assume that human-made resources are preferable to natural resources.

Passage 11: Steady-State Economics

What Makes It Difficult?

Long paragraphs present difficulty, and lest you rejoice too soon at the eight point haul, notice that there are only two global and detail questions; the global question is almost as long as the passage, and two questions are "LEAST"/"EXCEPT" variations, which will be more time consuming than their standard cousins. The passage itself is lacking in specific examples to help flesh out ideas such as "an economy is a closed system involving only the circular flow of exchange value between producers and consumers" (lines 6–8). And for those economics majors out there who breathe a sigh of relief at the familiar subject matter, there's a different, and perhaps more insidious, danger; be absolutely sure to answer the questions based on the passage content and not on your outside knowledge of the subject.

> An Advanced test taker uses his own knowledge to help him understand an author's ideas, but never replaces the author's ideas with his own.

Key Points of the Passage

Purpose and Main Idea: The author's purpose is to describe some fundamental principles of a new school of economic thinking by drawing contrasts with the tenets of the "reigning" model, neoclassicism. His main point—it's difficult to call it a "Main Idea" since the author allows little or no personal opinion to come through—is that the steady-state economists take issue with the idea that economic growth can be unlimited. They want to effect a balance with nature and limitations on growth, confident that humanity's ability to satisfy wants won't be compromised.

Paragraph Structure: Paragraph 1 lays out the battle lines right away: A new economic school is challenging the reigning one. The rest of the paragraph details the neoclassical definition of economy (a closed loop) and its fundamental (as far as the passage is concerned) principle, namely that "growth has no limits" (line 8). Growth should not be checked; growth indeed is necessary for solving economic problems.

Paragraph 2 offers the steady-staters' reply to that position. To them, economics is not a closed loop because the outside forces of nature intervene: Nature, whose resources run out and whose ability to process waste, is limited, too. In sharp contrast to the "Growth: Yes" tenet of neoclassicism, the central steady-state belief is that unlimited growth tends to "impoverish rather than enrich," and so steady-staters want to see a balance made with nature. The author brings in the neoclassicists one more time, in lines 30–36, where we hear their answer to the above: Nature is not a separate, outside force, but part of the entire picture, and new resources can be created should natural ones run out.

Paragraph 3 shifts from the broad lines of steady-stater argument to a specific though related concern: Some believe, probably to the fury of the neoclassicists, that optimum growth has already been reached, or in other words, that an "equilibrium with nature" had better be made pretty darned quick. Their proposal for doing so includes conservation, the focus of the final 10 lines. Growth is "quantitative" (More! More!) while conservation is "qualitative" (Better! Better!); the latter is but one "alternative to growth" that, say the steady-staters, can satisfy human wants and still keep nature and economics balanced.

Answers and Explanations

1. D 2. A 3. E 4. B 5. C 6. C 7. D 8. B

1. D

Not withstanding the unconscionable length of the choices, what we need in the answer to a "main point" question is a focus on the steady-state school, and an emphasis on the key issue of growth. Only (D) provides both of those things while still managing to characterize the passage's ideas acceptably. It properly alludes to the steady-stater view (as outlined in paragraph 2) that growth must be limited, and sums up the notion (presented in paragraph 3) that there are alternative means to growth that can keep satisfying humanity. Let us see where the others go wrong:

(A) sums up the neoclassical position pretty well, but in speaking of steady-staters merely in passing, it fails utterly as the main point. It is, after all, steady-state ideas that are explored in the greatest detail (and rightly so: They are the new kids on the block, the ones with the new ideas); steady-staters begin and end the passage.

On top of all that, (A) reflects almost nothing of paragraph 3. These are all key reasons for rejecting (A) decisively. (B) It is all, not "some" neoclassicists who believe in unlimited growth. And anyway, the substance of (B) ends at passage line 13. Fully 47 lines of text go unreflected by (B).

(C) It is all, not "some" steady-staters who argue against unlimited growth. And they never concede the potential of such qualitative strategies as conservation to lead, even temporarily, to "stagnation" (a term used only by the neoclassicists in opposition to the steady-state view, lines 44–47).

(E) spends half of its length on similarities between the two economic schools, when the entire passage is devoted to separating them! And (E) never mentions the key issue of the passage—that of economic growth—whatsoever.

2. A

This question is the LSAT equivalent of a tongue-twister. Better unpack it before proceeding further. "The neoclassicists would believe that steady-staters are wrong to believe . . . " So: The question is talking about sentiments that the steady-staters hold but that neoclassicists would oppose. And there are four of them; this is an "all of the following EXCEPT." So: Four of the choices are both consistent with steady-stater philosophy and contradictory to neoclassicism. What do steady-staters believe? In limits to growth. In the dangers of growth. In our dependence on nature. And in the need for alternatives to growth, such as conservation, to ensure that though growth is limited we can still satisfy human wants and needs. We can expect to see such ideas reflected in the wrong choices.

(A) Surely the steady-staters believe that natural resources—what (A) calls "the environment's ability to yield raw material"—are going to run out sometime. And the neoclassicists don't disagree. Oh, sure, the old school is sanguine about humanity's ability to replenish whatever is lost (cf. Q. 21, below), so neoclassicists aren't worried about nature's resources running out. But they do acknowledge that it may happen. That makes (A) what we want for this question. All of the other choices, as expected, reflect steady-state ideas that are anathema to the Old Guard: (B) Lines 30–32 vs. lines 19–22. (C) Line 8 vs. lines 26–28. (D), (E) Lines 7–8 vs. lines 37–44.

3. E

Ask yourself: Where does the "danger" idea come in? If you don't recall that it's mentioned about halfway, simply skim the passage in search of the word, and there it is at line 28. The Conclusion Keyword "thus"—"Steady-state economists thus believe that etc."—sends us backwards to find the evidence for that conclusion, in the previous sentence: Once the economy hits optimal growth, further growth "would increase the cost to the environment at a faster rate than the benefit" (lines 23–24). This is virtually (E) word for word.

(A), (B), (C), and (D) All four choices' "faster rates" are utterly distinct from line 28 and its preceding context. So none of them can be correct. Period.

4. B

If the right answer is least likely to be endorsed by a steady-stater, it follows that the four wrong choices are more likely to get his endorsement—meaning that four of the choices would help to reduce growth while satisfying human wants. All of that must send us to paragraph 3, and specifically to lines 47 and beyond, where the steady-staters' proposals, so to speak, are described. "Conservation" is named as one of the alternatives to growth "that still . . . [satisfy] human wants" (lines 48–49), and the author describes "conservation" as "qualitative, not quantitative": It involves better management of resources "rather than an increase in the amount of resources" (i.e. rather than more growth). Dollars to donuts, four of the choices will match up to that qualitative ideal. Let's see: (A) Recycling is smart resource management. This would please the steady-stater. (B) Cheaper fuel has nothing to do with better management of resources, though it's likely to save the manufacturer money. So it's probably the odd-man-out correct answer. Let us check the others—but not with respect! We must assume that they are incorrect, that they support the conservationist ideal, because (B) does not. (C) Quality control, to reduce the number of defective products, is smart resource management. (D) So is a switch to greater fuel efficiency. (Note the sharp contrast to (B), which saves money only.) (E) Reducing output to avoid overproduction couldn't be smarter. As anticipated, (B) is the odd man out.

> An Advanced test taker knows that when he thinks he's found the correct answer, it's worth taking a look at the other four choices, but not with real consideration; if one is right the other four must be absolutely wrong. Answer choices are never "more right" than one another.

5. C

The word "success" appears towards the end of paragraph 3, line 56, but even if you didn't recall it you still could have inferred an answer to Q. 18 by appealing to the passage's broadest ideas. We know that the steady-staters want to limit growth; we know they want to see a balance with nature; and we know that they don't want to inconvenience or deprive mankind in the process. All of that leads us to (C), which of course is directly echoed in the final sentence: "One measure of . . . success" will be a balance between helping nature by checking growth and the satisfying of wants. (A) is a principle that sounds more in line with the neoclassical argument, dealing as it does with the prospect of utilizing man-made resources. The steady-staters seem to believe that if measures like conservation are successful, the resources provided by nature can go a long way. (B) Want creation isn't part of the passage's scope. Want satisfaction is. (D) The steady-staters want to limit growth because if unchecked it would threaten the earth's balance. That doesn't mean they oppose all growth. (D) is just too extreme, even radical, for the views here, and distorts those views to boot. (E) The phrase "spur growth" should be a tipoff that this is a neoclassical idea, and hence just the opposite of the way in which a steady-stater would define success.

6. C

This question is tricky in that while it sends us to line 7, the information needed to answer it is to be found nowhere near line 7. Indeed, the question in its subtle way really does get at much broader issues separating the steady-staters from the neoclassicists. The issue in question is the notion of "noneconomic constraint." As we've discussed, pargraph 2 more or less acts as a direct answer to the neoclassical definition of economy outlined in paragraph 1. Well, it is early in paragraph 2 that we learn a chief difference between the two schools: To the neoclassicist, nothing outside of the economy acts as a check on growth, whereas to the steady-stater, there exists one huge outside check on growth, and that's nature, on which lines 14–16 assert the economy is "dependent." The limited ability of nature to "regenerate new material and absorb waste" (lines 20–21) is the basis of the steady-staters' denial that growth is unlimited—and is the basis of correct choice (C) to boot. Further support for (C)—in the admittedly unlikely event that you kept reading down to the end of paragraph 2 for a question that began at line 7—is offered at lines 30–32: Neoclassicists "consider nature to be just one element of the economy rather than an outside constraint," implying that to the steady-stater, nature is such a constraint. (C) is the only choice that alludes to a facet of nature.

7. D

We thought about the purpose and thrust of paragraph 3 back when we read it. It describes the somewhat apocalyptic opinion of some steady-staters that optimum growth has already been reached, the reaction of neoclassicists ("Don't inhibit growth! That could be disastrous"—lines 44–47), and the proposal of the steady-staters to switch from an emphasis on growth to an emphasis on conservation, from the quantitative to the qualitative. This analysis matches up with the abstract language of (D): The "objection" comes in lines 44–47, the "additional policy" is conservation, and the "goal an economy must meet," as lines 47–49 and the final sentence point out, is the satisfaction of human wants. (A)'s wording is weird: It "contradicts" the ways in which the two schools interpret data? Don't they mean "contrasts"? (Not that paragraph 3 does any such thing.) And the author shows no interest in "judging between them," criterion or no criterion. (B) Since the author takes no stand on whether either school has a weak or strong position, and makes no recommendations either, (B) cannot possibly be correct. (C), like (B), implies a bias on the author's part (towards the neoclassicists, in this case) that appears nowhere in the text. (E) seems to think that paragraph 3 is mostly about neoclassicism, when it is not; the "prevailing economic school" is mentioned once, in passing. And both schools agree on "the basic goal an economy must meet"—satisfying human needs—so (E) is off on that basis as well.

8. B

By now we have pinpointed the few locations in which neoclassical economists' views are expressed, and need only refresh our memory of them before searching for the one answer choice that is reflected somewhere in those locations. Correct choice (B) comes out of paragraph 2 and lines 30–36, the assertion that the "process of unlimited growth" can go on by replacing depleted natural resources "with other elements—i.e. human-made resources." Unlimited growth would only be possible if human-made resources were equally unlimited. (A) The very fact that the neoclassicists have a remedy in mind (outlined in lines 30–36) for the depletion of natural resources indicates that they do not believe (A) to be true. (C) "Growth has no limits" (line 8), remember? (D) And because "growth has no limits," neoclassicists are granting no necessary condition for growth such as (D) describes. In any case, as far as the passage goes, management inefficiency is a steady-state concern (cf. line 54). (E) No such preference is even hinted at. The neoclassicists will just roll with the punches: If natural resources run out, we'll simply replace 'em with the man-made kind.

An Advanced test taker remembers, even when time is running short, not to cut corners by answering from memory. The test makers build in wrong answer choices to appeal to test takers who do so!

What's Next?

One more passage to go, and this one delves into one of the most common places abstract philosophy rears its head on the LSAT—the Law passage. Remember that this is the LSAT, not the bar exam, and you aren't expected to know anything about law; then plunge ahead fearlessly.

PASSAGE 12

Ronald Dworkin argues that judges are in danger of uncritically embracing an erroneous theory known as legal positivism because they think that the only alternative is a theory that they (and Dworkin) see as clearly
(5) unacceptable—natural law. The latter theory holds that judges ought to interpret the law by consulting their own moral convictions, even if this means ignoring the letter of the law and the legal precedents for its interpretation. Dworkin regards this as an
(10) impermissible form of judicial activism that arrogates to judges powers properly reserved for legislators.

Legal positivism, the more popular of the two theories, holds that law and morality are wholly distinct. The meaning of the law rests on social
(15) convention in the same way as does the meaning of a word. Dworkin's view is that legal positivists regard disagreement among jurists as legitimate only if it arises over what the underlying convention is, and it is to be resolved by registering a consensus, not by
(20) deciding what is morally right. In the same way, disagreement about the meaning of a word is settled by determining how people actually use it, and not by deciding what it ought to mean. Where there is no consensus, there is no legal fact of the matter. The
(25) judge's interpretive role is limited to discerning this consensus, or the absence thereof.

According to Dworkin, this account is incompatible with the actual practice of judges and lawyers, who act as if there is a fact of the matter even
(30) in cases where there is no consensus. The theory he proposes seeks to validate this practice without falling into what Dworkin correctly sees as the error of natural law theory. It represents a kind of middle ground between the latter and legal positivism. Dworkin
(35) stresses the fact that there is an internal logic to a society's laws and the general principles they typically embody. An interpretation that conforms to these principles may be correct even if it is not supported by a consensus. Since these general principles may
(40) involve such moral concepts as justice and fairness, judges may be called upon to consult their own moral intuitions in arriving at an interpretation. But this is not to say that judges are free to impose their own morality at will, without regard to the internal logic of the laws.
(45) The positivist's mistake, as Dworkin points out, is assuming that the meaning of the law can only consist in what people think it means, whether these people be the original authors of the law or a majority of the interpreter's peers. Once we realize, as Dworkin does,
(50) that the law has an internal logic of its own that constrains interpretation, we open up the possibility of improving upon the interpretations not only of our contemporaries but of the original authors.

1. Which one of the following most accurately expresses the main point of the passage?

(A) Dworkin regards natural law theory as a middle ground between legal positivism and judicial activism.

(B) Dworkin holds that judicial interpretations should not be based solely on identifying a consensus or solely on moral intuition, but should be consistent with the reasoning that underlies the law.

(C) Dworkin argues that the internal logic of the law should generally guide judges except in instances where consensus is registered or judges have strong moral intuitions.

(D) Dworkin's theory of legal interpretation is based on borrowing equally from natural law theory and legal positivism.

(E) Dworkin validates judges' dependence on moral intuition, reason, and the intent of the authors of a law, but only in cases where a social consensus is not present.

2. What is the main purpose of the second paragraph?

(A) to explain why legal positivism is so popular
(B) to evaluate the theory of legal positivism
(C) to discuss how judicial consensus is determined
(D) to identify the basic tenets of legal positivism
(E) to argue in favor of the theory of legal positivism

3. Which one of the following most accurately characterizes the author's attitude toward Dworkin's theory?

(A) confident endorsement of its central assertions

(B) caution about its potential for justifying some forms of judicial activism

(C) modest expectation that some of its claims will be found to be unwarranted

(D) quiet conviction that its importance derives only from its originality

(E) enthusiasm that it will replace legal positivism as the most popular theory of legal interpretation

4. According to the passage, which one of the following is a goal of Dworkin's theory of legal interpretation?

   (A) to evaluate previous legal interpretations by judges influenced by legal positivism
   (B) to dispute the notion that social consensus plays any role in legal interpretation
   (C) to provide a theoretical argument against the use of moral intuition in legal interpretation
   (D) to argue that legal decisions must be based on the principles of the original authors of the laws
   (E) to validate theoretically the method commonly used by judges in practice

5. The passage suggests that Dworkin would be most likely to agree with which one of the following statements?

   (A) Judges and lawyers too often act as though there is a fact of the matter in legal cases.
   (B) Judges should not use their moral intuition when it conflicts with the intentions of those legislators who authored the law being interpreted.
   (C) Legal positivism is a more popular theory than natural law theory because legal positivism simplifies the judge's role.
   (D) If there is consensus about how to interpret a law, then jurists should not examine the internal logic of the law being interpreted.
   (E) Legal positivists misunderstand the role of moral intuition in legal interpretation.

6. It can be inferred that legal positivists, as described in the passage, agree with which one of the following statements?

   (A) Judges sometimes ought to be allowed to use personal moral convictions as a basis for a legal interpretation.
   (B) Disagreements about the meaning of a law are never legitimate.
   (C) The ultimate standard of interpretation is the logic of the law itself, not moral intuition.
   (D) The meaning of a law derives from jurists' interpretations of that law.
   (E) There is no legal fact of the matter when jurists have differing moral convictions about an issue.

Passage 12: Dworkin and Judicial Interpretation

What Makes It Difficult?

Even admitted attorneys would be hard pressed to explain "natural law" or "legal positivism," so remember that there's no way you can be expected to unless you're told. Focus on the repetition of these unfamiliar terms to help work your way through the passage. It's ok on the first pass through to just know that Dworkin dislikes both and has a different idea; in terms of what these two theories actually are, that can wait until—if—there's a question that requires you to know. If that's the case, it's time to research, which you would do anyway. Right?

With no examples to help guide you, be relentless in focusing on structural keywords and hot words as you read and build your Roadmap. This focus is the secret to finding your way through the most abstract passages and this one is no exception.

Key Points of the Passage

Purpose and Main Idea: The author's purpose is to explain Dworkin's theory of judicial interpretation, which is a middle ground between natural law and legal positivism. His main idea? That Dworkin (correctly) views judicial interpretation as governed by law's "internal logic." While the author's view only surfaces at the very end, don't miss the language the author uses—"we open up the possibility of improving. . . "

Paragraph Structure: The passage begins in paragraph 1 with Dworkin's indictment of not one but two approaches to theories of judicial interpretation: the "erroneous theory known as legal positivism" and the "clearly unacceptable [theory], natural law." As good critical readers we should be quick to ask the passage, "What's the gist of each?" and "What does Dworkin propose in their place?" Paragraph 1 defines the second of the two, the idea that judges ignore all precedents and the letter of the law and just follow their moral code.

Paragraph 2 defines the first and more popular theory, which is pretty much the opposite: Follow the letter of the law; ignore moral considerations; and if jurists disagree, look for a consensus to work it out. Neither, to Dworkin, will do, the former because it nullifies the legislature's work (lines 9–11), the latter because it flies in the face of how judges actually do business (lines 27–30).

Paragraph 3 continues with Dworkin's proposal, a kind of amalgam of the two ("middle ground," line 33). His feeling is that there is reason—"internal logic," line 35—at work in the law, logic that should arbitrate disputes between precedents (rather than morality or consensus, as the other two theories would have it). Judges may use morality, and judges may follow the law's letter, but only in the context of the law's logic.

Paragraph 4 adds the author's take, so far missing but an element you should always ask about mentally (even though the author may never show his hand). The author clearly believes here that Dworkin gets it right.

An Advanced test taker asks himself while reading, "what should I expect to see next?"

Answers and Explanations

1. B   2. D   3. A   4. E   5. E   6. D

1. B

When a passage espouses a strong point of view, quickly reject any choices that fail to reflect it. Only (B) even comes close to reflecting Dworkin's strong repudiation of both the natural law and legal positivism theories, as well as his equally strong espousal of the "legal reasoning" theory. Natural law is not the middle ground (A); it's one of the two extremes that Dworkin rejects. (C) is a hopeless 180; in fact, lines 39–49 make it quite clear that the internal logic of a society's laws should trump both consensus and a judge's own moral intuition. It's not so much that Dworkin has "borrowed from" the two theories he rejects (D) as that he finds a middle path—a way that is more sensible than either of the others. (E) lumps together three disparate elements and subordinates them all to "consensus," a concept that Dworkin isn't even wild about; (E) is a train wreck.

2. D

Use your Roadmap to predict the purpose of a paragraph. As we've already seen, paragraph 2 explains legal positivism. And that's all that's there; no critical evaluation. (D) is therefore correct. The theory is described but its popularity (A) is only mentioned in passing, not explored. The "evaluation" (B) of the theory comes later, in lines 27–30 and lines 45–49. Yes, legal positivism does depend on consensus being reached (C) but the scope of the paragraph, and indeed that of the passage as a whole, does not encompass how that might be done. And since the theory is one that Dworkin rejects, (E) is a 180.

3. A

If you feel that an author's attitude is negative, there MUST be evidence of the same; it can't just be a "hunch" on your part. Up to now our discussion of the passage and questions has lumped together the author's views and Dworkin's views as if they were indistinguishable. And so they are; Dworkin's critiques and new theory are presented with not a bit of demurral. (A) has it right. There's no evidence of caution (B) in the author's treatment of Dworkin. (C) is even more negative. (D) and (E) are positive but otherwise go wrong. (D) marginalizes the appeal of Dworkin's theory solely to originality, and (E) wrongly implies that the author cares about which theory is "most popular."

> An Advanced test taker understands that even the hardest passage will have some easier questions.

4. E

"According to the passage" and categorical language ("is a goal") should signal you to retrieve your answer right out of the text. Paragraph 3 is where Dworkin's middle ground theory is presented, and it's there stated flatly that the theory "seeks to validate" the practice followed by judges and lawyers. You don't actually have to understand that practice (acting "as if there is a fact of the matter") to recognize that (E) has it right, that Dworkin is trying to justify in theory that which is done in practice. (A)'s thrust is backward, to past legal interpretations, but Dworkin's thrust in putting forth his theory is forward. (B) goes too far in accusing Dworkin of wanting to dispose of the idea of social consensus. (In the passage, he only goes so far as to forbid consensus to trump the law's internal logic.) Since Dworkin's theory sees a role for judges' moral intuition (lines 41–42), (C) is a 180. And (D) sounds much more like a positivist idea (i.e. "the letter of the law") than one that Dworkin, with his insistence on underlying logic, would espouse.

5. E

"Most likely to agree" signals inference. There's no point in trying to make a prediction about the right answer, but we can predict something about the wrong ones—they will either deviate from the passage's scope, or reflect natural law or legal positivist ideas. (A), for instance, is a view held by legal positivists (lines 23–24) and rejected by Dworkin. (B) would be fine if it ended ". . . if it conflicts with the law's internal logic," but as written does not reflect Dworkin's ideas at all. (C) brings up that popularity issue again; has any one word thrown into an LSAT passage ever generated quite so many wrong answers in the past? (D) is a 180 because it has things precisely backward: To Dworkin, internal logic must trump consensus rather than vice versa. Lines 39–49 support (E), which properly credits Dworkin with the idea that the legal positivists are wrong to discount all morality in judicial interpretation. As long as it's constrained by the logic of the law, morality has a place.

6. D

"Legal positivists . . . agree" also signals inference, but be sure to keep the different views separate. As we might expect, the wrong answers here will either reflect natural law or Dworkin ideas, or distort the text or scope. (A) is certainly a natural law idea (cf. lines 5–7). Contrary to (B), "disagreements" must be legitimate to the legal positivists because they have a theory about their resolution (lines 16–20). (C) is a Dworkin idea, plain and simple—his main point, actually. Correct choice (D) is a paraphrase of lines 45–49, and is supported by paragraph 2 as well. For the record, (E) can be quickly rejected because it gives credence to judges' moral convictions, even though (lines 16–20), to legal positivists, morality plays no role.

An Advanced test taker expects to be tested on the different points of view in the passage, and keeps them all straight. The test maker is likely to create wrong answers from another viewpoint than the one the question asks about.

CHAPTER FIFTEEN

Comparative Reading

One of the four passage sets that comprise the Reading Comprehension section of the exam will be a Comparative Reading passage set that consists of two passages. According to LSAC, this passage set evaluates how well test takers utilize skills such as comparison, contrast, synthesis, and generalization in order to understand arguments from more than one text—a significant element of law school study.

Because the Comparative Reading question type is so new, there simply aren't a lot of real examples available. So our team of expert LSAT instructors has studied the examples we do have of the new Comparative Reading passage set in close detail, and created three challenging practice passages to get you in the comparative reading zone. Once you've tackled those, move on to Passage 16—a real Comparative Reading passage set from a recent LSAT administration.

For the very latest information on the LSAT test changes, please visit us at www.kaptest.com/LSAT.

THE PASSAGES

The two passages are clearly labeled "Passage A" and "Passage B," and together, are roughly the same length as a single Reading Comprehension passage (about 500 words). They also cover the same four categories—social sciences, natural sciences, humanities, and law—used for single-passage sets. According to LSAC, the passages are typically adapted from two different published sources written by two different authors. The authors do not necessarily respond to each other—they may be opposed or in agreement—and the passages are separate works. LSAC also states that while the passages cover the same or similar topics, they may relate to each other in different ways. For example, one passage may present theories or beliefs in a general way, while the other applies them to specific circumstances.

THE QUESTIONS

Comparative Reading passages are followed by five to eight questions, just like the single-passage sets. Most questions are about both passages, however there may be a question concerning only one of the passages.

PASSAGE SET 13

Passage A

The passage of the Bankruptcy Abuse Prevention and Consumer Protection Act (BAPCPA) was the culmination of a decade of lobbying, debate, and proposed legislation. The
(5) new law seeks to screen prospective bankruptcy petitioners more carefully to determine whether or not filing is really necessary, and to prevent abusive filings. Congress had previously passed significant bankruptcy reforms, but President
(10) Clinton vetoed those reforms in 2000. The current administration gained support from certain factions and presented the passage of "bankruptcy reform" in 2005 as a victory, but the new law almost immediately showed signs of failing to achieve its
(15) stated goals and is unlikely to have a long-term impact on consumer bankruptcy filing rates.

BAPCPA does nothing to alleviate the economic stresses at the root of the bankruptcy problem, such as uninsured medical expenses,
(20) that are most likely to trigger bankruptcy filings. Although recent studies indicate that lost work time, medical expenses, and other costs associated with illness and injury are responsible for approximately half of all consumer bankruptcy
(25) cases, BAPCPA is aimed almost exclusively at reducing "abusive" filings by increasing pre-filing hurdles and screening.

Furthermore, the pre-filing credit counseling requirement is too little, too late; U.S. Trustee-
(30) approved credit counseling agencies report that by the time potential bankruptcy petitioners reach them, fewer than 5 percent have any other viable option, and even the Government Accountability Office has recently questioned the value of the
(35) requirement.

The Chapter 7 means test, presented as the centerpiece of the reform and the primary means of preventing abusive filings, and the Chapter 13 allowable expense calculations both apply
(40) artificial figures, or actual figures which may be outdated and irrelevant, resulting in payment obligations that may have little or no relationship to the debtor's actual ability to pay.

Passage B

With consumer bankruptcy filings well in excess of 1 million per year, it was clear to nearly everyone that reform was necessary. The beleaguered consumer credit industry appealed to
(5) Congress for help, and despite obstacles—including the veto of significant reforms in 2000, due in part to the influence of Harvard law professor Elizabeth Warren on Hillary Clinton—lawmakers passed the Bankruptcy Abuse Prevention and Consumer
(10) Protection Act (BAPCPA) in 2005. The goal was to tighten up consumer bankruptcy filing requirements and discourage the practice of running up credit card and other debt in anticipation of defaulting on accounts and discharging obligations in bankruptcy.

(15) The new law imposes the requirement that each debtor must complete a credit counseling briefing administered by a U.S. Trustee-approved agency before even filing a bankruptcy petition. Then, if the consumer still wants to file for Chapter 7
(20) bankruptcy protection, he or she must qualify under a means test that first compares his or her income to the median income in the consumer's state and then, if the consumer's income exceeds the median, applies Internal Revenue Service figures
(25) to determine whether or not he or she has sufficient income to make partial payment to creditors. This forces debtors who have the ability to pay to make good on at least some of their debts.

The law took effect in October of 2005, and
(30) the new provisions have been extraordinarily successful in alleviating the bankruptcy problem. In the first quarter of 2006, there were only 65,397 consumer Chapter 7 bankruptcy cases filed, compared with 289,239 during the same
(35) period a year earlier.

1. Which of the following most accurately expresses the main point of Passage A?

    (A) Most consumer bankruptcy cases are not the result of abuse, but are filed by people who have suffered setbacks due to medical problems.

    (B) The numbers applied in bankruptcy calculations such as the Chapter 7 means test do not lead to a realistic picture of the debtor's ability to pay.

    (C) The bankruptcy reforms enacted in 2005 are flawed, and as such are unlikely to achieve their stated goals.

    (D) The passage of the 2005 bankruptcy reforms was intended more for political gain and to build support for the current administration than to address an actual problem in the U.S. economy.

    (E) The 2005 bankruptcy reforms are unlikely to have a significant long-term impact on consumer bankruptcy filing rates because they do not go far enough in cracking down on fraudulent claims.

2. Which of the following is identified in Passage A, but not in Passage B, as an issue key to the development of successful bankruptcy reform?

    (A) A requirement that bankruptcy petitioners explore other options with a qualified professional before filing a bankruptcy petition

    (B) Screening of income and expenses to determine which consumers really need to file for bankruptcy protection and which can afford to pay back some or all of their debts

    (C) Addressing the financial and life issues that cause people to file for bankruptcy protection

    (D) Cutting down on fraudulent filings by more thoroughly investigating the income and assets of people filing bankruptcy petitions

    (E) Eliminating the political incentive for the passage of laws so that lawmakers can focus on the actual issues at hand rather than currying favor with interest groups

3. Which one of the following most accurately describes the relationship between the use of the phrase "bankruptcy problem" in Passage A (line 19) and the use of the same phrase in Passage B (line 31)?

    (A) In both passages, the phrase refers to the unnecessarily high rate of bankruptcy filings in the United States in recent years.

    (B) In Passage A, it refers to the failure of bankruptcy reform to address the core underlying issues, while in Passage B it is used to describe high filing rates.

    (C) In both Passage A and Passage B, it refers to the economic stresses that contribute to the high bankruptcy filing rates.

    (D) The reference in Passage B is strictly to high bankruptcy filing rates, while the author of Passage A uses the term more broadly.

    (E) In both passages A and B, the phrase refers to the difficulty of and delays involved in passing bankruptcy reform provisions.

4. If the author of Passage A were to read Passage B, which of the following objections would he or she be likely to raise regarding the analysis in Passage B?

    (A) It is unfair to require consumers to explore other options before allowing them to file for bankruptcy protection.

    (B) The reforms vetoed by President Clinton in 2000 would have been no more or less successful than the statute enacted in 2005.

    (C) The bankruptcy filing statistics for the first quarter of 2006 are too low to be accurate.

    (D) The figures used in the means test calculations do not always yield accurate information about the amount of income available to pay creditors.

    (E) Discouraging consumers from filing for bankruptcy protection after running up credit card and other debts is not a valid objective.

5. The author of Passage B would be most likely to agree with which of the following statements?

   (A) Hillary Clinton should not have exerted influence over President Clinton's decision regarding the 2000 bankruptcy reforms.
   (B) There are better solutions to problems like unexpected medical bills and job loss than filing for bankruptcy protection.
   (C) The new screening tools and income and expense calculations are generally accurate in determining which consumers really need bankruptcy protection and which do not.
   (D) The number of bankruptcy filings each quarter will continue to decline in the wake of BAPCPA; ultimately, eliminating consumer bankruptcy entirely.

6. It can be inferred from the passages that the authors of both passages would agree that

   (A) the primary cause of the high rate of consumer bankruptcy filing in recent years is that ecnomic stresses and unavoidable personal crises like medical problems have left them little option.
   (B) the bankruptcy reforms, which were enacted and took effect in 2005, have already been successful in curbing excessive bankruptcy filings
   C) the rate of bankruptcy filings in the United States by the early 2000s was cause for concern.
   D) President Clinton should not have vetoed the bankruptcy reforms passed by Congress in 2000.
   E) the credit counseling requirement in the new bankruptcy law does little to address the bankruptcy problem.

7. Which of the following best describes a way in which the two passages are related to one another?

   (A) The two passages present conflicting statistics in support of their conclusions.
   (B) The authors reach differing conclusions, but do so without presenting contradictory evidence.
   (C) Passage B presents statistics that, if accurate, disprove the predictions made in Passage A.
   (D) Each passage uses identical data to project very different outcomes.
   (E) Passage B provides a point-by-point rebuttal of the weaknesses alleged in Passage A.

8. Based on their titles, which of the following pairs of documents relates in a manner most analogous to the relationship between Passage A and Passage B?

   (A) "Homeowner's Association Policy Falls Short of Addressing Key Issues"; "New Homeowner's Association Policy Already Making a Difference in the Neighborhood"
   (B) "Questionable Motivation in the City Council's Recent Actions"; "City Council Scores a Resounding Victory with New Ordinance"
   (C) "Why We Need an Anti-Smoking Ordinance"; "Anti-Smoking Ordinances and the Downfall of Freedom in the United States"
   (D) "Proposed Alternatives to the Current Expense Reporting System"; "How to Make the Most of Our Expense Reporting System"
   (E) "Mortgage Foreclosure Rates Skyrocketing Across the United States"; "Mortgage Foreclosure 'Crisis' Blown Out of Proportion by Media"

Passage 13: Bankruptcy Abuse Prevention and Consumer Protection Act

What Makes It Difficult?

The structure of Passage A doesn't provide much guidance—the author's main point is presented in the middle of the first paragraph, and then the rest of the passage is simply a mass of supporting details. Because the passage neither begins nor ends with the key point and it's mentioned quite briefly, it's very easy to miss the global issue in this passage and get caught up in the details. Those details are full of unfamiliar terminology. It's not as intimidating at a glance as some science (and even law or social science) passages can be, because it's all plain English, but terms like "Chapter 7 means test" will be unfamiliar to most test takers, and it's easy to get caught up in those new concepts and waste time. Passage B is more straightforward in terms of the author's presentation of his or her main point, but of course that question wasn't asked.

Eight questions make this a time challenge, aside from the difficulty of identifying the main point and purpose of Passage A. There's only one Global question and one Detail question among them, while open-ended inference questions like question five give no direction and require the greater time investment of evaluating each answer choice.

Key Points of the Passage

Like all Comparative Reading passages, these two have the same topic: the 2005 bankruptcy reforms. They also share a scope: the efficacy of those reforms. Next, we have to identify the purpose/main idea for each passage independently:

- Passage A: The author's main idea is that the bankruptcy reforms enacted in 2005 aren't likely to be effective in the long run due to various flaws. His or her purpose is simply to argue or advance that point.

- Passage B: The main idea in Passage B is that the reforms have been a resounding success. Again, the author's purpose is simply to demonstrate that that's the case.

Having assessed topic, scope, purpose, and main idea (T/S/P/MI) just as we do in regular passages (except that we have two purposes/main ideas), we move on to the one step that differs in reading comparative passages: before moving to the questions, we need to get a handle on the relationship between the passages.

The best starting point for that is to examine each passage's purpose/main idea. Passage A points out flaws in the bankruptcy reforms and predicts its failure, while Passage B presents evidence to support the idea that it's already a success. However, each author writes as though unaware of the other—one passage isn't responsive to the other or a direct rebuttal.

Answers and Explanations

1. C   2. C   3. D   4. D   5. C   6. C   7. B   8. A

1. C

This is a global (main idea) question, and it relates to only one passage, so we have every reason to attack it first. In addition, just as in a single reading passage, we've already identified the main idea, so we should be able to simply refer to our groundwork and match up our prediction with the answer choices. That's answer choice (C).

(A) Choice (A) is a distortion—we do hear about medical problems triggering bankruptcies, but not that they're "most" of the cases; further, it's only a detail, one of multiple flaws listed, not the main idea.

(B) This choice is tempting, because it's not only lifted directly from the passage, but it's also from the last paragraph—the paragraph many test-takers assume to be the author's conclusion.

(C) Correct! We said the main idea "the bankruptcy reforms aren't likely to be effective in the long term because of certain flaws." That fits with this choice.

(D) Another distortion—the author says that the current administration gained favor, but not that currying favor was its motivation; like (A) and (B), this is also too narrow to be the main idea.

(E) The first half of this answer choice looks like a clear winner, but it falls apart after "because." The author lists three reasons why the current reforms probably wouldn't work, and none of them have anything to do with fraud.

2. C

This is just a twist on the old "EXCEPT" detail question format. Here, however, we're going to have to check both passages and it may be time consuming. The fact that the question relates to both passages is reason enough to leave it for later; the fact that it requires us to check every answer choice strongly reinforces that idea.

(A) The requirement that bankruptcy petitioners explore other options with a qualified professional is mentioned in both passages; it's part of the new bankruptcy law. However, neither presents it as a key issue. The author of Passage A presents it as a measure in the new bankruptcy law that isn't likely to have the intended impact.

(B) Again, neither author actually says this is a key feature. The author of Passage B presents it in a positive light, but the author of Passage A only says that it's not being done very effectively—he doesn't make any suggestion that it must be or even should be done at all.

(C) Bingo! The first reason Author A offers for the projected failure of bankruptcy reform is the failure to address those issues (such as medical crisis).

(D) Passage A never mentions fraud.

(E) Distortion; beware of familiar language that's not responsive to the question.

3. D

Again, the question requires reference to both passages, so it shouldn't be one of the first ones you attack. However, once you've finished the single-passage and global questions, the line references make this one fairly inviting. You'll definitely want to go back to each passage and explicitly determine how the phrase is used in each passage independently before trying to determine the relationship, just as we did with the purpose and main idea before determining the relationship between the passages as a whole.

(A) While the phrase does refer to the high number of bankruptcy filings in both passages, the word "unnecessarily" here should be a red flag. We have no reason to believe that Author A thinks the high number of bankruptcy filings were unnecessary. In fact, he or she has used the phrase in a paragraph citing a legitimate and largely unavoidable bankruptcy trigger.

(B) This one might be tempting, and illustrates the importance of the work we did on this question before looking at the answer choices. Passage A surely refers to the failure of bankruptcy reform to address the core underlying issues, but we're asked about something much narrower: how this particular phrase is used.

(C) Passage B makes no mention of economic stresses as a contributing factor to bankruptcy.

(D) In Passage A, the author refers to the "bankruptcy problem" as having roots in socio-economic problems. Clearly, this relates to the high number of bankruptcy filings, but Author A has tied it into the larger issue. Author B, on the other hand, tells us the "bankruptcy problem" has largely been solved. The evidence for this is strictly limited to a reduced number of filings, so this author is using the term much more narrowly: the "bankruptcy problem" was that too many people were filing. That's a match for answer choice (D).

(E) Both passages mention the difficulties and delays in passing the new bankruptcy laws, but neither uses the phrase "bankruptcy problem" in that context. Moreover, context is everything when it comes to this question; there are several points and issues that could be classified as "bankruptcy problems," but we have to find the one that each author attached to that term.

4. D

Again, this question involves both passages, so it should be left for later. We're really looking for a point of disagreement, even if Author A hasn't explicitly addressed the issue.

(A) This is a distortion—the author of Passage A says the pre-filing credit counseling requirement doesn't help, but he or she doesn't say that it's unfair, only that it's ineffective.

(B) We don't have enough information to know either author's position on this issue; because Author B didn't make any statements about it, there's no basis to invoke objections from Author A.

(C) This one might have given you pause because Author A says the reforms won't work and the statistics presented in Passage B seem to indicate that they are working. However, the author of Passage A actually said that the reforms wouldn't work long term, and the statistics offered are from a time period ending less than six months after the law took effect; Author A can accept these statistics without contradicting his or her doubts about the long-term impact.

(D) This is it—both authors talk about the calculations to determine whether or not a debtor can afford to pay back his or her creditors. However, the author of Passage B touts this practice, while Author A suggests that the numbers employed lead to inaccurate conclusions.

(E) We have no information about what Author A would consider a valid objective; Passage A only addresses the likelihood of effectiveness.

5. C

This is another inference question that relates to only one passage. The question stem doesn't give us any direction, so we'll have to examine the answer choices one by one.

(A) This choice might be tempting, both because Hillary Clinton's involvement led to a result our author didn't agree with and because it's an issue most of us have heard raised before, but the author is simply reporting the history of bankruptcy reform at that point in the passage, not voicing an opinion.

(B) Choice (B) blends the overall outlook of the author—all those bankruptcy filings weren't the right answer—with another issue he or she doesn't address at all; we don't even know whether the author of Passage B believes that medical expenses are a significant problem, nor whether he or she thinks they're a legitimate reason for bankruptcy. Author B focuses on "unnecessary" filings.

(C) Correct—the author says that these calculations force those debtors who have the ability to pay to make good on at least some of their debts, so he or she must believe that the calculations are successful in identifying those who have the ability to pay.

(D) This choice is a distortion; the author gives us data meant to demonstrate that BAPCPA is already working, but doesn't make any predictions as to a continuing decline in filings.

(E) Choice (E) is extreme. The author never says that bankruptcy should be entirely eliminated; his or her focus is on eliminating unnecessary filings. In fact, the author represents over 65,000 filings in a quarter as a victory!

6. C

We're looking for common ground between the passages, but because this is an inference question, it may not be explicitly stated (or at least, not in both passages). Can we predict an area of agreement between our authors? The only thing they seem to agree on is that there's a "bankruptcy problem." That's enough to identify correct answer choice (C), but if you didn't have a prediction at hand, here are the rationales.

(A) Author A certainly told us that a large number of bankruptcy filings were attributable to such crises, but Author B gives no indication that he or she is on board with that idea. Author B implies that he or she thinks the problem is irresponsibility.

(B) Author B tells us that the bankruptcy reforms that were enacted and took effect in 2005 have already been successful in curbing excessive bankruptcy filings, but this directly contradicts the main point of Passage A.

(C) Author A clearly believes that there's a problem with the high number of bankruptcy filings; he or she thinks that we haven't adequately addressed the underlying causes. Author B explicitly tells us there was a problem and that it has been solved. Don't be fooled by the fact that Author A thinks there's still a problem—the answer choice doesn't limit the problem to the early 2000s.

(D) Neither author takes a clear position on this, although both mention the 2000 veto.

(E) We know that Author A believes this, but Author B doesn't talk about the efficacy of the provision directly. He or she lists it as a positive development, and so we can infer that the author doesn't think it's largely useless, but we don't even have to go that far—simply note that Author B didn't say anything to indicate that he or she thought it did little to address the problem.

7. B

We've already determined that the two passages have the same topic and scope, but differing purposes and main ideas. In fact, their purposes/main idea and the conclusions they draw are virtually contradictory: Author A wants us to know that bankruptcy reform in its current form won't work; Author B wants to demonstrate that it's already working. The answer choices here are phrased generally, so it may take a little more work to find what we're looking for. Let's generalize the relationship we've already determined—they reach opposite conclusions.

(A) What are the conflicting statistics? We didn't see any of those, only differing key points and predictions for the future.

(B) Correct! We already identified the different conclusions, but the authors don't dispute each other's facts.

(C) When in doubt, fill in the specifics that match each piece of the general statement. What is the prediction in Passage A? This new bankruptcy law won't work to reduce filings in the long run. The language in this choice is strong: we're not looking for evidence that weakens the prediction, but that disproves it. Did Author B give us any statistics that would prove this new law was going to keep filings down in the long-term? No it did not, therefore toss it out.

(D) Close, but the passages, though they don't contradict each other factually, don't actually employ identical data. **Note:** When you see two answer choices as similar as this one and correct answer choice (B), look at the difference between them. Here, it's the suggestion that the authors use "identical" data—an extreme-sounding term that should set off alarm bells.

(E) We established at the outset that Passage B wasn't directly responsive to A, but if you have any doubt here, just check. Where did Passage B take on the issue of underlying economic causes like medical problems? It didn't, so eliminate this.

8. A

We already determined that the relationship between Passages A and B was that they reached differing conclusions about the effectiveness of the law, though they didn't directly contradict one another's evidence.

(A) This is a perfect match! Both titles relate to the same policy; one says it's flawed and the other says it's working already.

(B) The first title talks about motivation, the second about success. These aren't conflicting positions on the same issue as our authors took.

(C) These are contradictory positions about the need for a law, which is entirely different from assessment/prediction of success or failure. Therefore, you can eliminate this choice.

(D) Although both of these titles are on the same topic, there doesn't appear to be any direct relationship between them, particularly not a contradictory one; one could advocate an alternative and still be looking to maximize the effectiveness of the current system in the interim.

(E) These two titles do take contradictory positions as our authors do, but there is a subtle difference: these documents are addressing the problem (or lack thereof) itself, whereas our authors—and the authors in answer choice (A)—are assessing the effectiveness of a solution and coming to opposite conclusions.

PASSAGE SET 14

Passage A

The form of a work of art is merely the means of expression of whatever message, representation, analogy, or other content the artist wishes to bring before the viewer; whatever value
(5) a work might possess is found in its content. Much attention has been given in recent years to the artistic form, and critics and philosophers alike have advanced arguments suggesting that aesthetics are at least as important as content. The
(10) truth is that a painting or other work of art that fails to say something to the viewer can hardly be classified a work of art at all.

All that remains to be determined is the correct approach to the assessment of the meaning and
(15) resulting value of a work of art. Upon this issue there has been much disagreement throughout the history of the arts. Plato would have had us believe that art was of little or no value. In his view, the objects themselves were only imitations,
(20) and thus an artistic representation of an object one step further removed from the truth. When beds, chairs, and water pitchers are viewed as something less than real, the copy of the copy becomes all the more detached. Most who retain an interest
(25) in the issue in modern times agree that art—or at least some art—has value, but the standard for determining that value, and for assessing the meaning conveyed by the creator, remains a point of contention.

(30) When one critic interprets a work as a literal representation, another as a religious allegory, and still a third as a psychological expression of the artist's own issues and experiences, only one can be correct: the mere fact that they arrive at
(35) opposing conclusions illustrates that. However, as yet a clear standard has not emerged for determining which the artist actually intended, so in those cases where the artist has not explicitly shared that information, there will always be
(40) contention about the true meaning and value of an individual work—not to mention the issue of the possible disconnect between the artist's intention and that which is actually conveyed.

Passage B

Susan Sontag's statement about artistic interpretation, "To interpret is to impoverish, to deplete the world—in order to set up a shadow world of 'meanings,'" sums up everything
(5) important about the issue. Despite the strength of that statement, her criticism of particular types of criticism was harsher, as well it should have been. She suggested that Freudian symbolic interpretation necessarily reflected dissatisfaction
(10) with the work, a desire to substitute for it. If the viewer-critic had responded deeply to the actual work of art, then he or she would have had no need to create some alternate meaning or interpretation to impose value upon it.
(15) Nevertheless, where such dissatisfaction exists, is it necessarily indicative of a flaw in the work? The flaw, if there is one, may be in the viewer, or rather in the urge to interpret and the preconceived form of interpretation that makes
(20) it impossible for the viewer to experience the work fresh and unfettered. Thus, it seems that the very standards and analysis that we apply in an effort to determine the meaning and value of a work of art may become the screen that clouds
(25) the true meaning and value, making an accurate assessment of the worth of a work impossible.

1. Which of the following assumptions is common to both passages?

   (A) Freudian interpretation does not yield an accurate view of the meaning and value of a work of art.
   (B) There is an objective answer to the question as to whether or not a work of art has value.
   (C) Interpretation is a negative approach to art that does not help to determine the meaning or value of a particular work.
   (D) The artist's intention is the key to the valid interpretation of a work of art.
   (E) Plato was incorrect in viewing art as an imitation of an imitation.

2. Which of the following is mentioned by the author of Passage A, but not by the author of Passage B, as a problem with the current state of artistic interpretation?

   (A) Interpretation is destructive to the original work, in that it seeks to replace it with something outside the work.
   (B) The effort to interpret obscures the true meaning of a work.
   (C) Too much emphasis is placed on what the artist intended and not enough on what the work actually conveys.
   (D) There is no clear standard for assessing the value and meaning of a work of art.
   (E) Modern interpretation seeks to project value onto works of art, which are inherently limited in value because they are simply imitative.

3. The authors of the two passages would be most likely to disagree about

   (A) the standards for arriving at the best formula for interpreting the meaning of a work of art accurately.
   (B) the validity of Freudian interpretation as a means of deriving important information about the meaning of a work of art.
   (C) Plato's assessment of the value of art overall.
   (D) the importance of the artist's intentions in assessing the value of a work of art.
   (E) the possibility of arriving at a "correct" system of artistic interpretation.

4. The primary purpose of Passage A is

   (A) to point out the weaknesses in the standards set forth by particular philosophers and critics for interpreting artistic creation.
   (B) to propose elements of a system by which the value of a work of art can be determined accurately and consistently.
   (C) to argue that artistic interpretation should be avoided, as it necessarily distracts from the authentic experience of a work of art.
   (D) to suggest the need for a clear and consistent system of artistic interpretation.
   (E) to refute Plato's assessment of the value of art overall.

5. The author of Passage B would be most likely to make which of the following criticisms about the analysis contained in the last paragraph of Passage A?

   (A) It places an unwarranted value on the intention of the artist.
   (B) It assumes that there is a form of artistic interpretation that will yield valuable and accurate information about a work of art.
   (C) It underestimates the role of literal representation in most artwork.
   (D) It lists only a small fraction of the possible methods of interpretation.
   (E) It misstates the relationship between content and form in a work of art.

6. The relationship between Passage A and Passage B is most analogous to the relationship between the documents described in which of the following?

   (A) A position paper that encourages the creation of an accepted set of standards for remodeling an existing structure and one offering the opinion that remodeling would not be beneficial at all
   (B) An article supporting a new school of thought about educational processes, and an article arguing that the current processes are superior to the proposed changes
   (C) An article describing three conflicting schools of thought regarding musical interpretation and an article advancing one of those three schools as clearly superior to the others
   (D) An article describing the sociological impact of art on early cultures and an article detailing the timeline and technical aspects of early art
   (E) A criticism of avant-garde fiction as a genre and a criticism of conventional fiction as outdated and stale

7. The author of Passage A most likely included the reference to Plato in order to:

(A) demonstrate how unworkable individual systems of artistic interpretation are in arriving at an objective determination of the value of a work of art.

(B) help illustrate the wide range of conflicting views on the value of art and how it is best determined.

(C) show how misguided the approach to artistic interpretation was during Plato's lifetime.

(D) refute the generally accepted view of artistic interpretation as subjective.

(E) contrast his or her outlook with Freud's to emphasize the spectrum of philosophies regarding artistic interpretation.

8. Which of the following most accurately describes the relationship between the argument in Passage A and the argument in Passage B?

(A) Passage A makes vague claims without providing supporting evidence, while the conclusions in Passage B are based strictly on specific illustrations.

(B) Passage A and Passage B come to the same conclusion, but arrive at it through very different analyses.

(C) Passage A warns about the dangers and weaknesses of a much broader spectrum of approaches than Passage B, which is more limited in scope.

(D) Passage A seeks a workable set of standards to apply to a process that Passage B suggests cannot be addressed productively regardless of the standards applied.

(E) Passage A provides examples that are used by the author of Passage B to prove a very different point.

Passage Set 14: Interpretation of Art

What Makes It Difficult?

Abstract concepts and minimal structural clues render both of these passages tough to break down. In Passage A, we don't find any indication of the scope and purpose of the passage at all in the first paragraph, and Passage B is one long mass of text that's difficult to sort out. To complicate matters further, the scope of the second paragraph is a bit different from the first; these aren't conflicting views on the right approach to interpretation, nor on whether or not interpretation is desirable at all—the focus of Passage B disputes an assumption inherent in Passage A, not its key point.

There are eight questions associated with the passage, which is undoubtedly a more time-consuming read than the average passage as well. This one can be a time killer if you're not careful. The questions are tough too. There's only one detail question, and it's a tricky one. The global questions may require more work than in most passages because the main points and purposes of the passages are harder to pin down than in a more tightly structured passage.

Key Points of the Passage

Of course, both passages have the same topic: the interpretation of art. The scope of the passages is slightly different, though: in Passage A we're primarily concerned with the best approach for assessing art, while Passage B focuses on the value of artistic interpretation overall.

- Passage A: The author's main idea is that there is currently no clear standard for assessing the meaning and value of art. Author A's purpose is simply to identify this problem.
- Passage B: The main idea in Passage B is that the interpretation isn't a valuable exercise. The author's purpose is simply to argue that point.

Having assessed topic, scope, purpose, and main idea (T/S/P/MI) just as we do in regular passages (except that we have two purpose/main idea questions), we move on to the one step that differs in reading comparative passages: before moving to the questions, we need to get a handle on the relationship between the passages.

The best starting point for that is to examine each passage's purpose/main idea. Passage A points out the need for clearer standards in order to make artistic interpretation valid and useful, while Passage B asserts that it is, by nature, neither. However, there isn't a direct connection between the two passages—each author writes as though unaware of the other.

Answers and Explanations

1. B   2. D   3. E   4. D   5. B   6. A   7. B   8. D

1. B

This question refers to both passages, and it's not a global question, so it's not going to be the first one you attack, even though it's printed first. "Assumption" has the same meaning that it does in Logical Reasoning questions, so we're looking for something both authors treat as true without directly stating. There isn't much point of agreement between the two authors, but predicting may still be a challenge here, so you may have to assess the answer choices.

(A) What did each author tell us, or imply, about Freudian interpretation? The author of Passage A doesn't talk about it at all, nor does he or she make any blanket statement about interpretation that could be extended. Eliminate this answer choice.

(B) Correct! What does Author A think about this? Author A wants us to find the "correct" appoach to determining value, so he or she obviously thinks there's a right answer to the value question. What does Author B think? This one is a little trickier, but he or she tells us that the method of interpretation may be the screen that obscures "the true meaning and value" and may make an "accurate assessment of the worth of a work" impossible—Author B, too, thinks there is a "true" answer to the value question.

(C) Author A wants us to find a clear approach to interpretation, so he or she must think it's a valuable undertaking. Therefore, eliminate this answer choice.

(D) Author A seems to believe this, because he or she presents as a problem the fact that we lack a clear standard for determining the artist's actual intention, but Author B makes no reference to the artist's intention. Eliminate this answer choice.

(E) Author A mentions Plato's perspective, and disagrees with it—but not with this part. His or her issue with Plato had to do with art being valuable, not being imitative. Author B doesn't talk about Plato or his or her theory at all. Either is sufficient to eliminate answer choice (E).

2. D

This is a specific detail question, but one that requires reference to both passages.

(A) This theory should sound familiar, but it's not Author A who advances this theory; it's Author B. Watch out for answer choices that cover the right perspectives, but attach them to the wrong passage.

(B) Again, this is stated directly in Passage B, so it sounds familiar and might be tempting, but we're looking for something that's not mentioned in Passage B.

(C) Author A does talk about the artist's intention, but this isn't his or her position—rather, Author A says we need better ways to determine the artist's actual intention. Eliminate this answer choice.

(D) Correct! Our authors are in agreement that there isn't a clear and consistent standard, so you might have been tempted to gloss over this one. That's a good reminder never to lose sight of exactly what the question has asked us for: we're looking for something Author A presents as a problem and Author B does not. Author B is against interpretation altogether, so he or she certainly won't see lack of a clear standard for interpretation as problematic.

(E) That's Plato's view, but not one shared by either of our authors. Eliminate this answer choice.

3. E

This is an inference question that, again, requires reference to both passages.

(A) What do we know about our authors' views of the "best formula"? For Author A, absolutely nothing—Author A wants consistency, but he or she doesn't advocate for a particular approach. That alone may be enough to eliminate this choice, but if you're not sure, look at Author B—Author B doesn't have a view on a "best" approach at all, because he or she thinks interpretation is a negative.

(B) Author A doesn't take a position on the validity of any particular school of thought—or say anything at all about Freud. Therefore, you can eliminate this answer choice.

(C) Plato thought art was without value, or at least of very limited value. However, both of our authors talk about the ways in which the "true value" of a work of art can be assessed, so both clearly reject Plato's idea that it's without value—no disagreement on this point. Eliminate this answer choice.

(D) Only Author A talks about the artist's intentions; he or she clearly thinks they're significant, based on the last sentence of the passage. However, we get no indication of Author B's view of the significance of artist's intentions, so we have no evidence that they'd disagree. Eliminate this answer choice.

(E) Correct! Author A laments the fact that we haven't yet arrived at the correct approach, so clearly he or she thinks there is one; Author B, however, thinks we shouldn't be interpreting at all, so he or she will hardly believe that there's a "right" way to do it.

4. D

This question should have been the first one answered, because it focuses on only one of the passages and it's also a global question that we should have answered already—the prediction is already made! We said Passage A was about the author's perception of a problem: the lack of consistent standards for artistic interpretation.

(A) This is tricky—our author does describe the beliefs of one philosopher (Plato) in some detail, an says that we're without a workable system. His or her goal, though, isn't to establish the weaknesses of any particular approach, but to lament the lack of a clear and consistent standard for interpretation.

(B) This choice is tempting. The author definitely asserts the importance of a consistent approach that will help us determine the true value of a work, but he or she doesn't propose the elements; Author B simply sets forth the need for a system.

(C) This refers to the wrong passage: it's the author of Passage B who suggests that we shouldn't be interpreting at all.

(D) Correct; this is a match for our paraphrase!

(E) The author certainly disagrees with Plato—he or she says art has little or no value, while seeing a system to assess that value accurately. It's just a detail, though, and one that's slightly outside the author's primary focus at that.

5. B

The last paragraph of Passage A says conflicts arise when different interpretive approaches are applied. We don't have a clear idea what the artist intended, so it's hard to get a handle on the real meaning and value of the work. What would Author B say about all that? Well, the only thing we really know about Author B is that he or she thinks this whole interpretation thing is wrong-headed and unhelpful. Thus, we can predict that the part he or she will take issue with is the idea that with a little consistency and better information about the artist's intent, we could get a handle on the meaning and value of a work.

(A) Author B doesn't take any identifiable position on the importance of the artist's intention. Therefore, you can eliminate this answer choice.

(B) Correct! Author A is looking for the "right" approach, but Author B doesn't believe there is a "right" way to interpret.

(C) This is just one interpretive approach, and Author B seems to disdain them all equally—we have no reason to believe he or she would like more emphasis on this one. Additionally, literal representation isn't even addressed in the piece of the passage the question stem points us to. You can eliminate this answer choice.

(D) It's true that Author A lists only a small fraction of the possible methods of interpretation, but would it be a problem for Author B? We have no reason to believe it would, so eliminate this answer choice.

(E) The discussion of content and form in Passage A takes place in the first paragraph, not the last. In addition, the author of Passage B doesn't address the issue at all, so we don't know where he or she would stand. Eliminate this answer choice.

6. A

Before jumping into the choices, review the relationship between our two passages. Passage A says we have a problem because we don't have clear standards with which to interpret art and thus determine its meaning and value. Passage B says we don't need interpretation; it does more harm than good.

(A) This choice is a perfect match: the first document says we need accepted standards in order to do something, the second says we shouldn't be doing the something at all.

(B) Author A doesn't support any particular school of thought, and Author B doesn't praise the current processes—eliminate this on both counts.

(C) Passage A does mention three conflicting interpretations, but doesn't really describe them; more importantly, Passage B definitely doesn't advocate for one of the schools mentioned in Passage A. Eliminate this answer choice.

(D) Our passages aren't this disparate; their scopes are much closer, and neither provides detailed historical or technical data. Eliminate this answer choice.

(E) This answer choice involves criticisms of two different genres of fiction; our passages address the same issue from different perspectives, and don't provide a broad criticism of a particular genre or school of thought. Eliminate this answer choice.

7. B

This is one of two questions relating to a single passage, and also should be answered early. It's a logic function question asking simply "why is the author talking about Plato in Passage A?"

As with every function question, we have to keep the author's primary purpose and the purpose of the paragraph clearly in mind in answering this question. Our author's concern is finding a "valid" and consistent system of artistic interpretation. Look at the second paragraph: the author tells us we need a system, and then points out that historically there's been much conflict. The Plato reference is an illustration of one pole of the conflict.

(A) Although the language seems in keeping with the author's view, answer choice (A) is wrong for multiple reasons: the author doesn't attack individual systems, merely says that we need agreement; in addition, Plato didn't attempt to employ a system to assess the value of individual works of art—his view described here applies to art generally.

(B) This is correct—the author tells us that opinions have been all over the place, then launches into one extreme, Plato's suggestion that art just didn't have much value in any case.

(C) The author's focus is on our present need; his or her reference to the past is only to set the stage for the confusion created by many conflicting (though not necessarily misguided) views.

(D) There's no indication that subjectivity is the "generally accepted view"—and the author isn't introducing Plato to refute anything, because he or she clearly disagrees with him.

(E) Freud isn't mentioned in Passage A—another plug for focusing on the single-passage questions first.

8. D

Like the previous question, this one deals with the relationship between the passages overall, and like the previous question, it asks us to extract the concepts in order to find the right answer. However, this question calls our attention more to the structure of the arguments than to the substance, as illustrated by the answer choices.

(A) You might have been tempted by "very specific illustrations" at first glance, because Passage B contains direct quotes, but in fact there is no illustration to support the contentions of Author B. Eliminate this answer choice.

(B) What would "the same conclusion" be? Author A concludes we need clearer standards, while Author B thinks we should leave interpretation alone. Eliminate this answer choice.

(C) It's true that Passage A mentions various approaches, while Passage B does not, which might have made this choice tempting. However, Passage B is not limited in scope when compared with Passage A—to the contrary, it includes all interpretation. Eliminate this answer choice.

(D) Correct! Passage A says we need clear rules of interpretation. Passage B says interpretation isn't going to work out, regardless of the rules we apply.

(E) Passage B doesn't draw on any examples from Passage A, so we can eliminate this answer choice.

PASSAGE SET 15

Passage A

The morphological, biochemical, and behavioral characteristics that make living organisms well-adapted for life in a particular environment arise through the impact of selection
(5) on genetic variation. Genetic variation isn't limited to a single process; it may occur through mutation and through recombination. Mutation takes place when the replication process is flawed and DNA is not copied perfectly. Recombination,
(10) on the other hand, is a natural function of sexual reproduction and occurs when separate DNA contributed by two individual parents is "shuffled" in the offspring.

Certainly random fluctuations impact gene
(15) frequency, but natural selection has a clear and demonstrable effect on the adaptive process we term "evolution." Certain genes result in behavioral or physiological characteristics that tend toward the enhancement of better survival
(20) skills. These characteristics may be as far flung as higher intelligence, better eyesight, a scent or coloring less easily detectable by predators, features that make them difficult to eat or are toxic to predators, and physical characteristics
(25) that enhance strength and speed. There is nothing therefore counterintuitive about the fact that those organisms with the superior survival mechanisms generally survive to produce greater numbers of offspring, and those offspring in turn have a
(30) greater chance of survival and tend to reproduce in greater numbers. As such, the percentage of the population with the "useful" genes increases over time, creating better adaptation within the general population and, often, a characteristic that
(35) becomes common to the species as a whole.

Passage B

Left uninfluenced and not acted upon by external forces, chemical compounds ultimately break down into simpler materials rather than increasing in order and complexity. It is not
(5) impossible that through a significant expenditure of energy, one or more outside forces might on occasion increase order for a time, but this cannot sustain; freed from the outside force, processes tend back toward deterioration and disorder.

(10) The theory of evolution through natural selection requires the precise reversal of this natural trend, which is universally applicable and forms the foundation of the second law of thermodynamics.

(15) Natural selection assumes an increasingly complex and effective order, a process precisely— or very nearly so—the inverse of the breakdown that actually occurs throughout nature. Scientists who subscribe to the theory of evolution maintain
(20) that it is not inconsistent with the second law of thermodynamics because the earth is an open thermodynamic system: a system that exchanges heat, light, or matter with its surroundings. Specifically, the earth receives outside energy
(25) from the sun. However, observation of the impact of the sun's energy on dead matter contradicts the idea that it is this external energy that prompts an increase in order and complexity. When the sun's energy sets to work on a dead plant or a dead
(30) animal, the organism tends to decay and break into its simplest components; in other words, the sun's energy speeds the disorganization process, rather than encouraging an unnatural trend toward organization.

1. Which of the following best describes the main point in Passage B?

    (A) The evolutionary process of living organisms has not been accurately described by scientists who subscribe to the theory.

    (B) The second law of thermodynamics demonstrates that processes on earth are not impacted by external energy from the sun.

    (C) The theory of evolution is inconsistent with the universal trend toward disorganization set forth in the second law of thermodynamics.

    (D) The external energy exerted by the sun acts to break down organisms and speed their decay, not to increase organization or complexity.

    (E) The natural tendency to disorder in accordance with the second law of thermodynamics provides a foundation for the theory of evolution of organisms on earth.

2. If the author of Passage A were to read Passage B, he or she would be most likely to disagree with which of the following points?

    (A) Free of outside forces such as the exertion of external energy upon an organism, nature tends toward simplicity rather than toward complexity.

    (B) The sun's energy leads to more rapid decomposition in certain dead organisms such as plants and animals than those organisms might experience in the absence of external energy.

    (C) The earth is an open system that exchanges energy with outside sources such as the sun.

    (D) Evolution is inconsistent with the second law of thermodynamics, in that it requires a trend toward greater order that is contrary to the natural trend toward disorder.

    (E) An increase in order is required for organisms to evolve in beneficial ways; organisms never derive positive attributes from a decrease in order.

3. It can be inferred from the passages that the two authors would agree that

    (A) it is unlikely that natural selection impacts the evolution of organisms.

    (B) the earth is an open thermodynamic system that exchanges with its surroundings.

    (C) the sun's energy is a destructive force when applied to organisms on earth.

    (D) change is a natural and expected process.

    (E) certain genetic characteristics result in superior chances of survival.

4. Which of the following best describes the relationship between the two passages?

    (A) Passage B provides a direct rebuttal to the theory set forth in Passage A.

    (B) Passage B provides an alternative explanation for the process described in Passage A.

    (C) Passage A provides the missing pieces that resolve the apparent contradictions in Passage B.

    (D) The passages address different aspects of the same process and are in no way inconsistent.

    (E) Passage B raises an issue that calls into question the explanation offered in Passage A.

5. The main purpose of Passage B is to

    (A) demonstrate that the theory of evolution is inconsistent with known scientific principles.

    (B) show that the impact of the sun's energy on the earth is destructive rather than productive, in that it actually hastens the breakdown and decay of certain organisms.

    (C) prove that evolution is possible, although the process by which it is most likely to occur differs significantly from the manner that most scientists suggest.

    (D) describe and explain the second law of thermodynamics and how it operates.

    (E) describe the role of the second law of thermodynamics in the process of natural selection

6. The attitude of the author of Passage B toward the theory of evolution through natural selection can best be described as

(A) uncertainty.
(B) cautious endorsement.
(C) extreme skepticism.
(D) partial acceptance.
(E) condescension.

7. The relationship between Passage A and Passage B is most analogous to the relationship between which of the following sets of documents?

(A) A report on the projected impact of global warming on coastal lands and a report from another source suggesting that the impact would be less significant than the original report indicated.

(B) A description of the process by which an ancient civilization cultivated crops and an essay asserting that the civilization in question had never had the capacity to grow food.

(C) A scientific paper hypothesizing that the dinosaur extinction was caused by a meteorite and another scientific paper advancing the theory that the extinction of the dinosaurs was caused by volcanic eruptions.

(D) Two papers describing the same phenomenon, but offering alternative explanations of the scientific factors bringing about the phenomenon.

(E) An explanation of the way genetic characteristics are passed from parent to child and an explanation of the role of DNA in asexual reproduction.

Passage Set 15: Evolution

What Makes It Difficult?

Language, language, language! Science passages can be intimidating to a lot of LSAT test takers, and these are chock full of language that's probably unfamiliar, right from the first sentence. In addition, the first passage has only two paragraphs, providing little or no structural guidance to help sort out the unfamiliar terminology. Passage B provides a little more structural help, but then it counteracts that with the introduction of the second law of thermodynamics and a discussion of the tendency toward disorder in the universe. It also makes unnecessary use of a lot of negative language and long introductory or modifying clauses that make sentence structure tough to follow.

An understanding of the second law of thermodynamics isn't necessary, of course, and it's only one small and relatively simple point that's applicable in the passage—if you can wade through the terminology and sort it out.

The questions themselves aren't especially difficult, except for some long answer choices incorporating some tough language. Breaking down the passages is the big hurdle.

Key Points of the Passage

Of course, both passages have the same broad topic: evolution through natural selection. The scope and purpose of the passages is slightly different, though: in Passage A the author sets forth an explanation of how evolution through natural selection works, while Passage B sets out to rebut the idea that it occurs at all.

- Passage A: The author's main idea is that natural selection impacts evolution. His or her purpose is to explain how that occurs.
- Passage B: The main idea in Passage B is that the idea of evolution through natural selection contradicts scientific law (the second law of thermodynamics, in particular). The author's purpose is to demonstrate the unlikelihood of evolution through natural selection.

Having assessed topic, scope, purpose, and main idea (T/S/P/MI) just as we do in regular passages (except that we have two purposes/main ideas), we move on to the one step that differs in reading comparative passages: before moving to the questions, we need to get a handle on the relationship between the passages.

The best starting point for that is to examine each passage's purpose/main idea. Passage A explains how evolution through natural selection works, while Passage B tells us that it doesn't—and can't—work. There isn't a direct connection between the two passages—each author writes independently. However, Passage B contradicts the theory set forth in Passage A.

Answers and Explanations

1. C   **2. D**   **3. D**   **4. E**   **5. A**   **6. C**   **7. B**

1. C

This is a global question that asks about only one passage, so we're definitely going to want to jump on this one right up front. We've already determined the main point of Passage B—this whole natural selection thing contradicts the laws of science.

(A) This answer choice is tempting, perhaps—the author of Passage B definitely thinks the scientists who are describing evolution are inaccurate, but this answer choice presumes that the author of Passage B believes there is an evolutionary process to be explained accurately; we don't know that. You can eliminate this answer choice.

(B) Again, a piece of this looks right—the author definitely uses the second law of thermodynamics as the basis of his or her challenge. However, what is Author B challenging? It's the idea of natural selection, not the impact of the sun's energy; therefore, you can eliminate this answer choice.

(C) This is the correct choice. All of the evidence the author offers is to support the central idea that evolution through natural selection can't happen because the natural trend is to break down.

(D) The author cites this, but it's just a detail offered as supporting evidence, not his or her main idea. Don't be fooled by familiar language. You can eliminate this answer choice.

(E) Again, half of what we're looking for is there—the natural tendency to disorder—but it's the author's evidence against evolution, not for it.

2. D

These two authors disagree about nearly everything, so you probably won't be able to predict an answer; just start working through the choices.

(A) The author of Passage A doesn't make any representations about what occurs "free of outside forces," so we don't know what his or her position on this would be.

(B) This is another point the author of Passage A doesn't address at all; he or she would undoubtedly disagree with the conclusion the author of Passage B draws based on this data, but we have no reason to think Author A would dispute the data itself.

(C) Again, we have no reason to believe that Author A would disagree with this.

(D) Correct—Author A believes that evolution through natural selection is taking place, and even explains how it works, so he or she clearly doesn't believe that it's impossible or violates the laws of nature.

(E) Author A doesn't address the order/disorder issue at all.

3. D

There's very little common ground between these two authors, so you should be able to move through these choices quickly.

(A) This answer choice directly contradicts Author A, so you can eliminate it.

(B) Author A doesn't mention this at all. He or she may believe it, but we can't infer that from what we've read so we can eliminate it.

(C) Again, only Author B takes a position on this; we don't know what the author of Passage A would say.

(D) This is the correct choice. Author A believes the change is the result of genetic variation and natural selection, and that it leads to evolution; Author B believes that change is a process that moves toward the simple over the complex, a breaking down. However, both point to a natural trend toward change—only the direction of that change differs.

(E) Author A clearly believes this, but Author B doesn't address particular characteristics or likelihood of survival.

4. E

When determining the relationship between two passages, revisit the purpose and main idea of each. Here, Passage A sets forth an explanation of how evolution through natural selection works, but then Passage B suggests that it doesn't, in fact, work at all.

(A) Passage B does attempt to demonstrate that natural selection can't occur, but not in direct response to Passage A—there's no direct response to the points raised in Passage A or any indication that the author of Passage B is even aware of Passage A. You can eliminate this answer choice.

(B) The process described in Passage A is evolution through natural selection; far from providing an alternative explanation, Passage B says it doesn't occur at all. You can eliminate this answer choice.

(C) Passage A doesn't address the issues—in particular, the second law of thermodynamics and the natural tendency toward simplicity and disorder—raised in Passage B at all. You can eliminate this answer choice.

(D) Passage B directly suggests that the process described in Passage A can't occur in nature; they're definitely inconsistent. You can eliminate this answer choice.

(E) This is the correct answer. The natural tendency toward disorder raises questions about the natural selection process described in Passage A.

5. A

A global question relating to only one passage—this one should have been answered right after question 1. We already know the main purpose of Passage B—it's to persuade us that the second law of thermodynamics rules out evolution through natural selection.

(A) This is the correct choice: the second law being the "known scientific principle."

(B) The author of Passage B does make this argument, but it's simply an example meant to illustrate his or her main point, not the purpose of the passage. You can eliminate this answer choice.

(C) Author B never suggests that evolution is possible in another manner. You can eliminate this choice.

(D) This answer leaves out the core issue of the passage (evolution); therefore, you can eliminate it.

(E) This answer choice contains all the right key words, but Author B doesn't believe there is a "process of natural selection"—he or she sets out to use the second law to demonstrate that there's no such process. Therefore, you can eliminate this answer choice.

6. C

This is another single passage question that should have been answered early. We can predict the attitude of the author of Passage B toward the theory of evolution through natural selection: he or she doesn't believe in it, so the answer will not convey a positive attitude. Now we just have to walk through the answer choices to eliminate words that contradict Author B's position.

(A) Uncertainty: Author B is very clear on his or her position, so we can eliminate this choice.

(B) Cautious endorsement: This has a positive connotation, so we can eliminate this choice too.

(C) Extreme skepticism: The negativity conveyed by this choice makes it jump right out as correct. Plus, the author clearly conveys his or her disbelief.

(D) Partial acceptance: This is a complete contradiction to Author B's position, so it can be eliminated.

(E) Condescension: While this word has a negative connotation, consider the tone of the passage—it's professional and scientific, not editorial.

7. B

"Relationship between the passage" questions seem to be common in Comparative Reading passages; sometimes they're straightforward, as is question 4, but others look for a parallel relationship. Defining the relationship in the abstract before looking at the potentially parallel relationships is critical. Here, we've already said that Passage B raises issues that call into question the whole process described by Passage A.

(A) The second report here questions only the degree, not the existence, of the situation described in the first, so it can be eliminated.

(B) This is a match—the first document describes a process, and the second suggests the process doesn't occur at all.

(C) Two different theories explaining the same event—there's no suggestion that the event itself didn't occur, so you can eliminate this answer choice.

(D) Again, there's no disagreement about the phenomenon, only the explanation for it. You can eliminate this answer choice.

(E) Don't be tempted by the genetics talk; these are simply two different explanations of different aspects of a broader topic. There's no necessary or apparent disagreement between them. You can eliminate this answer choice as well.

PASSAGE 16

The following passages on freedom of information are adapted from texts published in the United Kingdom.

Passage A

We have made a commitment to openness in government, and now it is essential that we strengthen that commitment with legislation that guarantees public access to government
(5) information. This is something that the previous Government conspicuously failed to do. What resulted was a haphazard approach based largely on nonstatutory arrangements, in particular the Code of Practice on Access to Government
(10) Information. Those statutory requirements for openness that were in place applied only in certain areas, such as environmental information, or were limited to particular sectors of the public service. We could have scored an early legislative
(15) achievement by simply enacting the Code of Practice into law, but it does not ultimately provide a satisfactory guarantee of openness. Some of its significant drawbacks, which our proposed legislation seeks to remedy, are that:

(20) • It contains too many exemptions—more than any of the main statutory freedom of information regimes elsewhere in the world. This inevitably makes it complex for applicants to use, and encourages accusations that
(25) Departments "trawl" for possible reasons for nondisclosure;

• Its wording encourages the use of a "category-based" approach toward exemptions by which whole classes of information or records are
(30) protected against disclosure, leaving no scope for partial disclosure of documents of those types (after deletion of sensitive material);

• It often requires assessing the relative weights to be assigned to the harm that a
(35) disclosure could cause and the public interest in disclosure. But the "public interest" is not defined, making it difficult for government staff, as well as for those who may be unfamiliar with the Code and with effective
(40) disclosure practices, to assess what would constitute harm to that interest.

Passage B

There is, of course, room for disagreement as to how best to achieve freedom of information, but there are a number of features common to all genuinely successful freedom of information
(5) regimes. The statute (or other legal instrument) creating the regime must contain a general presumption in favor of disclosure. There must be a general right of access to information held by public authorities that relates to their public
(10) functions. This right must be made subject to exemptions in order to protect specified public interests such as public health or public safety. These interests must, however, be narrowly drawn and disclosure refused only where it can
(15) be shown that disclosure of the particular piece of information withheld would cause harm to one or more of those interests. Many advocates of freedom of information would add that even where there is potential harm to a specified
(20) interest, disclosure should only be refused where the harm can be shown to outweigh the public's interest in disclosure of the information in question. Lastly, there must be the possibility of appeal to an independent body or official
(25) against refusals by public authorities to disclose information. This body or official must have the power to redetermine applications independently and to make binding decisions.

1. Which one of the following most accurately expresses the main point of passage A?

    (A) The current government is fully committed to openness in government, whereas the previous government was not.
    (B) The Code of Practice has many weaknesses that the current government's proposed legislation is designed to avoid.
    (C) There must be a general right of access to information held by public authorities that relates to public functions.
    (D) The previous government was more interested in scoring a legislative victory than in providing a suitable approach to openness in government.
    (E) Freedom of information regimes should not depend on nonstatutory arrangements that grant large numbers of exemptions.

2. Which one of the following is identified in passage B, but not in passage A, as a necessary component of an effective guarantee of freedom of information?

    (A) a category-based approach in which certain classes of information are declared exempt from disclosure requirements
    (B) a mechanism for appealing government denials of requests for specific information
    (C) a statutory guarantee of public access to government information
    (D) a government agency devoted solely to the processing of requests for government information
    (E) a limit to the number of exemptions from requirements to release government information

3. Which one of the following most accurately characterizes how the use of the word "regimes" in passage A (line 22) relates to the use of the word "regimes" in passage B (line 5)?

    (A) In passage A it refers to formal hierarchies within a government, whereas in passage B it refers to informal arrangements that evolve over time.
    (B) In passage A it refers to governments that have been in power at particular times, whereas in passage B it refers to statutes that are enacted by those governments.
    (C) In both passage A and passage B it refers to governments that have been in power at particular times.
    (D) In both passage A and passage B it refers to sets of laws or other policy mechanisms that impose particular duties on governments.
    (E) In both passage A and passage B it refers to political ideologies underlying the policies followed by various governments.

4. If the author of passage B were to read passage A, he or she would be most likely to draw which one of the following conclusions regarding matters addressed in passage A?

    (A) The Code of Practice did not allow sufficient public access to information.
    (B) It would have been premature for the previous government to have enacted statutory measures to guarantee freedom of information.
    (C) The measures recommended by the current government are unnecessarily complex.
    (D) Freedom of information laws ought not to allow sensitive material to be deleted from any document before disclosure of the document.
    (E) The current government's proposed legislation depends too heavily on the questionable assumption that "public interest" can be clearly defined.

5. Passage A differs from passage B in that passage A displays an attitude that is more

   (A) partisan
   (B) tentative
   (C) analytical
   (D) circumspect
   (E) pessimistic

6. It can be inferred from the passages that both authors hold which one of the following views?

   (A) Freedom of information laws should not compel governments to comply with all requests for disclosure of information.
   (B) "Public interest" is too vague a concept to be cited in justifying freedom of information laws.
   (C) Freedom of information laws should unequivocally specify the categories to which they apply, so that case-by-case determinations are unnecessary.
   (D) Noncompulsory freedom of information policies are often sufficient to guarantee adequate public access to government information.
   (E) There should be a presumption in favor of disclosing government information, but only in explicitly specified branches of government.

7. Which one of the following most accurately describes a way in which the two passages are related to each other?

   (A) Passage A contains reasoning of a kind that passage B suggests is fallacious.
   (B) Passage B presupposes that information given in passage A regarding specific events is accurate.
   (C) Passage A contains an explanation that, if valid, helps to resolve a paradox suggested in passage B.
   (D) If all of the claims made in passage A are true, then some of the claims made in passage B are false.
   (E) If the assertions made in passage B are valid, they strengthen the position expressed in passage A.

8. Based on what can be inferred from their titles, the relationship between which one of the following pairs of documents is most analogous to the relationship between passage A and passage B?

   (A) "What the Previous Management of the Midtown Health Club Left Undone", "The New Management of the Crescent Restaurant Has Some Bad Policies"
   (B) "A List of Grievances by Tenants of Garden Court Apartments", "Why the Grievances of the Garden Court Apartments Tenants Are Unfounded"
   (C) "How We Plan to Improve the Way in Which This Restaurant Is Managed", "Standards of Good Restaurant Management"
   (D) "Three Alternative Proposals for Our New Advertising Campaign", "Three Principles to Be Followed in Developing an Effective Sales Team"
   (E) "Detailed Instructions for Submitting a Formal Grievance to the Committee", "Procedures for Adjudicating Grievances"

Passage 16: Openness in Government

What Makes It Difficult?

These two passages, while brief, are filled with dense legalese (phrases like, its "wording encourages the use of a "category-based" approach toward exemptions) and lacking in concrete examples. Passage A has an unusual structure, to boot; the bullet point form is one you likely haven't seen before now. And in such short passages, it might be difficult to get enough of the author's argument to formulate his purpose and main idea.

Eight questions make this a time challenge, and only two of those are Global and Detail questions. You're asked to compare attitudes, give one author's attitude about something the other author says, and find a pair of parallel titles for the passages—an unusual way of asking, even if the question itself is not totally out of the blue. Remember that while the Comparative Reading questions may be more time consuming, you have both passages to use to eliminate wrong answer choices.

Key Points of the Passage

Like all Comparative Reading passages, these two have the same topic: "openness in Government" from lines 1–2. But that's about the only thing that'll apply to both passages. Passage A is one of the most obviously partisan passages we're likely to see on the LSAT. That's fitting, considering that its Scope is the failures of a party that just lost power. The author is clearly a member of the new government, and wastes no time in detailing what went wrong under his predecessors. In fact, Paragraph 1 does little else, focusing on the "haphazard" Code of Practice (line 7). The author of Passage B is far more neutral. We can find the Scope of her passage in lines 3–5, "features common to all genuinely successful freedom of information regimes." Next, we have to identify the purpose/main idea for each passage independently:

- Passage A: The author's purpose is merely to explain exactly what the problems with the current system are, not to detail how his party's "proposed legislation" (line 19) will solve them. That leads us to a very specific Main Idea: our proposed legislation must fix these problems in the Code of Practice.
- Passage B: In a single long paragraph, the author walks us through all the things that she believes must be true for a genuinely successful freedom of information regime. As she does so, it becomes clear that her Purpose of this passage is to outline all of those necessities. By the end of the paragraph, it should be clear that the author isn't going to shift the scope of the passage at all, and that her Main Idea is that a successful freedom of information regime must include all of the details she lists.

Having assessed topic, scope, purpose, and main idea just as we do in regular passages (except that we have two purposes/main ideas), we move on to the one step that differs in reading comparative passages: before moving to the questions, we need to get a handle on the relationship between the passages.

The best starting point is to examine each passage's purpose/main idea. Passage A reveals the problem with the current system, and calls for these problems to be fixed, while Passage B details what must be included for a successful system. You could think of Passage A as identifying the problem, and Passage B providing a potential solution.

Answers and Explanations

1. B   2. B   3. D   4. A   5. A   6. A   7. E   8. C

1. B

We almost wouldn't recognize that we're dealing with Comparative Reading based on this first question. We can treat this one just like a regular Global question that asks us for the Main Idea. Looking back to our Roadmap, we can predict an answer to this question: the new party's legislation must fix several problems in the old government's Code of Practice. The closest match in the answer choices is (B).

(A) gets the tone of the passage spot on, but goes even further than the author does. In line 1, the author says that his party has "made a commitment to openness in government," not that they are fully committed.

(C) pulls a detail from lines 8–10 of Passage B.

(D) The author spends a fair amount of time beating up on the previous government, but he never says they were more interested in scoring legislative victories than in anything else. This comparison is irrelevant.

(E) repeats the first bullet point from the passage. This detail is too narrow to be the author's main point.

2. B

Comparative Reading questions will often ask you to compare and contrast the details of the passages. We could approach this question two different ways: We could eliminate the choices that appear in Passage A, or we could check each choice against Passage B and see which ones are mentioned. Our Roadmap makes the second approach much faster. We can just jump from "must" to "must" in Passage B and eliminate any choice that isn't mentioned. Let's try that:

(A) isn't mentioned in Passage B. In fact, exemptions from disclosure are one of the flaws listed in Passage A (lines 20–26). Eliminate.

(B) is the final point made in Passage B, lines 23–26. Let's see if we can eliminate the other choices and be sure that this one is correct:

(C) Both passages suggest that a statute would be a good method of creating a freedom of information system, but Passage B explicitly allows that some "other legal instrument" (line 5) could be sufficient. Eliminate.

(D) The type of government agency mentioned in this choice is outside the scope of both passages.

(E) Both passages mention limiting exemptions from requirements to release government information—Passage A suggests this in lines 20–26, and Passage B suggests limiting exemptions in lines 13–17. Only (B) remains, so it must be correct.

3. D

The context is key to answering this question; or rather, the difference (or similarity) between the contexts. In line 22, the author refers to "freedom of information regimes," using the word in question to refer to government or bureaucratic systems; and in line 5, the second author uses the word in question in exactly the same way. This fact alone is enough to eliminate two of the choices. The second author further clarifies her use of the word "regime" in lines 6, noting that it is a system created by a "statute or other legal instrument." The choice which correctly identifies this use of the word is (D).

(A) and (B) claim that "regimes" is used in different ways in the two passages, but the usage is actually the same.

(C) The author of Passage A is careful to use "government" whenever he refers to a government in power. He uses "regime" for a different purpose.

(E) The context in Passage B tells us that the author is referring to the implementation of government policies, not the ideology underlying them.

4. A

Be sure to understand how each author would respond to the other.

Let's imagine for a second that the order of the passages was reversed, and that instead of showing up on the LSAT, they were presentations in a public debate on freedom of information. Once Author B has had his say about the best ways to guarantee freedom of information, Author A gets up and delivers his presentation on all the problems with the previous government's system. Then Author B has a chance to respond. What would she have to say about it? That's essentially what this question asks us: how would Author B respond to Author A? Well, Author A lays out a bunch of violations of Author B's principles. Once we realize that, we can see that Author B would respond by saying, "Yes, those certainly are flaws in the Code of Practice. That nasty Code of Practice doesn't really satisfy any of my requirements, so it's not a very good system for freedom of information."

(A) says this in a slightly more scholarly manner, just as Author B probably would.

(B) Author B doesn't speak to the timing of introducing her measures; in fact, she'd probably say that timing doesn't matter when you're talking about necessary components of a system.

(C) Passage A never mentions the measures recommended by the current government—it only speaks to the problems these measures are meant to correct. (C) is outside the scope of this passage.

(D) is a 180. Passage B explicitly allows exemptions from disclosure "to protect specified public interests" (line 11).

(E) is another 180—Passage B offers a suggested definition of "public interest," so its author must believe that "public interest" can be clearly defined.

5. A

Even though question 5 asks about the difference between the attitudes of the passages, it really asks about Passage A. The differing attitudes of each passage should have been clear from their tones: Passage B was fairly neutral, but Passage A backed a specific political party's legislation and denigrated the actions of the previous government. Passage A was far more partisan, (A).

(B) The passages were equally sure of themselves; neither was more tentative than the other.

(C) is a 180. If anything, Passage B is more analytical than Passage A, not vice versa.

(D) Neither passage is circumspect; both of them are direct.

(E) Don't be fooled by the fact that Passage A points out flaws in the previous government's system—that doesn't make it pessimistic. Both passages ultimately make positive recommendations.

6. A

Don't be fooled by differences in tone. The author of Passage A is a fire-breathing politician and the author of Passage B sounds more like a political science professor, but that doesn't mean they won't agree on something. Here, it sounds like they're both in favor of greater freedom of information. They also agree on several ways to achieve that goal. The only difference is that Author B cites them as characteristics of an ideal freedom-of-information regime, while Author A points to violations of those ideals that must be corrected. Only (A) cites a point that both authors agree on: even the best freedom of information regimes have exemptions for certain material. Author A points out that "sensitive material" should be redacted in line 32, and Author B argues in favor of certain exemptions to a general rule of disclosure "to protect specified public interests." (line 11). (A) is thus correct.

(B) Both of the authors argue in favor of defining public interest to avoid vagueness in the term; this suggests that each author would actually disagree with (B), making this a 180.

(C) and (E) Both authors definitely disagree with these choices, arguing in favor of "a general presumption in favor of disclosure" (line 7) and against "too many exemptions" from such a presumption (line 20).

(D) Both authors argue in favor of a statutory "or other legal" (line 5) method of creating freedom of information policies. This suggests that neither would favor noncompulsory policies.

7. E

We can answer this question by treating the two passages as one big one, and asking how the two halves of it are connected. They'll obviously have similar scopes, but the tone of each is very different, and that tone will key us in to the relationship between them. Passage A gives us a partisan view and has a very negative tone, but it still makes some worthwhile suggestions about a specific piece of legislation. Passage B has a far more neutral tone, and nearly all of its recommendations are general and positive. These general ideas make several of the same points as the author of Passage A. Passage B would thus bolster Passage A's argument, as suggested in (E).

(A) Passage B isn't the one that points out flaws—that's Passage A.

(B) Passage B doesn't refer to any specific events from Passage A, so it can't assume anything about them.

(C) There is neither an explanation in Passage A nor a paradox in Passage B.

(D) While the authors of the passages might differ in their ultimate legislative goals, none of their ideas are mutually exclusive.

8. C

Don't be intimidated by the fact that this is a Parallel Reasoning question; it's still vulnerable to the Kaplan Method. In fact, you may find the Parallel Reasoning questions in the Comparative Reading passages easier than those on the Logical Reasoning section, since you've already spent so much time thinking about the relationship between the passages.

We'll attack this using our Logical Reasoning skills. First, we'll think about the overall conclusions of the passages: Passage A, the partisan passage, lays out the specific flaws that "we" should fix; and Passage B, the neutral passage, tells us the general principles behind a good system. The relationship between these passages is most like that in (C).

(A) starts off well, with Passage A's discussion of the previous management's flaws, but Passage B doesn't suggest that the new management has its problems as well. (A) is half right, half wrong.

(B) The two passages in (B) are directly at odds, instead of complimenting each other like Passages A and B.

(D) Passage A doesn't give three alternative proposals, it details three problems in a previous system.

(E) The characterization of Passage A in this choice is far too neutral. Eliminate this distortion.

A Special Note for International Students

In recent years, U.S. law schools have experienced an increase in inquiries from non-U.S. citizens, some of whom are already practicing lawyers in their own countries. This surge of interest in the U.S. legal system has been attributed to the spread of the global economy. When business people from outside the United States do business with Americans, they often find themselves doing business under the American legal system. Gaining insight into how the American legal system works is of great interest around the world.

This new international interest in the U.S. legal system is having an effect on law schools. Many schools have developed special programs to accommodate the needs of this special population of lawyers and students from around the globe. If you are an international student or lawyer interested in learning more about the American legal system, or if you are considering attending law school in the United States, Kaplan can help you explore your options.

Getting into a U.S. law school can be especially challenging for students from other countries. If you are not from the United States, but are considering attending law school in the United States, here is what you'll need to get started.

- If English is not your first language, you'll probably need to take the TOEFL® (Test of English as a Foreign Language), or provide some other evidence that you are proficient in English. Most law schools require a minimum computer TOEFL score of 250 (600 on the paper-based TOEFL) or better.

- Depending on the program to which you are applying, you may also need to take the LSAT (Law School Admissions Test). All law schools in the United States require the LSAT® for their J.D. programs. LL.M. programs usually do not require the LSAT. Kaplan will help you determine if you need to take the LSAT. If you must take the LSAT, Kaplan can help you prepare for it.

- Since admission to law school is quite competitive, you may want to select three or four programs and complete applications for each school.

- You should begin the process of applying to law schools or special legal studies programs at least eighteen months before the fall of the year you plan to start your studies. Most programs will have only September start dates.

- In addition, you will need to obtain an I-20 Certificate of Eligibility from the school you plan to attend if you intend to apply for an F-1 Student Visa to study in the United States.

KAPLAN ENGLISH PROGRAMS*

If you need more help with the complex process of law school admissions, assistance preparing for the LSAT or TOEFL, or help building your English language skills in general, you may be interested in Kaplan's programs for international students.

Kaplan English Programs were designed to help students and professionals from outside the United States meet their educational and career goals. At locations throughout the United States, international students take advantage of Kaplan's programs to help them improve their academic and conversational English skills, raise their scores on the TOEFL, LSAT, and other standardized exams, and gain admission to the schools of their choice. Our staff and instructors give international students the individualized attention they need to succeed. Here is a brief description of some of Kaplan's programs for international students:

General Intensive English

Kaplan's General Intensive English classes are designed to help you improve your skills in all areas of English and to increase your fluency in spoken and written English. Classes are available for beginning to advanced students, and the average class size is 12 students.

TOEFL and Academic English

This course provides you with the skills you need to improve your TOEFL score and succeed in an American university or graduate program. It includes advanced reading, writing, listening, grammar and conversational English. You will also receive training for the TOEFL, updated for the TOEFL iBT, using Kaplan's exclusive computer-based practice materials.

LSAT Test-Preparation Course

The LSAT is a crucial admission criterion for law schools in the United States. A high score can help you stand out from other applicants. This course includes the skills you need to succeed on each section of the LSAT, as well as access to Kaplan's exclusive practice materials.

Other Kaplan Programs

Since 1938, more than three million students have come to Kaplan to advance their studies, prepare for entry to American universities, and further their careers. In addition to the above programs, Kaplan offers courses to prepare for the SAT®, GMAT®, GRE®, MCAT®, DAT®, USMLE®, NCLEX®, and other standardized exams at locations throughout the United States.

APPLYING TO KAPLAN ENGLISH PROGRAMS

To get more information, or to apply for admission to any of Kaplan's programs for international students and professionals, contact us at:

Kaplan English Programs
700 South Flower Street, Suite 2900
Los Angeles, CA 90017
Phone: If calling from outside the U.S.: (213) 452-5800
Phone: If calling from within the U.S.: (800) 818-9128
Fax: (213) 892-1364
Email: world@kaplan.com
Web: www.kaplanenglish.com

FREE Services for International Students

Kaplan now offers international students many services online—*free of charge*!
Students may assess their TOEFL skills and gain valuable feedback on their English
language proficiency in just a few hours with Kaplan's TOEFL Skills Assessment.
Log onto www.kaplanenglish.com today.

---

*Kaplan is authorized under federal law to enroll nonimmigrant alien students. Kaplan is accredited by ACCET (Accrediting Council for Continuing Education and Training) and is a member of FIYTO and ALTO.

NOTES

NOTES

NOTES

NOTES

NOTES

NOTES

NOTES

NOTES

NOTES

NOTES

NOTES

NOTES

NOTES

NOTES

NOTES

NOTES

The Key to 1L Success

You made it to law school! The success you have had as an undergrad will translate into law school. Right? Not so fast. No matter what your background and success habits were as an undergrad, law school is different. It is as different as college was from high school. The faster you embrace the differences the better your chances are of success in law school. You may be smart, but so is everyone else.

Don't let this unnerve you. You've got Kaplan PMBR on your side to help you succeed. We provide invaluable guidance for all three years of law school, and *then* we help you pass the Bar Exam. Kaplan PMBR offers the most realistic, complete, up-to-date, and effective bar review prep through live courses, home study material, and small group tutorials. The following pages provide just a small preview of the insights and advice, tools and tactics that you'll receive in Kaplan PMBR's 1L Success Program. Visit our website at kaplanpmbr.com to learn more!

Your law school experience is likely to be the most challenging academic process of your life. Just remember, it can be done. Kaplan PMBR will help you do it. Good luck and we will see you on campus!

WHAT IS A "1L"? WHAT IS YOUR "SOL" ON YOUR "COA"? WHO IS THE "π"? WHO IS THE "Δ"?

If you answered these questions with a "Huh?" that is perfectly normal. Law school has its own language. A 1L is simply what first year law school students are called. "SOL" stands for statute of limitations. "COA" is your cause of action. π is shorthand for "Plaintiff", and Δ is shorthand for "Defendant". At first, it is a lot like learning Klingon, but you will learn quickly, and it is a language that will last you a lifetime. With a large legal dictionary in hand, you can create your own shorthand for note-taking and start using words like negate, moot, or sua sponte!

BE PROFESSIONAL

At first glance, law school seems to be very much like college. There are social events, a lot of studying, and new friends. However, keep in mind you are building a professional reputation that will follow you through the rest of your legal career. Your professors and classmates are learning who you are and those impressions last. Make sure they are good ones, and enjoy the process of becoming an attorney along the way.

NIGHT OWLS VS. EARLY BIRDS

Just because you've made it to law school doesn't mean you have to reinvent the wheel. In fact, don't. What and how you studied worked for you. If you study best at night, keep up that practice. If you study best first thing in the morning, continue to do so. Your study patterns have long been established and law school doesn't necessarily require you to change them. Stick with what works!

STUDY GROUPS AND STUDY MATERIALS

Two important issues you will face are whether you should join a study group, and when and how to use study aids.

Study Groups

Early in law school people usually scramble to get together to form study groups with other students. They are completely optional. Some groups will go fast, others slow. Others will study more of the social conditions in law school rather than anything substantive. To get the most from a study group, you must position yourself in the best group *for you*—should you choose to join one.

Study Materials

There are as many opinions about study aids. Used correctly, study aids can help you understand your class notes, let you see how things relate to each other, provide focus on the rationale of cases, and in the end, help you better understand the topic of law covered in class. Commercial outlines are prepackaged outlines in skeletal form of the law you need to know for a particular course. Hornbooks are the comprehensive and expansive overview of the particular course. They are also referred to as *treatises*.

Finally, there are the bar review programs. Don't let the term "bar review" fool you. True, Kaplan PMBR is a bar review company, but we also are a *law student* company. We have materials for first years, second years, third years, and *then* we help you pass the Bar Exam. For example, Kaplan PMBR offers substantive black letter law course outlines and audio CDs to help you prepare for classes. These are resources you will turn to again and again—throughout law school and beyond. Visit our website at kaplanpmbr.com to learn more or to enroll.

OUTLINES

What goes into an outline? Essentially, it contains the rules of law, exceptions, and defenses to it. As a brief example, a Battery is a harmful or offensive touching of another with Intent. Consent is a defense to battery.

You might choose to incorporate some of your professor's pet topics or the like to keep them in the front of your mind. They very well could show up on the exam. Sometimes students split up different sections of the course with each creating an outline for her or his portion. However, if you focus on only one portion of the course, you will likely have a good understanding of only that one area and must rely on someone else's perception of their section of the course. Make your own outlines for each course. This allows you to understand the material and how it relates together.

THE EXAM PROCESS

Your exam can include multiple choice questions, short answer, and most popular, essay questions. Your grade depends on how you perform on the exam. However, it is what you do prior to xam day that will have the most impact on your success. Developing a good outline, learning to spot issues, honing your exam skills by practicing on old exams, and designing your test strategy are all solid ways to get ahead of the game and likely many of your classmates as well.

Issue spotting

The first step is knowing the law. The next—issue spotting—is a real time test of your ability to identify legal issues or causes of action. Your professor will test you on material you covered in class and material you were assigned but didn't cover in class. Every law school exam is invented using complex situations that may involve multiple lawsuits or defendants, and usually the professor will ask multiple questions. Truly, some facts are trash while some are treasure. You'll have to decide which is which.

Practice Exams

Practice exams are an essential tool to building your law school success. Sample exams are an underappreciated and underutilized tool. Too often, in the heat of preparing for exams, they are overlooked or ignored due to time constraints. Not only are they are a great barometer of the issues the professor likes, the style of the exam, but you could luck out and one those questions could end up on your actual final exam. Remember to allocate the time to use them!